THE PHILOSOPHER
IN THE CITY

THE PHILOSOPHER
IN THE CITY

The Moral Dimensions
of Urban Politics

HADLEY ARKES

PRINCETON UNIVERSITY PRESS
PRINCETON, NEW JERSEY

For Peter and Jeremy Arkes
and
Leopold and Theresa Sonn

CONTENTS

CONTENTS

PREFACE

This book was written during the academic year 1976-1977, when I was a Fellow of the Woodrow Wilson Center of the Smithsonian Institution. The Wilson Center absorbed me into its care: it provided for my needs with its genteel facilities administered with a large nature; it furnished me with a corps of engaging colleagues; and it livened my work with a year filled by varied characters and seminars, by a series of occasions that stirred exertions of the mind and other minor excitements. More I could not accept because my financial support was already provided, with a decent generosity, by the National Endowment for the Humanities. I would like to express my gratitude to the Endowment—and to my government— for the interest they manifested at the time in the "moral sciences," and for the kind help that was offered me.

Not long after I had arrived at the Wilson Center, my colleague, Robert Conquest, asked me what my book was about, and I told him that it was a manuscript in which Immanuel Kant meets Mayor Daley. The book would offer a blending of the philosophic and the prosaic, and it was precisely my mission to show that the prosaic could not be understood without the philosophic. The argument would advance through a chain of problems that often show themselves in a pronounced way in the cities; but those problems became interesting only because they led back to some older questions about the standards of moral judgment. Moral judgments can be made only with principles of judgment, and the understanding of those principles requires a reflection that is distinctively philosophic. But that reflection also requires an occasion, and we are likely to be drawn to our most serious reflection in the presence of real disputes and controversies, where people are threatened with injustices or injuries, and we are compelled to consider, in a demanding way, the grounds on which we would claim to do justice.

And so the work I have spun together here puts its accent on cases and arguments—by which I mean, in part, cases in law, but also public disputes and arguments over policy that have never entered a courtroom. It should be evident, however, from the beginning that my purpose here is to use the cases as incidents that reflect and test our understandings about the principles of moral judgment. The materials in the book are drawn, therefore, from political theory and constitutional law, as well as from empirical studies that bear on the concerns of politics in the cities. I have made use, at different moments, of personal interviews, and the reader will occasionally find in the book numbers and accounts that have not been published elsewhere. But I hope it will be plain, also, that the book does not recommend itself to its audience primarily for the novelty of its empirical researches. I incorporate empirical findings because the exercise of moral judgment involves the wedding of principles to the facts that define the character of cases. But there is nothing about the *principles* of judgment, and there is nothing in the most fundamental strata of argument in this book, that could be affected in any way by late discoveries of an empirical nature which have not yet made it into print.

The purpose of this book is to offer a *perspective* on the city—or on politics itself—and to draw out the implications of this perspective for a number of substantive questions that arise in the politics of the city. It has been understood since the beginning of moral philosophy that the concern for what is good or bad, just or unjust, is a concern for the standards that guide our *practical* judgment. I would hope to relay that ancient recognition by reminding us of what a difference can be made by a philosophic perspective, even in those parts of our politics that are usually thought to be the most prosaic.

Beyond that, in the larger design of this work, I would try to clear up a confusion that has plagued the law for many years on the relation between "principles" and "injuries." As I will try to argue, the most important laws on our books could hardly be comprehensible if they were to be understood only in those contracted terms to which modern jurisprudence has sought to limit the province of law—that is, to the relief of material injuries and to the high-minded neglect of what are loosely called "moral questions." The project of modern jurisprudence, the aspiration to place moral questions beyond the law altogether, is an enterprise that begins in error. The commitment to restrict the law to the relief of material harms, and to the harms that people inflict on others rather than themselves, is a commitment that can be established and preserved only if one ceases to remember what is meant, in the strictest terms, by "morals" and "principles." Without the presence of that more rigorous understanding it would be impossible to explain why we choose to let pass most of the "hurts" that may be inflicted, say, by dentists and lovers, and why we choose to label other hurts as "injuries" that the law may reach. Our understanding of "injuries" depends ultimately on our understanding of the principles that define "injustices"; and once that recognition is absorbed, it will become easier to establish anew the understanding that the law finds its main mission in vindicating injustice, whether or not the wrong in any case is manifested in the suffering of a material harm.

The judgments I offer in this book must depend for their validity on the moral groundwork from which they are drawn. And so this study would have to point in turn to a more fundamental work, which could give itself over more fully to the task of explaining and justifying that moral groundwork. A project of that kind would be a venture in what is oddly known these days as "metaethics": it would set forth the axioms or first principles that must arise from the concept of morals itself, and it would have to consider, in an intensive way, the grounds on which we may claim to *know* anything at all in the domain of morals. That project is in fact the work to which I will next be turning. But to describe its aims is to recognize at once why they could not have been accomplished within the bounds of this book on the city. The present work will have done enough if it makes the point ineffaceable for its readers that "moral" questions are not confined to matters of sex and gambling; that moral judgments, in the most rigorous sense, form the central, pervasive problem in politics; and that the concerns of the law cannot be reduced to the sole end of securing people against material damages. It is only when readers are satisfied on these points that they will be drawn to the threshold of that further work on morals and law.

But in the meantime the source of the moral judgments in *this* book does not remain concealed. The ground of those judgments is set forth in Chapters II, III, and IX; it is given a further articulation in parts of Chapters XIII and XIV; and its implications are drawn through the rest of the book. I would not reveal, in a subsequent work, a ground of moral understanding that differs in any way from the ground I offer here as the foundation of my judgments. But I must postpone until a later time the task of elaborating the explanations and tracing matters back to "first things."

I have had the advantage of testing out parts of the argument in this book by publishing portions of the manuscript separately at an earlier stage. Most notably, a compressed version of Chapters II and III appeared in *The Supreme Court Review 1974* as "Civility and the Restriction of Speech: Rediscovering the Defamation of Groups." Parts of Chapters VI and XV appeared, in a different version, in *Commentary* magazine as "The Problem of Kenneth Clark." I would like to thank the editors of these journals, along with the editors of *The American Spectator*, the *National Review*, and *The Wall Street Journal*, for permission to use material that I published first under their imprint.

My piece in the *Supreme Court Review* appeared while Walter Berns was completing his redoubtable book on *The First Amendment and the Future of American Democracy*, and so I could not incorporate his arguments in the fabric of my own. As it turned out, our arguments were compatible and reinforcing, without being identical—or as Walter Berns put it in a letter to me at the time, "We had managed to say the truth about the [Supreme] Court without making the same points."

A number of colleagues and friends have been kind enough to read parts of the manuscript at different times and give me the benefit of their reactions. I would like to express my thanks here to Philip Kurland, Norman Podhoretz, George Kateb, Benjamin Ziegler, Austin Sarat, Dale Frederick Swartz, Steven Schlesinger, James Billington, Gertrude Himmelfarb, Fr. Joseph Sebes, Eva Brann, Robert Hawkins, Antonin Scalia, and Gordon Levin. Walter Berns, Carey Wilson McWilliams, and Seth Dubin read through the entire manuscript, and I hope I have succeeded in making the improvements that were suggested by their comments. I am grateful for the support and help that were offered by my friends, without implying, of course, that they always shared my judgments.

And speaking of those who have not always shared my judgments, I cannot fail to mention the people whose reactions had the most pronounced effect on the shaping of the arguments that are found in this book. There is no argument offered here that was not first presented and developed in the tension of the classroom, with my students at Amherst. Few experiences are more likely to cultivate the art of being disarming, or to foster the special effort to be persuasive, than the need to offer an argument to a band of skeptical and resourceful undergraduates. That is especially the case when the students are not apt to find all of the conclusions congenial. I think the arguments here have been improved overall through the discipline of these friendly abrasions. But the best compliment I can pay to my former students is that, as a result of our experience together, I find it hard to conceive of a life of writing, in my own case, that was not attended at least in part by the wholesome tension of the classroom.

He does not find a place in my footnotes, but Daniel Robinson has affected in many ways the understanding that informs this manuscript. In the years of our friendship Daniel Robinson has been, in effect, part brother, part tutor, part press agent. I could not begin to recount what he has imparted to me in years of conversations, and I could not number all the gifts he has made to me.

I made a general mention earlier of the Woodrow Wilson Center, but I would like to express my thanks, in particular, to James Billington, the Director of the Center, and to William Dunn and Frances Hunter. They managed to preserve, in the Center, a setting congenial at once to scholarship and friendship.

Dianne Kaplan has made a large impress on the Department of Political Science at Amherst since she became, in effect, its chief of administration. Once again she has done her characteristic, extraordinary job on my behalf in managing the work involved in typing the manuscript and preparing it for press. Sanford Thatcher, my editor at Princeton University Press, supported me in this project from the beginning; this is the second book he has guided through the Press for me. He continues to read me, I think, more closely than anyone else, and he has become that rarest of combinations: my constant advocate and my steadiest critic.

He is matched in these qualities only by my wife, Judy, who can still be pressed into service at times as an editor in her home as well as in her office. This book is dedicated to our children—and to the affectionate parents she brought me as an addition to my own. Leopold and Theresa Sonn were the quintessential young urbanites in the Vienna of the 1920's and 1930's, before they were ripped out of the cast of their lives with the advent of the Nazis. They came to know the barbarism of the Nazis in a direct, personal way, and they experienced a city in which the authorities were pleased to permit the streets to be used as theaters of combat. My parents-in-law have understood why I have chosen to begin a book on the city by considering the conditions of civility and the terms of principle on which a people live together. And I think they have understood intuitively the truth of what I have sought to argue here.

Not too long ago I participated in a conference on abortion and euthanasia, in which a biologist expressed his skepticism about the "population problem." He pointed out that if everyone in the world were somehow, magically, transported to Texas, there would be 1,500 square feet for every man, woman, and child in the world. It so happened that 1,500 square feet was the size of the lot on which the biologist's home stood in San Francisco, and with the population of the world concentrated in Texas, Texas would still have been *less dense* than San Francisco. A short while later, when

I rose to speak, I noted that I had always sought to avoid religious grounds for my arguments, but the projections for Texas had finally moved me to a recognition of personal faith. If all the people in the world were really moved to Texas—if there was no one in Europe, no one in Asia, no one in the Middle East, and no one in Africa— I still *believed*: there would be 700,000 Democratic votes *reported* from Chicago.

I have been transported, in my middle years, to a pastoral setting, but I remain a child of the city, and though there is much of late to challenge that faith, I still believe in the gods that watch over Chicago.

Amherst, Massachusetts
January, 1980

THE PHILOSOPHER
IN THE CITY

I

INTRODUCTION

All about us today urban life is celebrated, but largely for the wrong reasons. When the city is valued, it is valued as the theater of diversity, the center of a cosmopolitan culture, the breeding ground of freedom and tolerance. It is the place where cultures run up against one another; where couples find it easier to maintain mixed racial marriages; where homosexuals can find a society of their own and a shelter for their style of life. It is a place of specialty, movement, and color, of services tailored to the rarest taste.

But these virtues are the virtues of the marketplace or of the city as "hotel." What they leave out, conspicuously, is any sense of the city as a source of obligation—not an arena for pursuing wants, a place for indulging tastes of literally any description, with no governing sense of character, but a place where people learn the lessons of propriety and self-control. The commitment to diversity for its own sake, to the expansion of choices and the satisfaction of "wants," suggests no sense of substantive ends. It implies no measure of the difference between decent and indecent passions, or between the kinds of tastes that are more or less legitimate for people living in a civil society. What is lost, then, in this vision of the city as a shopping center is the sense of a people joined together in a perception of common ends; who found their common life on procedures they regard, by and large, as just; and who cultivate an understanding of justice and morals in one another through the things they hold up to the community with the force of law. What is lost, in a word, is the sense of the city as polity.

It may be rather unsettling, though, even to members of an older generation, to regard the city, in the more classic sense, as a source of moral instruction. But the discomfort with that notion in our own day is a measure of how far we have drifted from the original understanding of the connection between morals and law. Our difficulties in recent years can be laid most importantly to a confusion that has arisen over the meaning of "morals" itself in the strictest sense. There is a tendency in our public discourse to equate moral judgments with matters of religious belief, or to reduce them to questions of the most subjective personal taste. Either way, morals are removed from the domain of practical reasoning and they are attached to the sphere of the ineffable or the unknowable. On the one hand it is assumed that morals address the gravest questions as to how human beings ought to conduct their lives; but on the other hand it is taken for granted that morals are matters of the most personal belief, which cannot be used to judge or direct others.

This confusion has been reflected rather well in many of the college students I have known over the last decade. It was important to them to insist, for example, that the war in Vietnam could not be regarded merely as an enterprise plagued by poor management and bad luck, but that it was a thoroughly *immoral* venture. They were disposed to argue, in a more classic vein, that politics could not be marked off and ruled by some internal logic of its own, cut off from questions of morals. For political decisions could not help but imply something about the standards of judgment, and in that respect they had to be guided by some notions of the things that were in general good or bad, just or unjust. Politics could never be separated from moral understandings, because politics was, as the classics thought, a virtual school of ethics.

And yet as these students came to face many of the problems that arose in the city—problems of drugs, abortion, the censorship of literature and the arts—they became liberals in a rather old sense that they usually disdained. Their tendency then was to argue that the state of anyone's morals was not the business of the government—that morals were essentially matters of private taste and judgment. And so, if people wished to have abortions, that was something that they would have to be left free to decide, according to their own, private sense of what was best for themselves. Whether it was in fact good for people to become dependent on drugs or to earn their livings by prostitution were questions that seemed to turn ultimately on matters of the most subjective preference and the most personal taste.

The curious thing about this understanding of morals was that it reduced the indictment of the Vietnam war to the level of the utterly trivial. To have said that the Vietnam war was "immoral" was to have said, in effect, that the Vietnam war was simply not to one's taste (much as one might have said, for example, "I don't care, especially, for cabbage or squid"). By implication, however, others might tenably have liked the Vietnam war (just as they might have liked squid) if they happened to care for that sort of thing. The language of condemnation would have been strikingly out of place here, for one does not show outrage or indignation over disgreements that turn on the most subjective taste.

There is a hard difference in logic between a proposition on the order of "I don't like squid," and a proposition like, "The Vietnam war is wrong." In the first case one expresses only the most personal preference, and there is no implication that the preference ought to be shared by other people. There is no suggestion that those who take another view of the matter ought to be condemned, and still less is there any sense that the foundation has been laid in this statement for committing other people. But in the proposition on the Vietnam war, the logic would be notably different. There, one would indeed purport to do more than convey a merely personal view. One would be saying, rather, that the Vietnam war ought to be regarded as wrong by others as well as oneself, and that the grounds on which it is wrong would not depend for their validity on whether they are accepted by any person in particular, or even by a majority of those who form an opinion on the matter. For that reason, or with that logic, the opponents of the Vietnam war would have thought it proper to impose their views on others with the force of law if they had attained political power. They would have been willing, it is clear, to close down the war in Vietnam, even though the effects of this decision could have been felt throughout the whole society if their judgment had been wrong.

The same matter might be put with more vividness and point if we simply altered the direction of the statement and said that the war in Vietnam was in fact justified. In that event we would be establishing the foundation for committing people, through the law, to support the war, either by paying taxes or serving in the military. In that respect the logic of law follows rather closely from the logic of morals: moral propositions, in the strictest sense, move beyond matters of personal taste or subjective belief, and they claim to speak about the things that are more generally or universally "good." That is to say, they seek to establish the things that are in principle good or bad, right or wrong, for others as well as oneself.

When we presume to legislate for others we are implying, of necessity, that the law rests on considerations that are moral or "principled" in the most literal sense.[1] If that were not the case,

---

[1] It should become evident on reflection that it is the logic of morals that lies behind the notion of a "principled" argument. When a person tries to convert us to his views, it is thoroughly proper to consider whether his position is merely a

the law would represent nothing more than the opinions or interests shared by the majority; and if one refused to acknowledge any "moral" basis for the law, the majority could claim to rule the minority only by the license of numerical strength. The law would be reduced, in other words, to nothing more than a polite form of the rule of force or might. At that point one could ask, with Rousseau, just "what validity can there be in a Right which ceases to exist when Might changes hands?"[2] When we take it upon ourselves to legislate for others we must therefore imply that there is a moral foundation for our acts which could justify the presumption we display in commanding other people. We must imply that there are reasons we could give, principles we could cite, to establish that something was good or just, not merely for ourselves, but for others as well—including, in many cases, those who at the moment disagree.

When we consider our laws on murder, theft, and assault, it is plain even to the most advanced libertarians that the laws embody perspectives that are authentically moral. But moral judgments of one kind or another—large or small, valid or arguable—can be seen to underlie almost every other kind of law on the books, from copyrights and embezzlement to the regulation of insurance. Those moral judgments become even more important, of course, in the legislation that touches the most prominent questions of the day; but even the most urbane people have quite often been willing to withhold the recognition that moral principles are indeed engaged in these matters. In point of fact, though, the community is legislating morals when it removes the freedom of a homeowner to act on his own personal preference and discriminate against blacks in the sale or rental of his home. It is legislating morals also when it insists on implicating a taxpayer against his will in a situation he may regard as personally offensive, as would be the case, for example, if he were opposed to supporting, through his taxes, an unwed mother on welfare who continues to have illegitimate children. If public policy has a claim to bind everyone, it is because it

---

reflection of his self-interest or whether it expresses an understanding of what would be good or just for people in general. As a practical matter, then, we would ask whether his argument could be stated in the form of a more general rule which would be applied to all similar cases, now and in the future. If the argument could achieve the cast of a principle, it would come to have a moral standing, and the test would be whether the man who first offered the argument would also honor the principle when it cut against his interests.

[2] See Rousseau, *The Social Contract*, Bk. I, ch. 3.

claims to rest on moral principles, or on understandings of the public good, that amount to something more than the personal interests or opinions of those who rule.

Libertarians have sought to evade this understanding by insisting that, if the law does happen to coincide at many points with moral judgments, it nevertheless reaches only those matters that involve a material harm or a measurable injury. As we shall see, however, this is a perspective that can be preserved only by extinguishing from our current laws a recognition of the moral grounds on which they may rest. And so when we come to consider the laws that forbid discrimination on the basis of race in public accommodations, the disposition among lawyers and jurists has been to say that the issue at stake here for blacks is the question of getting access to the same goods and services that are offered to whites. The problem, as they see it, is that blacks are being deprived of food or lodgings. But in any strict assessment it would be hard to establish that black people are being denied food if they are turned away from a particular restaurant. For all one knows, they may able to obtain food next door or across the street, and in the case in which this issue was argued before the Supreme Court, the re-doubtable Ollie's Barbecue in Birmingham had a take-out counter serving blacks.[3] It makes no more sense to contend that a black person is being denied food in these kinds of cases than it would to claim that a person is being denied food when he is turned away from a restaurant for the want of a necktie. We accept the exclusion in the latter instance but not in the former, and our reasons have nothing to do with the deprivation of food. The question would turn, rather, on the ground of principle on which the exclusion is made in either case.

But to say that is to recognize that the issue of principle is more decisive in these cases than the estimation of material injuries. The estimate of material harms often depends on empirical evidence and conjectures, and on propositions of a statistical nature. It rests, in other words, on what we would have to call "contingent truths," rather than the kinds of truths or principles that "cannot be otherwise." I will press the argument later, in a Kantian vein, that any policy which claims the name of "law" cannot be grounded in "truths" of a merely contingent or statistical nature—that before the law can justify its claim to bind others, it must be established on a ground of principle that cannot be evaded. And if we accept

---

[3] See *Katzenbach* v. *McClung*, 379 U.S. 294 (1964).

the discipline of these requirements for the law, we come to discover also that the law achieves its firmest foundation when it is grounded in principles that are strictly necessary to the *idea of law* itself.

As Kant understood, "the idea of law . . . is present only in a rational being";[4] and in that respect he reflected the classic understanding of the problem: Law was the distinctive mark of a polis (or a polity), and the polity, as Aristotle taught, emanated from human nature. The polity was as much a "natural" association as the family was, but it was also, as Aristotle said, "prior in the order of nature to the family and the individual" in the way that "the whole is necessarily prior to the part."[5] But if it were true, as Aristotle wrote, that "man is by nature an animal intended to live in a polis," and if the polis was the most "sovereign and inclusive" association, then it seemed to follow that the polis was a reflection of the highest parts of human nature.

In Aristotle's understanding, polity and law did arise out of the highest and most distinctive attributes of human nature, and the nature of humans could be understood in the plainest way by considering the things that separated human beings most decisively from beings that were subhuman. As Aristotle put it, animals could emit sounds to indicate pleasure or pain, but human beings could go well beyond that: they could declare what was good or bad, just or unjust, which is to say that they could give reasons or justifications in matters of right and wrong. "It is the peculiarity of man," said Aristotle, "in comparison with the rest of the animal world, that he alone possesses a perception of good and evil, of the just and unjust, and of other similar qualities; and it is association in [a common perception of] these things which makes a family and a polis."[6]

[4] *Groundwork of the Metaphysics of Morals*, trans. H. J. Paton (New York: Harper's, 1964), p. 69; p. 401 in the standard edition of this work published by the Royal Prussian Academy of Science.

[5] Aristotle, *The Politics*, 1253a; and see generally 1252a-1253a.

[6] Ibid., 1253a. This is not to deny that animals may "communicate" in some sense, but it is to recognize that the communications of animals are not textured by the moral judgments and shadings that affect human language at almost every point. As was often the case, it fell to Thomas Reid to make the point most tellingly: "A fox," he wrote, "is said to use stratagems, but he cannot lie; because he cannot give his testimony, or plight his veracity. A dog is said to be faithful to his master; but no more is meant but that he is affectionate, for he never came under any engagement. I see no evidence that any brute animal is capable of either giving testimony, or making a promise." Thomas Reid, *Essays on the Active Powers of the Human Mind* (Cambridge: MIT Press, 1969; originally published in 1813), Essay V, ch. VI, p. 442.

The capacity for morals in the strictest sense can exist only where there is such a capacity to reason over matters of right and wrong. As I have suggested, there is a connection also between the logic of morals and the logic of law, and if one followed Aristotle closely it would be apparent that the connection is not accidental but necessary. For Aristotle, polity arises, along with law, from the capacity of human beings for morals. It might be said that law is the consequence that follows directly from the existence of morals, and the connection may be seen in this way: Once we come to the recognition, for example, that it is wrong to kill without justification, it would simply be inconsistent with the logic of the terms to say at the same time that "people should be left free, therefore, to kill or not kill as it suits their own preferences." If something can be established as a "wrong," it may properly be removed from the domain of personal choice and forbidden to people generally. It may be proscribed, then, as we would say, with the force of "law."

Conversely, when the community acts through the law it cannot help engaging in moral instruction; for it conveys to its citizens in a dramatic public way that there are matters of such gravity, of such incontestable standing as matters of right and wrong, that they can no longer be left to the freedom of personal choice. In the traditional understanding, a polity manifested its character through its laws, and the function of law was suited precisely to the distinctive end of polity. That end was not, as Aristotle was careful to explain, the mere encouragement of commerce or the protection of people against mutual injury. If those were the ends of the polity, then, as Aristotle observed, "the Etruscans and the Carthaginians [who were joined by agreements on these matters] would be in the position of belonging to a single state; and the same would be true of all peoples who have commercial treaties with one another."[7]

The United States and the Soviet Union have entered into treaties with one another in recent years for the purpose of enlarging trade and reducing the risk of mutual injury through war. If those ends represented the main purposes of political life, citizens within the same polity would stand in the same relation to one another as citizens of two different countries that were joined together through agreements that encouraged commerce and regulated armaments. And yet the polity cannot be reduced to a mere "alliance" or a system of contracts. As Aristotle understood, the problem in re-

---

[7] *The Politics*, 1280a.

ducing the polity to the condition of an alliance was that none of the parties in a contractual arrangement "concerns itself to insure a proper quality or character among the members . . . neither of them seeks to insure that all who are included in the scope of the treaties shall be free from injustice and from any form of vice; and neither of them goes beyond the aim of preventing its own members from committing injustice [in the course of trade] against the members of the other."[8] In a transaction of buying and selling, or in an agreement for the avoidance of conflict, the concerns of the parties are usually confined to the limited interests they both have at stake. Their interests are not assumed to encompass a concern for the moral character of the people they are dealing with. But a true polis, as Aristotle said, "must devote itself to the end of encouraging goodness. Otherwise, a political association sinks into a mere alliance . . . [and] law becomes a mere convenant . . . instead of being, as it should be, a rule of life such as will make the members of a polis good and just."[9]

The polis is, preeminently, a moral association. Its distinctive end is to cultivate a sense of morals or justice in its members, and it does that, in the most characteristic way, through the teaching of law. And so the question was raised: What kind of being does not stand in need of a polity? He would be a man who is already so perfect that he does not require the restraint of law, or he would be a being who is cut off decisively from those possibilities of moral instruction that are contained within the law. He must be, as Aristotle said, "either a beast or a god."[10]

But to recall the classic understanding is to notice how far it departs from the persuasion of our own day. The voice of our times is the voice of Justice Holmes, and Holmes thought it would be a decided gain "if every word of moral significance could be banished from the law altogether, and other words adopted which should

[8] Ibid., 1280b.

[9] Ibid. As Aristotle suggested, the case for oligarchy would be strengthened considerably if the ends of the polity were merely the accumulation and protection of property: for who should be better qualified in that case to lead the state but the people who had already demonstrated their acumen in collecting and preserving property? See 1280a. Similarly, if the end of the state were simply the protection of people against physical violence, then it would be the soldier who would have the preeminent claim to govern. But if we insist, with Aristotle, that the aim of the polity is not merely to preserve property and life but to encourage a "good quality [or character] of life," then the claim to lead the state would require something more than the skills of making money or waging war. Presumably we would look for people who had cultivated some notable competence in the arts of rendering justice.

[10] Ibid., 1253a.

convey legal ideas uncolored by anything outside the law."[11] In the modern understanding, the ends of polity and law have been reduced to the protection of people from material injuries, and in this perspective the question raised, for example, by racial discrimination has indeed been reduced to the problem of depriving people of material services.

And yet we introduce the gravest confusion about the grounds of our law when we insist that the law may reach only matters in which material injuries are either present or imminent. We would seem to suggest then, with Hobbes, that if the hurt is not "corporeal," it must only be "phantastical." But the problems of "the city" compel us to raise again for ourselves the question of whether we take the city seriously as a moral association, and whether, in fact, it is proper to constitute political life on any terms other than a commitment to establish the conditions of justice or morals. The study of the city may attain its highest effect when it helps us reach those larger questions about the relation in our law between "principles" and "injuries"; for when it does that, it would also move us toward a recognition of those substantive moral principles that ought to be dominant in political life.

With that purpose in mind, I have chosen to begin this book with a consideration of certain questions of civility, defamation, and the restraint of speech. These problems raise in almost the purest form the question of whether there are implicit, in the moral sense of a *civitas* or a civil order, any commitments that citizens can be legally obliged to respect. The question occurs in nearly a pure form because when we deal with many varieties of speech that degrade the climate of civility, we deal with cases in which material injuries are largely absent, or, at the most, rather speculative. That is especially true in cases involving the defamation of racial or religious groups. The offensive speech may be the source of serious material injuries as it puts the stamp of obloquy on a whole group of people, and yet it may be impossible to draw a clear empirical connection between any given instance of "hate literature" and the suffering of a hurt by a particular person. If the law can reach this kind of speech, it is only, as I would argue, because the offensiveness of the speech is grounded in certain principles that are necessary to the very ideas of law and morals.

[11] Holmes, "The Path of the Law," in *Collected Legal Papers* (New York: Harcourt Brace and Company, 1920), p. 179. See, by way of contrast, Roscoe Pound, *Law and Morals* (Chapel Hill: University of North Carolina Press, 1926), especially pp. 74-75.

For a variety of reasons, then, the question of civility and speech provides an appropriate place to begin a discussion of the grounds of principle that are necessary and sufficient in restraining personal freedom. This issue cannot be addressed, of course, without compelling us to get clear on our understanding of the First Amendment—that is, to understand the grounds on which speech may be restrained, with justification, in a constitutional order. But that question, in turn, cannot be addressed without establishing some understanding about the grounds on which personal freedom of any other kind may be restricted, legitimately, in a regime of law. In other words, the question of civility and law would have to be taken to its root, and in responding to the question it would be necessary to establish, in effect, one's understanding of the first principles of republican government.

As we moved, then, through the range of other problems that arise in the city, we would be compelled to reconcile our judgments on the restriction of speech with the judgments we are inclined to reach on other issues of public policy. It will be discovered, I think, with a cumulative force, that one cannot be a "libertarian" on the central issues of the First Amendment and at the same time be a "liberal" on the critical problems of policy that arise in the city. For if one denied the validity of all restraints on speech or expression, it would be that much harder to turn around and restrict the liberty of individuals in other areas of private choice. If it is insisted, in cases of speech, that there must be a substantial probability of material injury before the freedom of individuals may be restricted, it may be just as hard to show, by the same standards, that any material injury would arise from the exercise of personal freedom in other arenas—in the refusal, for example, of a white homeowner to sell his home to a black family, or in the refusal of white parents to send their children to an integrated school.

Whether we can reach these cases depends less on the demonstration of a material injury than on our ability to establish the principles that are being violated. In a regime of law we would have to say that the burden of proof rests with those who would restrict freedom in any of its forms. That understanding, of course, flows from the character of a "liberal" political order, but in this respect the commitments of a liberal order merely express the logic of the connection between morals and law: In the most demanding sense there would simply be no justification for binding others through the law unless the legislation were established on a ground of moral principle—that is, unless it rested on a moral proposition that held true, as a matter of necessity, for others as well as oneself.

When that test can be met, as it could be, for example, in our laws on civil rights, then the laws may be enforced with their full vigor.

But there are many important laws on our books that could not survive a stringent test of that kind, and we come to recognize here what we should have known all along: that a political community which takes itself seriously as a moral association is not obliged to extend its reach until it governs almost everything. It need not be driven to find "moral" implications in every matter of dispute; it need not be impelled to enlarge the domain of "political" life and bring every matter of consequence within the reach of its powers. The requirements of a moral argument are in fact very demanding, and a government that understood the moral grounds on which its own authority rested could end up, in many cases, doing less rather than more. But when the requirements of a moral argument can be satisfied, a government would be obliged to respect the logic that attaches to moral principles and to set about vindicating the interests of justice.

One or two friends who would generally share the perspective I represent here have nevertheless urged me to point out that the classic understanding of the polis is not quite in accord with the understanding that informed the creation of the American republic. They would counsel me to record my recognition that the Founders sought to render the problem of government more tractable by scaling down the ends of the political order: the polity fashioned by the Founders would not seek to address the highest questions—questions about the purpose or the proper ends of human life—and it would not find its chief mission in cultivating the moral character of its citizens. Governments that sought in this way to address the highest questions were governments that bred divisiveness and civil wars, and if they presumed to answer these questions in an official way, the polities they produced were likely to be anything but libertarian. And so, instead of directing political life to its highest ends, the Founders settled (in this view) for the rather more modest aims that were consistent with the Lockean vision of politics: The polity would confine itself to the task of preserving the lives and property of its citizens, and securing for them the liberty they would require to pursue their own self-interest.[12]

But as the energies of men were directed toward the acquisition

[12] This argument was set forth with more calibration and elegance by the late Martin Diamond in "Democracy and *The Federalist*: A Reconsideration of the Framers' Intent," *American Political Science Review*, Vol. 53 (March 1959), pp. 52-68.

of property, they would be diverted into channels that were conducive to the preservation of civic peace, and in that sense the problem of politics would be eased. As Tocqueville observed, "violent political passions have but little hold on those who have devoted all their faculties to the pursuit of their well-being."[13] The passions of acquisition and commerce are passions that can be domesticated: they can be satisfied without war; they can fuel undertakings that raise the standard of living and solve the problem of want; and anything that solves the problem of want can soften many other conflicts in society. The conflicts may be softened, of course, because the ends of politics, or the common concerns that defined the character of the community, would no longer embrace any matter of moral consequence. In the classic polis, citizens were to find their connection to one another through the ties of a common moral commitment; but in the commercial republic citizens would be bound together mainly through the ties of dependence and mutual interest. In this way, as Walter Berns remarked, "acquisition [would] replace the morality that formerly constituted the community, the cement that bound men into a community. . . ."[14]

And yet, as it was said in the Federalist #49, even "the most rational government will not find it a superfluous advantage to have the prejudices of the community on its side." Even citizens who are bound together through a common moral understanding may not find it useless to have, in the ties of industry and commerce, a set of interests that support their moral attachments. A respect for the logic of moral principles does require, as I have said, the commitments of law; but it also requires at the same time that people be left free to pursue their own wants and interests, including their taste for acquisition and commerce, so long as those interests are legitimate (that is, so long as they do not violate any moral principle in the strictest sense). There is nothing incompatible, then, between the moral premises of a real polity and the conditions that describe a free economy with a vigorous commercial life. In that respect we are reminded that the conditions of a free economy are merely another manifestation of a regime that respects personal freedom

[13] Tocqueville, *Democracy in America* (New York: Vintage, 1954), Vol. II, p. 265. If one perceives, as Tocqueville said, "that the Americans are on every side unceasingly engaged in the execution of important and difficult plans, which the slightest revolution would throw in confusion, [one] will readily comprehend why people so well employed are by no means tempted to perturb the state or to destroy that public tranquillity by which they all profit." Ibid., p. 127.

[14] Walter Berns, "Thinking About the City," *Commentary* (October 1973), pp. 74-77, at 76.

in all of its forms so long as that freedom is not directed toward ends that are unjustified or illegitimate.

When the Founders spoke of "natural rights" and the ends of government, it is true that their understanding was usually rooted in the notion of individuals animated by a natural impulse to seek their own "self-preservation." The Founders did indeed speak in the language of Locke and Hobbes, but their minds were furnished also from other sources. They drew upon a tradition of writing that ran back from Locke to Hooker to Aquinas to Aristotle; their discussions were informed by a sense of ancient history and philosophy; and even though their language was often the language of "moderns," their conception of the ends of government was critically affected by a classic understanding. That understanding was more likely to be found, though, in the things the Founders did not think it necessary to make fully explicit. The writings of the Founders were persistently textured by such qualifications as the "just" powers of the government or the "legitimate" interests of the state, and that language marked a frame of mind in which moral distinctions always mattered. It also marked what the Founders decorously took for granted. And so, Madison could argue in the Federalist #10 for the largest measure of freedom for people to pursue their own interests, but it went without saying that this freedom could be claimed only in the service of legitimate ends. Presumably, the people who derived their incomes from prostitution would not be free to advertise their wares in public merely because they could claim to possess a commercial "interest." Nor would the question have been affected in any way if a majority of the population had manifested a demand for this particular commerce.[15]

---

[15] It is worth recalling that when Madison argued against the establishment of religion, he pointed out that states with religious establishments were often plagued by the same vices that afflicted states without established churches. The antidote to vices was not to be found in the establishment of religion (which would only corrupt the churches), but in laws that were designed "to cherish virtue." Madison supported the traditional responsibility of local governments to act for the health, welfare, and "morals" of the population—the mandate under which local governments restricted cockfighting and horse-racing and dealt with criminality in its more prosaic forms. But beyond that, Madison was willing to use the taxing power of the federal government to put a levy on rum and discourage the use of spiritous liquors. He wisely opposed schemes of prohibition that would have banned outright the use of hard liquors; but he had no doubt that governments in the United States could properly use their powers for the sake of suppressing those things that have been classified traditionally as "vices." See Joseph Hartt Nesler, "Madison, the Ancients and the Moderns: An Inquiry into the Ends of Republican Government," Senior thesis, Amherst College (1978), pp. 75, 76, 105.

The Founders, in other words, were not prepared to draw their judgments of propriety from the play of the marketplace. They apparently assumed that the law would perpetually do what the law must always do: make distinctions between the things that are justified or unjustified and the kinds of occupations that are legitimate or illegitimate. James Wilson explained in his lectures on jurisprudence that the purpose of government was to secure and expand "natural rights"—the rights of a man, for example, "to his property, to his character, to liberty, and to safety."[16] But that was to say, in effect, that the protection of natural rights encompassed the protection of people from virtually all species of injustice—that is, from almost any harm inflicted on them without justification. As Madison summed it up, "Justice is the end of government. It is the end of civil society."[17] But once this understanding is in place, the premises of political life are conceived in terms that were understood by the classics—the only terms, one soon discovers, that are ultimately coherent or practicable. The function of the law is to declare what is right or wrong, just or unjust, and the task of the legislator is to come to an understanding of the principles that define the proper ends—and limits—of the law.

But even if it is true that a classic view of the city may still be pertinent to our own politics, Aristotle's understanding of "the city" was probably closer to our current sense of the nation-state—the most sovereign and inclusive association in any territory—than to those things we regard today as "cities." And yet the attribute of sovereignty or the size of the community are not as critical in this matter as the exercise of political authority and the *perspective* that arises on the problem of politics when the polity is taken seriously as a moral association. Governments at the national and local levels will often reach different objects, but anyone who exercises lawful authority over others must be obliged to consider the grounds of principle on which he would impose public law and displace private choice. To the extent that officials at the local level are free to make decisions of their own, their decisions must raise questions about the principles that underlie their judgments, and the standards by which they distinguish between ends that are good or bad, legitimate or illegitimate. The nature of this inquiry is irreducibly philosophic, whether or not political men recognize what is truly required of them. And the discipline of moral judgment

[16] *The Works of James Wilson*, ed. Robert G. McCloskey (Cambridge: Harvard University Press, 1967), Vol. II, p. 593.
[17] *The Federalist* #51 (New York: Modern Library, n.d.), p. 340.

remains the same, it retains the same essential properties, whether it takes place at the local or the national level.

It makes a certain sense then to view the cities as polities, even though they may be polities that are immured in a larger political order. For one thing, we may put the accent in the right place, on the right set of questions. We are all too often inclined to find the presence of the city in those services that press immediately on our lives, such as the cleaning of streets or the regulation of traffic. But the city may mark its character more sharply as it reaches certain questions of moral judgment which are far more important for its citizens in establishing the kind of people they wish to be. And so the city may face the question of whether the Nazis should be restrained from marching into Jewish neighborhoods; whether patterns of discrimination by race should be abetted or resisted; whether abortion clinics should become subject to regulations that are very encouraging or restrictive.

Different cities have obviously rendered different judgments on these matters. They have also been affected in their character by different arrangements in the structure of legal and political power, and by different levels of what we may call the "urbanity" and discipline of their own people. But this variety of experience provides still another reason for viewing cities at times as small political orders in themselves. Wherever there is a real political process at work, wherever officials at the local level are free to make decisions on their own in matters that count, the possibility exists that the local community can manifest its character in its public policy and in the structure of its politics. The character and power structure of Chicago have been noticeably different over the years from those of either New York or Los Angeles. The Chicago of Richard Daley was far different from the New York of John Lindsay or Abraham Beame in its experience with labor unions and strikes in the public service. The disciplined party government of Chicago could hardly be mistaken for the weak party system of Los Angeles; the police of Chicago or Albany, with their ties to ward politics, could not be confused with their highly bureaucratic and "professionalized" counterparts in Los Angeles. There are some cities that have taken a very tough attitude toward gambling and prostitution, while other cities have been known as "open towns," where the official attitude toward vice is more tolerant or casual. In this respect there was a difference in the past between Boston and St. Louis that one could hardly fail to notice, even though the two cities found their place within the same national polity. These differences that are still possible in the political character of our cities are distinctions that can still affect in vital ways the tone and style and habits of daily life and what it means even today to be the citizen of a city.

The perspectives of the classics on the problem of politics recall a connection between morals and law that was understood more clearly at an earlier time, even in our own country. And my contention here is that the alternative which is presented in the classic perspective can become more evident if we return, initially at least, to the more circumscribed arena of the city. In this respect there may be a lesson hidden in the fact that it is municipal government in the United States that still retains an explicit residue of the older understanding about the ends of a polity. It is local government in this country that still claims a responsibility under the "police powers" to act for the "health, welfare, and *morals*" of the population. A large measure of that responsibility has already been undermined by the federal courts, and yet it is still the local governments that bear the main responsibility, for example, in protecting people against lawless assaults (including verbal assaults and defamation); establishing the conditions of propriety that govern the use of the public streets; defining the principles that shape public education; restraining the incidence of prostitution; and exercising a broad, but limited, supervision over the character of public displays and entertainments.

The business of the city reminds us that questions of morals and justice come to us always in the form of cases. It is curious that, in recent years, we have had a resurgence of works in political theory on a grand scale—works that unfold with calibration, design, and no trifling sweep; and yet, whether they argue for "equality" or for the "freedom" of the "minimal state," these works are usually spun out at a very abstract level, almost wholly unrelieved by the discussion of specific cases. Throughout these works, which include our very best, one feels a hunger for something like cases in law—for some effort, in other words, to sort out conflicting claims and to show how principles of moral judgment may actually bear on the real world. In short, one comes to wish that those who propound theories of justice would move along a series of cases and possibly show, in a chain of demonstrations, just how their theories may actually succeed in rendering justice.

It is from that kind of abstraction, it seems to me, that the city, as a vantage point, may save us. We might say that the city gives us a certain handle or lever by which we may move from the circumstances of the real world to the lasting principles that ought to govern that world. I tend to doubt, for my own part, that there is anything very different about the nature of politics when it occurs in an urban place. But as I have suggested, there may be something about a city that poses in a much sharper form some of the older questions of political theory. The questions come to us in this setting with a certain familiarity and vividness, through the palpable incidents of our daily lives; and in putting the matter to us in this way, through the things we can readily touch, there may be something in the nature of a city that helps to remind us of what some of those older questions were. If the problem of the city also moves us to recall the classic view of the polis, and the classic understanding of the relation between morals and law, it may put us in touch again with a perspective that would have to be understood today as that of "neither Nozick nor Rawls."[18] The angle of vision here would serve as an alternative, in our own time, to the perspectives of those who would reject the classic tradition, as it were, from the Right as well as the Left.

That is not to say that a book of this kind, which makes its way to political theory from the politics of the city, can really take the place of a more intensive work on the principles of morals and politics. But in the course of performing its own tasks it may succeed in drawing out many of the substantive moral truths, as well as the forms of moral reasoning, that would fill out those principles of morals and justice; and it may stand, withal, as a summons to that further work. It may help to show just how much a moral perspective may count in understanding the questions raised by the politics of cities. And it may compel us finally to conclude that Plato was largely right when he had Socrates say of himself in the *Gorgias* that he was the only statesman in Athens, the only one engaged in the true political art.[19] In the last analysis it may indeed be only the philosopher who is capable of addressing, at their root, the practical questions of public policy that arise in the city.

What is ironic in our own day is that when we consider the training that ought to be given to the men and women who would govern cities, our attention has been drawn to such things as the principles of traffic management or the principles of accounting, or perhaps, at most, to the principles of "city planning." And yet

---

[18] I have in mind, of course, those two estimable works: John Rawls, *A Theory of Justice* (Cambridge: Harvard University Press, 1971), and Robert Nozick, *Anarchy, State and Utopia* (New York: Basic Books, 1974).

[19] 521d.

if it is true that, whatever else a city is, it is also, in its own limited sphere, a polity, then it is quite as plausible that the people who govern cities ought to know something, too, about the principles of justice. That indulges an assumption, of course, which was held more securely in an earlier time: that there are in fact moral truths that are as knowable and as certain as mathematical truths. If that understanding has become less secure in our own time, it is not because the truths have ceased to be true, but because that original understanding has grown faint among the very people in the academy and public life who have borne the largest responsibility in the past for preserving the tradition of moral philosophy. It may be at once the shortcoming and the advantage of our own day that it requires the politics of the city to remind us of the enduring things we once knew.

ONE

THE COMMITMENTS OF CIVILITY

II

POLITICAL DISCOURSE AND THE DEFAMATION OF GROUPS

In the late 1960's James Q. Wilson reported a survey that was carried out in Boston among more than one thousand homeowners, who were asked what they thought was the biggest problem facing the city. The "usual" kinds of urban problems—housing, transportation, pollution, urban renewal—were a major concern of only 18 percent of those who were questioned. Only 9 percent mentioned jobs and unemployment, even though many of the persons interviewed had incomes at, or even below, what was often regarded as the poverty level. The issue that concerned people more than any other was described rather variously in terms of things like crime, violence, rebellious youth, racial tension, public immorality, delinquency. The concern held among blacks as well as whites, liberals as well as conservatives, and although it might have looked on the surface like a reaction to "crime in the streets," many of the things that were mentioned were not criminal in any strict legal sense. They involved what one might call forms of incivility or of public indecencies: verbal assaults in the street; unconstrained, rowdy teenagers; lurid advertisements in front of neighborhood movies; tawdry paperbacks and magazines. As Wilson summed it up, the concern seemed to be for improper behavior in public places[1] and the apparent disintegration of any standards that might claim to govern one's behavior in a public place according to some understanding of civility.

It has traditionally been thought that a man who can restrain himself out of respect for some other interest than his own, someone who shows in the ordinary course of his life a sense of obligation to family, friends, or community, is a far better man, a far more humane and civilized being, than one who respects no law beyond his own self-interest. In the strictest sense a polity would not be possible if it were composed of people who refused to accept obligations to others, and so it should not be surprising that most

[1] James Q. Wilson, "The Urban Unease," *The Public Interest* (Summer 1968), pp. 25, 27.

people tend to measure the goodness of cities by the conditions of civility rather than the supply of amenities. The love affair that many Americans have had in the past with London arose from the presence of attributes that were increasingly missing in American cities in the 1950's and 1960's: a pervasive climate of civility, gentleness, and restraint; a release from the imminent expectation of violent crime; a freedom to send children abroad in the city on their own, without fears for their safety.

But when we speak of civility we speak, really, about the fostering of moral codes and of the prospect of teaching something in a public way about the kind of life, the manners, even the modes of making a living that we hold up for emulation—about the occupations that are more or less respectable for people who are suited to live in a civil society. And not the least of what we teach, in giving some insight into ourselves and our standards, are the things we regard as respectable to say in public.

Madison warned in the Federalist #10 that the greatest threat to civility in a republic found its sources in the character of the regime itself: In a regime of personal liberty, where individuals and groups were free to press their interests in public, the violence and calumnies of faction promised to be an enduring part of the public arena of politics. The demands and interests of groups may provide the raw materials of politics, and it is no wonder then that the assault and defense of groups may occupy a prominent place in what passes for our public discourse on politics. As factional conflict expands in the freedom that a republican regime affords, one can expect, too, that the public rhetoric of the day will get less, rather than more, subtle, and that speech may become almost conventionally libelous, routinely hateful. If one adds to that the conditions of a modern urban society, where the transitions are rather abrupt, and differences of race, culture, class, and ethnicity may confront one another rather sharply, the collision of groups may reach a level at times that is truly explosive. In this setting, as Justice Frankfurter came to observe, the attack on racial and religious groups may not only promote civil strife, but "tend powerfully to obstruct the manifold adjustments required for free, ordered life in a metropolitan, polyglot community."[2]

[2] *Beauharnais* v. *Illinois*, 343 U.S. 250, 259 (1952). The best modern example is the race riots in Chicago in 1919. For the background and analysis of these riots, see Chicago Commission on Race Relations, *The Negro in Chicago* (New York: Arno Press, 1968; originally published in 1922); St. Clair Drake and Horace R. Cayton, *Black Metropolis* (New York: Harcourt Brace, 1970), pp. 8-18, 31-65; and

The question of civility might be posed, then, with the greatest consequence for a society in the defamation of groups, or what has become known more commonly as group libel. But the problem has a special force in relation to those groups defined by race, religion, and nationality; and it is the questions raised in the law by the defamation of these kinds of groups that take the problem of restricting speech to its philosophic root. For other groups, the current understanding in the law seems sensible enough and quite adequate to its ends: Actions for libel will hold more easily to the extent that the group is smaller and that an individual can be identified more readily as a member of the group.[3] With this variety of libel, the remedy has been, quite properly, a civil suit in which individuals may seek an award for personal damages. But there are certain kinds of defamation that cannot be dealt with reasonably through civil suits, and the injuries they produce are not always so immediate or direct that they can be weighed instantly in the courts. They are not for that reason, however, any less real as injuries. For them the criminal law would provide a more suitable instrument; but one would have an obligation then to be even more careful and explicit about the grounds on which the criminal law would rest in these cases. Not the least of the complications is that the speech involved here has moved quite patently beyond the level of individuals to the defamation of whole groups, and so it has moved beyond the plane of private quarrels to involve disputes that are more nearly public and "political" in nature. Therefore, the prob-

---

on a more impressionistic, but very evocative, level, James T. Farrell's *Studs Lonigan* (New York: Vanguard Press, 1935).

[3] In one notable case, for example, suits were brought against the authors of *U.S.A. Confidential* for charging in their book that some of the models and salesgirls in the Neiman-Marcus store in Texas had often served as "call girls," and that most of the male salesmen were homosexuals. Suits were brought by nine models, who made up the entire staff of models at the time the book was published; by fifteen salesmen out of a group of twenty-five; and by thirty saleswomen out of a group of three hundred eighty-two. The defendants did not contest the suit brought by the models, but they moved to dismiss the claims made by the salesmen and saleswomen. The court rejected the motion to dismiss as to the salesmen, because the group was small and the allegation had been made that "most" of the men were homosexuals. However, the court did reject the suit brought by the saleswomen. It pointed to the large size of the group, and it argued that "no reasonable man would take the writer seriously and conclude from the publication a reference to any individual saleswoman." *Neiman-Marcus* v. *Lait*, 13 F.R.D. 311 (1952). See also Philip Wittenberg, *Dangerous Words* (New York: Columbia University Press, 1947), chs. 11, 12; Mason C. Lewis, "The Individual Member's Right to Recover for a Defamation Leveled at a Group," 17 *U. Miami L. Rev.* 519 (1963).

lem raises, in a much sterner test, the question of whether speech can ever legitimately be restricted out of a regard for civility—out of a regard, that is, for those moral commitments that are simply implicit in the idea of law and a civil order.

Since the 1930's and 1940's, when fascist organizations were engaged in the systematic defamation of racial and religious groups, the interest in group libel statutes has declined markedly. There are only four state laws on the books now in this country,[4] prosecutions have been rare, and convictions even rarer.[5] Indeed, the concept of group libel itself seems to have fallen into disfavor among legal scholars.[6] To put it mildly, it is not treated any longer with the same plausibility or even esteem that it held in the 1940's.[7] Among "professional" civil libertarians, the concept is treated as an anachronism, and its general disuse in recent years is taken as a sign of its ultimate inaptness in our constitutional law. For spokesmen of the American Civil Liberties Union, it has been a matter both of principle and strategy that group libel be held in disgrace, and they have expressed alarm on those occasions when the concept has shown even a flickering sign that it is still alive.[8]

And yet the irony, as we shall see, is that there are important parts of our public policy today, including sections of our recent Civil Rights acts, that would be hard to understand or justify on anything other than group libel grounds. The deeper irony is that both the American Civil Liberties Union and the Justice Department, in their tendency to avoid the group libel argument as a ground of justification, have fallen back on formulas which are far more threatening to free speech, and which should be even more suspect to civil libertarians. What is involved here, of course, is the old distinction that has been drawn between political and com-

[4] Conn. Gen. Statutes, Sec. 53-37 (1958); Ind. Stat. Ann., Secs. 10-914 (1956); Mass. Gen. Laws, Ch. 272, Sec. 98(c) (1956); and West Va. Code, Sec. 55-7-14 (1966).

[5] A venerable survey on the subject can be found in Joseph Tanenhaus, "Group Libel," 35 *Cornell L. Q.* 261, 276, 286 (1950).

[6] See, for example, Harry Kalven, *The Negro and the First Amendment* (Columbus: Ohio State University Press, 1965), ch. 1.

[7] On this latter point there is no better example than David Riesman's classic series of articles on "Democracy and Defamation" in 42 *Columbia L. R.* 727, 1085, and 1282 (1942). Even Joseph Tanenhaus, who was more apprehensive about the effects that group libel laws might have in restricting legitimate forms of expression, could still regard group libel, much in the way Riesman did, as a serious concern of a liberal society and a fit object of legal remedy. See note 5 above.

[8] See John Pemberton, Jr., "Can the Law Provide a Remedy for Race Defamation in the United States?" 14 *N.Y.U. Law Forum* 33 (1968).

mercial speech, and the willingness to rest with an unjustified serenity on the "clear and present danger" test in cases where the
danger test would tend to work with effects that are decidedly less
than libertarian.

Beyond that, we will find that the choice in the group libel problem is not between the restraint of free expression and the absence
of restraint. It is more of a choice, rather, between two forms of
restraint: one carried out by private groups operating outside the
law, usually with a more diffuse effect and a much vaguer sense
of limits (a form of restraint, in fact, that is closer to censorship
than to the kind of restraint we associate with the law of libel);
and another kind of restriction, of a more limited nature, carried
out by the legal authorities under the discipline of working with
a formal statute. In the earliest writings on libertarian thought, the
host of repressions carried out in society outside the law were no
less to be feared than a program of censorship imposed by the
government, and in some respects they could be vastly worse. As
Mill wrote in *On Liberty*:[9]

> Like other tyrannies, the tyranny of the majority was at first,
> and is still vulgarly, held in dread chiefly as operating through
> the acts of the public authorities. But reflecting persons per-
> ceived that when society is itself the tyrant—society collectively
> over the separate individuals who compose it—its means of
> tyrannizing are not restricted to the acts which it may do by
> the hands of its political functionaries. Society can and does
> execute its own mandates; and if it issues wrong mandates
> instead of right, or any mandates at all in things with which
> it ought not to meddle, it practices a social tyranny more
> formidable than many kinds of political oppression, since,
> though not usually upheld by such extreme penalties, it leaves
> fewer means of escape, penetrating much more deeply into the
> details of life. . . . Protection, therefore, against the tyranny
> of the magistrate is not enough: there needs protection also
> against the tyranny of the prevailing opinion and feeling;
> against the tendency of society to impose by other means than
> civil penalties, its own ideas and practices as rules of conduct.
> . . .

In the present period, the consent of the majority is often taken
to mean the appeasement of the minority whose interests are more

---

[9] John Stuart Mill, *On Liberty* (Oxford: Basil Blackwell, 1946), p. 4.

directly engaged in any case, and who are more likely to take action to protect their interests. If one puts in the place of Mill's amorphous "majority" the organized minorities and "veto groups," which may exercise extraordinary leverage in their relations with newspapers and the broadcast media, one may find the forces that comprise the "majority" that Mill suspected, and which produce, in combination, the "social tyranny" he anticipated in the regulation of the most ordinary things. That these small acts of censorship may be carried on in the name of "responsiveness to the local community" is no warrant for their innocence. That we are more inclined to let them pass unnoticed, out of the mistaken belief, quite often, that there is nothing public policy can do to affect them, says something more about the limits of our sensitivity as libertarians than about the triviality or the harmlessness of these private intimidations.

1. THE PROBLEM OF GROUP LIBEL:
Beauharnais v. *Illinois*

The question of group libel came before the Supreme Court for the first time in 1952, in the case of *Beauharnais* v. *Illinois*,[10] and since that time the Court has not faced the question directly again.[11] The Court in *Beauharnais* upheld a statute in Illinois that established criminal penalties for the defamation of "a class of citizens, of any race, color, creed or religion." The defamation of groups took place, of course, in the familiar forms, through published or spoken insults that were directed at a particular class; and because defamation was a species of assault (or "insult") there was a traditional concern also that it could stir tumults and violence in the community. In the case of *Beauharnais*, the offense took the form of leaflets which were distributed in a busy section of Chicago, and which branded blacks as a group of congenital robbers and rapists. The leaflet sought to excite opposition among whites to the movement of blacks into white neighborhoods, but it took an overly literal reading of the leaflet to see it as a publication confined to the question of housing. If the leaflet happened to counsel, in this instance, a resistance to blacks as neighbors, that counsel flowed from a teaching of universal, unmeasured hostility toward any semblance of

---

[10] 343 U.S. 250 (1952).

[11] There were other cases, though, which were not appealed to the federal courts, in which statutes were sustained that allowed criminal prosecutions for the defamation of groups. See *People* v. *Turner*, 28 Cal. App. 766 (1914); *Crane* v. *State*, 14 Okl. Crim. 30, 166 P. 1110 (1917); *Alumbaugh* v. *State*, 39 Ga. App. 559, 147 S.E. 714 (1920); and *People* v. *Speilman*, 318 Ill. 482, 149 N.E. 466 (1925).

civil relations between blacks and whites. The "political" import of this leaflet was as evident in 1952 as it is in our own day, and yet it was understood by the Court at the time that the "political" character of this publication was not enough in itself to invest this form of expression with the protections of the First Amendment.

But a serious question can be raised as to whether the Court would still hold today to its understanding in *Beauharnais*, particularly after the landmark decision in *New York Times* v. *Sullivan*[12] and the cases that followed in its train. In the *Times* case, the Court explicitly rejected for the first time the concept of seditious libel (i.e., the defaming of the government) and it restricted the freedom of public officials to make use of the laws of libel for the purpose of silencing their citizen-critics. The Court argued in that case for a certain "breathing space" for speech on the understanding that political speech is often heated and exaggerated, and that it often takes place in the public streets, under conditions of excitement, where it might not be possible to verify every assertion that is made, as though one were working in a library on a piece of scholarly research. The Court contracted the grounds of libel then to a very narrow test of "malice": the allegedly defamatory statement had to be made with knowledge that it was false, or with "reckless disregard" of whether it was false or not.[13]

With a few short steps over the next three years, the Court went even further in rolling back this coverage of the law of libel. From public officials it moved to "public figures" (that is, celebrities who may not, however, hold office at the moment),[14] and then finally even to the inadvertent subjects of publicity, who just happened to be involved in events that one of the news media considered newsworthy.[15] Over the past few years, however, the Court has steadily reclaimed some of the protections of the law of libel that it seemed to be discarding, in a surge of novelty, in its earlier decisions. It has restored the protections of the laws on libel to public figures and even to the inadvertent subjects of publicity who became public figures merely because they were covered in the press.[16] At the same

[12] 376 U.S. 254 (1964).

[13] Ibid. at 280; see also *St. Amant* v. *Thompson*, 390 U.S. 727 (1968).

[14] *Associated Press* v. *Walker*, 388 U.S. 130 (1966); see also Harry Kalven, "The Reasonable Man and the First Amendment: Hill, Butts and Walker," 1967 *Supreme Court Review* 267.

[15] *Time, Inc.* v. *Hill*, 385 U.S. 374 (1966).

[16] See, in this vein, *Gertz* v. *Robert Welch, Inc.*, 418 U.S. 23 (1974), *Time, Inc.* v. *Firestone*, 424 U.S. 448 (1976), and *Hutchinson* v. *Proxmire*, 61 L. Ed. 2d 411 (1979).

time the Court has made it clear that it does not regard the test of "malice" as too infirm in its definition to be taken seriously. The Court has shown, in this respect, a willingness to take evidence on the facts that were known to the people who published the alleged libel. To the dismay of many editors and reporters, the Court has been compelled to point out very recently that this test of malice may well have to include evidence on the reasons that underlay decisions on research and editing.[17]

But in the wave of change that followed *Times* v. *Sullivan* it appeared for a while that the traditional restraints on libel would be swept away. It was readily presumed, in this mood, that the decision in *Beauharnais* would go the way of all of those other parts of the law which affirmed, in one way or another, the claim of the law to restrict defamation and other forms of verbal assault. And yet, less than a year after the decision in *Times* v. *Sullivan* the Court mentioned *Beauharnais* approvingly, and it seemed to suggest then that the decision in *Beauharnais* was not really threatened by the lines of doctrine that were emerging from the *Times* case.[18] That intimation brought a sharp dissent from Justice Douglas, who had apparently thought that *Beauharnais* had been silently laid aside by the *Times* case. He railed against *Beauharnais* as a "misfit in our constitutional system," a decision that was out of line with "the dictates of the First Amendment," and if it had not been overruled earlier, he thought the Court should waste no time in overruling it now.[19]

The question of *Beauharnais* has lingered, and it has been raised in a dramatic way more recently by the dispute over the American Nazis in Skokie. That case became the object of a fierce debate throughout the country in the summer of 1977, when a contingent of American Nazis sought to stage a march in a suburb of Chicago that contained a large proportion of Jews (including many former refugees who had survived the Holocaust). The Village of Skokie sought to prevent the march and it succeeded at first in gaining an injunction from a county court. But after a series of appeals to the state and federal courts the injunction was dissolved. In June 1978 the Supreme Court refused to order a stay of the judgment handed down by the federal court of appeals in Illinois, which had removed the injunction and cleared the way, in effect, for the Nazis to march.

But if it was understood in *Beauharnais* that words and gestures

---

[17] See *Herbert* v. *Lando*, 60 L. Ed. 2d 115, especially note 6 (1979).
[18] *Garrison* v. *Louisiana*, 379 U.S. 64, 70 (1964).
[19] Ibid. at 82.

could become vehicles of assault, then that concern was clearly raised by the prospect of Nazis parading with the symbols of genocide (with the swastikas on flags and uniforms) through a community that contained survivors of the Holocaust. If it was recognized in *Beauharnais* that speech could be used to stir up hatred toward members of particular racial or ethnic groups, then that condition, too, was present in the case of the Nazis. The march through Skokie was hardly less assaulting in character or less precise about its target than the "hate literature" that was directed against blacks in the case of *Beauharnais*. And so if *Beauharnais* still retained its validity twenty-six years later, here was a signal case, marked by wide public interest, in which the Supreme Court had the chance to settle its judgment and teach an important public lesson. But the Court did nothing more than decline to order the stay—and decline to protect the victims of the assault in this case—without providing, however, the benefit of reasons. The omission did not pass entirely without notice: Justice Blackmun rightly pointed out to his colleagues in dissent that there was "some tension" after all between the decision of the court of appeals and the decision of the Supreme Court in *Beauharnais*. If the decision in *Beauharnais* stood, then the Court was preventing the Village of Skokie from vindicating the rights of the victims and providing the protections that were sanctioned in the law. And as Justice Blackmun reminded his colleagues, the decision in *Beauharnais* still in fact stood. "*Beauharnais*," he wrote, "has never been overruled or formally limited in any way."[20]

The deeper irony in the case of Skokie is that the Court has never overturned the precedents that provided the foundation at an earlier time for the restriction of injurious speech, including the precedents that were decisive for *Beauharnais*; and it is these same precedents that the Court has used in recent years when it has sought to confirm the authority of local governments in restraining obscenity and public lewdness. At those moments the Court has been compelled to explain in a traditional, familiar voice that not all forms of speech and expression can claim the protection of the Constitution.

And so the question raised in *Beauharnais* is very much a live question at this moment in our law and our public life. As we have seen in the case of the Nazis in Skokie, it is an issue that can still tear a community apart, and it has this effect precisely because it does touch the core: because it raises questions about the moral

[20] *Smith* v. *Collin*, 57 L. Ed. 2d 1131 (1978).

premises on which the law, and the political community itself, may
be constituted. But because the question is still open, there is the
chance to look again at *Beauharnais*—to remind ourselves of the
issues of principle it raised and to reestablish its authority, if we
can, by stating the case anew.

Section 224a of the Illinois Criminal Code, Ill. Rev. Stat., 1948,
made it unlawful to:[21]

> manufacture, sell, or offer for sale, advertise or publish, pre-
> sent or exhibit in any public place in this state any lithograph,
> moving picture, play, drama or sketch, which publication or
> exhibition portrays depravity, criminality, unchastity, or lack
> of virtue of a class of citizens, of any race, color, creed or
> religion which said publication or exhibition exposes the cit-
> izens of any race, color, creed or religion to contempt, derision,
> or obloquy or which is productive of breach of the peace or
> riots. . . .[22]

Joseph Beauharnais was the president of the White Circle League,
with headquarters in Chicago. In January 1950, he gave out packages of leaflets to volunteers who offered to distribute them on
street corners in downtown Chicago. Beauharnais himself organized and directed this effort, and on January 7, 1950, the literature
was in fact distributed as he had planned. The leaflet, which was
cast in the form of a petition to the mayor and City Council, called
upon the officials of the city "to halt the further encroachment,
harassment and invasion of white people, their property, neighborhoods and persons, by the Negro—through the exercise of the
Police Power. . . ." The leaflet went on to urge "one million self-
respecting white people in Chicago to unite under the banner of
the White Circle League" to support the petition and resist the
national campaign carried on by "Truman's infamous civil rights
program and Pro Negro Organizations to amalgamate the black
and white races with the object of mongrelizing the white race!"
It was suggested, fruther, that "if persuasion and the need to prevent
the white race from becoming mongrelized by the Negro will not
unite us, then the aggressions . . . rapes, robberies, knives, guns and
marijuana of the Negro, surely will." The statement ended with the

---

[21] C. 38, Div. 1, sec. 471.

[22] The legislation was later repealed, though not, apparently, because of any weakness or lack of precision in the statute itself. It is worth noting that the Illinois law
compared rather favorably with other "model" statutes on group libel that were
being proposed in the 1940's. See Tanenhaus, note 5 above, at 293ff.

declaration that "the first loyalty of every white person is to his race" and that "the hour has struck for all normal white people to stand up and fight. . . ." Beauharnais's name appeared at the bottom of the text, along with a coupon that could serve as an application form for membership in the White Circle League.[23]

Beauharnais was arrested under the group libel statute, and in the trial that followed, the judge confined the jury to the narrow factual issues of whether he was in fact guilty of manufacturing, publishing, or distributing the leaflet, as proscribed in the law. The judge found that the leaflet was indeed defamatory within the terms of the statute; and therefore he refused either to submit that question to the jury or to follow the request of the defendant and let the conviction hinge upon a finding by the jury "that the article complained of was likely to produce a clear and present danger of a serious substantive evil that rises far above public inconvenience, annoyance or unrest."[24] Under these holdings, and with the evidence at hand, Beauharnais was convicted rather easily and assessed a fine of $200.

On appeal, Beauharnais argued that the statute abridged the freedom of speech and of the press that was protected in the First Amendment and guaranteed against the states by the due process clause of the Fourteenth Amendment. Beyond that, he contended that the law was too vague, under the requirements of the due process clause, to support a conviction.[25]

Among the dissenting judges, the issue of vagueness was taken up only by Justice Reed, and in his opinion for the majority Justice Frankfurter was able to move through that question without too much resistance. Frankfurter would recall the history of racial riots in Illinois, from the violence that erupted in Springfield in 1908, to the Cicero riots of 1951, and which included, along the way, the bloody rioting that took place, first in East St. Louis in 1917, and then in Chicago in 1919. The historical record in Illinois made the prospect of racial violence something more than an abstract question, but even without placing the prime weight on the experience in Illinois Frankfurter found the statute sufficiently clear, both in its drafting and its application, to survive a constitutional challenge. "The statute before us," he wrote, "is not a catchall enactment left at large by the State court which applied it":

[23] 343 U.S. 252-53, 276.

[24] Ibid. at 253. As Frankfurter noted in his opinion for the majority, the action of the trial court here followed the set rule for the prosecution of libels in Illinois and other states. See ibid. at 254 and n. 2.

[25] Ibid. at 251-52.

It is a law specifically directed at a defined evil, its language drawing from history and practice in Illinois and in more than a score of other jurisdictions a meaning confirmed by the Supreme Court of that State in upholding this conviction. We do not, therefore, parse the statute as grammarians or treat it as an abstract exercise in lexicography. We read it in the animating context of well-defined usage . . . and State court construction which determines its meaning for us. . . .[26]

There could not have been much serious question about the kind of speech and publication that the statute sought to restrict. The real issue, rather, was whether the statute sought to restrain speech that could not justly be restrained. The decision was bound up then with other disputes that ran more deeply in the Court over the standards of judgment and the conditions that would have to exist before one could ever be justified in restraining public speech.

2. ON LIBELS, INJURIES, AND POLITICAL SPEECH: THE BLACK DISSENT

In the case of *Beauharnais*, as in many other instances, the descriptions that the judges offered of the case did not represent a mere statement of the facts, but a reflection of the judgments they had reached on the substance of the case. Frankfurter viewed Beauharnais and his White Circle League and the literature bristling with charges against a whole racial group, and he saw the issue as a matter of group libel. Justice Black responded to the presence of an argument and the apparent absence of violence, and he insisted that the case involved a group of citizens out "peacefully [to] petition" the government. And so, according to Black, what the Court was restricting in *Beauharnais* was the freedom "to petition for and publicly discuss proposed legislation."[27]

The complaint in Black's opinion was that all the facts that added texture to the case were dissolved once it was assimilated to the law of libel. And if there really was an alternative way of conceiving the case, then there were even more compelling reasons, in Black's estimate, for avoiding the concept of "group" libel. He contended that criminal libel had been restricted in the past, with good reason, to charges that were made against individuals and not against "huge groups." With that perspective, the punishment of speech and expression had been confined "to the narrowest of areas involving nothing more than purely private feuds." But every expansion of

[26] Ibid. at 253.　　　　　　　　[27] Ibid. at 267-68, 275.

the law of libel threatened to punish "discussions of matters of public concern" and invade the area of speech protected by the First Amendment.[28] The argument here, again, bore the imprint of the Federalist #10, or at the very least it was deepened by an awareness of a regime of public competition: where the demands of groups became the very stuff of politics, it might be impossible to talk about political things in public without assaulting or defending the interests of identifiable groups—unions, real estate boards, civil rights groups—and if political discourse was often intemperate, one could expect that a good deal of it would involve the maligning of groups in public. In that event how could one prosecute for the defamation of groups without touching at many points the kind of speech that is constitutionally protected, or, as Black put it, without making it "very dangerous indeed to say something critical of one of [these] groups."[29]

It is not likely, though, that Black's argument rested on the assumption that speech directed at individuals was less "public" or "political" than speech directed at groups. That assumption was far too problematic, and it could not in itself explain the grounds on which Black could still regard an action for libel as something he could accept in principle. A further guide to his understanding might have been found in his comments about the size of the group and the wisdom of narrowing the scope of the libel. Altogether they suggest a second line of argument, which might have been stated in this way: Traditionally it has been the test of individual injuries that has added concreteness and discipline to prosecutions for libel (and it is only when those qualities are present that libel becomes a comprehensible offense which may be vindicated in courts). But as soon as one considers the libel of whole groups, the remarks get more and more general, the target becomes larger and more diffuse, and it becomes that much harder to argue that anyone *in particular* has been libeled. If someone went on national television and made disparaging remarks about blacks in general, it would be absurd, say, to let the Reverend Jesse Jackson go into a court in Chicago, seeking personal damages.[30] Once the connection to individual in-

---

[28] Ibid. at 271-72.   [29] See Black, ibid. at 273.

[30] It may be as unworkable, in this respect, as the suit brought by the Mexican-American Anti-Defamation Committee against the makers of Frito corn chips. A television advertisement for Frito Banditos had a stereotyped cartoon character, a Latin American with sombrero, mustache, and accent. The Anti-Defamation Committee claimed that the advertisement reenforced a harmful stereotype of the Mexican-American, and it sought $100 in punitive damages for every Chicano in the United States. See *The New York Times*, January 1, 1971, p. 31.

juries is lost—or so, at least, the argument may go—the charge of libel becomes so vague that it may be nothing more than an arbitrary warrant for cutting off speech that is critical of certain groups.

If we consider, first, the matter of confining libel to the test of individual injuries, it is worth setting forth more precisely just what that argument can or cannot establish. It would probably establish rather clearly that a suit for personal damages would be highly inappropriate as a form of remedy for the problem posed in *Beauharnais*. It *would* be hard to show special damages or injuries to an individual, and so a civil suit in a case like this would be either clumsy or inapt.[31] But if the injuries are hard to demonstrate through the conventional tests of a civil suit, would that establish also that there are no injuries involved in these cases: that there is no such thing as the libel of a group, or that no serious injuries may arise for the separate members as a result of being stigmatized as a group?

The question one is forced to raise is whether there is not some plausibility in the argument made by Frankfurter (and David Riesman)[32] that it is indeed possible to be libeled through a group: that a libel directed at a group may defame no less because it is directed at the group as a whole; that in fact it may defame even more, because it sweeps with a broader brush. In resisting this argument, the most difficult bodies of evidence one would have to deal with are the data that confirm the vigor and widespread presence of racial and religious stereotypes.[33] When blacks were commonly turned away from hotels and other public accommodations—the

---

[31] On the more precise meaning of "special damages," see *Terwilliger* v. *Wands*, 17 N.Y. 54 (1858), where Judge Strong mentioned, in the way of examples, "the loss of a marriage, loss of hospitable gratuitous entertainment, preventing a servant or bailiff from getting a place, the loss of customers by a tradesman." It is worth noting, too, as a partial counter to Justice Black's argument, that after the advent of libel as a separate tort, special damages became pertinent only when the words were not actionable in themselves or clearly defamatory in nature. See Willaim Holdsworth, *A History of English Law* (London: Methuen, 1926) Vol. 8, p. 365; and cf. *Terwilliger* v. *Wands*, 17 N.Y. at 57.

[32] See note 7 above.

[33] See, for example, Gordon Allport, *The Nature of Prejudice* (Cambridge: Addison Wesley Publ. Co., 1954); Bruno Bettelheim and Morris Janowitz, *Dynamics of Prejudice* (New York: Harper, 1950), chs. 2-3, and for a later work that reprinted the older study with some additional material, their *Social Change and Prejudice* (New York: Free Press of Glencoe, 1964), ch. 1; see also Angus Campbell, *White Attitudes Towards Black People* (Ann Arbor: Institute for Social Research, 1971), pp. 109-10.

black middle class and professional people as well as the poor and uneducated—one may seriously wonder whether the clerks behind the counters were responding to these people as individuals, with their own character and merits as individuals, or whether they were responding largely to a category into which these people had been thrust, and in which they had been stigmatized as a group.

The argument advanced by Frankfurter and by Riesman would be impossible to reject unless one were also willing to reject this proposition: that certain minority groups in this country have in fact suffered serious injuries in the past as a result of racist stereotypes that have been perpetuated in the public mind. I should be frank and say that, in my own judgment, the case against the defamation of groups would have to rest ultimately on a ground of principle far less problematic than the estimate of empirical injuries. But the notion that injuries are indeed likely to arise in the long run for stigmatized groups is an understanding that is hard to resist. And yet anyone who acknowledges the plausibility or likelihood of those injuries cannot reject out of hand the concern that has traditionally existed in the law for the libel of groups.

It is precisely because group libels may sweep with a broader brush that they can be that much harder to avoid; and in that respect, there are some groups that are clearly more difficult to disengage from than others. As Frankfurter remarked at one point in his opinion, it may be hard to deny the assumption that was possibly held by the Illinois legislature, that

> a man's job and his educational opportunities and the dignity accorded him may depend as much on the reputation of the racial and religious group *to which he willy-nilly belongs,* as on his own merits. This being so, we are precluded from saying that speech concededly punishable when immediately directed at individuals cannot be outlawed if directed at groups with whose position and esteem in society the affiliated individual may be *inextricably* involved.[34]

There is a major difference between groups of an almost primordial nature (groups into which one is virtually born) and organizations of a more voluntary nature, such as political parties and trade associations, from which it is possible more easily to withdraw. It is not quite as easy to "contract out" of one's race or even one's religion, and for that reason it can be far harder then

[34] 343 U.S. at 263. Emphasis added.

to evade the force of the libel. And so there is some point, too, in Frankfurter's argument that the law in Illinois was limited to groups of a less voluntary nature (groups defined by "race, color, creed, or religion") and that the law goes only as far as it intends to go when it covers only these groups, which have been the perennial objects of the fiercest loyalties and the fiercest calumnies. That is to say, it may be possible for the law to strike at the most serious sources of the problem without spilling over, as Justice Black had feared, to affect groups like political parties. And in that case it may be possible to avoid a situation in which the law is invoked all too casually in restricting speech that is more conventionally political.[35]

One ought to be clear, though, that the injuries involved in these cases are injuries that arise out of a climate of opinion, and so it may be hard to make a precise connection in any case between the suffering of a harm and any particular publication that might have helped to sustain (or create) a climate of prejudice from which injuries may arise. In the nature of things, the lines of causation here cannot be drawn with exactness between particular events, and many of the harms that result from the defamation of groups may not crop up until years after the fact. One recalls a story told of the first time that blacks appeared in a New Hampshire town— and were refused rooms at the hotel! The impulse to exclude black people in this way did not arise from some inveterate local custom; and if one searched for the sources of this disposition to discrim- inate, one would probably be led to certain attitudes or perspectives that were given a certain currency in the culture. The hotel clerk might have been acting from personal experiences or exposures in this climate of opinion that might have run back twenty or thirty years. The lines of connection may be impossible to chart empiri- cally, and yet it can be grasped in principle that the connections exist, and those connections are not without their palpable effects. If one were concerned to protect people from the assaults or injuries that may be inflicted on them as a result of racial or ethnic ani- mosities, there would probably be a noticeable difference between a society in which leaflets like Beauharnais's are encouraged until they flourish, and a society in which publications of that sort cannot command the indulgence of respectable opinion.

If the matter were gauged with strictness and consistency it would soon be discovered that the problem of charting empirical injuries, and justifying the restrictions of law, would not differ very much

[35] On this point, see Frankfurter, ibid. at note 18.

from what it is in many other areas in which social policy is supported by legal penalties. One need only consider, as a single example, the case of a man who claimed moral objections and refused
to pay that part of his federal income tax that went into the support
of people on welfare who kept on having illegitimate children. It
is clear that his objections would never be honored as a ground of
privilege for gaining exemption from the law, and if this citizen
persisted in his refusal to pay he would suffer penalties far more
severe than the fine that was leveled at Beauharnais.[36] And yet, the
failure of one taxpayer to pay his taxes could not possibly threaten
a serious harm to any recipient of public welfare; and even if a
handful of taxpayers succeeded in opting out, the effect would still
not be discernible.[37]

The most commonly heard retort, of course, is "What if everyone
did that? What would the consequences be?" But that kind of retort
fails, really, as a moral test because it offers an empirical question
in place of a question of principle. We do not know that all citizens
would be in a position to hear about this breach of the law, and
even if they were, it is not clear that they would all react in the
same way, by refusing to pay taxes for welfare or for some other
policy that they found uncongenial. To the extent that the law
would be made to rest on the prediction of injuries in the future,
it would not be very different from a law based on a prediction of
the injuries that arise from the defamation of groups. But the law
cannot find a proper ground of justification if it rests on anything
as problematic as these empirical conjectures. And so if we insist
on compelling people to pay taxes and keep supporting, say, the
welfare system, we ought to be clear that it is *not because of any
material injury that can be shown to result from* the refusal of any
person in particular to pay his taxes.

Similarly, one would discover that the problem of proving injury

[36] For the failure to pay one's income tax on the appropriate date without a
reasonable excuse or justification, the law stipulates a fine equal to the amount of
the unpaid tax plus 5 percent for the first month, and 5 percent for each additional
month that the tax remains unpaid, up to a level of 25 percent of the original tax.
26 U.S.C.A. Sec. 6651(a).

[37] This argument would be reinforced by Mancur Olson's analysis in *The Logic
of Collective Action* (Cambridge: Harvard University Press, 1965). The courts conceded the same point indirectly in the early cases on "standing." See, for example,
Frothingham v. *Mellon*, 262 U.S. 447 (1923), where the court denied a taxpayer
standing to sue, on the grounds that the tax payments of any one person would
represent such a minute fraction of the whole that one's "support" of any program
would be largely a fiction, and one's degree of injury, then, as a result of being
compelled to support a program, would be virtually insignificant.

would be quite as difficult even in cases of individual libel, where Black assumed that the injuries would be far easier to assess than in cases involving the defamation of whole groups. For even where there has been no doubt about the identity of the person being libeled, the courts have recognized that it is probably beyond their means to establish in any rigorous sense a causal connection between the words that were uttered and the behavior that produced the injuries. If it were said of an automobile dealer, for example, that he was a dishonest dealer, the usual approach of the courts has been to look at his sales figures to see if there was a drop-off in the man's business. But it is entirely possible, of course, that the two events—the alleged libel and the decline in business—were independent of one another. Even if this one business were suffering while auto dealers elsewhere were prospering, the decline might still have taken place for reasons unrelated to the libel. (It might have been, very simply, that the service at the garage had become notably poor.)

A more sensitive and precise instrument for getting at the question would be survey research—a more scholarly and rigorous version of the research methods that have been popularized in the public opinion polls. We would have a very precise test if we could estimate, from a sample of the local population, the proportion of people who were exposed to the libelous statement and who were moved on that account to withhold their business. One reason for casting the net so widely is that it would not do, really, to confine the survey to established or former customers who decided not to come back; it would be necessary also to estimate the number of *potential* customers who might have come forward, but who held back as a result of the libel. But in any general sample drawn at random from a city, the number of people who had heard the libel, who were in the market for a car, and who were affected in their decision on buying, would probably be very small. Most likely it would be too small to support any reliable inferences about the size of the population in the city that was in the market for a car, but which was scared off by the libel. To get a more realistic sense of the dimensions of the injury, a survey would have to take in a large sample composed entirely of these potential buyers. And yet, to collect enough people of that description would require a vast increase in the size of the original sample. By that point the scale and expense of the survey could well exceed the level of any damage award that is likely to come out of the trial.

Whether the courts have been aware of these considerations or not, they have been willing to settle for rather modest tests, such as a fall-off in aggregate sales.[38] For the rest, they have been willing to stand on the inference that certain expressions, like "Brown is a dishonest car dealer," if they have any tendency at all, have a tendency to harm rather than help. But that is simply to say that the courts have acted, in effect, on the etymological connection between "injury" and "injustice": what their decisions may recognize is that an injury is constituted, strictly speaking, by the suffering of an "injustice." As we shall see later, when we arrive at the question of racial discrimination, an "injustice" is committed, a wrong is done, when a moral principle is violated, and it is not always the case that the injustice will be attended by a material injury. (Some people, as it turns out, may actually be better off in certain instances as a result of suffering discrimination—as, for example, when they are barred, on the basis of race, from the purchase of a home and end up finding a better house in the same neighborhood at a better price. Nothing in the material outcome, however, effaces the wrong that was done to them.)

In the case of libel the courts have shown a disposition that has not been uncommon in other parts of the law as well: they have been inclined to assume that, if an injustice is productive of consequences, the consequences are likely to be malign rather than benign. Of course that assumption cannot claim the force of a necessary truth, and the result quite often is a certain awkwardness as the courts try to calculate compensation for material damages that may remain highly speculative. Many points of awkwardness, and, as we shall see, no small number of confusions in the law, might be removed if the courts could come to a clearer recognition of what they have been doing all along: viz., that they have made the inference of an injury *after* they have drawn the judgment that a person has suffered an injustice—in the case of libel, that he has been defamed, as it were, unjustly. As Holdsworth commented in his famous history of the English law, "the publication of written defamation was regarded as a wrong to reputation from which damage *could be presumed*," and the consequence was "to make the insult a more prominent element in the tort than the damage."[39] Once the libel was established, "the defendant was shown to be a wrongdoer, and the plaintiff could recover damages because the commission of such a wrong implies damages."[40] And in judging

[38] See *Smith* v. *Godfrey*, 102 N.Y.S. 2d 251 (1951), and *Ellsworth* v. *Martindale-Hubbell Law Directory*, 68 N.D. 425, 280 N.W. 879 (1938).

[39] Holdsworth, note 31 above, p. 365, emphasis added.   [40] Ibid.

whether a wrong had been committed, the courts put the decisive weight on the nature of the words that formed the defamation. They came to speak eventually of words that were libelous or defamatory *in themselves*.

It may be argued then that the principle engaged in these cases— the principle which defines the nature of the "wrong"—must be regarded as more decisive than the measurement of material injuries. Whether the libels are directed at individuals or groups, the main task is to establish in any case whether a wrong had been done: whether the content of the speech was defamatory; whether the defamation was unwarranted; and whether a harm was inflicted for the sake of ends that could not be justified. These kinds of judgments can flow only from principles of moral judgment, and those principles are virtually indifferent to the question of whether the victims of the defamation are individuals or groups. That the difference between individuals and groups has little moral relevance may be borne out once again if we return to Justice Black and recall the remaining strand in his argument. The libel of groups, in Black's judgment, was too much like the stuff of political speech, too close to matters of public, rather than merely private, dispute, and it could be restricted (he argued) only at the peril of closing off speech that was authentically political.

But if Black's concern was with the restraint of political speech, it is hard to see how the problem would have been ameliorated in any way by confining the law to the libel of individuals. It should be evident that political speech is involved just as much in attacks on individuals as on groups, and a good deal of this speech pierces to the level of character as well as policy. It is enough to think here of the attacks on Lyndon Johnson and Richard Nixon—the charges of racism, murder, and corruption, the satires that were obscene even by contemporary standards. And as the Supreme Court came to take a more expansive view of the kind of speech that may be legitimate in politics, it also reduced that zone of privacy which had been claimed in the past even by political figures. As Justice Stewart has put it, somewhat tartly, "A candidate who . . . seeks to further his cause through the prominent display of his wife and children can hardly argue that his qualities as a husband or father remain of 'purely private' concern."[41]

To confine libel to individuals is not to confine it to an area that is in all cases more personal and less public, and it does nothing

[41] *Monitor Patriot Co.* v. *Roy*, 401 U.S. 265, 274 (1971).

to avoid the problem of restricting political speech. For that reason there was a critical tension in Black's argument: If he had been truly committed to an absolutist position in protecting all political speech, the logic of his commitment should have moved him to reject individual libels as well. And in fact, ten years later, he did just that. He brought his position to a point of seemingly perfect consistency by declaring himself in opposition to all libel laws as incompatible with the character of the First Amendment.[42] I say "seemingly" perfect consistency, because one could argue that there was a flaw in the structure of his thought here, which gave rise to some strange paradoxes. Despite everything Black was later to say about libels, he was still willing throughout his career to restrict speech of the clearest political import; and the curious part is that the grounds he was content to accept in these cases were virtually identical with the grounds that were decisive in *Beauharnais*.

Exactly what those grounds were becomes clearer as one considers more closely the differences that separated Black and Jackson. For it would become more apparent at the same time just what separated Jackson from the judges in the majority, and it will help to establish rather precisely the grounds that had to be decisive in the main opinion.

3. The Question of Truth and the "Danger" Test

Initially, at least, it might have appeared that Justice Jackson was preparing the kind of framework that could support the conviction of Beauharnais (as, to some extent, he was). He began with a carefully drawn statement against the "incorporationist" position, or the view that the Fourteenth Amendment had "incorporated" the first eight amendments and made them binding on the states. Jackson had no doubt that the First Amendment applied with full stringency against the federal government, and he thought it was a matter of some significance that the Court had never sustained a federal law of criminal libel.[43] He was also willing to concede that the Fourteenth Amendment imposed some limits on the ca-

---

[42] See "Justice Black and First Amendment 'Absolutes': A Public Interview," 37 *N.Y.U. L. R.* 549 (1962). For an expression of this view in his formal opinions, see *New York Times* v. *Sullivan*, 376 U.S. at 293-97 (1964); also, *Rosenblatt* v. *Baer*, 383 U.S. at 94 (1966) (concurring and dissenting), *Curtis Publishing Co.* v. *Butts*, 388 U.S. at 170-72 (1967) (dissenting), *Monitor* v. *Roy*, 401 U.S. at 278 (1971) (separate opinion).

[43] 343 U.S. at 288-90.

pacity of the states to regulate speech; but having said all that, he was nevertheless persuaded now, with Holmes and Brandeis, that the "liberty" protected against the states "may be accepted with a somewhat larger latitude of interpretation than is allowed to Congress."[44] That latitude had to be larger, he was convinced, because the responsibilities of the federal and local governments were not really comparable in the protection of those substantive interests that were threatened most directly by the misuse of speech. The criminality of defamation, for example, was predicated on the "power either to protect the private right to enjoy integrity of reputation or the public right to tranquillity."

> Neither of these are objects of federal cognizance except when necessary to the accomplishment of some delegated power, such as protection of interstate commerce. When the Federal Government puts liberty of press in one scale, it has a very limited duty to personal reputation or local tranquillity to weigh against it in the other. But state action affecting speech or press can and should be weighed against and reconciled with these conflicting social interests.[45]

Therefore it did not follow for him that if Congress could not have been permitted to enact this statute on group libel, the state of Illinois (or the city of Chicago) had to be constrained in the same way. And it was clear, for example, that the restraints of "ordered liberty" had never foreclosed the power of the states to enact criminal libel statutes.[46]

But if the Fourteenth Amendment offered a wider latitude to the states, it still imposed on them some basic tests in the regulation of speech, and Jackson was not at all convinced that those tests had been met in this case. Among the authorities that he found critical were Fox's Libel Act of 1792, which permitted the jury to determine whether a publication was libelous, and Lord Campbell's Libel Act of 1843, which allowed truth to be proved as a defense. The American precedent came in *People* v. *Croswell*,[47] where Justice Kent had ruled on appeal that the trial court was obliged to submit the libelous character and intent of the article to the decision of the jury, which had to be allowed then to decide both the questions of law and fact.[48] In *Beauharnais*, however, the libelous character of

[44] *Gitlow* v. *New York*, 268 U.S. 652, 672 (1925), quoted in 343 U.S. at 291.
[45] 343 U.S. at 294-95. [46] Ibid., 288, 292.
[47] 3 Johns (N.Y.) 337 (1804).
[48] The significance of this case is considered more fully by Walter Berns, "Freedom

the publication had been decided by the judge as a matter of law. Evidence as to the truth of the charges contained in the pamphlet, as well as explanations bearing on the motives of the defendant, were all ruled out of the trial and in that way barred from the purview of the jury.[49]

A second point of objection for Jackson arose over the "clear and present danger" test, the one addition that the Court had made in the past to the restraints that many of the states had adopted for themselves in the regulation of speech.[50] Jackson's concern was that speech had been punished in this case without any effort, either on the part of the judge or the jury, to consider the context in which the speech had occurred: no evidence had been taken of any injuries, or any breach of the public peace; nor had there been any attempt to weigh the potential for violence or the imminence of any injuries to specific persons. "The leaflet," said Jackson, "was simply held punishable as criminal libel *per se* irrespective of its actual or probable consequences."[51]

The separate points here were accurate enough as far as they went; the only question, though, was whether they could preserve their plausibility or their aptness as the issue moved from the libel of individuals to the libel of groups. The truth of the publication was indeed excluded from the inquiry of the trial, but in the nature of the case one wonders how the test of truth could ever have been more than a gesture without consequence as it was applied to the libel of groups. In the law of defamation, the test of truth has usually proceeded in a framework in which the statement, if it is defamatory, is presumed to be false, and the burden of proof is given over to the defendant. Moreover, the requirement has been that the truth be provided in exacting detail; that it be proved directly about the plaintiff, and not merely about the accuracy of any secondary account concerning the plaintiff or his reputation; and that it be proved in every respect that is at all relevant to the charges.[52]

---

of the Press and the Alien and Sedition Laws: A Reappraisal," *Supreme Court Review 1970*, pp. 109, 150-59. See also ch. 3 in his *The First Amendment and the Future of American Democracy* (New York: Basic Books, 1976).

[49] 343 U.S. at 296, 300.

[50] Ibid. at 298. As Jackson phrased it here, "where expression, oral or printed, is punished, although it has not actually caused injuries or disorders but is thought to have a tendency to do so, the likelihood of such consequences must not be remote or speculative."

[51] Ibid., 302.

[52] See Charles Gregory and Harry Kalven, *Cases and Materials on Torts* (Boston:

In the case of Beauharnais and the libel of a racial group, the charges had to be proved true of the whole group to which they were directed. It was possible, of course, that Beauharnais could have cited some statistics in support of his views; he could have shown, very likely, that the rate of illegitimacy was indeed higher in black areas, as were the rates for murder and other serious crimes. In this respect the defense might have claimed that Beauharnais was saying nothing very different in substance from the findings that many social scientists had reported; and it might have been argued, in addition, that when statements of this kind are made about whole groups or collectivities, they are understood to be general statements, which carry an implicit sense of exceptions.

That argument, however, is not satisfying, because it belies the understanding held by Beauharnais himself as to what it was he was trying to convey. Assuming for the moment that Beauharnais might have made use of many of the statistics cited by scholars, it was never a part of his purpose to warn, as a scholar probably would, that the figures he was reporting about blacks described only the characteristics of an aggregate: it was plainly not his intention to counsel that it was hazardous and even illegitimate to draw inferences about the merits of individuals from the statistical profile of a population. Nor would he have been disposed to point out that there was, of course, some overlap among populations, so that there were classes of whites who had higher crime rates than blacks as a group, and many blacks who had never been implicated in a crime.

For a number of reasons a scholar was not likely to have produced the kind of caricatured view of blacks that was offered by Beauharnais, and not the least of the reasons lay in the radical falsity of the understanding contained in the pamphlet: that is, in the very nature of things, Beauharnais's lurid charges could not be supported by any of the statistical evidence that people might have been inclined to bring forward. But the absorption of the falsity, the molding of the caricature, were integral to Beauharnais's ends. He was not saying, after all, that one ought to look at the particular black

---

Little Brown, revised edition, 1969), pp. 1019ff. The editors call particular attention to *Sharpe* v. *Stevenson*, 34 N.C. 348 (1851), which contained this headnote: "In an action for slander . . . for charging that the plaintiff had criminal intercourse with A. at a particular time and place, the defendant cannot justify by showing that she had such intercourse with A. at another time and place." For a criticism of this view, see Courtney, "Absurdities of the Law of Libel and Slander," 36 *Am. L. Rev.* 552, 563 (1902).

who moves in next door as an individual who must be judged on his own merits. Beauharnais's counsel, rather, was a counsel of resistance—to all blacks, to any black, who moved into a white neighborhood—and it had to be based on assumptions about blacks as a group that were fully as sweeping, and as lacking in equivocation, as the nature of the resistance he was urging. It was precisely the intent of Beauharnais to say that one could indeed start from the aggregate characteristics of a group and draw inferences about the moral character of particular members: that if one simply knew, for example, the race of the family next door, one would also know what the probability was that they would have a tendency to crime and violence. But of course even probabilities do not govern particular cases. Even if 99 out of every 100 blacks were proven criminals, one would still not be justified in excluding a particular black family from the neighborhood on the assumption that they are likely to be criminals. It was that understanding that Beauharnais sought directly to deny, and it is that which finally explains the injustice that is immanent in the very nature of group libel.

Racial and ethnic groups are not voluntary associations composed of people who share common commitments, and who may be depended on to act according to a common code. They are not, in that respect, either like the Jesuit Order or a team of terrorists. Nor are racial groups equivalent to certain classes or "groups" that are defined by their performance of criminal acts (e.g., arsonists, rapists) or their suffering of disabilities (e.g., the mentally incompetent). It would therefore be an error far graver than a mere technical mistake if one were to attribute to racial groups, as corporate groups, a tendency toward criminality or immorality. One would have to imply in that case that the group exerts a kind of *deterministic* control over the moral acts of each member: that the individual cannot disengage himself from the ethic of the group; that he cannot draw himself back on occasion and reach a judgment of right and wrong quite apart from the views that are dominant in the group. What the libel of groups would deny at its root is the moral autonomy which is the distinctive feature of human beings and the premise on which law itself is founded. The very notion of jurisprudence assumes the existence of individuals with a capacity for morals, who are free in essential respects to make choices over matters of right and wrong, and who can be held responsible for their own acts. For that reason the wrongness of group libel does not depend on any material injuries it may happen to cause; the wrong derives, rather, from the concept of morals itself. And so it could be said in all strictness that, if the premises of group libel are not wrong, nothing can be wrong, *for there can then be no such concepts of right and wrong for which individuals can be held responsible.*

But all of this may simply fill out the understanding that was set forth long ago by Kant: viz., that any valid proposition in the domain of morals and law must be derived from the very nature of a rational being, which is to say, a being that has the capacity to give and understand reasons in matters of right and wrong. As Kant observed, the "idea" of morals and law is present only in a rational being, and "since moral laws have to hold for every rational being as such, we ought . . . to derive our principles from the general concept of a rational being as such, and on this basis to expound the whole of ethics. . . ."[53] To put it another way, the moral laws may be drawn as inferences from the nature of that creature which can grasp, in the first place, the idea of morals, and which has the freedom, therefore, to choose between right and wrong. And if the wrongness of any act rests on a proposition that is simply implicit in the idea of morals itself, then that act must indeed be wrong under all circumstances and contingencies. The wrong would be, in a word, *categorical*; and moral laws, as Kant wrote, must be categorical, for "otherwise they would not be laws."[54]

The libel of racial groups stands out, categorically, as a wrong because its wrongness is defined by propositions that trace back ultimately to the idea of morals itself and the nature of that creature which has the capacity for moral judgment.[55] It would betray a serious misunderstanding then about the nature of the wrong involved in the defamation of racial groups if one sought to weigh evidence in every case and consider whether the libel of such a group might have been "true" or justified. And so when Justice Jackson insisted in *Beauharnais* that the "truth" of the libel must be argued out before a jury, he was insisting on the emptiest of rituals. For his own part, Jackson himself realized that Beauharnais had no prospect of establishing the "truth" of his publication.

[53] Kant, *Groundwork for the Metaphysics of Morals*, 401, 412; these numbers refer to the pages of the standard edition of Kant's works published by the Royal Prussian Academy of Science (Berlin, 1902-1938). They can often be found in the margins of more recent editions of Kant's works.

[54] Kant, *Critique of Practical Reason*, trans. Lewis White Beck (Indianapolis: Bobbs-Merrill, 1956), Bk. I, ch. I, p. 18.

[55] See also Chapter IX below ("Segregation, Busing, and the Idea of Law"), and my piece on "reverse discrimination" in "Bakke: The Legal Profession in Crisis," *The American Spectator* (February 1978), pp. 5-8.

Ostensibly, he was willing to go so far as to overturn the conviction because the matter of truth had not been submitted to the jury, and yet he conceded that, in his own estimate, "this defendant [did not stand] even a remote chance of justifying what impresses me, as it did the trial court, as reckless and vicious libel":

A publication which diffuses its attack over unnamed and impersonal multitudes is likely to be harder to justify than one which concentrates its attack on named individuals, but the burden may properly be cast on an accused and punishment follow failure to carry it.[56]

The burden was to be cast upon the accused even though, apparently, he had no chance of carrying it. One would think that a conclusion of that kind would have been sufficiently paradoxical that it should have raised a serious question about the substance of the reasoning that supported it.[57] Given Jackson's own reservations about his argument on this point, it would seem that his dissent rested even more importantly on his concern that there had been no attempt to apply the "clear and present danger" test. That explains, more than anything else, why Justice Black could not have joined Jackson's opinion (and why Jackson, in turn, could not have joined his). With the "clear and present danger" test, the court would have had to consider whether the words that were used were likely to bring about a substantive evil that the state had a right

[56] 343 U.S. at 300, 301.

[57] In a similar vein Roscoe Pound once warned against the dogmatic insistence on the test of truth in those instances when it was evident that the truth of the publication could not be proved, and when the insistence on forming a jury to try the matter of truth formed the greatest obstacle to the use of injunctive relief in cases of defamation. See Roscoe Pound, "Equitable Relief Against Defamation and Injuries to Personality," 29 *Harvard L. Rev.* (1916), pp. 640, 556-57, 664-65. Beyond that, the law has recognized a number of instances in which the truth of an account would still not be enough to justify its publication. The published report may reveal intimate and embarrassing details of a private life, but there may be no legitimate public interest in publishing the account, even if it were true in all respects. In an older view, then, it was necessary also to show good motives or the absence of malice in order to justify publication. Alexander Hamilton offered a strong statement for this position even as he argued for the defense in *People* v. *Crosswell*, 3 Johns (N.Y.) 337, 355 (1804). For a statement of more recent vintage see Bertram Harnett and John V. Thornton, "The Truth Hurts: A Critique of a Defense to Defamation," 35 *Virginia L. Rev.* 425 (1949). If that argument may be plausible in regard to individuals, one wonders why it would not be plausible also for the defamation of groups, which may take the form quite often of political pornography, and inflict embarrassment on the innocent to an even greater degree.

to prevent; and for that, one had to pay close attention to the particular details and circumstances of each case.[58] But it should be evident now that the same reasons that made the test of "truth" superfluous rendered the test of "clear and present danger" inapt: the nature of the wrong inhered in the principle underlying the defamation itself, and not in any material consequences that the defamation might be thought to produce.

And in fact, by Jackson's own account, the danger test would have applied to the case of Beauharnais in a form that in no way resembled its character in other kinds of cases. As Jackson explained, the danger test would have been satisfied for him if Beauharnais's leaflet had "caused injury to any individual Negro, such as being refused living quarters in a particular section, house or apartment, or being refused employment."[59] Yet these were injuries that would not necessarily have been detectable by the time of the trial, and they were rather beyond the scope of the danger test as it was strictly and narrowly applied. These were closer to the kinds of injuries I described earlier, which may be quite delayed in their occurrence, and which would be very hard to trace to their cause. If Jackson were willing to bring these kinds of injuries within the purview of the danger test, one would have to say that it was not a test that would add as much discipline to the prosecution as he suggested, and it is hard to see how he would have been separated by any real issue of substance from Frankfurter and the judges in the majority.

But to the extent that he insisted on the application of the "clear and present danger" test in any form, he foreclosed any concurrence on the part of Black. For Black the danger test was a form of empiricism run wild: in most instances it would dissolve into a mere exercise in "balancing" the claims of speech against other social interests, and if one believed, with Black, that there were fundamental liberties involved, then these were not things to be "balanced" away from case to case. From the time Black finally declared himself for an "absolutist" position in the protection of First Amendment rights, he became equally adamant in rejecting

[58] It bears saying, though, that in the earliest applications of the "clear and present danger" test, the relation between the words or publication and the substantive evil they were thought to be threatening could be rather remote. See *Schenck* v. *United States*, 249 U.S. 47 (1919) and *Abrams* v. *United States*, 250 U.S. 616 (1919), along with the dissent by Holmes, joined by Brandeis, at 624-31. Cf. the refinement of the danger test in the language of Learned Hand in *Masses Pub. Co.* v. *Patten*, 244 Fed. 535 (1917) and Justice Harlan in *Yates* v. *United States*, 354 U.S. 298, 321.

[59] 343 U.S. at 302.

the danger test and its preoccupation with "balancing."[60] In the same way that he would refuse later even to look at the motion pictures in cases involving censorship of the movies, he feared a movement away from the strict grounds of principle as soon as the judgment was thrown open to more and more details of the case.[61] He did not care to know, then, any more than he had to know in order to dispose of the case, and what he had to know, he thought, was very limited. If he could only identify the issue, if he could determine, for example, that he was dealing essentially with a problem of political speech, then that was all he had to know, and he could resolve the matter right there without looking further into the details of the case.

That was a position, however, that most of his colleagues were never able to accept (and there is a serious question as to whether Black himself really held to it consistently, except in dissent). In *Beauharnais*, Black was able to classify the leaflet under the heading of political speech, and he was willing to protect it on that basis, because it had the form, in part, of a petition; it was addressed to the mayor of Chicago. But as Jackson pointed out, the leaflet also contained a coupon to be clipped for the purpose of taking out a membership in the White Circle League and sending in a contribution.[62] And so it might have been quite as tenable to argue that the leaflet was an advertisement or a solicitation as much as it was a petition. As far as anyone could tell, the address to the mayor might have been added largely for dramatic or rhetorical effect, and as Jackson suggested, one could not be allowed to save an otherwise scurrilous publication merely by cloaking it in the form of a petition.[63]

Black's scheme for the protection of political speech could resolve itself, then, into a formal exercise, which turned largely on the way one came to describe an event of many parts that might have been described, really, in several ways. It had the appearance of a more impartial or objective method, which depended on a simple act of description rather than any exercise of judgment. And yet it is clear that Black did not proceed simply by describing the case to himself

[60] See Black, "The Bill of Rights and the Federal Government," in Edmund Cahn, *The Great Rights* (New York: Macmillan, 1963), pp. 43 and 53ff.; *Adamson* v. *California*, 332 U.S. 46, 89-92 (1947) (dissenting); *Barenblatt* v. *United States*, 360 U.S. 109, 134, and especially 143-44 (1959) (dissenting).

[61] See *Kingsley International Pictures* v. *Regents of New York*, 360 U.S. at 690 (1959); also, see Black's comment in *Curtis Publishing Co.* v. *Butts*, 388 U.S. at 171 (1967).

[62] 343 U.S. at 301.   [63] Ibid.

and then recording the decision that the description entailed. It is probably more accurate to say that the descriptive label he finally pinned on the case reflected his reading of the circumstances, and his sense of the facts that were most "essential" in defining its character; and to an important extent, also, it reflected his judgment on the issues. When Black encountered varieties of speech and assembly that seemed to him far less justified in their context—such as the wearing of black arm bands in school to protest the Vietnam war,[64] or the holding of demonstrations in front of Mayor Daley's home[65]—he was quite capable of declaring that these were not matters of speech at all, but matters merely of "conduct," which were not, of course, protected in the First Amendment.[66] He could reach these decisions without betraying a sign of reservation, despite the fact that the expression and assembly involved in these cases were unmistakably political in their nature. It was, to put it mildly, a rather paradoxical view, and it could produce at one time this paradoxical expression: "The First and Fourteenth Amendments [said Black] take away from government, state and federal, all power to restrict freedom of speech, press, and assembly *where people have a right to be for such purposes.*[67]

Jackson was undoubtedly right to avoid the kind of mechanical approach that Black held out, for he recognized that it really offered no alternative to the necessity of looking separately at the facts of each case. But in making the danger test the critical point on which his dissent turned, Jackson also clarified the grounds of his difference with Frankfurter and the opinion of the majority. For despite the use, in part, of language that was associated with the danger test, it was not the danger test that was decisive in the opinion of the Court.

Frankfurter did mention the history of race riots in Illinois, and he did not think it unreasonable for the Illinois legislature to conclude that "in many of these outbreaks utterances of the character

---

[64] *Tinker* v. *Des Moines*, 393 U.S. 503 (1969), and see also 520, where Black tries to distinguish his judgment in Tinker from his concurrence in the decision of the Court in *West Virginia School Board* v. *Barnette*, 319 U.S. 624 (1943), in which he seemed to agree at the time with the majority that a flag salute was not merely "conduct" but a form of expression covered by the First Amendment. For his opinion in *Barnette*, see 319 U.S. 643-44.

[65] *Gregory* v. *Chicago*, 394 U.S. 111, 113 (1969) (concurring opinion).

[66] See ibid. at 124; also, *Cox* v. *Louisiana*, 379 U.S. 536, 555 (1965); *Giboney* v. *Empire Storage and Ice Co.*, 336 U.S. 490, 502 (1949).

[67] *Cox* v. *Louisiana*, 379 U.S. 536, 578 (1965); italics in original.

here in question . . . played a significant part."[68] He noted that the Supreme Court of Illinois had characterized the words prohibited in the statute as those "liable to cause violence and disorder," and that the language paraphrased "the traditional justification for punishing libels criminally, namely their 'tendency to cause breach of the peace.' "[69] In these passages, Frankfurter seemed to be writing in the tradition of group libel that came down from the classic case of *King* v. *Osborne* (1732).[70] In *Osborne*, a publication charged that Jews who were recent arrivals from Portugal, and who were living near Broad Street in London, had burned a Jewish woman to death when she bore a child out of wedlock by a Christian man. It was alleged further that such acts of retribution occurred frequently. As an apparent result of these stories, which were spread by publication, Jews were assaulted and beaten in various parts of the city, and the peace was actually breached. The Court observed that, in contrast with an earlier case in which the targets of the defamation were not clearly known,[71] here "the whole community of Jews are struck at."[72]

But to recall that case is to notice how far it departed from the circumstances of *Beauharnais*. In *Beauharnais* the offending leaflets were handed out in downtown Chicago in a patently nonselective way; they were not distributed in an area that was undergoing racial transition, or which might have been tense already with racial conflict. There was no evidence, then, of a potential for violence that might have been ignited by the systematic spread of this literature. As far as one could tell, the leaflets could not be connected with any breach of the peace or, for that matter, with any other act of an illegal nature; and so, if the danger test had been applied in any strict sense, Beauharnais could never have been convicted.

Frankfurter's opinion did indeed cover the issue of incitement to a breach of the peace, but very clearly, also, it could never have been confined to the danger test—and that, precisely, was the point of Jackson's disagreement. Frankfurter's opinion was based on an understanding of certain words or expressions as *defamatory in themselves*, words that by their very utterance were likely to inflict injury. And if they did not inflict injury in themselves, they might incite to a breach of the peace or, at the very least, they would

---

[68] 343 U.S. at 259.   [69] Ibid. at 254.

[70] 2 Barnardiston 138; 94 Eng. Rep. 406.

[71] *King* v. *Alme and Nott*, 3 Salk, 224, 91 Eng. Rep. 790 (1700); also called *King* v. *Orm(e) and Nutt.*

[72] 2 Barnardiston at 166.

degrade the climate of civility and make future harms more likely. The authority he relied on for this understanding was the old *Chaplinsky* case,[73] and the key passage he cited there was the most memorable in Justice Murphy's opinion:

> There are certain well-defined and narrowly limited classes of speech [wrote Murphy], the prevention and punishment of which have never been thought to raise any Constitutional problem. These include the lewd and obscene, the profane, the libelous, and the insulting or 'fighting' words—those which *by their very utterance inflict injury* or tend to incite an immediate breach of the peace. It has been well observed that such utterances are no essential part of any exposition of ideas, and are of such slight social value as a step to truth that any benefit that may be derived from them is clearly out-weighed by the social interest in order and morality.[74]

These passages in the *Chaplinsky* case have continued to provide the rationale by which a government may legitimately withdraw the protections of law from speech that constitutes, in its public aspect, a species of unjustified assault. In our own day there has been a serious erosion in the conviction that surrounded the teaching in *Chaplinsky*; but as I will try to show, the doctrine in that case is still necessary to any explanation of the grounds on which a lawful government may restrain those acts of gross incivility in public which can convert the streets of the city into theaters of assault and intimidation. The decision on group libel eventually hinges then on the doctrine in *Chaplinsky*: the restriction of group libel is plausible only if libel itself can be defined, but that problem simply leads in turn to the question of whether it is possible to identify, in something more than a subjective way, those forms of expression that are assaulting or defamatory. To that question philosophy, as it turns out, yields an unambiguous answer. Oddly enough, it is the doctrine in *Chaplinsky* that remains consistent with the more matured understandings of analytic philosophy in our own time, while the recent attack on *Chaplinsky* depends on doctrines that have been rejected in the schools of philosophy over

---

[73] *Chaplinsky* v. *New Hampshire*, 315 U.S. 568 (1942); for Frankfurter's reliance on this case, see 343 U.S. at 255-58.

[74] 315 U.S. at 571-72. Emphasis added. In this passage Murphy leaned significantly on Zechariah Chafee, *Free Speech in the United States* (Cambridge: Harvard University Press, 1941), p. 149; and this reliance was the subject of critical comments by Harry Kalven in *The Negro and the First Amendment*, pp. 49-50.

the past thirty years. The problem of *Beauharnais*, therefore, has to be traced back to its solution in *Chaplinsky*: the question of group libel must dissolve into the more general question of civility and the law, and it is the teaching in *Chaplinsky* that brings the matter to its philosophic foundation.

III

THE PHILOSOPHIC FOUNDATION FOR
THE RESTRICTION OF SPEECH

1. *Chaplinsky* AND THE PREMISES
OF REPUBLICAN GOVERNMENT

It often occurs with legal cases viewed over a distance of many years that the judgment rings with a firmness that the case itself may lack when seen in its particulars, and we may be faced with a paradox of this kind: The principle articulated in the judgment may turn out to be indispensable, even though we would be far less certain as to how we would dispose of the matter if the circumstances of the case ever presented themselves again. Such is the state, I think, of that venerable decision of the Court in the *Chaplinsky* case. Chaplinsky was a member of the Jehovah's Witnesses, and on a busy Saturday afternoon in Rochester, New Hampshire, he was distributing literature which attacked all religion as a "racket" (except, presumably, his own). A hostile crowd began to form, and a complaint was made to Bowering, the city marshal. Bowering took care to explain that Chaplinsky was acting within his legal rights; but at the same time, he warned Chaplinsky that the crowd was getting restless. Somewhat later, a disturbance occurred on the street, and Chaplinsky was led away by a traffic officer. Heading toward the station, Chaplinsky and the officer met Bowering, who was on his way now to what he thought was the scene of a riot. The marshal repeated at that moment the warning he had made to Chaplinsky earlier. With that, Chaplinsky allegedly called Bowering a "racketeer" and said that he was "a damned Fascist and the whole government of Rochester are Fascists or agents of Fascists."[1] Chaplinsky was charged with a verbal assault on Bowering, and was convicted under a state law proscribing insults in a public place.[2]

[1] 315 U.S. at 569-70.

[2] Chapter 378, Section 2 of the Public Laws of New Hampshire read: "No person shall address any offensive, derisive or annoying word to any other person who is lawfully in any street or other public place, nor call him by any offensive or derisive name, nor make any noise or exclamation in his presence and hearing with intent

Now it is not clear that we would consider the same words actionable today when directed against a policeman, who might be in the class, after all, of a public official.[3] In some respects, that may be a measure of our own callousness, of how much more it takes today to pass the threshold we have established for serious verbal assaults. Yet there may be room to argue, even today, that these actions cannot be ruled out entirely. For it is not certain that the police are less deserving of the protections of civility in a public place than ordinary citizens are, and there are some verbal assaults that are so provocative and malicious that we would not wish to drape them in innocence merely because they are directed at the police.[4] But if there may be some uncertainty over the way in which we would dispose of the case today, the principles of *Chaplinsky* stand on firmer ground, and they have established some points of durable import for the regulation of speech in the public streets. The case established that certain forms of speech or expression may constitute an assault in themselves, *even if they are not accompanied by overt acts that involve a physical assault.* It reminded us that, traditionally, "assaults" have not required bodily contact:[5] they may be carried out just as effectively by assailants who deliberately stop short of touching the body, as in the case of someone who strikes at a person and intentionally misses,[6] or one who points a

---

to deride, offend or annoy him, or to prevent him from pursuing his lawful business or occupation." Ibid. at 569. On the construction that was given to the statute by the highest court of New Hampshire, see 315 U.S. at 572-73.

[3] Cf. Justice Powell (concurring) in *Lewis* v. *New Orleans*, 408 U.S. 913 (1972).

[4] For some prurient cases in point, see Chapter IV, Section 3, "The Police and the Violence."

[5] Blackstone wrote that "[A]ssault [is] an attempt to offer to beat another, without touching him: as if one lifts up his cane, or his fist, in a threatening manner at another; or strikes at him but misses him; this is an assault, insultus, which Finch describes as an 'unlawful setting upon one's person.' This also is an inchoate violence, amounting considerably higher than bare threats; and therefore, though no actual suffering is proved, yet the party injured may have redress by action of trespass *vi et armis*; wherein he shall recover damages as compensation for the injury." St. George Tucker, *Blackstone's Commentaries* (New York: Augustus M. Kelley, 1790), Vol. 3, p. 120.

The Restatement of Torts defines a "battery" in this way: "An act which, directly or indirectly, is a legal cause of a contact with another person or with anything so closely attached thereto as to be customarily regarded as a part thereof and which is offensive to a reasonable sense of personal dignity, although involving no bodily harm. . . ." 1 Restatement of Torts, Section 18.

[6] *I. de S. and Wife* v. *W. de S.* (1348) [or 1349], reprinted in Charles Gregory and Harry Kalven, *Cases and Materials on Torts* (Boston: Little, Brown; revised edition, 1969), p. 918.

loaded, or for that matter, even an unloaded, pistol at another person.[7] The assaults, in these acts, are implicit in the gestures, and they may be punished even without waiting for bodily injury.[8] In that sense, the case helped to remind us, too, that there is in fact such a thing as psychological injury, which may be quite as grave, and as much of a concern in the eyes of the law, as an assault on one's body or a broken leg. When these points were taken together, *Chaplinsky* suggested in a rather compelling way that people have a claim to be protected from an unprovoked assault (including a verbal or psychological assault) when they venture into a public place.

That is not all there was to *Chaplinsky*, as we shall see more fully in a moment, but it does suggest the features that made this such a durable case. In a manner far more satisfying than in any other decision, *Chaplinsky* was able to account for the grounds on which we would be justified in calling the police, for example, and ordering a crowd to "move along" or disperse, in cases where nearly everyone would agree that the crowd should, in decency, be dispersed, even though there was only speech involved. Consider two hypothetical cases, which are not very far from incidents we have already experienced. In the first case, a crowd gathers all night before the house of the first black family to move into the neighborhood. No violence arises; no rocks or bottles are thrown. The

[7] *Allen* v. *Hannaford*, 138 Wash. 423, 244 Pac. 700 (1926).

[8] In interpreting the statute involved in *Chaplinsky*, the Supreme Court of New Hampshire declared that no words were "forbidden except such as have a direct tendency to cause acts of violence by the persons to whom, individually, the remark is addressed." Later it added: "The statute, as construed, does no more than prohibit the face-to-face words plainly likely to cause a breach of the peace by the addressee, *words whose speaking constitutes a breach of peace by the speaker. . . .*" Quoted in 315 U.S. at 573 (emphasis added). For the sake, apparently, of avoiding the notion that someone may be punished for "mere" words, the court sought to assimilate the words themselves to an act of violence, and it did that largely by importing language which suggested an almost certain connection between the utterance of the words and the outbreak of violence.

All of this was based, of course, on the assumption that most people would be moved to violence by certain classes of "fighting words"—an assumption that may be highly problematic in any case, even though people may uniformly take offense at the words. The understanding that the courts—and many commentators—have seemed anxious to avoid is that the inference of injury is being made from the words themselves, and from nothing more. Harry Kalven seemed to be pursuing much the same kind of exercise when he said, in explaining the *Chaplinsky* case, that "a certain class of face-to-face epithets are regulatable *per se* because they are, so to speak, *per se* freighted with a clear and present danger." Harry Kalven, *The Negro and the First Amendment* (Chicago: University of Chicago Press, 1965), pp. 49-50.

crowd merely stands there, chanting in a low tone, and as it stays on through the night it makes almost no sound at all. There is no breach of the peace, nor even anything that fits the usual notice of a public disturbance. The crowd simply stands in silence through the night, intimidating by its very presence.[9, 10]

In the second case, a young black child or a group of black children are on their way to school as part of the first cohort of blacks in a previously all-white school. As they walk along, they are followed by a larger crowd of whites, who shout epithets and do everything in their power to harass and intimidate the children, short of using violence. Or, as in the first case, the crowd may say very little or nothing; it takes care to avoid anything that might resemble a disturbance of the peace, and it tries instead to work its intimidation largely through its very presence.

In both cases the crowds refrained from violence, and so it might be said that they were engaged in peaceable assembly, or, at their most unruly, in a form of public protest. For despite the fact that harassment was aimed at private individuals, these acts could not be dismissed as mere private quarrels that had not political significance, and no claim therefore to the status of political speech. The aim of these acts was to have a larger effect on the character of the community by keeping blacks out. In pursuing these forms of in-

[9] Since I have had the occasion to mention this "hypothetical" case in print, I have been told of a real incident that resembled this case rather closely. Maynard Wishner, in Chicago, recalls a situation on the South Side of Chicago in the late 1940's, in which a crowd gathered outside the home of one of the first black families to move into the neighborhood. The crowd chanted songs, including old Negro spirituals (done, of course, in mockery), along with tunes like "Carry Me Back to Ole Virginny." Spokesmen for the crowd insisted, when they were confronted by the police, that they were simply engaged, in a "peaceable" way, in public singing. But the Chicago police would have none of it.

[10] The Restatement of Torts, Section 21(1) defines an assault as "An act *other than the mere speaking of words* which, directly or indirectly, is a legal cause of putting another in apprehension of an immediate and harmful or offensive contact. . . ." (Emphasis added.) In commenting on this problem, Kalven and Gregory have acknowledged that "the relevance of verbal conduct to assaults has proved to be a somewhat troublesome point. It has been frequently said that words alone cannot constitute an assault. . . . But this is almost certainly an oversimplification. If the point is that words normally convey a future threat, this formulation is then an oblique and ambiguous way of saying that an assault requires the apprehension of immediate harm. If the point is that no reasonable man would interpret words, however threatening, as carrying the danger of immediate use of force, unless accompanied by gestures, then it does not seem to make sense. In any event, *is it true that standing still can under no circumstances be considered a gesture . . .?*" Charles Gregory and Harry Kalven, *Cases and Materials on Torts*, p. 926.

timidation outside the law, the object was to discourage blacks from exercising rights that were theirs in the law, or to frustrate the ends of a public policy that sought to bring down the barriers to racial integration.[11]

For the most part, then, these acts would have been peaceful; they would have comprised mainly speech or expressive gestures; they would have had a dimension that was clearly political; and finally, one could not have pretended that these acts were punishable because they were likely to provoke the victims to a breach of the peace. Realistically speaking, the chances were rather remote that either the children on the way to school, or the family inside the house, would take the initiative in assaulting the crowd. We clearly strain the limits here of the old fiction that the law may touch these cases only because it is necessary to forestall private acts of reprisal.[12] If the law can reach these cases, it must be because we recognize that there is something in the nature of the words or gestures themselves that constitute an assault. No government that would call itself a decent government would fail to intervene in these cases and disperse the crowd, and it will not do, at those times, to slough off the matter of justification and say that we are simply "balancing" one right against another, or giving more weight to the interests of those who appear to be outnumbered. The metaphor of "balancing" explains nothing here—first, because it says nothing about the standards that are used to measure and balance, and second, because it implies that the claims we are balancing are equally plausible or that they are of a comparable order of dignity.

That is to say, "balancing" tends to suggest an intuitive and, possibly, idiosyncratic judgment, which might come out just as defensibly on one side as the other. But there can be no such parity for the claims involved in these cases. The rights of the crowd in the street cannot really stand on the same plane as the rights of the family inside the house or the children on the way to school. One

[11] An argument might be made that there is still a sensible distinction to be drawn in these cases between the home of a public official and that of a private citizen. Yet that argument would be weakened by the fact that the distinction between the official and the private citizen has already been blurred in the law (see above, Chapter II, p. 29), and it is not clear that we would wish to withhold these protections from public officials. In Justice Black's view, even a public official like Mayor Daley had some right to enjoy the privacy of his home as a "sacred retreat" from the clamor of demonstrators. See *Gregory* v. *Chicago*, 394 U.S. at 125 (1969).

[12] For a fuller discussion of the subject, see John W. Wade, "Tort Liability for Abusive and Insulting Language," 4 *Vand. L. Rev.* 63 (1950).

set of rights is incontestably more fundamental than the other, and its standing as a class of fundamental rights is unaffected, in principle, by the differences that separate one form of government from another. The claims involved here are the claims, as we have suggested, that any government is obliged to respect if it is to be regarded as a decent or legitimate government. We are dealing in this instance with the protections that governments have an obligation to render to both citizens and noncitizens alike, and when we speak in this way in a language that is not textured by the gradations of privilege or the sense of discrimination among polities, we are speaking of rights that come closer to the level of natural rights. No government, whether it is a Czarist government in Russia or a popular government in the United States, may stand back and allow a man to be run down and lynched in the public streets. Nor may a government stand by and permit a local mob to intimidate blacks from making use of the liberty that is theirs to secure property where they can and live where they choose. No government may hold back in these instances and properly claim the allegiance of its citizens, for if we may use an older phrase, it would have shown itself at that moment to be destructive of those ends for which governments are instituted. It would have defaulted then on the first obligation of government as it was understood by the men who framed the Declaration of Independence: to protect its subjects from lawlessness in the taking of their lives, the abridgement of their liberty, or the destruction of their property.

Depending on the circumstances, of course, it may be justified to take a human life or to restrict both liberty and property, but the point is that these acts have to be justified. They cannot be done in a lawless way, that is, without reasons or justifications that can be given under the discipline of lawful procedure. What Lincoln said in explaining the grounds of objection to lynching may apply with equal force to other kinds of lawlessness that visit punishment in this way without the constraint of procedure. As he warned in his famous speech to the Young Men's Lyceum,

> When men take it in their heads today, to hang gamblers, or burn murderers, they should recollect, that, in the confusion usually attending such transactions, they will be as likely to hang or burn someone, who is neither a gambler nor a murderer [as] one who is; and that, acting upon the example they set, the mob of tomorrow, may, and probably will, hang or burn some of them, by the very same mistake. . . . [T]he

innocent, those who have ever set their faces against violations of law in every shape, alike with the guilty, fall victims to the ravages of mob law. . . .[13]

A trial, with its formal rationality, may not always produce a verdict that is substantively rational or just,[14] but with its stricter controls on the presentation and assessment of evidence, a formal trial bears a firm connection in principle to the end of making reasoned discriminations between the innocent and the guilty. (On that account it may also stand a better chance in the long run of producing verdicts that are just.) But to treat the difference between the innocent and the guilty as a casual matter must be the mark of a polity that is disordered in a fundamental sense. For no government could claim to call itself a decent or lawful government if it were not committed to recognizing, in the first instance, the differences that separate the innocent and the guilty, the decent and the corrupt. And it shows its respect for these differences in the most serious manner when it insists on making discriminations between the innocent and the guilty only in the most sober, reasoned way.

All this goes beyond, of course, any facts that arose in the *Chaplinsky* case. But the questions raised here are the questions that must, of necessity, arise if one merely follows through the implications of *Chaplinsky*. In principle, that case cut far more deeply than we have often suspected, and it was tied up, perhaps more closely than we thought, with the things that are necessary to any decent society.

As I have tried to show, the validity of *Beauharnais* turned most decisively on the argument in *Chaplinsky*. Therefore, the question of whether *Beauharnais* is good law depends significantly on the question of whether *Chaplinsky*, at this moment, is itself good law. But *Chaplinsky* has recently been threatened, if, indeed, it has not been undermined, by the decision of the Court in *Cohen* v. *Cali-*

---

[13] Address before the Young Men's Lyceum of Springfield, Illinois (January 27, 1838) in *The Collected Works of Abraham Lincoln*, ed. Roy Prentice Basler (New Brunswick: Rutgers University Press, 1953), Vol. I, pp. 108-15, pp. 110-11. For an excellent analysis of this address, see Harry Jaffa, "The Teaching Concerning Political Salvation" in his *The Crisis of the House Divided* (New York: Doubleday, 1959), ch. 9.

[14] *Max Weber on Law in Economy and Society*, ed. Max Rheinstein, trans. Edward Shils (Cambridge: Harvard University Press, 1954), pp. l-li, 59, 63-64; also, Hadley Arkes, *Bureaucracy, the Marshall Plan, and the National Interest* (Princeton: Princeton University Press, 1972), pp. 352ff.

fornia[15] and a series of recent cases that have been controlled by the judgment in *Cohen*.[16] There is no space here to treat *Cohen* fully, but it is worth considering for a moment those parts of the opinion that presented the most radical challenge yet to the premises on which *Chaplinsky* rested, for they provided a far more critical test of the grounds on which the restriction of speech in any case would have to be defended.

2. *Cohen* v. *California*: THE END OF PROFANITY

In April 1968, Paul Robert Cohen was visiting the Los Angeles County Courthouse, and as he went through the corridors of this public place he wore a jacket that bore the inscription "Fuck the Draft." He was arrested, and subsequently convicted, under a state law that prohibited, among other things, "maliciously and willfully disturb[ing] the peace or quiet of any neighborhood or person, . . . by . . . offensive conduct . . . or us[ing] any vulgar, profane, or indecent language within the presence or hearing of women or children. . . ."[17]

In reversing the conviction, Justice Harlan assumed at the outset that he was dealing with a class of speech that was presumptively "political."[18] That was already a considerable leap from the premises of *Chaplinsky*, and I shall have more to say about it in a moment; but once the shift in presumptions was made, a new burden was placed on the kind of evidence that was needed for conviction. The Court was not disposed to assume, without the benefit of supporting evidence, that Cohen had shocked the sensibilities of those around him or that his words were likely to have led to the outbreak of violence. Not only was it necessary to show now that someone had in fact taken offense at Cohen's sign, but it was necessary to demonstrate also that the person who had been offended had been "powerless to avoid" Cohen and his jacket.[19] Gone, in other words, was the sense that came out of *Chaplinsky*, that one had some right to be protected against a verbal assault, or the knowing infliction of a psychological shock, when one entered a public place. The burden was on the side of the potential victim now rather than the assailant: it was apparently more rea-

[15] 403 U.S. 15 (1971).
[16] See *Gooding* v. *Wilson*, 405 U.S. 518 (1972); *Rosenfeld* v. *New Jersey*, 408 U.S. 901 (1972); *Lewis* v. *New Orleans*, 408 U.S. 913 (1972); *Brown* v. *Oklahoma*, 408 U.S. 914 (1972).
[17] 403 U.S. at 16.   [18] Ibid. at 18, 19.   [19] Ibid. at 22.

sonable to ask the auditors to turn away or to make some effort to avoid the offensive speech—something that was not always easy to do in public streets or buildings—rather than ask the speaker to accept some restraints on his behavior in public.

The understanding of injury was narrowed to the most personal and immediate terms, and to accomplish that end, the meaning of *Chaplinsky* also had to be narrowed. In Harlan's hands, the scope of *Chaplinsky* was reduced to encompass only face-to-face encounters and "those personally abusive epithets which, when addressed to the ordinary citizen, are . . . inherently likely to provoke violent reaction."[20] But the danger of a violent reaction was only one-half of the formula in *Chaplinsky*: what Harlan left out was the understanding of "words . . . which by their very utterance inflict injury," even without inciting a breach of the peace.[21] The question of immediate danger was, of course, a prominent test in cases of insults and "fighting words," because the context was often as important as the words in establishing the overall meaning of the act. But when the danger test is made the exclusive test in these cases, the emphases will be placed even more heavily on the personal encounter rather than the offense, and the results may often be unfortunate.

For example, let us suppose that instead of Cohen we had someone with a jacket saying "Fuck the Jews." Let us suppose further that, like Cohen, he is in a courthouse, or perhaps in a line at the Internal Revenue Service, where he has an appointment to consider his tax returns. Most of the people around him are probably there on business that leaves little freedom for rescheduling, and so if they are standing in line somewhere behind the person with the jacket, waiting to take up the question of their taxes, they may not feel they can afford to leave the line if they happen to take offense at the jacket. Now it is conceivable that, within the terms of Harlan's opinion, it would be possible to reach this case. In relation to Cohen's statement about the draft, Harlan thought that "no individual actually or likely to be present could reasonably have

20 Ibid. at 20.

21 That the holding in *Chaplinsky* does indeed extend much farther has been recognized recently by Mr. Justice Powell in his dissenting opinion in *Rosenfeld* v. *New Jersey*. Writing, as it were, against the line of argument emerging from the *Cohen* case, Powell pointed out that "*Chaplinsky* is not limited to words whose mere utterance entails a high probability of an outbreak of physical violence. It also extends to the willful use of scurrilous language calculated to offend the sensibilities of an unwilling audience." 408 U.S. at 905.

regarded the words on the appellant's jacket as a direct personal insult."[22] But for any Jew who is present, it is plausible that the sign "Fuck the Jews" could be taken as a "direct personal insult"; and since the rule embraces any individual "actually or likely" to be present, it allows the authorities to anticipate that any Jew who enters the room is likely to feel personally affronted.

But the assumption that Jews are likely to enter the room is quite problematic or speculative and, for that reason, a rather weak peg on which to hang a prosecution. By insisting on the test of a direct personal assault, Harlan ruled out the possibility that someone could take offense at this statement about Jews even though he was not himself Jewish and would not have been the object of a direct personal assault. If there were a cause of action in this case, it would have to arise from the nature of the words themselves; and if there was a valid interest to be asserted, it could only be an interest in preserving the climate of civility, regardless of whether the ingredient of a personal insult were present. That becomes even clearer with a statement like "Fuck the Draft," which attacks only an impersonal institution and does not single out any particular persons for ridicule. To come forward at that point and ask someone to remove his jacket, one would have to take seriously the notion that there truly is something like a climate of civility, which is important in itself, and which can be degraded only with costs that are by no means trivial.[23]

With Harlan's opinion in *Cohen*, the Court resolved for the first time that the preservation of civility was simply not substantial enough as an interest of the state to warrant any restrictions on speech that had even the slenderest pretense of being "political."[24]

[22] 403 U.S. at 20.

[23] There is a danger here of confusing the issue of principle with the question of the particular penalty that is applied. The issue of principle would be established if it were conceded that the authorities would have been acting with propriety had they merely asked Cohen to remove his jacket in a public place. Everything after that amounts simply to a dispute over the reasonableness of the penalty. In other words, one may accept in principle the restraints on certain kinds of speech, and yet at the same time, one may prefer that Cohen were given a warning or request in the first instance, rather than being subjected to an immediate arrest. Or, if he refused to remove his jacket, Cohen could have been given a light fine or some penalty far less severe than the one that was prescribed in this case, which was thirty days in jail.

[24] For another critical view of the *Cohen* case in a similar vein—and a commentary I did not see until after my own argument had appeared in print—see Walter Berns, *The First Amendment and the Future of American Democracy* (New York: Basic Books, 1976), pp. 190-96.

There could be no room for claims of civility because Harlan's opinion denied at its root that there was any longer such a category as profane or libelous speech. Speaking of the profanity on Cohen's jacket, Harlan asked, "How is one to distinguish this from any other offensive word?" Surely the state would not have a right "to cleanse public debate to the point where it is grammatically palatable to the most squeamish among us"; and yet he saw no way to avoid that result once one conceded the right to restrain offensive speech, for there was "no readily ascertainable general principle" by which one could draw a distinction.[25] Which is to say, there was no reasonable way of distinguishing the profane and defamatory from forms of speech that were either neutral or inoffensive. It was all, in the final analysis, a matter merely of personal taste: "One man's vulgarity," said Harlan, "is another's lyric," and it was precisely "because governmental officials cannot make principled distinctions in this area" that the Constitution left these "matters of taste and style so largely to the individual."[26] What Harlan denied no less was the existence of any standards for identifying offensive speech, because the offensiveness of the words depended entirely on the subjective feelings of the people who heard them. And therefore it could only be, as he had said earlier, that the decision as to what language is fit for a public place must be left "largely [in] the hands of each of us."[27]

There was a slight, but telling, discord, though, in Harlan's opinion between the argument he was forced to make for the radically subjective nature of all offensive and defamatory words, and the assumptions that led him into the case and defined his initial break from *Chaplinsky*. As I have noted, Harlan had begun by turning the presumptions in *Chaplinsky* around: instead of presuming that profane or defamatory speech was beneath constitutional protection, he presumed that the speech was protected and that the burden of proof lay with those who would restrict it. The speech acquired a new claim to protection because it was seen to be "political," and it was seen to be political because it was assumed now by Harlan that the jacket was presenting an argument over public policy. According to Harlan, what Cohen was doing with his jacket was "asserting [a] position on the inutility or immorality of the draft."[28]

The properly irreverent question is, which one, precisely, did

[25] 403 U.S. at 25.
[27] Ibid. at 24.
[26] Ibid.
[28] Ibid. at 18.

Cohen mean when he said "Fuck the Draft"? Did he mean that the draft was "inutile," or that it was "immoral"? One wonders if some point might be served in noting that "Fuck the Draft" may not mean either one of those things, and that very probably it meant neither. The profanity on the jacket, like most expressions that have acquired the status of swear words, had a certain grossness to it that was an important part of its meaning and of the purpose for which it was used. By its nature, it lacked the precision of analytic prose, particularly when it was applied to questions of public policy, where it mocked through its gross lack of relevance. But was this not, in fact, what Justice Murphy had in mind when he wrote in *Chaplinsky* of utterances that were "no essential part of any exposition of ideas" and which were "of such slight social value as a step to truth"[29] that they might be restrained, with no serious harm, for the sake of preserving other values that were at least as important, and perhaps even more compelling, for a civil society?

All one could safely infer from Cohen's jacket was that, for some reason his language was incapable of disclosing, Cohen disliked the draft and strongly condemned it. But it was quite evident, even at the time when *Chaplinsky* was decided, that profane and defamatory statements were usually charged, as Justice Harlan put it, with "emotive" meaning, and that they were capable of conveying a powerful sense of likes and dislikes, approval and condemnation. The sense that came out of *Chaplinsky*, though, was that these statements conveyed nothing of substance that could not be conveyed in some other way; and since it was possible to express the same substance in another manner, it did not seem to threaten the free flow of ideas if we asked someone to avoid the grosser forms of profanity and defamation in public, and indeed if we insisted on restraining this kind of speech out of a respect for the sensibilities of others in a public place.

In *Paris Adult Theatre* v. *Slaton*, Chief Justice Burger raised the possibility of a " 'live' performance of a man and woman locked in a sexual embrace at high noon in Times Square," and he observed that the performance would not be "protected by the Constitution [even if the two people] simultaneously engage in a valid political dialogue."[30] The problem could be presented in a "purer" form if the action took place on the steps of the Capitol and the dialogue were removed, so that we would have a case of "symbolic speech" (comparable, say, to the wearing of an arm band or the burning

---

[29] 315 U.S. at 572.   [30] 413 U.S. at 67 (1973).

of a draft card). The scene would be virtually the same as one that was carried out on the steps of the royal palace in Stockholm in the film, *I Am Curious (Yellow)*, where the political import of the act was unmistakable. In any event one cannot read Burger on this point without finding in his words a reproach to Mr. Justice Harlan in the *Cohen* case; for within the terms of Harlan's opinion there was no principled way of reaching the couple having intercourse in public. As long as there was a residue of political significance in the act, it would have a claim to be protected as symbolic expression, and the burden would fall to passersby to avert their eyes. Yet, the law should probably be obliged to restrain this "expression," and it is Murphy's opinion in *Chaplinsky* that explains, far more persuasively than anything else, the grounds on which the law may be exercised in such a case. That is to say, anyone who conceded that performances of this kind ought to be restrained could not pretend that they were forms of expression without a political meaning; and therefore he would find himself following the logic of *Chaplinsky*, even if he preferred to conceal it from himself and call it by another name.[31]

The case for rejecting that older view and protecting Cohen's jacket is one that argues that the profanity was an integral part of the meaning in something that was, after all, a political statement, and that the expression would lose its meaning as a political statement if the profanity were removed. This view would pretend, in other words, that as far as the Constitution is concerned, Cohen's jacket lies on the same plane as the Federalist #10: They are both political "statements." Cohen's jacket presented a statement, as Harlan argued, because it asserted a position on the draft. The case for protecting the jacket, and treating it in that respect as though it were the Federalist #10, had to rest then on the surety with which one could tell that Cohen was in fact taking a position and condemning the draft.

For the sake of argument it is worth raising a challenge to that view for a moment and asking, how does one know for sure that

[31] It has been suggested, for example, that problems like that of the couple having intercourse in public may be handled under regulations for "aesthetic" zoning. The difficulty, however, is that the law becomes productive of grievous faults when the grounds on which it would dispose of a case diverge markedly from the ground on which it defines the nature of the wrong involved in the case. Whether we choose to call a certain public act a violation of "aesthetic" standards, or whether we place it under some other category, we are still dealing with expression that may have political import, and we are obliged to give an account of the grounds on which we would be justified in restricting expression of that kind.

Cohen was *condemning* the draft? Why could it not be argued, for example, that even though "Fuck the Draft" has the form of an imperative, it is really nothing more than a descriptive statement, in the same vein as many of the older, more classic statements that are found on bathroom walls? It cannot claim protection, then, as a political statement, because (as the argument may go) the phrase does not convey any positive or negative judgment at all. But, of course, this is all scarcely believable: no one is really prepared to accept that kind of arbitrariness in the meaning of words. Almost anyone knows that if he wandered into the street and used Cohen's language in a more personal way to the first person he met, the consequences would probably be, if not dire, then at the least rather vexing. And yet, to say that is to concede the most consequential point that would have to be made against Harlan's argument. It would be to admit, in fact, that there are certain words that are established very clearly in our ordinary language as terms of con- demnation or assault, and that *their meaning, therefore, cannot depend entirely on the subjective feelings of the people who hear them.*

With that, one would have arrived, I think, at the proper answer to Harlan by backing into the argument that was eventually offered by philosophers in rejecting logical positivism. And it is the same argument that finally proves decisive in establishing our ability to recognize those words "which by their very utterance inflict injury." I cannot, of course, review here, in its proper detail or sophisti- cation, the challenge raised by the positivists to ethical theory.[32] The main point of connection to Harlan's argument in *Cohen* lies in the insistence of the positivists that the only meaningful state- ments were either empirical (i.e., statements that could be confirmed or falsified with empirical evidence) or analytic (i.e., statements that could be established as true or false by examining the definition of their terms, as in the sentence, "All triangles are squares"). As the positivists argued, propositions that were neither empirical nor an- alytic were literal "nonsense," and unless ethical judgments could be converted into verifiable statements—unless they could become closer, in that respect, to the propositions of empirical science—

---

[32] The name "logical positivism" was first used by A. E. Blumberg and Herbert Feigl in 1931 to describe the ideas of the so-called "Vienna Circle" of the early 1920's. Among the major works have been Moritz Schlick, *Problems of Ethics* (New York: Prentice Hall, 1939); Rudolf Carnap, *Philosophy and Logical Syntax* (Lon- don: K. Paul, Trench, Trubner & Co., 1935); and A. J. Ayer, *Language, Truth and Logic* (London: V. Gollancz Ltd., 1936; rev. ed. 1946).

they could be the object of no reliable knowledge, and would have to fall into this category of literal "nonsense." But as the positivists saw the matter, ethical judgments could not be reduced to empirical statements; they were closer to statements on the order of "I like parsley." They were expressions of taste, or they were reports on the state of one's emotions,[33] but they were too subjective in nature to be proven true or false. Whether slavery was in principle wrong, whether all men ought to be free, were propositions that could not, ultimately, be confirmed or denied. It was possible to take notice of the dominant force that these propositions exerted in the lives of men, but it could not be said that they were right or wrong, justified or unjustified, any more than it could be said that one ought to like parsley. As A. J. Ayer wrote:

> [I]t is impossible to find a criterion for determining the validity of ethical judgements. It is not because they have an 'absolute' validity which is mysteriously independent of ordinary sense-experience, but because they have no objective validity what-soever. If a sentence makes no statement at all, there is obviously no sense in asking whether what it says is true or false. And we have seen that sentences which simply express moral judgment do not say anything. They are pure expressions of feeling and as such do not come under the category of truth and falsehood. . . .[34]

On the other side of the argument, it is hard again to do justice to the fullness of thought, or to trace back, step by step, every important point at which the logical positivists were engaged by their opponents. The task is made doubly hard by the fact that the refutation was not accomplished by one or two philosophers, who managed to do it all with the stroke of a major book. The enterprise was carried on, rather, by a number of writers, who published shorter essays and articles over a period of many years.[35] In offering

---

[33] See Charles Stevenson, "The Nature of Political Disagreement," *Sigma* (Conoscenza Unitaria), Vol. 1, p. 469 and especially pp. 473-76, and his *Ethics and Language* (London: Oxford University Press, 1944).

[34] Ayer, *Language, Truth and Logic*, p. 108.

[35] In looking back to the antecedents of this "post-positivist" school, some scholars have given credit to G. E. Moore for his early attack in *Principia Ethica* (Cambridge: Cambridge University Press, 1903) on the "naturalistic fallacy" (or the tendency to reduce moral standards to strictly empirical measures). But as important as Moore undoubtedly was, his writing contains only a dim anticipation of the kind of argument that Richard Hare was able to develop later. While no one book stands as the definitive work, there are a few notable contributions that collect the most

an overview of the arguments, it may be best to begin by noting that, in sharp contrast to the positivists, their critics started with an awareness of the profound differences that separated moral judgments from statements of merely personal taste. A statement on the order of "I like parsley" is notably different in its logic from propositions like, "It is wrong to hurt others for the sake of one's own self-interest," or, "We would be justified in going to war, and using conscription, to resist Hitler." The latter two statements speak about the things that are good or bad, right or wrong, for others as well as oneself. They may also establish the ground on which to commit other people as well as oneself to a common policy.

But when we presume to speak about the kinds of commitments that ought to be accepted by others, we would enter a new universe of obligations. We could be obligated now to give reasons, to bring forth evidence and considerations that are not merely subjective or idiosyncratic, but accessible to others as well as ourselves. If a person had been urging the United States to join the war against Hitler, he might have been moved to say a number of things in explaining his judgment. He might have pointed to those features of life in Nazi Germany that stamped the government as totalitarian. He might have explained why totalitarian governments are in point of principle objectionable and why it is undesirable that any people should suffer the injustice and barbarism that is implicit in these regimes. He might have suggested also that governments constituted on terms of principle that are radically opposed to our own are also likely to be committed over the long run to ends and interests that are adverse to our own. Each of these arguments might have brought responses from people who were inclined to dispute the facts or the premises, or who were inclined to grant the facts but resist the conclusion that we ought to go to war. As the discussants went on in this way, setting forth their reasons, what they would be doing, in effect, is clarifying the empirical evidence and the considerations of principle that stand behind their judgment that it would be justified (or unjustified) to go to war. In this manner it becomes evident that moral preferences represent something more than arbitrary expressions of personal taste which cannot be ex-

---

important arguments and make substantial statements in their own right. See, for example, R. M. Hare, *The Language of Morals* (Oxford: Clarendon Press, 1952); and *Freedom and Reason* (Oxford: Clarendon Press, 1963); Stephen Toulmin, *An Examination of the Place of Reason in Ethics* (Cambridge: Cambridge University Press, 1950); and more recently, Richard E. Flathman, *The Public Interest* (New York: Wiley, 1966).

amined or judged by others. And it becomes possible then to speak of a moral discourse that could in fact persuade people to alter their moral judgments.

However, it is one thing to say that moral terms have the function of drawing attention to empirical evidence in any case; it is quite another to insist that their meaning is entirely descriptive. When someone says, "That is a 'good' (or 'just') war," it should be evident that "just" or "good" is more than a shorthand expression for "a war that is fought against a totalitarian country." It should be clear that, in addition to describing the war, the speaker would also be *commending* or *justifying* it. If that were not the case, then the meaning of "good" (or "just") would be frozen into its current political cast (its meaning would be tied indefinitely to the circumstances that inspire the moral judgment) and there would be no possibility of enlarging or revising moral judgments over time in response to new evidence or more mature reflection. If the standards of "good theater" had been codified in ancient Rome, they might have included the slaughtering of a martyr or the staging of a live crucifixion. And if "good theater" was nothing more than a descriptive term, those standards would have been fixed for time. Henceforth, we would not have been justified in labeling any dramatic performance as "good theater" if it did not include these features; nor could we have called a play anything but "good" if it contained them.

But obviously, moral terms cannot be restricted in that way. They must have the capacity to disengage themselves from the current standards of what is good and call those very standards into question. That is to say, moral terms must have an empirical or substantive content, and part of their function is in fact to describe; but this descriptive function can never exhaust their meaning. They must have, in addition, a prescriptive or commendatory function, which allows them to commend what current opinion has not yet accepted (or to condemn what current practice has sanctioned). Even in the face of a very careful effort to clarify the meaning of "good," we would still claim the freedom to hold ourselves back and say, for example, "Yes, you've defined all the ingredients of what you regard as 'good' theater, but still we can't bring ourselves to agree that the kind of theater you describe is something we could call 'good.' There are certain considerations you've overlooked, certain perverse points in your reasoning, which prevent us from agreeing now that this is a form of drama that even you should have found acceptable."

If we can do that—if we can detach moral terms from the current definitions of what is good and use them to commend something different—it is only because the prescriptive meaning of the terms has been planted very firmly in our ordinary language. Words, of course, may change over time, but if morals are to continue to exist as an ongoing inquiry into the standards of what is good, the functions of commending and condemning must be present in the language, and at any given time the words that serve these functions must be recognized rather clearly. Frankfurter wrote in *Beauharnais* that "no one will gainsay that it is libelous falsely to charge another with being a rapist, robber, carrier of knives and guns, and user of marijuana."[36] Not everyone would agree today that it is defamatory on its face to be called a "user of marijuana," and of course many other words like "robber" or "thief" may be uttered in jest, or in circumstances that render them rather innocent. (The New Hampshire court in *Chaplinsky* was very much aware of the effect of context on meaning, and it sought to incorporate that understanding in its decision when it wrote of words that were used "without a disarming smile"—that is, without those attendant gestures or circumstances that could alter the meaning of the words.)[37] But at any given moment, anyone who has had to live with a language in his everyday life should have a fairly reliable sense of the words that are established rather plainly as terms of insult and defamation and the words that may be on the borderline between derision and neutrality. It so happens that juries have been fairly good at making judgments of this kind about the meaning of words, as well as the context in which they are used, and they seem to have been reasonably effective in cases of insult in separating the frivolous from the serious claims.[38] But whether the decision is made

---

[36] 343 U.S. at 257-58. [37] See 315 U.S. at 573.

[38] See Reynolds C. Seitz, "Insults—Practical Jokes—Threats of Future Harm— Now New as Torts?" 28 *Kentucky L. J.* 411, 413 (1940).

In his dissent in *Beauharnais*, Justice Reed declared that he would have reversed the conviction on grounds of vagueness, because the Illinois statute contained words like "virtue," "derision," and "obloquy" which had, he thought, "neither general nor special meanings well enough known to apprise those within their reach as to limitations on speech." 343 U.S. at 283-84. But I hope it would be clear from what I have said already that any attempt to fill out the meaning of "virtue" in a definitive, empirical way would have been quite as fruitless—and as unresponsive to the nature of morals—as any effort to fix the meaning of "good" once and for all. Given any awareness of the concepts of commending or condemning, applauding or maligning, "derision" and "obloquy" should not have presented any problem that a trip to the dictionary would not have been able to resolve. In any event, as Frankfurter understood, there could have been no serious question as to what the state of Illinois was

by a judge or a jury, the exercise of judgment on the defamation of groups would proceed from the same foundation as the exercise of judgment in other cases of injurious speech in public: the judgment would ultimately rest in any case on our ability to recognize some of the clearest things that are given to us in our language.

If one still tends to doubt that the standards are clear, or that anyone ought to be trusted to make these judgments, a fairly simple test comes to mind from an incident of several years ago. In the heat of a presidential election year, with the primaries getting underway and alliances starting to form, George Romney referred to Charles Percy as an "opportunist." Percy took offense, and Romney was obviously embarrassed that his comment had made its way into the press. In an effort to repair the damage, Romney tried to explain later that all he had meant was that Percy was an intelligent man who took advantage of his opportunities. That is, he was merely *describing* Percy rather than judging him, and if anything, he suggested, his remark was complimentary rather than critical: he was actually commending Percy for his alertness in seizing opportunities!

In the final analysis the matter may be put simply in this way: The measure of our willingness to believe that moral words are entirely subjective and arbitrary—that terms of defamation and commendation depend on nothing more than the feelings of the people who hear them—is our willingness in this case to accept Romney's account of what he meant.

3. THE DILEMMAS OF A LIBERTARIAN ALTERNATIVE

Natan Lerner noted that when the Council of Europe was considering a statute on the defamation of groups, a question arose on the point of separating the incitement to hatred from incitement to a breach of the peace. It was argued by the Italian representative, Januzzi, that the two were really very separate:

---

forbidding; the only matter to be judged was whether *Beauharnais* properly fell within the ambit of the law.

One year after the decision in *Cohen*, the Supreme Court voided on its face a Georgia statute that made it a misdemeanor to use "without provocation . . . opprobrious words or abusive language, tending to cause a breach of the peace." This statute was at least as clearly drawn as the law involved in *Chaplinsky*, but the Court struck it down, in part because it had permitted a conviction in 1905 (!) for the remark "You swore a lie," and in 1913 for the phrase "God damn you, why don't you get out of the road." *Gooding* v. *Wilson*, 92 S.Ct. 1103, 1107 (1972).

These [incitements to a breach of the peace] are not factors that must be taken into consideration as contributory to the offense of incitement to hatred, inasmuch as that offense might equally well exist without violence, insult, or breach of *ordre public* or of the peace. . . . Incitement [to hatred] is, thus, an independent offense at law which might be accompanied by such others as violence, threats, insults, breach of *ordre public*, but which nevertheless must have its own special character-istics, its own objective consistency, its own criminal intent.[39]

For all practical purposes, this was the same understanding that lay behind the decision of the Court in the *Beauharnais* case, and it may explain just why the concept of group libel still holds a special usefulness in the law today, even as the statutes on group libel have virtually disappeared. It would be better, for several reasons, if those statutes were still present and if there were a willingness to make use of them. But our experience also suggests that, even though group libel may not have much life in our sta-tutory law, we may be forced, in a number of practical situations, to reinvent the concept anyway. As I have already suggested, there are important parts of our public policy today that would be hard to understand or justify on anything other than the grounds that underlie the rejection of group libel. I shall discuss this point more fully later, when I consider the problem raised by statutes that restrain "discriminatory advertising"—that is, notices that declare an intention to discriminate on the basis of race in the sale or rental of housing. These proscriptions on advertising have existed even in instances in which discrimination in housing has not been made illegal; and so they have stood on their own as restraints on expres-sion pure and simple.

But beyond that, there are moments that arise quite often in the preservation of public order where the concept of group libel would be especially apt and where the alternative standards for restraining

---

Justice Blackman was quite justified when he complained that "the Court, despite its protestations to the contrary, is merely paying lip service to *Chaplinsky*." (Ibid. at 1113.) But he was merely late in recording here the implications that should have been apparent already at the time *Cohen* was decided. The Chief Justice added, with some point, that after the decision in *Gooding*, "it is difficult to imagine how a State could enact a statute more clearly and narrowly aimed at regulating the type of conduct that the unanimous holding of *Chaplinsky* tells us may be regulated." Ibid. at 1112.

[39] Quoted by Lerner in "International Definitions of Incitement to Racial Hatred," 14 *N.Y.U. Law Forum* 49, 53 (1968).

speech may bear serious defects in principle. One notable case may stand as an example. In March 1962, eight members of the American Nazi party decided to picket a movie theater in downtown Chicago which was showing a film with Sammy Davis, Jr.[40] The eight men appeared before the theater at the height of the evening rush hour with placards and leaflets advertising a mock "correspondence course" for blacks. "Niggers!" the leaflet read, "You Too Can Be A Jew . . . It's Easy! It's Fun . . . Sammy-the-Kosher-Coon Shows You How. . . . In Ten Easy Lessons!!" "In Just Minutes A Day!" it said, "Be One of Us Chosen People . . . Here's Some of the Things You Learn: Jewish customs and traditions such as how to force your way into social groups, how to be obnoxious and arrogant, how to throw orange peels around in a professional Jewish manner . . . How to make millions cheating widows and orphans . . . How to Hate-Hitler and get people believing he killed six millions of us even though we are all over here living it up on the dumb Christians. . . ."

Thrown into the "offer" was a kit of "working tools," including a *"Special piece of extra nose*, handsomely tinted black, from our New York Jewish Beak-bank, for grafting on so you will look more like a *real* Jew. . . . *Synagogue bombing kit*, for keeping the anti-semites under control. . . . *Thumb screws*, or a manual on Jewish business methods." Immediately following was a section on "Testimonials," which contained statements over names like "Rastus Rosenberg," and "Uncle Moses Ginsburg," and which were accompanied by pictorial caricatures. Finally, a section near the end, set off to resemble a coupon, read, "Yes! I want to be a Jew-Nigger and get equal right away! . . . Name . . . Address . . . Nose size . . . Prefer Blondes?"

It was, on the whole, a pamphlet of rare edge and exemplary viciousness. Within fifteen minutes, in the heavy rush hour traffic, about 200 people had gathered around the small band of marchers. Complaints were heard in the crowd, particularly from blacks and Jews, and men were seen in different places picking up bats and other objects to use as weapons. The police sergeant on the scene was informed by another patrolman that a crowd was gathering on Lake Street and that it was likely to try to attack the pickets. The sergeant approached Malcolm Lambert, the leader of the self-proclaimed Nazis, and urged him to have his group disperse. Lambert refused, however, to issue that command. In the meantime an

---

[40] *Chicago v. Lambert*, 197 N.E. 2d 448 (1964).

officer went to observe the group forming on Lake Street and found about 40-60 people who were apparently not to be constrained. They told him, as he testified later, that they would not leave until something had been done about the marchers. As the action shifted back to the theater and the tension seemed to be mounting, the marchers were asked again to disperse; again they refused, and this time they were arrested.[41]

In the exchange between the policeman and the crowd on Lake Street, it appears that a question was being raised as much as a threat. With more or less explicitness the question was being put: "Must we really do these things, must we really move ourselves to the point of violence and make the first step toward taking the law into our own hands, before the police can do anything about these men?" And, pursuing the same question from the other side, if there were no clear grounds for an arrest before the situation grew menacing, what was there in the mere willingness of a crowd to assemble and take up weapons that provided any clearer warrant for the arrest of these men? Here, as in other cases,[42] the insistence on waiting for the first signs of violence works with a clear antilibertarian effect: it makes the rights of the speaker contingent on the sufferance of a hostile audience. The speaker becomes a hostage to the first rock that is thrown, or to the first heckler who cares to instigate a fight and stir a commotion in the audience. Under the conditions of a crowd, it may often be hard to remove scattered hecklers without bringing on the very disturbance that the police are trying to avoid (and that the hecklers may be trying to create). And so it may be all too easy, under the formula of the danger test, to deprive the speaker of his audience and make a mockery out of his right to speak.[43]

Not only is the danger test, in this sense, highly questionable as a libertarian device, but it teaches the worst lessons that a regime of law could possibly teach. It suggests that, before citizens can

[41] Ibid. at 452-53.

[42] See, for example, *Feiner* v. *New York*, 340 U.S. 315 (1951).

[43] Cf. *Terminiello* v. *Chicago*, 337 U.S. 1, 16, 22 (1949), where the police acted first to remove the disorderly "spectators" from the crowd, both inside and outside the hall, before they judged that the speaker himself was responsible for provoking the crowd to violence. In other words, the police sought to avoid a situation in which the rights of the speaker would have depended on the sufferance of a hostile audience. They tried to deal with the heckling and the violence where they could, but they were compelled also to judge the nature of the words used by the speaker, in the context in which they were used, as a measure of his own intentions and responsibility.

expect the law to protect them or to vindicate their interests, they must be prepared themselves to use violence outside the law. More than that, it encourages the private use of force, as it did in the case of Lambert, for the purpose of inducing the authorities to make an arrest. All things considered, this kind of ritual rather alters our sense of the bases on which arrests ought to be made.

And yet it is precisely the clear and present danger test that has been urged on the courts by civil libertarians. The Lambert case in particular was picked out several years ago by John Pemberton, Jr., of the American Civil Liberties Union, who offered it up as an example in which the clear and present danger test would have provided the most salutary ground for a judgment.[44] Pemberton was moved to speak out on this case because the court in *Lambert* had placed its reliance on the holding in *Beauharnais* and avoided the use of the danger test. In this disposition, the court showed better judgment than Mr. Pemberton. But in view of the serious antilibertarian effects that may come along with the danger test, one may wonder why libertarians would not prefer to have the law step in earlier and respond to the offense itself rather than let matters hinge upon the reactions of crowds.

The answer seems to be that, as high as the cost may be in principle, it is a price that libertarians are nevertheless willing to pay for the sake of avoiding an alternative they regard as far worse in principle, namely, that it may be legitimate to restrict speech by judging the content of the speech itself. The point is frequently made on the libertarian side that one does not trust judges or policemen (or anyone else) to make decisions about the kind of speech that is so lacking in substantive value that it falls beneath constitutional protection. At the root there is still a tendency to believe that the law has no standards in these cases that are anything but hopelessly subjective, and that there can be no way of restraining Lambert and his neo-Nazi band without imperiling all speech and writing of a critical nature.

But as I have sought to show, the premise itself is misconceived. The meaning of words cannot be so arbitrary and subjective. There may, of course, be borderline cases that are difficult to judge; but there are borderline judgments to be made in all kinds of cases, including murder, assault, and rape. Even though the injuries are unambiguous in these cases, they cannot be enough in themselves to determine the verdict. Whether a killing is a murder or a "jus-

---

[44] John Pemberton, Jr., "Can the Law Provide a Remedy for Race Defamation in the United States?" 14 *N.Y.U. Law Forum* 33 (1968).

tifiable homicide" will depend, by definition, on the case that could be made in justification. It will become necessary then to consider matters of intention and provocation, and these things can be judged only by reading the circumstances of the case. But the facts of the case, as we know, are not always unequivocal. Testimony may be in conflict, key points of mitigation may not be fully documented, and so a decision, when it is finally made, may have to rest on an educated hunch—an estimate of character or an exercise of conjecture, which may be quite as slippery and "subjective" as anything that is likely to be encountered in cases of speech or verbal assault.

Not all murders present borderline cases, but the point is that neither do all cases of speech. There are cases of verbal assault, as in *Lambert*, that are far more unambiguous, and far easier to judge, than some cases of murder and many cases of rape. Our standards for recognizing a verbal assault or an act of defamation are no more uncertain than the standards we have for the recognition of other kinds of assaults. If anything, the language itself may present a measure of intention that is even more precise and reliable than the measures that are available to us in other cases.

Some cases in fact are so patent, and the distinctions so obvious, that we would never doubt for a moment our capacity to judge, and therefore we may not even be aware that we are making judgments at all. We may find, for example, that the admissions officer of a college induces despair in a young applicant when he calls him on the phone and informs him that he was not admitted to the college. We find another person who excites fear in other people by disturbing them in the middle of the night with obscene phone calls. In both cases it may be said that a hurt is inflicted through the use of speech, and yet the law reaches one case and not the other. The law may punish the obscene caller but not the dean of admissions, and the difference turns on the nature of the words that were used and the ends that animated these acts of speech. In the case of the dean of admissions, the speech that induced the hurt feelings was the necessary byproduct of a process of selection that could be shown to be legitimate in its objects and its methods. In the case of the obscene calls, a hurt is inflicted for no reason other than the sadistic pleasure (or, possibly, the self-interest) of the caller, which is to say that it is inflicted for the sake of an end that cannot be justified.

Worldly people without training in law are called upon to make judgments of this kind all the time in their daily lives, and they often wonder why questions of justification that must be accessible to men of ordinary intellect should be found so inscrutable by so many lawyers and libertarians. The fact that mistakes may be made at times in judging matters of speech can no more stand as an argument against the law than the mistakes made by juries in cases of murder and assault can establish the essential injustice of having laws on murder and assault. The most disturbing part of the libertarian argument is not that it promises to let quite a lot of degrading speech flourish, but that it denies, in principle, the very possibility of judging. If it is impossible to judge the content of Lambert's pamphlet, it is impossible to judge anything. If there are no grounds on which one could distinguish between the decent and the indecent in cases like *Lambert*, then there are no grounds on which one could make distinctions of that kind in any other area of public policy.

Unlike *Beauharnais*, there was not the thinnest pretense in *Lambert* that the leaflet was presenting either an argument or a petition. That it was very much political, however, in its intention and effect, is something that cannot be denied. The case can only press one to consider, in a more sober way, whether it is possible to claim protection for anything that has political relevance, no matter how distant it may be from the substance of argument, and how unrelievedly malicious it may be in its character. Of course, there is no defensible way for the law to touch Lambert and his group without passing judgment on the leaflet itself, and it is not clear that *Cohen v. California* would offer any help. There was nothing here to suggest a direct personal assault: the leaflet was ostensibly aimed at Sammy Davis, Jr., but Davis himself was not even in Chicago at the time. Besides, the attack on Davis was the most transparent formal device, a vehicle for a much larger purpose of defamation that the court was very quick to recognize. The evident purpose of the pamphlet was to defame blacks and Jews, and it was obviously understood in that way by many blacks and Jews who were present, despite the fact that they were never mentioned personally in the leaflet.

The only satisfying way, then, of resolving this case was to return to the original ground of the ruling in the *Chaplinsky* case, a ground that permitted the law to respond to forms of expression that were in principle (or in themselves) offensive, regardless of whether they produced an outbreak of violence. A republican order was not obliged to let the public peace be used as a plaything by combat groups in the street; nor was there any need for a lawful government to stand by while decent citizens were moved to violence through provocations borne of no good motive or justification. To speak of testing the truth of ideas in the marketplace is patent nonsense in cases of this kind: the premises of Nazism cannot be regarded as plausible or legitimate without denying the self-evident truths that underlie democratic government itself. For that reason the offensiveness of the Nazis is not to be measured merely by the personal reactions of bystanders. It would be established, rather, in the very principles that define a regime of civil liberties. And so, if it is possible to say that obscene phone calls may be restricted because their ends are not justified, the task of judging the speech of the Nazis cannot represent a difficult problem in the science of moral judgment.[45]

In any event, the holding in *Chaplinsky* provided an instrument for bringing all these recognitions to bear on cases in law. It prepared the most defensible grounds on which one could have restrained the speech of a Lambert; and it would explain, more recently, the grounds on which the authorities in Skokie, Illinois were justified in their efforts to prevent the Nazis from staging a march in their community. It is at least somewhat revealing that, in the *Lambert* case, the court in Illinois placed its main accent at first on the danger test and the breach of the peace; but as it sought to justify its decision it moved away from standards that put more emphasis on the reactions of the crowd than on the responsibility of the marchers. The justification began to turn, in other words, on the nature of the leaflet, and as the court came over to the view that the danger of violence was really inherent in the words that were used, the opinion of the court came rather near to the language of the statute in *Beauharnais*:

> Persons may express their feelings on matters of public interest but action calculated to asperse and degrade other persons because of their race or religion can and do provoke breaches of the peace, violence, riots or other public disturbances. . . . A mere reading of the leaflet refers to Negroes and Jews as

---

[45] For a fuller statement of this argument—and its application to the problem of the Nazis in Skokie—see my piece, "Marching Through Skokie," *The National Review* (May 12, 1978), pp. 588-92. At the time I was writing, Philip Kurland was also raising the question, ". . . [H]ow many times does the Constitution command that this bloody, depraved credo of Aryan Supremacy has to be brought to the marketplace of ideas before it is deemed bested by 'truth'?" Philip B. Kurland, "Village of Skokie v. National Socialist Party of America: A Dissent" (unpublished address, 1978).

people possessing various criminal tendencies, unchastity and degrading sexual inclinations, all of which are 'fighting words' liable to cause violence and disorder between the races.[46]

There is a measure of irony in the fact that the court could find itself filling out a rationale along the lines of group libel in the same year as the legislature in Illinois repealed the statute on group defamation that had formed the basis for the prosecution in *Beauharnais*. Of course there was nothing said by the court in this instance, in upholding the restraints on the Nazis, that could not have been said with equal force more recently in restraining them from marching in Jewish neighborhoods. In this way the *Lambert* case helped to teach an enduring lesson: viz., that there is a class of problems in the law that the concept of group libel is precisely fitted to address, and that the courts may be compelled, enduringly, to apply the logic of the concept even if all the statutes on group libel should happen to vanish from the books.[47]

4. The Flight from Legal Restraint

But even if the understanding I have set forth here is correct, it is still possible to argue that it would be better not to deal with these problems of defamation through the formal instruments of the law. The intervention of the government carries the portents of censorship, and rather than take that risk, it would be better, in this view, to search for voluntary restraint and rely on informal processes of negotiation. It might be argued, for example, that even without the help of the government a great deal of offensive material is already screened from the public media. Ethnic and religious associations have often been quite effective in having material censored when members of their groups have been portrayed in foolish or defamatory stereotypes. The Italian-American Civil Rights League has

[46] 197 N.E. 2d at 455.

[47] And so Philip Kurland suggested that the courts could still make use of the doctrine of group libel in restraining the Nazis from marching in Skokie, Illinois, even though the statute on group defamation had not been restored. The authority for this judgment Kurland found, quite sufficiently, in *Beauharnais*. The Federal District Court in the Skokie case thought it was "widely believed by First Amendment scholars that [Beauharnais] is no longer good law." But Kurland cited the academic disagreement on this point and he observed that the judgment in *Beauharnais* was still, after all, the "law of the land." He reminded the Court that *Beauharnais* had never been overruled and "neither scholars nor lower federal courts are charged with the power to overrule Supreme Court decisions." Kurland, note 45 above.

managed to have a number of commercials removed from television, including one done for Alka Seltzer that had a man saying, "datsa somma spicy meatball." More significant, the League succeeded in having the words "Mafia" and "Cosa Nostra" expunged from a series on the F.B.I. that was carried by the American Broadcasting Company.[48] Not long after that, Jewish groups brought pressure on the Columbia Broadcasting System over a series called "Bridget Loves Bernie." Both Orthodox and Reform rabbis took the lead in this movement to have the program taken off the air because of the heavy use of Jewish stereotypes and because the show treated intermarriage in a favorable light.[49]

In Chicago, two years earlier, an alliance of community action groups withdrew petitions they had filed with the Federal Communications Commission to deny a renewal of broadcast licenses to WBBM-TV and WBBM radio. The withdrawal came after an agreement was reached between the stations and the community action groups for what was described as "upgraded community broadcast services." According to the report in *The New York Times*, the stations agreed, on their part, to advise the community groups of job openings as soon as they became available, to open business accounts in two weeks with Chicago firms owned by blacks, and "to meet with the community groups regularly over the next three years to discuss politics and programming; to screen advertising for demeaning references to ethnic and racial groups."[50]

There is little reason to doubt, then, that private groups in this society can be quite effective in protecting their interests and screening material from the media, even without the help of the government. But instead of weakening the case for legal restraints, this state of affairs only sharpens the sense of the problem: for it is plain that the choice, as we suggested earlier, is not between re-

[48] *The New York Times*, March 24, 1971, p. 44.

[49] *The New York Times*, February 7, 1973, p. 79.

[50] *The New York Times*, March 3, 1971, p. 71. In 1973 station KHJ-TV in Los Angeles began receiving lists of movies that were considered "off limits" by the Japanese-American Citizens League and by Justicia, an organization of Mexican-Americans. In other places, Chinese-Americans have opposed Charlie Chan movies, and black groups have succeeded in keeping off the air certain movies made by Shirley Temple and Will Rogers, which contained the actor, Stepin Fetchit, in his characteristic role as a rather slow-witted black. See *The New York Times*, November 28, 1973, p. 90. For the successes also of the Gay Activists Alliance in having certain lines struck from a network television show ("Marcus Welby, M.D."), see *The New York Times*, February 21, 1973, p. 87.

straint and free expression; it is between two kinds of restraint, one carried on outside the law by private groups, and another administered by the government and carried out under the authority of a formal statute. Between these two kinds of restraint it is by no means clear that we should always choose the informal, as though it were somehow more benign and less coercive for being outside the law.

From the examples we have already seen, it is apparent that a system of extralegal censorship may move well beyond matters of racial and religious defamation to reach issues of a more contentious political nature. Instead of operating in a precise and limited way, they have worked with diffuse and uncontained effects. But all this was understood with notable clarity by the Supreme Court when it addressed the same problem in a slightly different form in 1963 in *Bantam Books* v. *Sullivan.*[51] In that case the Court dealt with the Rhode Island Commission to Encourage Morality in Youth, an organization that was charged by the legislature to educate the public on obscene materials that could tend to corrupt young people. As part of its responsibilities the Commission was "to investigate and recommend the prosecution of all violations" of the laws on obscenity.[52] The Commission had no formal powers of prosecution, but when it "advised" a distributor that certain books or magazines had been found objectionable for young people under the age of 18, a prudent distributor did not have to be told twice. Field agents would be sent out to the various retailers, where they would pick up all the unsold copies, and the books would be returned to the publisher. As one distributor testified, there was a strong incentive to act immediately on the receipt of the notice, "rather than face the possibility of some sort of court action against ourselves, as well as the people that we supply."[53]

A group of publishers finally pressed a suit and charged that the Commission was engaged in a scheme of censorship without the usual safeguards of the legal process. In writing for the Court, Justice Brennan acknowledged that the Commission had been limited to "informal sanctions," but the record amply showed that the Commission had set out to suppress publications that were considered "objectionable" and that it had succeeded rather thoroughly in its aims. "We are not the first court," he said, "to look through forms to the substance and recognize that informal censorship may

[51] 372 U.S. 58 (1963). [52] Ibid. at 59-60.
[53] Ibid. at 63.

sufficiently inhibit the circulation of publications to warrant injunctive relief."[54]

The distributors had been free, of course, to disregard the warnings of the Commission in the sense that, if they had refused to comply, they would have violated no law. But threats of prosecution were not to be lightly disregarded, especially when they came from a body that apparently enjoyed such a close relation to agencies of the government. As Brennan remarked, one had to be naive to credit the assertion of the state that "these blacklists are in the nature of mere legal advice, when they plainly serve as instruments of regulation independent of the laws against obscenity":[55]

> Herein lies the vice of the system. The Commission's operation is a form of effective state regulation superimposed upon the State's regulation of obscenity and making such regulation largely unnecessary. In thus obviating the need to employ criminal sanctions, the State has at the same time eliminated the safeguards of the criminal process. Criminal sanctions may be applied only after a determination of obscenity has been made in a criminal trial hedged about with the procedural safeguards of the criminal process. The Commission's practice is in striking contrast, in that it provides no safeguards whatever against the suppression of nonobscene, and therefore constitutionally protected, matter. It is a form of regulation that creates hazards to protected freedoms markedly greater than those that attend reliance upon the criminal law.[56]

The fact that this system of censorship went on outside the law, without the direct use of legal penalties, did not make it, for that reason, any more gentle or liberating. On the contrary, it produced a form of restraint that was far more stringent in its effects than anything that was likely to have occurred if the authorities had been forced to work instead under the discipline of a formal statute. Without the need, as a matter of course, to face a challenge in court and justify its decisions, the Commission could get along fairly well with standards that were rather gross and unarticulated. Publications were listed simply as "objectionable," without any further word of explanation.[57] The attorney general of Rhode Island conceded, for example, in his oral argument that several of the books

[54] Ibid. at 67, and see also note 7 on the same page for further references on the problem of "informal censorship."

[55] Ibid. at 68-69.　　　　[56] Ibid. at 69-70.　　　　[57] Ibid. at 71.

listed by the Commission would not have met the criteria used by the Supreme Court in defining obscenity.[58] And while that point might not have been as momentous as it was made out to be, it was nevertheless true that a system designed for the purpose of keeping certain materials from a youthful audience was having the effect, in this case, of suppressing publications in the state as a whole, for adults as well as adolescents.[59] The system worked, then, in an unconstrained way, and it could reach publications that the authorities would have been powerless to forbid if they had been compelled to work their will through an explicit statute.[60] Altogether, the experience seemed to bear out Mill's admonition that, for the true libertarian, there were worse things to be dreaded than the acts of the public authorities. There was the need for protection, too, "against the tendency of society to impose by other means than civil penalties, its own ideas and practices as rules of conduct."[61]

In that sense the *Bantam Books* case had the advantage of setting several things in order, which apply just as well to the defamation of groups and to other problems in the regulation of speech. It suggested, for example, that one may still share the concerns of the libertarian, even as one regards the defamation of groups as a fit object of restraint which deserves to be treated with the most solemn and formal processes of the law. The two concerns are not necessarily in conflict; they may be reconciled by the way in which the presumptions are finally placed in the enforcement of the law. If we were resolved, for example, to eradicate every sign and vestige of group defamation, we might presume, even in all doubtful cases, that it is better to arrest and convict. On the other hand, our aim may be to reach only the most egregious cases, where the offense is unambiguous; and in that event our presumptions would be turned around. Instead of presuming in favor of prosecution, we would presume now, in all doubtful cases, that we ought to let the matter go. The change may seem slight, but the difference may be profound as far as the consequences are concerned. The shift in presumptions creates a different structure of action, in which the

---

[58] Ibid. at 64.

[59] See Brennan's argument on the point, ibid. at 71.

[60] As a forerunner of the Bantam Books case where the censoring body in question (the Watch and Ward Society of Boston) had an even more remote relation to the formal agencies of government, see *American Mercury, Inc.* v. *Chase*, 13 F. 2d 224 (1926), especially 225.

[61] Mill, *On Liberty* (Oxford: Basil Blackwell, 1946), p. 4.

bias is placed in favor of one set of outcomes and the burden of proof is given over to the other side.

In the case of regulating speech, the presumptions could be set in favor of free expression, and the burden of proof could be placed on the side of those who would restrict free speech. Without too much difficulty, the police can be coached to hold back on these matters and to act only when they have an unmistakable case. And in those situations where a judgment has to be made about the intentions of a speaker, we could encourage the police to be even more circumspect. We could take a leaf from the "stop and frisk" cases and caution the police to wait for those "specific and articulable facts" which, when combined with the "rational inferences [drawn] from those facts" could reasonably justify their decision if the matter were reviewed in court.[62]

By arranging the presumptions and incentives in this way, we could preserve an active arena of public discourse, while at the same time allowing ourselves to reach the most odious cases of group defamation, or the cases that are so public and offensive that they cannot be avoided. Again, there is no need to overreach ourselves. It is quite enough if we confine our actions to the most obvious cases, which raise the clearest issues of principle. For in doing that, we would demonstrate once again that it is indeed possible to judge; and when we judge, as we would here, with all the force and attention of public authority, we would hold up an example to others that goes well beyond the matter of group libel. We would encourage confidence in the discipline of judging itself, and we would encourage others to make judgments as well, not simply on group defamation, but on many other matters that, in one form or another, raise questions about propriety and decency and the obligations that individuals may have to one another.

We should expect, of course, that mistakes in judgment will be made, as they are made in other areas of adjudication. But the possibility of abuse has never been a sufficient ground for the denial of a power that is otherwise legitimate. By that reckoning there is not a set of laws on the books that could survive (including the laws that provide for voting and aid to dependent children). That

---

[62] The phrases are drawn from *Terry* v. *Ohio*, 392 U.S. 1, 21, 22 (1968), and see also 5-6, 22-23, for a recitation of the facts that were able to satisfy the formula in this case. Cf. also the facts in *Terminiello* v. *Chicago*, 337 U.S. 1, 13-22, especially 16, 22 (1949) (Jackson, dissenting), which could have satisfied this test and upheld the decision of the police.

mistakes should occur at all is something that can only be regretted. But when the ends of the law are legitimate, and when the means are aptly tailored to their ends, we can live with the occasional mistakes. Thirty years ago, when *Chaplinsky* was decided, our laws were a great deal more vigorous than they are today in the regulation of obscenity, as well as other forms of offensive speech. Yet few people doubted at the time that, in the world of 1942, the United States held out, along with Britain, the example of a healthy democracy, where civil liberties were generally protected and the range of political dissent could be rather wide. Even today, in Britain, the courts have been far sterner than their American counterparts in the treatment of libel, and as recently as the mid-sixties the Labour Government secured the passage of a statute on racial defamation, at a time when the matter was being regarded in the United States as a relic of a benighted past.[63] And yet, it would be hard to assert that the public discourse of politics is any less vigorous or substantive in Britain than it is in the United States. Nor has anyone been able to argue that these restraints on speech have had such an inhibiting effect on political expression that the alternatives presented by the parties in Britain have been in any degree narrower, or less significant in their reach, than the alternatives that have been offered by the American parties.

All things taken together, it is just that much harder to believe now that we would lose our character as a constitutional democracy if a number of cities and towns suddenly took a harder line on the matter of racial and religious defamation, or if a policeman, say, in Chicago, moved a shade too quickly one day and took an antiblack speaker off a public corner. The sense endures, somehow, that we could survive errors of that sort without impairing the basic character of this regime or absorbing flaws that reach to the level of principle. Or at least, it may be said that we could survive those mistakes more easily than we could survive the consequences of making no judgments at all, or professing no recognition of any standards by which we could ever hope to judge.[64]

[63] For an account of the background and nature of the British Race Relations Act of 1965, see Anthony Dickey, "English Law and Race Defamation," 14 *N.Y.U. Law Forum* 9 (1968).

[64] In 1973, after the argument in these chapters was first set down, the Supreme Court affirmed a scheme of regulation for pornography that was rather similar to the scheme put forth here. See *Miller* v. *California*, 413 U.S. 15 (1973) and *Paris Adult Theatre* v. *Slaton*, 413 U.S. 49 (1973). The Court moved to give more latitude to state and local governments; and whatever can be argued in favor of this arrangement in regard to pornography can be argued with comparable force in regard

5. CONCLUSION

I should say that, along with many other people in the mid-sixties, I was very much affected by the late Harry Kalven's noted article on "The Central Meaning of the First Amendment," and by his insistence that the issue of seditious libel stood at the heart of the definition of democratic government. "Political freedom ends," wrote Kalven, "when government can use its power and its courts to silence its critics. . . . [D]efamation of the government is an impossible notion for a democracy."[65] Kalven's argument, in short, was that whatever else a government may be, it cannot be a democratic government if officials are permitted to make casual use of the laws of libel for the sake of silencing their "citizen-critics." I was, as I own, very much impressed at the time by the force of the observation and the sweep of the analysis. But while Kalven was justified in many of his concerns about the concept of seditious libel, I am no longer persuaded that the issue of seditious libel would have to represent, as Kalven said, the "touchstone" that defines the regime itself. One might as tenably say that whatever else a government may be, it cannot be a democratic government if it permits officials to make casual use of the laws on traffic and commerce in order to prevent innocent citizens from going about their lawful callings.

As far as one can see, there is no logically necessary step that places the issue of speech at the center of the definition of a democratic order. What seems plainer to me on reflection is the elementary point that a democracy must be a regime of law before it is anything else. As we saw in the discussion of Lincoln, a lawful government manifests its character most importantly by preserving the conditions of justice and honoring the differences that separate the innocent and the guilty: its first obligation is to protect people against harms that may be inflicted on them unjustly, through assaults carried on outside a process of law. Those injustices can be

---

to the regulation of speech more generally. It is notable in this respect that when the Court framed its decision on pornography it returned to the old Roth case (354 U.S. 476 [1967]) and to the reliance that was placed there on *Chaplinsky*. See 413 U.S. at 20. In fact, it is hard to read the opinions of the Chief Justice in these cases without discerning some intention on the part of the majority to firm up precedents that had been seriously weakened in cases like *Cohen* v. *California* and its progeny. See notes 16 and 21 above.

[65] Kalven, "The New York Times Case: A Note on the 'Central Meaning of the First Amendment,' " in Philip B. Kurland, ed., *The Supreme Court Review 1964* (Chicago: University of Chicago Press, 1965), pp. 191ff.

found in a variety of forms, in acts of coercion that may restrict freedom, take property, or endanger lives.

The question, in that case, is whether injuries (or "injustices") can be inflicted through the use of speech; and for most of our history the answer to the question seemed obvious. There was nothing about speech itself that rendered it categorically innocent or incapable of doing harm. There was nothing in the freedom of speech that made it more productive of good or less productive of evil than any other species of freedom. It was well understood traditionally that certain kinds of expression (such as defamatory and insulting statements) could represent assaults in themselves even if they were not accompanied by acts of physical force. The *Chaplinsky* case had the merit of reminding us of that ancient recognition. It encouraged us to look at verbal assaults in the way we looked at other kinds of assaults: the question had to be raised, in any given case, of whether the assault could be justified or excused; and if it could not be, the speech could be restrained and the speaker could be punished, in much the same way as the law dealt with other kinds of assaults. If there is an obligation then to restrict speech, even in a democratic regime, it is because speech can be a medium of injustice along with a variety of other devices. And if we have the capacity to judge whether harms are inflicted justly or unjustly, we do not lose that capacity to judge when the harms are inflicted through the use of speech.

If there is any case that marks the limits of the argument I have offered here, it would probably be found in a species of the "Jabberwocky" problem: it is not hard to identify the words that are established in our language as terms of defamation and insult; but what would we do in a case where the words are arrayed in such a context that the language serves a defamatory function, even though the words themselves are literally innocent or meaningless? In Lewis Caroll's "Jabberwocky," it is easy to tell just which words are the nouns, and which the verbs and adjectives, even though the sounds themselves are literally nonsense: " 'Twas brillig and the slithey toves did gire and gimble in the wabe. . . ." (It was, after all, the "toves" that *did* "gire and gimble" in the wabe.) Might something similar be done in a conscious way to employ innocent words, but with the purpose of achieving a defamatory effect? In Florida, in 1950, George Smathers managed the very difficult task of defeating the incumbent, Claude Pepper, in the Democratic primary for United States Senator. In the course of the campaign,

Smathers delivered these remarks to a rustic audience in the Florida panhandle:

> Are you aware [he said] that Claude Pepper is known all over Washington as a shameless extrovert? Not only that, but this man is reliably reported to practice nepotism with his sister-in-law, and he has a sister who was once a Thespian in New York. Worst of all, it is an established fact that Mr. Pepper, before his marriage, practiced celibacy.[66]

Here we may decide, with Aristotle, that we would be wise not to push our principles to the limits of their logic. It is enough, as we have said, if we reach only the most egregious cases, the cases that raise the deepest concern and that call out in the most urgent way for the response of a decent society. If we can live with mistakes borne of an excess of diligence, we can live, too, with certain borderline cases. We may find in the end that we have come to agree after all with Holmes—if only we had leave now to recall him in a voice slightly gentler than his own—that the law does all it needs to do when it does all it sensibly can.

[66] Quoted in William F. Buckley, Jr. and L. Brent Bozell, *McCarthy and His Enemies* (Chicago: Henry Regnery Co., 1961), p. 304.

IV

URBAN DISORDERS I:
CHICAGO 1968

The disorders that surrounded the Democratic Convention in Chicago in 1968 have already achieved a certain standing as an "event" in our recent political history. They have been stamped in the public mind with a rather definite meaning; in some instances they have been taken to mark the character of the period or of the American regime itself. In the surveys that were taken at the time, the public was quite emphatic in its judgments on the event—as emphatic, one might say, as it was divided in its understanding of the facts. In this respect, the division of opinion may simply reflect the seriousness of the issues in dispute, for it was realized, even at the time, that questions were being raised here of a more enduring nature about the conditions of rendering justice in the city. They were questions, in part, about the principles that governed the political use of public places, but they led outward to questions about the preservation of civility; the terms of principle on which a community lives together; and the restraints that citizens may be obliged to respect, as well as the rights they can decently claim.

That tangle of happenings which made up the events in Chicago was impossible to grasp in its fullness. There was, of course, a structure imposed by the Convention itself and its schedule of business: the Convention provided, at once, a target for the various acts of protest against the war in Vietnam and a timetable around which the protesting groups could arrange their activities. But even though there were a number of central events that gave the appearance of a structure to the incidents of the week, the action dissolved into myriad confrontations among individuals at the periphery (demonstrators, policemen, reporters, even pedestrians and motorists who just happened to be passing by) so that the events in their entirety simply could not be documented. To cast a judgment on these events as a whole, one would presume to judge a host of minor wars in the street, which were bound up in turn with many provocations and villainies that remained unseen.

And yet in spite of all the hazards to a reliable judgment, most

Americans seemed to suffer little equivocation as they came to settle the meaning of the event for themselves. According to the Survey Research Center of the University of Michigan, the divisions of opinion in the public were associated most importantly with race, age, and the number of years spent in school. Blacks were far more disposed on the whole than whites to think that the police used too much force against the demonstrators. That view was held by 63 percent of the blacks who were sampled, a figure that was equaled among whites only by people between the ages of 21 and 29 who held graduate degrees. The tendency to be critical of the police advanced, among whites, with each step along a scale of formal schooling; but it was only among whites under 40 that the possession of a graduate degree produced majorities that found fault with the police.[1]

For most whites, then, including whites with a college education, the responsibility for the violence lay with the lawlessness of the demonstrators. According to the report of the Survey Research Center, the Democrats lost more votes in 1968 among those people who thought that the police had *not* used enough force in dealing with the demonstrators.[2] And what is more startling, even among those people who could have been classified as "doves" on the Vietnam war, 70 percent rejected the proposition that too much force had been used by the police. Among the respondents in the sample as a whole, the most frequent response (offered by 40 percent of the people) was that *not enough* force had been used.[3] As the researchers suggested in the way of an explanation, the same people in this country who seemed most disturbed by the prospect of unabating violence abroad seemed highly alarmed also by what they saw perhaps as cognate forms of violence and lawlessness in the streets.[4]

The question naturally arises as to what can be made of these differences. Should it be assumed that younger people with college degrees were more informed and enlightened in their reaction to these events? Or should it be assumed that the older people who condemned the demonstrators spoke with a more rigorous sense

[1] See John Robinson, "Public Reaction to Political Protest: Chicago 1968," *Public Opinion Quarterly*, Vol. 34 (Spring 1970), pp. 1-9, at 7.

[2] Ibid., p. 9.

[3] See Philip Converse et al., "Continuity and Change in American Politics: Parties and Issues in the 1968 Election," *American Political Science Review*, Vol. 63, no. 4 (December 1969), pp. 1083-1105, at 1087.

[4] Ibid., p. 1088.

of principle? The short answer is that, in the absence of any evidence as to what in fact any of these people knew, there is no basis for treating the views on either side as anything more than mere "opinion." If personal experience is admissible, it can be reported that even the most select college students, armed with the records of the case,[5] have a very hard time setting the facts in order. And even when they manage to notice the full range of facts that bear on the main issues, they are not clear on the questions of principle that must be brought to the facts for the purpose of forming a judgment.

Still, the disorders in Chicago became enveloped in significance for so many people because they *were* thought to be examples on a dramatic scale of things that were, *in principle*, wrong. What occurred in Chicago was quite evidently more than a matter of traffic control, or of two rival groups fighting it out in the streets. It was a situation that raised questions of public rights and duties, and it was clear that it was not the last time they would be raised.

The official commission that studied the disorders in Chicago issued its report under the title of *Rights in Conflict*. In that way it seemed to convey its understanding that the task it set for itself— the task of getting to the source of the problem and helping to prevent disorders of this kind in the future—depended on the prospect of settling the rights and wrongs of the matter. In that purpose, however, the report conspicuously failed (as indeed it might have been expected that a committee would fail at a task which required reflection of a judicial and philosophic kind). It took a rather coarse reading of the record in order to say, as the Walker Commission did, that the right engaged on the side of the protesters was the "right to dissent"; and it betrayed a certain want of imagination to suggest that the right involved on the other side was nothing more than "the right of a city to protect its citizens and its property."[6] It was the expectation of the Commission that the facts, when they were brought out, would largely speak for themselves. They did not; but the Commission at least furnished a record, and it preserved the possibility that others may look at the same documents again, with a somewhat different set of questions, and reach a more calibrated set of judgments.

I will limit my own discussion here to three problems, which take in, I think, the most important questions that were raised by

[5] *Rights in Conflict*: The Walker Report to the National Commission on the Causes and Prevention of Violence (New York: Bantam Books, 1968).
[6] Ibid., p. xvi.

the events of Chicago. As we shall see, also, any attempt to render a judgment on these questions would be affected in a serious way by the understandings and precedents that were established in the previous two chapters. I will deal first with the problem presented by Rennie Davis and his group in their efforts to obtain permits from the city for demonstrations and rallies. From there I will turn to the question of whether the city should have permitted Lincoln Park to be used for the week as a dormitory or hotel for the various protest groups that were drawn to the city. The third section will involve the period during the Convention, after the cords of civility were snapped, and I will consider there the reaction of the police.

1. RENNIE DAVIS AND THE QUESTION OF PERMITS

The Spring Mobilization Committee was formed by David Dellinger and A. J. Muste in the latter part of 1966 with the purpose of setting plans in motion for demonstrations against the war in Vietnam. The fruits of the planning were two large demonstrations held in New York and San Francisco in April 1967. The demonstration in New York drew an estimated 100,000 people, and it offered the chance to a variety of protest groups to cultivate their own capacities as organizations. After the success of the demonstrations, the Spring Mobilization Committee gave way to the National Mobilization Committee to End the War in Vietnam, which came into being with a list of the organizations that had participated in the spring marches.

Trying to build its momentum, the Committee launched into the planning for new demonstrations. The most important project to emerge was the famous march on the Pentagon, which took place in October 1967. This event attracted about 50,000 demonstrators, but unlike the larger demonstration in New York the previous spring, the encounter at the Pentagon gave rise to some disruption and violence. A group of about 2,000 demonstrators had shoved their way up to the entrance of the Pentagon; another 3,000 or so had broken through the lines of police to charge another entrance, with some of them actually getting into the building. By the time it was all over, about 600 people had been arrested.[7]

At about the same time, in October 1967, the officers of the National Mobilization were looking ahead to the Democratic Convention, which would be occurring the next summer. By February 1968 the Committee had raised enough money to open an office

[7] Ibid., pp. 21-22.

in Chicago, and set to work preparing for the Convention. The responsibility for acting as the Chicago "coordinator" was given to Rennie Davis, a young man in his mid-twenties, who was working at the time as a "community organizer" for the Students for a Democratic Society (SDS). It was Davis who would bear the burden of negotiating with representatives of the city over the routes for parades and demonstrations.

Davis's proposals called for two major parades, one right up the middle of State Street to the edge of the Loop (that is to say, in the heart of the downtown area), and another, alongside the Convention hall itself, moving down Halsted Street, between 39th and 47th Streets. Davis also sought the use of ten parks for "meet-ins" (with sound equipment) and six park areas for sleeping. These were not modest demands, and it was only to be expected that the city would treat these proposals with marked caution.

Off and on, between the middle of June and the first week in August, Davis met informally with Al Baugher of the Chicago Commission on Youth Welfare, and David Stahl, the administrative assistant to the mayor. One gathers that Baugher was anxious to achieve some accommodation with the dissident groups, and Stahl, though rather hard to get to see, was at least willing to take notes and listen patiently. Still, there seemed to be a certain stalling from above, and Davis could not make headway at any point. Mayor Daley turned down efforts at mediation, and for a while, in July, the administration seemed to be impenetrable. A meeting was arranged with Baugher and Stahl, but the two failed to appear. Stahl's office refused to respond to telephone calls from the New Mobilization. Later on, in August, Stahl and Baugher appeared at a meeting, but the meeting failed to draw the heads of other departments in the city, whose cooperation would be necessary to the demonstrators.[8] On the following day an application for park permits was mysteriously laid aside in the meeting of the Park Commission, and the request failed to appear on the agenda.[9]

[8] Ibid., pp. 64-65. The record of the Walker Commission is not clear on the point of whether *any* representatives from these agencies managed to attend the meeting.

[9] Ibid., p. 65. See also pp. 73-75 for some similar, though far more equivocal, experiences of the Committee for an Open Convention (COC), as it sought to get permission from the city to hold a large demonstration in Soldier Field during the week of the Convention. In fairness, the Walker Commission reviews some of the considerations that had to be applied by the city in leasing a facility as large as Soldier Field. Apart from parking, transportation, and utilities, there were problems of arranging liability insurance, ambulance services, and medical care. These matters were usually arranged long in advance by professional promoters, and as the Walker

For his own part, David Stahl was put off at times by the public comments made by the people with whom he was supposed to be negotiating. Rennie Davis had declared in a television interview that he was asking the Justice Department to investigate the Chicago police (on the grounds that they were preparing to use violence against the demonstrators). Stahl asked, in irritation, whether it was worth holding meetings with people who made statements of that kind. A sense of prudence would prevail and the negotiations would go forward again; but nevertheless there was a distrust of Davis and his allied groups that could not be effaced. The officials of the city were very much aware that the National Mobilization had sponsored the march on the Pentagon in October 1967, and that the march had broken out into violence and disorder. They were willing to accept the view that Davis and Dellinger were not themselves committed to violence, but they seriously doubted that either man had the ability to restrain all the people who were responding to their call and heading for Chicago. Beyond that, the request for sleeping accommodations was soon connected with the so-called Festival of Life which was being planned for Lincoln Park, and the people who were prominent in the planning were Jerry Rubin, Abbie Hoffman, and the New York Yippies. As the Walker Commission noted, in what must stand as a classic understatement, Rubin and Hoffman "had impressed the city negotiators as militant and unpredictable. Their association with the Stony Brook raid and the Grand Central disturbances in New York had not gone un-noticed."[10] Nor could David Stahl have avoided doubts about the seriousness of the people he was dealing with when some of the Yippies warned, in one meeting, that a "most dangerous social problem" would result if their demands for the use of Lincoln Park were not met, but then offered to call the whole thing off for $200,000![11] Altogether, then, even men in City Hall who were more sympathetic with the demonstrators would have moved very slowly, and made efforts to discourage the frivolous, before they turned over large public facilities to the use of these groups.

Matters moved along indecisively until suddenly the National Mobilization brought things to a head and pressed a suit against the city in a federal court. The dissident groups charged in their

---

Commission noted, "The COC rally promoters had not evidenced the organization, experience or inclination to meet the planning demands which such arrangements required." Ibid., p. 74. What is more, these considerations were not entirely without point in relation also to Rennie Davis and his request for the use of ten public parks.

[10] Ibid., p. 60.   [11] Ibid., p. 72.

suit that the mayor had been conspiring with other officials of the city to deny them the right to assemble, and that the failure of the city to act upon their requests had effectively denied them the equal protection of the laws.[12] The suit was eventually dismissed by Judge Lynch, but it had the advantage of forcing the city back into negotiations. The corporation counsel of the city came forward now with the offer of four specific routes for a daytime parade. But before considering those routes, and the response of Davis and his group, there are one or two points that are worth noting for the sake of setting the boundaries of the problem. Despite the controversy that arose over permits, it was not necessary to have a permit in all cases before an assembly could be held. The Park District had designated four park areas in which assemblies could be held without permits. They were: Burnham Park on Northerly Island, Garfield Park, Washington Park, and Lincoln Park.[13] These parks were clustered in the near-south and near-north sides (that is, in the more central parts of the city), and the last three in particular had been mentioned by Rennie Davis in some of his earlier discussions with Al Baugher.[14]

What was at issue, then, was not, in any strict sense, the First Amendment right to assemble. There was no constraint on the right of the National Mobilization, or any other of the antiwar groups, to hold assemblies of protest wherever they could find a private hall for hire. Clearly, too, there was no restraint on their freedom to present a petition to City Hall, and as the record showed, they suffered no incapacity to gain access to officials of the city. Nor were they denied the right to assemble in a public place, in parks that belonged to the city. What was at issue, as Judge Lynch later noted, was the application for permits "for the particular places and at the particular times" sought by Davis and his group.

It has been established for many years now in our case law that the power to grant permits for the use of the streets or parks may not be employed by the local authorities as a virtual license for restricting the expression of views they find uncongenial.[15] The regulations that govern the use of public places must apply in a neutral way; they must bear a rational relation to some legitimate end of government; and they must be, as the saying goes, "reasonable." It would not do, for example, if the authorities simply tried to be clever and used a variant of what might be called the "Death

[12] Ibid., p. 65.   [13] Ibid., p. 75.   [14] Ibid., p. 61.
[15] See, for example, *Hague* v. *CIO*, 307 U.S. 496 (1939), and *Cox* v. *New Hampshire*, 312 U.S. 569, 576 (1941).

Valley" strategem—that is, granting to a group of people the privilege of demonstrating, but assigning them to the local equivalent
of Death Valley as far as the news media are concerned. The authorities might well accomplish this ploy if, perhaps, among all the
parks in the city, they made available only one small park, on the
outskirts of town, where it would be very hard for any demonstration to attract notice.

In the case of Chicago, however, the parade routes that were
offered by the city could hardly be faulted on these grounds. In
considering the streets that could be closed off for the use of the
demonstrators, the city suggested these alternative plans:

(1) Assembling at the McCormick Place parking lot, north on the
    Outer Drive (one or two lanes only) to the Grant Park band-
    shell;
(2) Assembling at Lake Shore Park, Chicago Avenue and the Outer
    Drive, south on the Outer Drive (one or two lanes only) to the
    Grant Park bandshell;
(3) Assembling at Wacker Drive and Jackson Boulevard, east on
    Jackson to Columbus Drive to the Grant Park bandshell; and
(4) Assembling at the Monroe Street parking lot (in Grant Park)
    marching south along Columbus Drive to the Grant Park band-
    shell.[16]

These locations were all rather central; they were not in the heart
of the downtown area, but they were at important junctures in a
major traffic artery and, it might be added, they were also in some
of the most attractive settings in the city. Taking all things into
account, the demonstration surely would have been noticed if it
had moved along any one of these routes. Rennie Davis said that
any one of the four routes would be acceptable for the daytime
demonstration on August 28.[17] That did not, however, satisfy all
of the requests of the demonstrators. What Davis sought, in addition, was a parade and rally alongside the Convention hall itself,
which would take place at the very time that the nominations were
being made. He was told then by the corporation counsel that
parades were prohibited by state law for the interval between 4
p.m. and 7 p.m. (the period that roughly coincided with the "rush
hour"). But the city would permit a parade at night on any route
except the one Davis requested, along Halsted Street from 39th to
45th Streets. As the counsel explained, that area had been placed
off limits by the police and the Secret Service for reasons of security.

[16] Walker Report, note 5 above, p. 66.   [17] Ibid.

Davis raised then the possibility of using the parking lot of a shopping center at the corner of 47th and Halsted, or, as an alternative, the parking lot of the Amphitheatre, where the Convention was being held. The shopping center lot was, of course, private property and out of the hands of the city. As it turned out, the shopping center was scheduled to stay open that night, and so the parking lot was needed for its customers. The parking lot of the Amphitheatre was reserved for the Democratic National Committee, and in any event it would have been covered by the same considerations of security that barred demonstrations from the area of the Convention hall. It was suggested though, again, that other areas of the city could be used for an assembly, including places such as Lincoln Park, Garfield Park, and the Grant Park bandshell. But Davis was quite emphatic in his view that these sites were not at all adequate to the real needs of his group. The location for the evening rally had to be within "eyeshot" of the Amphitheatre if it was to have, as the Walker Report paraphrased it, any "psychological impact." If the demonstration could not be close to the Convention hall and to the delegates, then, as Davis said, the group might just as well "meet in Detroit."[18]

What Davis was claiming, then, was not a right of assembly or of free expression, for those rights were never brought into question. What he was claiming instead was a right to be "effective." Or to put it more precisely, he was claiming a right to go wherever one wished to go in a public place, without restraint, for the sake of pressing one's political views to the point of success. If the sense of the "rights" at stake here were to encompass anything less than that, then the complaint seemed to be that the right of expression would be reduced to harmless, formal acts, without the promise of a substantive result.

But when phrased in these terms, as a right to be anywhere in public, without restraint, as a means of becoming politically effective, the claims of Davis and his group would run directly counter to the principle in *Chaplinsky* and its corollary cases. In drawing

[18] Ibid. As Davis recalled, "We wanted to have legal and undisrupted demonstrations, and we felt the real power of our coming to Chicago would be around those public hearings at the Amphitheatre, and that's really what we wanted to secure. . . . We felt that . . . there was an important political presence that needed to be made on the eve of the nomination, as we anticipated at that time Humphrey would be nominated. . . . [A]n antiwar presence [was needed] outside the Amphitheatre. And . . . the political impact of that presence would be lost if we held a demonstration five miles from the Amphitheatre or held it in Detroit. I mean it was at the Amphitheatre where . . . that presence would be made and felt." Quoted in ibid., p. 63.

out the principle in the *Chaplinsky* case I suggested two analogues: the case of the crowd outside the house of the first black family in the neighborhood, and that of the crowd following the children to school. In both instances the political dimension of the cases was undeniable. There were larger purposes involved than the mere expression of hostility toward individuals, and since the crowds in these cases were engaged in nothing other than speech or expressive acts, they too might have claimed the right to station themselves in the one place where they were most likely to be "effective." They too might have claimed that if they were forced to express their feelings somewhere else, rather than make themselves directly visible or audible to the people they were trying to affect, they would not have had anything near the same impact and they might just as well have met "in Detroit."

If this analogy holds, one could not support Rennie Davis here without upholding in principle the claims of the crowds in those earlier cases. And as I argued earlier, the rights that were at stake on the part of the victims were so fundamental that no society could fail to protect them and still be called a decent or lawful society.

None of that is to say, of course, that Rennie Davis and his allied groups were identical at every point with the crowds that figured in the two cases that were mentioned earlier. They were identical in the most basic respect that their demands, in either case, could not be justified on terms that were compatible with a regime of law. Still, in the measures of justice, the thoughtless do not stand on the same plane with the malicious, and for all of their absence of reflection it would be hard to reckon Davis and his group as the equal of the crowd, say, that was out to harass the first black family in the neighborhood. As far as Davis and his allies were able to understand, they were not out to do injury or deprive someone else of his rights; and in that respect they differed from that crowd outside the house, which would have to know without much question the reason for its presence. And so, while there are ample grounds here for regarding the principle in the *Chaplinsky* case as controlling, one would wish to see a more rounded statement of the concerns on either side before one would consider the matter entirely resolved.

Taking the matter first from the side of the city, it could be said that its concerns in this case were not exclusively, of course, concerns of the city. The object of the municipal administrators was to secure the area of the Convention from violence and disruption, and in this respect the measures they took were probably guided as much by the Secret Service as by the judgment of the local police. That there was a potential for violence at the Convention was not something, at that time, which could easily be discounted. Martin Luther King had if been killed earlier in the spring, and then, in the beginning of June, Robert Kennedy had been assassinated. After the death of King, riots broke out in black areas scattered across the country, and Chicago itself had a somber taste of the destruction and the burning. With the murder of Kennedy, the antiwar groups lost the best hope they had that the Democratic nomination would be captured by a candidate whose views on the war seemed closest to their own. It could be expected that the dissatisfaction of these groups would mount as the Convention moved toward Hubert Humphrey; and with the increasing violence of political rhetoric and the politics of confrontation, the prospect of violence at the Convention could not be ruled out. Certainly it could not be ruled out if city officials gave any credence to reports appearing in the press. On August 13, for example, UPI reported that the "battle plan [of the National Mobilization] is to raise cain outside the convention hall. As their Chicago coordinator, Rennie Davis, warns, a storming of the convention hall itself is 'obviously not out of the question.' "[19]

The same general message was echoed in the local papers for months preceding the Convention, and it was amplified by such journals as the *New Left Notes, Liberation*, and the *Village Voice*.[20] One flyer of unknown origin, which circulated before the Convention, laid out in fuller detail the sense of what was likely to happen on Wednesday of Convention week, when the nominations would be made:

> We can be sure that the rally would be surrounded and contained by the Guard and the cops. This would mean that once the demonstration started people could neither enter nor leave the area. . . . There are a couple of contingency plans dealing with the problem of getting all of the people participating in

[19] Ibid., p. 90.

[20] The *New Left Notes* said in its issue of March 4, 1968: "To envision nonviolent demonstrations at the Convention is to indulge in unpleasant fantising [*sic*]. It should be clear to anyone who has been following developments in Chicago that a nonviolent demonstration would be impossible." An article in the *Village Voice* of June 20 remarked that "if the Central Committee gives us Humphrey anyway, then . . . We can leave the country, we can drift into quietism and tend our private gardens, or we can disrupt, disrupt, disrupt." Both cited in ibid. For a sampling of similar excerpts from other newspapers, see ibid., pp. 85-94.

this rally to the amphitheatre *en masse*. A mass march through the loop. . . . This would effectively tie up traffic in the loop and make our numbers seen and felt in a most effective way. . . . The other form of demonstration will be unofficial and not sponsored by the Mobilization Committee. The strategy of these actions would be that of employing mobile street tactics. The delegates will be entering the Amphitheatre via the parking lot. . . . The mobile demonstration (50, 100, 150 people in each group) would be involved in general disruption and more specifically in disrupting the delegates as they attempt to enter into the parking lot. . . .[21]

Whether the leaflet was authentic or not, it accurately anticipated the way in which many disruptions would occur during the week of the Convention. In the experience of that week, repeated several times over, one person or a group would come forward initially and make an open gesture in defiance of the law. Policemen would then step in to restrain them, and at that point the police would be rushed and engulfed by other demonstrators, the area would become impassable, and gas might have to be used to disperse the crowd. In hindsight it does not take much imagination to see that if a massive demonstration had run up against the gates of the Amphitheatre, and an attempt been made to climb the gate or breach the lines of the police, the result would have been a melee of uncontrollable dimensions. Hundreds of people caught in the strands of the crowd could have been injured, and the aim of disruption would essentially have been accomplished. For it might have been impossible then either to get in or out of the Convention hall, and if the demonstration had occurred early enough in the day, it might have been impossible to continue the work of the Convention. But even if it had failed to stall the Convention, the eruption of violence on this scale outside the hall could not have helped but make a deep impression on the delegates, and no matter what the precise outcome of the voting, it might have generated substantial powers of intimidation.

It cannot be said, of course, that the flyer quoted earlier had any authoritative standing as directions for the protest groups, and it is entirely possible that Rennie Davis did not say exactly the things that were attributed to him in the press (though there is no record in the Walker Report of any denials on his part). But whether these reports were accurate or not, no responsible leader in the city could

[21] Ibid., p. 91.

have afforded to dismiss them. The apprehension of violence or disruption at the site of the Convention was not an unreasonable fear, and if city officials seemed to be more excited than the situation might have warranted, it could also have been said on their behalf that they paid the demonstrators the compliment of taking their words seriously.

As for Davis and his group, what they wanted, very clearly, was to influence the decisions that were being made within the Amphitheatre. But what was there in their ability to bring large numbers of people into the streets that could establish any claim to influence the Convention? Why did they deserve to make an impact on the Convention that was independent, say, of the influence commanded by those delegates who shared their views, and who were in a position to make their arguments before the Convention? Conceivably, Rennie Davis and his group might have contended that the views they represented were the views of a popular majority, either in the country or the Democratic party, but that the majority was not being represented accurately in the Convention. We know now, though, that an argument of that kind would have been flatly untrue. We can probably assume that, as diverse as the groups were that formed the National Mobilization, they held certain basic tenets in common: namely, that the war in Vietnam was morally wrong and that the United States should remove its forces as soon as possible, regardless of what effect that might have on the outcome of the contest and the kind of regime that controlled the territory of Vietnam. By that measure, the antiwar groups never represented a majority, either in the Democratic party or in the electorate as a whole.[22] In fact, from the evidence we have, the tactic of moving into the streets with demonstrations provided a point of separation for those people in the country who could loosely be called "doves" on the war.[23] According to the Survey Research Center, a majority of the people that it was able to classify as "doves" on Vietnam had "negative" reactions to the antiwar demonstrators.[24] And if one combined categories, those people who were in favor of the

[22] The best evidence we have on this point was collected by the Survey Research Center at Michigan. See Converse et al., note 3 above, p. 1088.

[23] For the purposes of its survey, the Michigan research group marked off as "doves" on the war people who believed (a) that we had made a mistake in getting involved in the Vietnam War; and (b) that the preferable course of action at the moment would be to "pull out" of the country entirely. See ibid., p. 1087.

[24] Ibid., p. 1087.

demonstrators and reserved about the war in Vietnam accounted for only three per cent of the electorate.[25]

Whatever the claims, then, of Davis and his group, they could not have been "majoritarian" claims. Nor, one suspects, would Davis and his allies have been inclined to call off their demonstrations once it had been shown that they did not represent a majority, either in the country or the party. On what grounds, therefore, would they have claimed to guide the decisions of the Convention by demonstrating in a public way the depth of their feelings? Might the claim have been based simply on the intensity of those feelings? In any process of collective decision, there may be a large reservoir of people who are indifferent about the outcome, and at certain moments, the argument may go, those people ought to be willing to defer to a minority that may be outnumbered, but which feels the issue with far greater anguish. An argument of that nature does touch a familiar theme in democratic thought: we do tend to think that those people who are likely to be affected in the most direct way by the operation of any policy have a compelling claim to make their views known, and that their views, when known, ought to carry more than ordinary weight. We tend to think that people who have been directly injured by any policy are in a position to tell us something important about the way in which the principles behind our policies happen to be working in practice. But to say all this is not to say that decisions must be left in all cases to the judgment of those people who have the most direct personal or material stake in the outcome. If that formula were applied with any strictness, one would have to give the most decisive voice to the automobile companies and the auto unions in making regulations on pollution and safety in automobiles. When it comes to the matter of the schools and busing, one would be compelled, by the same reasoning, to give the greatest deference to the violent and resisting parents, who manifest their intensity of feeling by turning over buses. It is doubtful that Davis and the antiwar groups could even have qualified as the groups who were most directly affected by the Vietnam war. That they might have been moved by the most passionate intensity is something that no prudent statesmen should have failed to take into account. But to have assigned them, for that reason, a predominant voice in the making of decisions is a judgment that had no warrant.

And yet if the claims of Davis and his group could not have

[25] Ibid., p. 1088.

rested on majoritarian grounds, if they could not derive, in addition, from some principle of deference to those who feel most "intensely," on what ground could their claim to influence have rested? Again, it is worth being clear on the point that, in the demand for an "effective" demonstration, the authorities were not dealing with a plea to present an argument on the substantive issues involved in the Vietnam war. To engage in reasoned discourse is something that does not have to be justified, for no claim is made then to govern others except through the influence that can rightly be commanded on the strength of one's own reasoned arguments. There is a conspicuous difference between that kind of exercise and the act of merely massing people in the streets, and no one, least of all one who is fit to live in a constitutional order, can afford to be insensitive to that difference. The melancholy judgment would arise that, for Davis and his group, the sense of justification did not extend very far beyond their sense of political tactics: they were engaged in the warfare of politics, and as they understood it, politics moved most importantly through the application of power. Once they had committed themselves in the political contest, what else were they to do but throw every resource they had into the struggle? And what resource did they have other than the capacity to bring in against the authorities the power of "the people in the streets"?

But to recognize the nature of the act in these terms comes close to recognizing what we seek to gloss over today or conceal from ourselves with fictions—namely, that the justification even for ordinary demonstrations is far more problematic than we have usually supposed. A "demonstration" in the street provides neither an assembly for the discussion of issues nor a medium for the conveyance of a substantive argument. To the extent that it would claim to influence decisions that will touch everyone in the society with the force of law, it would claim to govern others ultimately on grounds that could not be admissible in point of basic principle.

Robert Kennedy once bade the young to look at things as they are and ask, "Why?"—and to consider things as they might be and ask, "Why not?" Demonstrations seem to have become now a part of the natural order of things. They have become so much a part of "things as they are" that it has become nearly impossible for some people even to understand the nature of the question if they are asked to explain what the justification for demonstrations might be. We almost require here the shock of a perspective drawn from an earlier time, before our attitudes toward public demonstrations had been lifted from the realm of convention and confounded with nature. Hobbes, for one, grasped the character of the problem long ago, and in his characteristic way managed to state the point with an unsettling directness. It was one thing, for Hobbes, when people assembled in large numbers in "the usual meeting of men at church, or at a public show"; but when people came into the public streets in numbers that were "extraordinarily great," one had to ask them to give an account or justification as to why they were there:

> It may be lawful for a thousand men to join to a petition to be delivered to a judge, or magistrate; yet if a thousand men come to present it, it is a tumultous assembly; because there needs but one or two for that purpose . . . When an unusual number of men, assemble against a man whom they accuse; the assembly is an unlawful tumult; because they may deliver their accusation to the magistrate by a few, or by one man . . . [A]n assembly, whereof men can give no just account, [is] a sedition, and such as they could not answer for . . .[26]

Hobbes wrote, of course, with the rudimentary logic of one who had not had the benefit of *The New York Times*. Making the proper allowances for him, his proposition, again, was this: It did not require a thousand people in order to present a petition or an argument, and if a petition were not being presented, if an argument were not being heard, what could be the legitimate purpose of bringing a thousand people into the street?

It is the measure of our current orthodoxies that it is almost embarrassing to acknowledge that there is some plausibility in this question. And yet, oddly enough, we have already conceded the force of Hobbes's argument in a number of places, though we have not brought the concession to the point of conscious recognition. Also, we have been reluctant, at the same time, to consider just how far the argument actually extends. In 1965, in the case of *Cox v. Louisiana*,[27] the Supreme Court sustained a state law that prohibited demonstrations and parades in front of courtrooms.[28] The picketing that was at issue in the case was carried out in support of the defendants in a trial involving leaders of the Communist

[26] Thomas Hobbes, *Leviathan* (Oxford: Basil Blackwell, 1960), Part 2, ch. 22, pp. 155-56.

[27] 379 U.S. 559.

[28] More precisely, the statute punished those who "with the intent of interfering with, obstructing, or impeding the administration of justice, or with the intent of influencing any judge, juror, witness, or court officer, in the discharge of his duty pickets or parades in or near a building housing a court of the State of Louisiana." Ibid., at 560.

Party. On technical grounds, and over the dissent of Justice Black, the Court overturned the conviction of the demonstrators.[29] But on the principle of barring demonstrations from the vicinity of court-rooms, the Court was firm in its position. As Justice Goldberg wrote for the majority, "A State may . . . properly protect the judicial process from being misjudged in the minds of the public." Under conditions of continuous picketing, judges and jurors could well be influenced in their judgments. But even if they were not, there was an important interest on the part of the state in dispelling the impression that might arise in these circumstances "that the judge's action was in part a product of intimidation and did not flow only from the fair and orderly working of the judicial process."[30]

Goldberg was quick to add that, in the absence of a specific statute that would cover other offices, "entirely different consid-erations would apply if, for example, the demonstrators were pick-eting to protest the actions of a mayor or other official of a city completely unrelated to any judicial proceedings, who just hap-pened to have an office located in the courthouse building."[31] But one would have to presume that, with the presence of a statute of that kind, the same principle would have to establish a comparable concern on the part of the Court to preserve the integrity of the executive and legislative departments, as well as that of the judi-ciary. If it is important to dispel the notion that the decisions of judges may be affected by the numbers of people who are brought into the street, it is no less urgent to remove that suspicion from the acts of other officers of the government.[32] For as Madison asked, "what are many of the most important acts of legislation, but so many *judicial determinations?*"[33] The fact that other officials are elected rather than appointed—that they are, in that sense, more "political" in our estimate than judges—does not give them a license to be less judicious or disciplined, or more open in their judgments to outside pressures. In the view of the Founders, it was the re-

[29] See ibid. at 570-73, especially 571, and cf. Justice Black's criticism of the ma-jority decision on this point, at 583.

[30] Ibid., at 565.　　　　　　　　　　　　[31] Ibid., at 567.

[32] In October 1979 a series of violent clashes erupted between black and white students in the public schools of South Boston. With tensions running high, a group of whites planned to hold a demonstration in front of City Hall; but fearing serious violence, Mayor White banned demonstrations from that vicinity. When demon-strators began to march from City Hall to the mayor's home, a cordon of police sealed off the street that led to the residence. *Boston Globe*, October 18, 1979, pp. 1, 27.

[33] *The Federalist* #10 (New York: Modern Library, n.d.), p. 56; emphasis added.

sponsibility of other statesmen to act more like judges. And what applies to men at the top of the state must apply to anyone, even one in a lesser office, who is discharging the public business. That responsibility may apply to local school boards as well as to the people who administer the Pentagon, and it may apply equally well to the delegates of a major party, who may be choosing the next President of the United States. It would be no less consequential for the nature of our public life if the impression became widespread that the nomination of a President could hinge at any point on the force of demonstrations in the public streets.

Given the opportunities that were available to Rennie Davis and his group to convey their opinions; given the alternative sites that were made available by the city; and given, too, the fact that people who shared the views of the National Mobilization had the chance to make their case within the Convention, it was not unreasonable for the city to have acted out of a concern for security and preserved that one area, adjacent to the Convention hall itself, as a space that would be free of disruptions.

As for Rennie Davis, he might have credited himself, in his own eyes, with some ground of moral advantage as a result of his personal rejection of violence. But at the same time, if one takes him at his word, he was almost ingenuously unaware of the true potential for violence that was inherent in the project, and of the coercion that was implicit in its meaning all along. One suspects, in the end, that he would have found the justification for his moves in the play of politics itself: pressure tactics and coercion seemed to be parts of the game as it was played, and it was fair to use them, apparently, against a party and a government that seemed willing enough themselves to accept coercion on a massive scale in Vietnam. And yet even if that argument were less problematic than it actually was, it was at best an excuse rather than a justification; it still provided no moral foundation for the course Davis was taking. The demands he pressed with such insistence may be seen as part of a search for advantage that went forward at the expense of his true interests—the interests that he shared with others in preserving the premises that underlie a regime of legal restraint.

2. The City is Not for Sleeping

At first sight, the matter of the sleeping accommodations did not seem to raise issues of principle in the same way that the question of the parade permits did. No one seriously claimed that there was a First Amendment right to a place to sleep, or that the city had an obligation to provide sleeping accommodations free of charge for all visitors to the city who were not able to arrange lodgings of their own. The mayor and his aides were not criticized for a want of principle here, but of prudence. The legal rights and wrongs of the matter were one thing; but responsible men, faced with a mass influx that they could not entirely restrain, and which they knew was quite beyond the capacity of the hotels, might have tried to work out some practical solution. The alternatives had been laid out by Rennie Davis in a threatening, but nonetheless realistic way. He explained to the corporation counsel of the city that he had found housing for about 30,000 people, but that 70,000 more were expected, and if there were no place for them to sleep, they would have to sleep in the parks:

> If people come to Chicago with no place to go, and begin to sleep in parks, or wherever they can find a place to sleep, and then will be forced out of the park, that entirely breaks down our ability to provide organization, which leads to the kind of disruption that you and I both want to prevent, and the issue of peaceful assembly becomes shattered against a practical reality that people have no place to go and will be confronted by police, leading to disruption and possible violence all through the week of the convention.[34]

The mayor was under no obligation to suspend the curfew and allow the demonstrators to sleep in Lincoln Park, but the question that has been raised is whether a prudent man might not have found in this instance that his larger interests would have been served by a measure of generosity. That is a rather limited indictment, though no less condemning for all of that. Yet the record would show that this indictment, too, was not borne out by the evidence; and if the case were considered more closely, this prosaic matter of the sleeping accommodations would not have been found wholly wanting in real questions of principle.

It seemed to escape the notice of most observers (even many, it appears, who studied the record) that the city did in fact propose some alternative sites for sleeping. The first discussions on this topic took place in January 1968 when the Youth International Party (or "Yippies") applied for a permit for the use of park facilities in order to put on their "Festival of Life." In March, David Stahl met

[34] Walker Report, note 5 above, p. 67.

with the representatives of the Yippies in Chicago (a group of hippies that was later called the "Free City" group), who informed him of their plans and made a request for the use of Grant Park. At the end of May, Stahl met with the group again and reported that Grant Park would not be possible after all as a site for the Festival. He intimated, however, that Lincoln Park might be made available. It was after this meeting that Al Baugher came forward with a list of suggestions, and it was those proposals that eventually put the matter in much clearer focus.

Baugher ventured the opinion that the chance of securing a permit for Lincoln Park would be "good," but he suggested also that a circus tent be used. As further possibilities, he suggested Soldier Field and Navy Pier, and for the sake of gauging their suitability he took the group on a tour of these facilities. Finally, some mention was made of the Edgewater Beach Hotel, a fashionable old hotel farther north on the Outer Drive, which happened to be closed just then in a state of receivership.[35] All of the sites were centrally placed in the city, with the exception of the Edgewater Beach Hotel (from which the transportation was excellent, though, by automobile). As it turned out, all of the sites were easily adaptable for housing. Navy Pier had been for many years the campus of the University of Illinois in Chicago. It extended a distance of about five city blocks into the lake, and it was within walking distance of Grant Park and the heart of the downtown area. It was also widely used as a convention center, with two ample floors of rooms and warehouse space. To what extent Baugher was really in a position to "offer" these facilities is not entirely clear from the record. The offers were never tested, however, because they were unequivocally rejected. According to the Walker Report, "The Festival planners . . . did not feel that these sites would be in any way appropriate for their Festival."[36]

But what was there about the Festival that made these sites so unsuitable? As the Walker Commission pointed out, the Festival was conceived as a "festive counter-convention." There would be entertainment, discussions, workshops on the problems facing dissident youth; but more than that, the Festival would be the celebration of a "counter culture." It was meant to portray what was called an alternative "life style"—the emancipation of youth from established conventions, their spontaneity, freshness, and creativity. The Festival had to be robust, open, as expansive as nature itself;

[35] Ibid., p. 69.   [36] Ibid.

it could not be constrained within walls and tents. It would be, as Abbie Hoffman said, "revolution for the hell of it," "theatre in the streets." As the Walker Report noted, "the stage would be the streets and the message would be a demonstration of disrespect, irreverence, and ridicule."[37] Abbie Hoffman described it:

> People will be attempting to use guerrilla theater techniques, people will be attempting to use satire, people will be attempting to talk to other people and people will be passing out newspapers, and some will be stoned and some will be fucking on the grass, and people will do whatever they want to do.
> . . .[38]

All of this was not lost on officials of the city. The Yippies were not the only ones, of course, who wished to make use of the parks for sleeping, and they could not be taken to stand for everyone that Rennie Davis had been representing in his own discussions with officials in the city. But the Yippies could not be excluded from the larger group, and it was they who intended to exploit their presence in the park and make it into something vastly more than a casual event. If any officials had lingering doubts on that score, they were free to draw their own inferences from the requests that were made later, after Baugher's offer of alternative sites had been rejected. The Free City group went on to seek a park permit, and they requested, among other things, that the curfew laws be suspended, along with the regulations that prohibited sleeping on the beaches. At the same time, they asked that arrests be suspended for violations of the laws on narcotics.[39] The curfew in the parks had been applied fairly flexibly in the past, but this event was shaping up now as something of rather new dimensions. As the Walker Report put it, with some restraint, "the Yippie program for Lincoln Park was considered a far cry from previous, more conventional requests for park usage."[40]

The Festival could not be muffled behind walls, because it had to be flaunted. Its very purpose was to assault the conventional "middle class" morality of the city and the nation, and for that reason it had to be carried on before the eyes of the city. As the city responded with its own proposals, the argument that seemed to be implicit in its offers could have been stated in this manner. There was something in the *combination* of *public visibility* and

[37] Ibid., pp. 41-42.　　　　[38] Ibid., p. 42.
[39] Ibid., p. 69.　　　　　　[40] Ibid., p. 60.

official support that implicated the city or lent a certain quality of legitimacy to the event which would not have been present if the event were managed in some other way: if, for example, the event were public and visible, but carried no official sanction; or if the event carried some sanction, but were not such a public spectacle. The public spectacle might have been avoided if the event went on behind the doors of the Edgewater Beach Hotel, or within the halls of Navy Pier. Under these conditions it would have been far easier for the city to disclaim any responsibility for the things that were likely to take place.

It was too much to expect, of course, that the press and television would not be present, and that the antics of the Yippies would not be highly publicized. But at least this sheltering of the event behind walls would have averted a situation in which people passing by might have come upon the Yippies in the throes of their occupations, unaware that the park was virtually in the custody that week of Abbie Hoffman and his group.[41] That there would still be some unsuspecting people of this kind remaining in the city (and that a few of them might even be on their way, perhaps, to see "Mary Poppins") was something one could always count on. That they stood a good chance of experiencing some psychological shock when they encountered Hoffman and the Yippies was something one could also expect. Apart from the mercy involved in avoiding these encounters, there was the likelihood, also, of avoiding that difficult situation in which citizens brought accounts to the police of what was going on in the park and then demanded to know what the city was going to do about it.

The alternatives proffered by the Administration had the advantage of avoiding these problems, and in doing that, they would have allowed a prudential compromise with the Yippies without forcing the city to support the whole enterprise in principle. The city was, in effect, addressing a plea to the Yippies and their allied groups, which might have been put in this way:

> We have another moral perspective, different from yours, perhaps radically different. We can't expect you to share it, but we, at least, would like to preserve it for ourselves, for this community, in this place. As a practical matter, it would probably be foolish to hold rigidly to the law in a situation that

[41] At the beginning of August the Free City group asked that Lincoln Park Zoo be closed during the week of the Convention and that the Park District keep all persons who were not hippies out of the park for that period! See ibid., p. 71.

overwhelms private and public facilities. And so we'll try to reach some practical accommodation with you and give you, as we can, what you need in this case. All we ask is that you respect our own commitments—that you accept a solution that doesn't assault our own understanding of morality, or which doesn't force us, on the other hand, to sanction yours. Grant us, if you would, the privilege of our own detachment: all we wish to do now is to hold up a standard of sorts as to what this community believes in as a community, and which we hope others will come to share—more readily, perhaps, because we have upheld these commitments in principle.

The argument, in this form, is not so foreign to us. We have encountered it in other places and other times where the means were not available to support the full commitment of the law. At those moments political men have been faced with the question of whether the ends should be given up in principle because they appear for awhile to be unattainable. The problem is a common one in politics, and there have been many cases in which leaders, out of a sense of prudence, have refrained from enforcing the law with the same strictness in all places, even while they have continued to uphold the law in principle. This is a phase of political experience that would be recognized at once by any practicing politician. For any working politician knows that principles have consequences. The mayor of a large city knows, for example, that if he gives one group the privilege of tying up a main intersection at the peak of the rush hour, other groups will come forward to claim the same privilege. (They may come forward for no better reason than to claim the same concession that had been gained by one of their rivals.) Beyond that, he knows that if he can avoid making concessions in principle on any matter, he can preserve a larger field of maneuver for himself. And he knows that if he can preserve a principle while making concessions on lesser matters, he will stand a better chance of acting on the principle more fully at a later date, when the means are more readily at hand.

All of this, as I say, would be readily understood by any seasoned politician. Therefore it is not so bizarre to find reflections of the same approach in the response of Mayor Daley and his aides to the problem of the sleeping sites. The position of the city was a guarded and prudent one, and it could be rejected in this instance only on a ground of principle. It could be rejected only if one dismissed the notion that the authorities of the city may be justified in acting in any case for the end simply of preserving a commitment in principle to a set of moral understandings. One would have to deny, in other words, that the authorities may act properly at times as the custodian of the interests of the city—not "the city" as a collection of streets and buildings, but as a civic body vested with a moral character.

3. THE POLICE AND THE VIOLENCE

This chain of judgment brings us finally to the question of the police and their behavior during the week of the Convention. No part of the events of that week generated more outrage and condemnation, and none, certainly, seemed to define more completely the faults that were attributed to the authorities in Chicago. At the same time, however, this part of the case is considerably more difficult to deal with because we are faced with a maze of interactions, in which the documentation is almost certain to be poor.

But if it is hard to lend structure to the events, it is worth the effort again to mark off the boundaries of the problem and to fix more precisely the area of our concern. Everyone would probably agree, first, that policemen and public officials ought to be as responsible to the law as other citizens, and that a policeman who commits an unjustified assault is every bit as much a criminal as any private offender. Beyond that, it may be argued that the police or public officials have an even greater responsibility than ordinary citizens to observe the law. There is something far graver, we have thought, about corruption in official places, because it reflects a conviction on the part of the authorities that the law is not really law in the strictest sense—that it does not represent a principle which must hold true universally, and which must therefore be universally respected. If a policeman or other official shows his contempt for the law, if he breaks it himself or stands back knowingly and does nothing while others all around him are breaking it, then the law will appear to be little more than a device of the rulers for controlling the ruled, and it may be hard to expect private citizens to preserve their own sense of obligation to the law.

In this older view, then, it is particularly harmful if officers of the law take a position of detachment in the face of criminal acts. It is one thing for private citizens to turn away at the sight of a crime, but the results may be even more destructive if the police make it clear, in a dramatic public display, that the laws will go unenforced.

That is, as I say, an old understanding, but it is worth recalling in its fuller expression here because it may bear on some of the harder cases that arose in the confrontation between the police and the demonstrators. It would probably not be as important in dealing with an event as clear as what occurred on Wednesday night of the Convention, when the police broke discipline on Michigan Avenue and charged a peaceful crowd. Up to that time the initiatives in these assaults had come from the demonstrators.[42] In the incident of Wednesday night, however, the police acted largely as a unit, in full view of their commanders; and in that respect it was quite different from the situation that was seen a number of times during the week, in which individual policemen would go berserk under pressure and begin swinging out wildly on their own. With the assault of Wednesday night, the record tells of malice and criminality pure and simple. The police who were guilty of assault should not only have lost their badges; they should also have gone to jail, and their commanding officers should have been held responsible in turn for this plunge into violence.

But most of the controversy about the events in Chicago has not surrounded incidents of that kind. It has centered, rather, on more ambiguous cases, in which the police responded to provocations on the part of demonstrators, or in which the demonstrators resisted the efforts of the police to enforce the law. There were two tiers of problems here, one which involved verbal or psychological assaults, and another, which moved to the point of actual violence.

In the first group of incidents there were the deliberate attempts to rattle the police. They ranged from sneering solicitations by young women in the crowd to taunts like "Who's fuckin' your wife this afternoon, pig?" . . . "We're fucking your wives and daughters while you guys are protecting your city" . . . "How would you like to fuck a man?"[43] Of a comparable quality were the taunts directed at members of the National Guard when they were called in on Tuesday. One assistant squad leader recalled a man walking along

---

[42] There was one exception, on Clark Street, Sunday night, when a group of 12 to 20 policemen broke from the police lines and used their batons on people who were retreating from Lincoln Park. There had apparently been no resistance or provocation on the part of the crowd, though it is true also that on other parts of Clark Street that night the police had been assaulted with rocks and bottles. And so a climate of tension might have built up among the police, who were being marshaled now, after all, to cope with a tense situation. In that respect, as well as in the number of police involved and their distance from their supervising officers, there was an important difference between the incident on Sunday night and the assault that occurred in full force on Wednesday. See ibid., p. 157.

[43] Ibid., pp. 143, 209, 276.

the line of Guardsmen who would "spit at us, flick cigarette ashes and lighted cigarettes at us. He would pick out the Jewish boys from their nameplates and make anti-Semitic remarks to them. He called me a 'kike.' I turned to a Polish boy standing next to me and asked him who the guy reminded him of. He answered, 'A Nazi storm trooper.' "[44] There is no need to recount all the separate jeers and details of these encounters; it is enough to recall just how vicious they could be, and how much they were capable of inflaming even the most hardened men.

In the second group of assaults, there were incidents like the one in Lincoln Park on Sunday night when a group of twelve police officers were backed up against the wall of a field house. Soon the crowd began to close in, throwing cigarette butts at first, but later bricks and bottles. Or, on a more dramatic scale, there was the situation Tuesday night in Grant Park (across from the Conrad Hilton) when the first clear assault was made on the police by the demonstrators. The mood of the crowd had grown uglier as the challengers in the Democratic Convention lost their fights over credentials. As the police set up a line on the east side of the street, objects of terrible variety, blends of artifice and malevolence, were thrown in large numbers: Pepsi cans filled with urine, beer cans filled with sand, ping pong balls with nails, plastic bags with urine and excrement. In these devices one may find the evidence of a premeditation that separates these acts from the desperate reactions of those individual policemen who broke down under pressure and began striking out in all directions. Even if there was no difference at all in the magnitude of the violence, there would be a significant difference in moral responsibility or blameworthiness, which would have to turn on the matter of intention and forethought. As Hobbes remarked on the point,

> A crime arising from a sudden passion, is not so great, as when the same ariseth from long meditation: for in the former case there is a place for extenuation, in the common infirmity of human nature; but he that doth it with premeditation, has used circumspection, and cast his eye on the law, on the punishment, and on the consequence thereof to human society; all which, in committing the crime, he hath contemned and postponed to his own appetite.[45]

[44] Ibid., p. 213.

[45] Hobbes, note 26 above, Part 2, ch. 27, p. 199. For some vivid accounts of the kinds of situations in which the police—or anyone else, for that matter—were likely to crack under pressure, see the Walker Report, note 5 above, pp. 150-51, 156.

In approaching these cases involving assaults on the police the most pertinent question to ask is whether the assaults and provocations that took place would have been punishable if they had been directed at private citizens. In the case of assaults with rocks and bottles and other contraptions, the answer is obvious. In the case of verbal assaults or provocations, the answer would again have to be yes, these assaults would have been punishable, *as long as one holds (as one must) to the principle that was settled earlier in the Chaplinsky case.* But if all this is true, then the question is, why would these acts not have been punishable when directed at the police? Is an assault of this kind somehow less serious when it is aimed at *them*? Do the police have a greater obligation to practice restraint or remain detached merely because the assaults are directed at themselves rather than ordinary citizens? It would have to follow, I think, from what I have said before, that the answer would be no. That is not to say, of course, that the police have a virtual license in any case to use unmodulated force. It means simply that if the police hold back in the presence of provocations, if they refrain from making an arrest and using the reasonable measure of force that may be needed to secure that arrest, the restraint they show would not be enjoined upon them by principle, but by prudence.

In most cases where the police hold back, they do that in order to prevent a bad situation from becoming worse. And so the National Guard, with considerable wisdom, refused to respond to the provocations of the people who were trying, often in the basest way, to bait them. To their credit, the police succeeded in holding back Tuesday night, when they were assaulted in front of the Hilton with the cans filled with urine and the bags filled with excrement. How long they could have kept it up is an open question, but fortunately they were relieved fairly quickly by the National Guard. It was not without some justification, then, that an observer from the police department in Los Angeles remarked at the time that "the restraint of the police both as individual members and as an organization, was beyond reason."[46]

But even though the police were the principal focus of assaults and provocations, it deserves some notice that private citizens were not sheltered from the violence. On Sunday night, for example, when the crowds of protesters were cleared out of Lincoln Park, a large group of them headed south along La Salle Street and

[46] Walker Report, p. 257.

eventually found their way to Michigan Avenue. From there they moved south along Michigan Avenue, heading for the downtown area. As the Walker Report described it, "They marched south down the center of the Avenue, occupying the entire width of the street, which is eighty feet from curb to curb. Vehicular traffic in both directions was unable to pass." As the marchers moved along, some were seen tipping over trash cans and inflicting damage on automobiles. One young man and his girlfriend were driving north on Michigan Avenue when they encountered the wall of marchers and realized that it was impossible to move forward. They decided then to stop in the massive current of people until it had moved past them. But,

> one of the marchers, and then about five others, climbed over the Volkswagen—a foot on the front hood, another on the roof, then the rear deck, the rear bumper and off. Other demonstrators were shouting: "Don't hurt the cars." Nevertheless, another demonstrator kicked in the windshield of the vehicle and others started kicking the doors and rocking the car.[47]

At other times, and in other incidents, demonstrators threw cherry bombs at a bus, including one bomb that went in the rear window. Some demonstrators (in a more literal sense) exposed their penises to passersby on the street and to people who were in cars stalled by the crowd.[48] In one instance, when a small group of demonstrators cast insults at people passing by and one of them had the rashness to answer back, five of the demonstrators charged onto the sidewalk, and as one witness reported, "knocked the pedestrian down, formed a circle around his fallen body, locked their arms together and commenced kicking him in a vicious manner. When they had finished . . . they unlocked their arms and immediately melted back into the crowd."[49]

The police, for their own part, were in a better position to protect themselves, and, as the Walker Commission reported, they showed considerable restraint, especially on Tuesday night near the Hilton when they were subjected to a severe wave of assaults. But if the police had managed to hold themselves back on Tuesday night, there *had* been a response by some members of the force the previous Sunday in Lincoln Park. A group of eight to twelve officers were backed against the wall of a field house, and under the large lights of the park they made an excellent target for a group of

[47] Ibid., pp. 150-151.   [48] Ibid., pp. 190, 276.   [49] Ibid., p. 244.

demonstrators who were gathered about them in a semicircle. The demonstrators kept up a running chant of things like "Mother fuckers!" "Shitheads!" "Pigs!" and other terms of art. As the Walker Report noted, "The police had not initiated the barrage of abuse, and they were not responding to it in any way." But with the attraction of the lights and the excitement, the crowd grew larger, and the verbal attacks on the police became more menacing. At first, the crowd kept a distance of about twenty feet, but as it grew in size, it seemed to grow also in confidence, and it began then to move further in. "Soon," as the Walker Commission said, "the police were clearly trapped. Someone on the roof threw a lighted cigarette at one of them. It landed on his bare right arm, but he didn't flinch. Others threw rocks."[50]

All of this—the throwing of rocks, the jeering, the imminent threat of the crowd pressing forward—went on for about half an hour, but the police still remained silent. Then, two squads of reinforcements arrived, and they were able to take up positions behind the original line of police. But the crowd, which had now grown to a size of about 150, kept moving slowly inward. Finally, and with great suddenness, the police charged. There had been a word of warning, something to the effect of "All right, get out of the way!" but of course, as the Walker Commission observed, "the crowd had no chance to get out of the way." The police struck out in rage, swinging at everyone within reach. The crowd staggered back, but it was charged again, and yet again. One VISTA volunteer reported that he had been hit in the stomach and back by the police. A volunteer medic on the scene described the action:

> When someone would fall, three or four cops would start beating him. One kid was beaten so badly he couldn't get up. He was bleeding profusely from the head. The kids scattered to the street as the police moved about 200 yards and then regrouped around the building. A couple of dozen Yippies were clubbed. I treated five myself.[51]

It was not without reason that the reactions of the police were regarded as "excessive," even granting the provocations that led to the violence. And yet the question that must be asked is, What was there that marked the essential wrongness or injustice in the reactions of the police? The answer, I would suggest, is that in the furious assault on the crowd, in the terrifying melee that followed,

[50] Ibid., p. 146.   [51] Quoted in ibid., p. 147.

the violence became nearly random. Under the conditions of a crowd fallen into disorder and panic, it was unlikely that the policeman in all cases could lay his hands on the precise person he aimed to catch—the person who had flung that rock, or who had spat at him with vicious insults. With the police striking out in mad vengeance, and with all restraints broken, it became impossible to distinguish clearly between the offenders and the bystanders, which meant that punishment was visited alike on the innocent and the guilty. But as I recalled earlier, that is the problem which informed the objections of Lincoln to the practice of lynching:

> [I]n the confusion usually attending such transactions, [men] will be as likely to hang or burn someone, who is neither a gambler nor a murderer [as] one who is . . . [T]he innocent, those who have ever set their faces against violations of law in every shape, alike with the guilty, fall victims to the ravages of mob law . . .[52]

The proper response to this problem was to insist on the importance of formal procedure or due process of law—not because it could be guaranteed, with a formal trial, that mistakes would never be made, but because a formal process, with its greater rigor and deliberation, is more likely than any random procedure to make reasoned distinctions between the innocent and the guilty. To state the argument in that way is to recognize that our objections to "informal justice" rest most importantly on the case for "orderly process"—that is, the "order" that is part of the familiar phrase, "law and order."

The question we are forced to ask is whether civilians are entirely without any "civic obligations" of their own in these matters. That is to say, for the sake of preserving a climate in which orderly process is dominant and the conditions are not established for indiscriminate violence, do civilians have no responsibilities of their own to observe the restraints of civility and lawfulness? Whatever must be said in this case against the police, it is hard to sustain the fiction that all of the people injured in the melee were hapless and unsuspecting victims who were caught up without warning in a surge of violence. Certainly, anyone who had been in the front line of those demonstrators who were facing down the police could not claim to have been a mere bystander. And anyone who remained

---

[52] *The Collected Works of Abraham Lincoln*, ed. Roy Prentice Basler (New Brunswick: Rutgers University Press, 1953), Vol. I, pp. 110-11.

in that position near the front of the crowd for half an hour after the rocks and bottles had been flying could not reasonably claim the defense of naiveté. He surely had to realize that if he remained in that spot, he remained at his own risk, and that the police, if they reached the limits of their endurance, could not have been expected to behave with the detachment and precision of judges in a courtroom. What can be said in this respect for the knowing bystander who decided to stay and lend his body to the crowd, must be said, too, with even greater force for those who actually armed themselves with rocks and bottles and took part in the assault. After helping to bring the situation past the threshold of violence, they were hardly in a position to complain of the unrestrained use of violence. Nor could they reasonably have claimed at that point the protections that orderly process confers.

It has been said quite rightly in the past that the law must be reasonable in its aims: it must not expect to eradicate all vice, or to demand from ordinary citizens the kind of virtue that can be expected only from saints. At the same time, it has been part of that understanding, also, that citizens themselves have an obligation to be reasonable, even in their relations with officers of the law. We could hardly expect those who enforce the law to disdain, in some saintly way, a concern for their own protection, or to be so firm in their own inner strength that they find no ground of resentment in the violation of their dignity. It was thought traditionally that a people who lacked a sense of lawful restraint could only be governed by despotism, and that in a true republic the obligation to civility and restraint had to be borne no less by citizens than by public officials. That understanding might not have been as important for aristocracies, where rulers were drawn from a rather small stratum of society and were subject to special conventions of their own. But where the rulers were drawn from the people themselves, the prospects for lawful government depended on the cultivation of citizens who possessed their own sense of self-control, people who carried within themselves, as Plato said, their own constitutional rulers.

V

URBAN DISORDERS II:
THE URBAN RIOTS

1. RIOTS AND REBELLIONS

The urban riots that spread across five summers in the mid-60's probably had a greater effect on our politics than the Vietnam War. They helped to create a new concern for the issue of "law and order" that candidates for the presidency were powerless to ignore.[1] They apparently diminished the tolerance for those opponents of the Vietnam War who were willing to push their protests into the streets at the cost of further violence.[2] And they fed the anxieties of people who feared that the dynamism in favor of the demands of blacks was moving far too quickly and in violent directions.[3]

The worst of the violence was concentrated in the period 1967-1968. In the first nine months of 1967 there were more than 160 disorders in 128 cities. After the assassination of Martin Luther King in April 1968 there was another series of riots in over 100 cities. It appears now that the cities which suffered more violent riots attracted a heavier outpouring of money from the federal government under the Model Cities program (and perhaps also a

[1] See, on this point, Theodore White, *The Making of the President 1968* (New York: Atheneum, 1969), pp. 189-90 and passim.

[2] See Philip Converse et al., "Continuity and Change in American Politics: Parties and Issues in the 1968 Election," *American Political Science Review*, Vol. 63, no. 4 (December 1969), pp. 1083-1105, especially 1087-88.

[3] Richard Scammon and Ben Wattenberg have argued, on the basis of surveys that were conducted in New Hampshire in 1968, that Lyndon Johnson was hampered very severely by a strong identification with the movement for black rights and with the agitation it was creating in the country. In one survey carried out by Louis Harris, the reaction to Johnson revealed a clear division along racial lines. Eighty-five percent of the blacks in the survey approved of Johnson and his performance, while the president received the approval of only 39 percent of the whites. By way of contrast, Eugene McCarthy was seen as a candidate who was less inclined to spur on activism over civil rights than Robert Kennedy, Hubert Humphrey, or even Nelson Rockefeller. This current was detectable elsewhere as well, and suggested that the issues of race and domestic violence had become far more important in the political primaries than the war in Vietnam. See Scammon and Wattenberg, *The Real Majority* (New York: Coward-McCann, 1970), p. 98.

slight increase of spending under the Poverty program).[4] But if the riots elicited more social spending, and if they provided a partial fillip to the Fair Housing Act of 1968, they also brought forth the Omnibus Crime Control and Safe Streets Act of 1968, and produced rather outsized budgets for the Law Enforcement Assistance Administration. There is no doubt that the riots induced an increase in federal spending and that they encouraged the federal government to work more closely with local police. But apart from this enlargement of federal activity there is no evidence that the riots produced any benign effect that could possibly offset, let alone justify, the wrongs that were done through the violence and looting.[5] And even those who have been eager to believe that the riots would prod the country into liberal acts have been willing to concede, nevertheless, that the net effect of the riots, politically, was to excite the electorate to a more retributive temper. As James Button wrote, "the ultimate irony [in the riots] was that the president who had done the most for black people in this century [Lyndon Johnson], and the federal agency that responded to the grievances of black rioters most emphatically [the Office of Economic Opportunity (OEO)], were both eventual casualties of the forces unleashed in part by the urban riots."[6]

But as in the case of other events that have become important as political symbols, the riots have often been invested with a meaning that suits the political interpretation that different commentators have been pleased to place on them. In one perspective the riots have been seen as self-conscious political acts, perhaps even authentic revolutionary acts, and they have been assumed to be responses of a measured kind to deprivations that are rooted in the American "system."[7] In a more sober view, they have been seen as

---

[4] See James W. Button, *Black Violence* (Princeton: Princeton University Press, 1978), pp. 57, 75, 77-78, 91-92.

[5] The absence of any evidence on this point represents a telling omission in James Button's book, *Black Violence*, note 4 above. Mr. Button received only divided and inconclusive results when he asked 58 officials in the federal government to reflect on the experience of the riots and consider whether "domestic violence can be helpful in effecting social change." (See pp. 169-171.) But of course if there had been a clear sense, in the first place, of the evidence that bore directly on this point, the evidence itself could have been consulted, and there would have been no need to canvass federal officials for their impressions.

[6] Ibid., p. 57.

[7] See, for example, Michael Lipsky and David Olson, "The Processing of Racial Crisis in America," *Politics and Society*, Vol. 6, no. 1 (1976), pp. 78-103. The authors refer to the riots as the "violent expression of political demands at the street level" (p. 80), "the most vigorous statement of discontent" (100), and as acts "related

acts of lawlessness without any larger plan or design,[8] except that they may reflect some new attitudes, diffusing through the society, about the conditions under which violence in America can be justified.[9]

One wag has observed that the Newark riot in 1967 was essentially like the race riots of old, with one exception: that this time the Italians were in blue. The remark was offered, of course, sardonically, but if it were treated seriously for a moment it would raise an interesting matter of analogies, which opens onto larger questions: Could it be said that the urban riots of 1964-1968 were rather like the disorders that occurred in Chicago around the Democratic Convention? Or were they closer in character to previous race riots, like the ones that took place in Chicago in 1919 and which gave rise eventually to the kind of legislation that was involved in the *Beauharnais* case? The difference is important. Depending on where we would place the riots—under which category we would subsume them—we would make an important judgment about the nature of these disorders.

In the case of Chicago in 1968, it was clear that people did not arrive on the scene randomly. The demonstrators who flocked to Chicago by car or train or bus came there intentionally and they came for a very explicit political purpose. Apart from the careful planning involved at different stages of the operations, the groups that sought to march on the Amphitheatre or parade in the downtown area had at least a focused sense of the policies they were trying to affect. In contrast, it would be hard to find anything near the same consciousness or political direction in the urban riots. In almost all of them, the violence flared up after a fortuitous incident that usually involved the police. (In Harlem in 1964, the outbreak of violence followed upon the shooting of a black teenager who had been wielding a knife; in Newark in 1967 it arose after the police had apparently subjected a black cab driver to harsh treatment.) It was not, in fact, until the spring of 1966 that the idea was advanced in black journals that the riots could be seen as

---

to real grievances and as strategies designed to gain redress" (91). The authors also offer the opinion that the black riots of the 1960's "represented levels of threat and challenge to governing elites and to the institutions they presided over unprecedented in this century, save possibly for the Great Depression of the 1930's."

[8] Edward Banfield, *The Unheavenly City* (Boston: Little, Brown, 1970), pp. 185-209.

[9] See James Q. Wilson, "Why We Are Having a Wave of Violence," *New York Times Magazine*, May 19, 1968, pp. 23ff.

"weapons" or "rebellions"; and as one student of the events has observed, they acquired their veneer of purpose after that, not from anything intrinsic to the acts, but from the militant rhetoric that was used in public to interpret them.[10]

That is not to say, of course, that these riots contained nothing of political significance. The record showed, for example, a certain hostility toward the police (though other evidence would warn us against assuming that this hostility was shared by a majority in the black community).[11] There was evidence, also, at times, of a particular animus toward whites, which could burst forth into violent expression; and in the reactions on the street, in the speed with which the violence followed upon the original incident, one could find a general unwillingness to give white officials any benefit of the doubt.

But to the extent that these ingredients were more important in the riots, the resemblance to the old race riots becomes stronger. The analogy is not satisfying at all points, but the comparison is worth considering for a moment. When whites hunted down blacks in Chicago in 1919, or when whites in the South went after blacks for the purpose of lynching, these events, too, were not without their political overtones. In Chicago, working-class whites and blacks were in competition for housing and jobs. In the South, as Hadley Cantril discovered, the frequency of lynchings bore a definite relation to the state of the economy or changes in the level of farm prices.[12] And yet, in confronting these cases of violence, the disposition at the time was not to take them as the portents of some revolutionary disturbance. There was no tendency to look first for their "underlying social causes," and no one came forward to sug-

---

[10] See Howard Hubbard, "Five Long Summers and How They Grew," *The Public Interest* (Summer 1968), pp. 3-24, especially 15-17. For some studies and perspectives on the riots, see Joe R. Feagin and Paul Sheatsley, "Ghetto Resident Appraisals of a Riot," *Public Opinion Quarterly*, Vol. 32, no. 3 (Fall 1968), pp. 353-62; Howard Aldrich and Albert J. Reiss, Jr., "The Effect of Civil Disorders on Small Business in the Inner City," *Journal of Social Issues*, Vol. 26, no. 4 (Winter 1970), pp. 187-206; Angus Campbell and Howard Schuman, *Racial Attitudes in Fifteen American Cities* (Ann Arbor: Institute for Social Research, 1968) [the study by the Survey Research Center, carried out after the riots of 1967], especially chs. 2, 3, 5, and 6; Edward C. Banfield, note 8 above; James Q. Wilson, note 9 above; Gary Marx, "Two Cheers for the Riot Commission Report," *Harvard Review* (Second Quarter, 1968), pp. 3-14; Edward C. Banfield, "Some 'Do's' and 'Don't's' of Riot Control," *Harvard Review* (Second Quarter, 1968), pp. 41-44.

[11] Campbell and Schuman, note 10 above, pp. 42-43.

[12] See Hadley Cantril, *The Psychology of Social Movements* (New York: John Wiley, 1941), pp. 83-85.

gest, in mitigation, that these acts of violence were "determined" most importantly by the state of the system itself. If the violence was traceable to the system, it was traceable for the most part, as Madison taught us, to those characteristics of the system that arose from its republican character. The violence of factions was an ominous and yet predictable feature in any society in which groups were free to press their interests and cultivate their antagonisms in public. And so, to recall Madison once again, one could not strike at the causes of faction without striking at the basic liberty which is, to conflict, what oxygen is to fire.[13] All one could hope to do was to move as quickly and energetically as possible to suppress the violence and limit the injuries. The hand of the law was not to be stayed from the suppression of the violence as men in authority cast about for larger social meanings in something as diffuse as a riot.

That there were a variety of influences at work, and that some people were more likely than others to fall into these patterns of violence, is something that was never in doubt. But until it was possible to sort out the causes, it had to be assumed that these people were still responsible for their acts. What was posed here again was nothing less than the issue of moral responsibility and social determinism: that is, the question of whether the actions of an individual are essentially "determined" by certain attributes that define his situation in life (as, for example, his class, education, income, or race), or whether the individual retains some autonomy as a moral actor to make choices between right and wrong. It was that same question about the implications of "morals" (and moral autonomy) that lay at the foundation of the problem raised in the law by the defamation of racial groups. And as we shall see later, the same principle would prove decisive also in settling the grounds on which the law may define the wrongness of discrimination and segregation founded on race.

The assumption of moral autonomy in human beings is logically necessary in all matters of law and morals, and it is the premise that must underlie the most important measures of public policy in the field of civil rights. That premise would have to bear just as well on the problem of the urban riots, and its application could be seen rather directly if the simple question were posed of whether the rioters, if they were caught, would deserve to go to jail. Surely punishment would not be justified if an individual had no control

---

[13] See *The Federalist* #10 (New York: Modern Library, n.d.), p. 55.

over his actions, or if his behavior had been determined by the force of certain stimuli that he was powerless to resist (as in the case, say, of someone caught in an hypnotic trance). Nor would it be right to punish someone if it were held at the same time that the riots, overall, were "justified" as political or social acts. To say that an act is "justified" is to offer grounds of exculpation. If it could be said that a particular rebellion were just, then one would have to concede in principle that the rebels did not deserve to be punished. They may be punished in fact anyway, but that would have more to do with outcome of the power struggle than with the justice of the case.

In weighing the matter seriously, I tend to doubt that most people would be willing to exempt the rioters from their personal responsibility on either one of these grounds: either on the ground that the rioters virtually lacked control over their own acts, or that there was something in their general condition—in their poverty, perhaps, or the sense of their own disparagement—that could justify the assaults they carried out against particular shops and businesses. One would probably find it hard to attribute a kind of "automatism" to the rioters or the looters, as though they had no moral sense of what they were doing. But that is to say that when most of us are pressed on the issue, we would probably be inclined to believe that no matter how badly off a person may be, he still retains, as a human being, the power to hold himself back and say, "This is wrong—this I may not do. It is not right to destroy or loot this shop and hurt someone who has done no injury to me." And yet to say that is to recognize again that human beings do not lose their capacity for moral judgment even if they fall into the most serious poverty. If it were otherwise, it would be necessary to grant a virtual exemption from the criminal law for all people who could be classified as "poor." At the same time, if there were any reason to believe that people do lose their moral competence when they become poor, there would be no stronger ground for removing the privileges of citizenship and voting. For citizenship may demand the exercise of morals and reason at their highest level, in decisions affecting the character of the community and the conditions of justice. It should go without saying that responsibilities of that kind could not be extended to people who lack the capacity for moral judgment, or indeed, who lack the rudiments of control over their own most important acts.[14]

[14] The same point was made in another way by Midge Decter in her account of the looting that took place in New York City following the blackout on July 13,

As to the matter of saying, overall, that the riots were justified, most people at a common-sense level would probably avoid a blanket judgment of that kind. Before we would exculpate a person from an act that stands out, on its face, as a serious crime, we would wish to know considerably more about the individual case: Were there extenuating reasons, perhaps, that lay behind the assault on a person or his property? Were there elements of accident present, which suggest the absence of a real intent to do harm? If an assailant had been moved, not out of the sense of a wrong that had been done to him by any particular person, but out of the sense of a grievance with the so-called "system" as a whole, would he have been justified in directing his attack at the owners of shops—or even on firemen and policemen? Were they really so much the agents of the society that one could strike at them and know that, by injuring them, one was sure to injure the system they supported?

It goes without saying that the plea for exculpation here would be a rather hard one to make, but the question, as we have faced it, carries its own point: How could we come to a sweeping verdict in the abstract, and judge the riots to have been justified in the large, when any sensible man would find it too hard to justify any one of the single acts that made up the whole?

If we return then to the question of analogies, the logic of the choice would seem to be this: If the riots were largely planless eruptions of violence, or if they were closer in character to the race riots of earlier years, we should probably have moved at once to suppress the violence and reserved for a later time our questions about "causes." But if the riots were really self-conscious political acts, if they were steps toward rebellion, or if they were at least as conscious in their political direction as the acts of the demonstrators in Chicago, then we should have to ask of the rioters precisely what we were obliged to ask of the demonstrators when they sought their

---

1977. Decter argued that the black youths who went on a spree of looting "had been given permission to do so by all the papers and magazines . . . —all the outlets for the purveying of enlightened liberal attitude and progressive liberal policy—which had for years and years been proclaiming that race and poverty were sufficient excuses for lawlessness. . . . Young blacks are getting the message from the liberal culture, more subtly but just as surely as from any old-time Southern sheriff, that they are, inherently and by virtue of their race, inferior. There are virtually no crimes they can commit that someone with great influence does not rush in to excuse on the grounds that we had no right to expect anything else. . . . The message they are given, in short, is that they are not fully enough human to be held morally responsible for their own behavior." Midge Decter, "Looting and Liberal Racism," *Commentary* (September 1977), pp. 48-54, at 53-54.

ends through a display of power in the streets: What precisely are
the grounds for your claim? What ends are you seeking, and what
is there, in the current state of things, that would justify this effort
on your part to extend your influence through the threat of force?
In other words, we would ask of the rioters no less than we would
ask of anyone who would act politically by pressing demands on
the community and breaking away from the restraints of law. We
would ask them to give reasons, to offer justifications.

It is revealing in this respect that in the public discussion of the
riots it was not common to speak of ends or purposes; there was
a disposition, rather, to speak of underlying *causes*. Where the task
of a political movement is to state ends and give reasons, the tendency here was instead to look for certain social characteristics or
"variables" that might explain why some people, more than others,
were willing to participate in the riots. In this way, some observers
sought to discover the forces that moved people to action, and in
disclosing the motive forces they seemed to assume, also, that they
would uncover the real "motives" or the "reasons." A second approach was to seek the sources of disorder or disintegration in the
nature of the "ghetto" itself and the conditions that sustained it.
I will look more closely at that phase of the analysis in the next
chapter, when I turn to the work of Kenneth Clark and the problem
of the ghetto. At this moment, however, I would take up the proposal implicit in the first approach and see what might be said
about the aims of the rioters if the evidence about their backgrounds
were taken as a source of clues to their complaints.

2. The Search for Motives and Causes: A Look at the Survey Evidence

One would be inclined to look first, of course, for signs of material
want and consider the evidence on income and unemployment
among those who participated in the riots. And yet, according to
the figures compiled by the Kerner Commission in relation to Detroit and Newark, there were no substantial differences in unemployment between the rioters and those members of the community
who did not take part in the violence or looting.[15] In Detroit the
rioters showed lower levels of unemployment than the uninvolved
(29.6 percent compared to 31.5 percent), while in Newark the

[15] *Report of the National Advisory Commission on Civil Disorders* (New York:
Bantam Books, 1968), p. 132. Hereafter cited as the *Kerner Commission Report*.

situations were reversed (29.7 percent of the rioters were unemployed, compared to 19.0 percent of the uninvolved).[16] In other words, there was no consistent trend; the *majority* of rioters were, in any case, employed; and so unemployment could not have been very critical in itself in determining just which people were likely to participate in the riots.

More rioters in Detroit had incomes below $5,000 than did the uninvolved (38.6 percent compared with 30.3 percent, while in Newark the corresponding figures were 32.6 against 29.4 percent). But the differences were not statistically significant, and they appeared to be largely a function of age, since the rioters were drawn disproportionately from younger people. When there was a control for age, the differences in income disappeared.[17]

In Newark more of the rioters professed to be dissatisfied with their jobs than did those who were not involved. But the number who were dissatisfied formed a majority in either group, and the figures probably ought to be set against the surveys in recent years which have shown a dominant sense among blacks that the job market, in general, will respond to the merits of individuals.[18] More of the rioters than the nonrioters thought it was impossible for them to get the kind of job they wanted. Yet here, too, the feeling was shared by a majority in each group, and so the degree of dissatisfaction with one's job could not have made much difference in determining the people who were more likely than others to participate in the riots.

There was a more substantial difference on the question of whether racial discrimination had been the main obstacle in the way of getting a better job. Whether or not the perception was justified in any individual case, 69 percent of the rioters thought they had been hindered by racial discrimination, while that view was held by 50 percent of the uninvolved. On the other hand, that figure has to be set against the even larger proportion of rioters (76.9 percent) who agreed that "getting what you want out of life is a matter of ability, not being in the right place at the right time,"[19] a response that has been confirmed by other surveys, involving many other cities than Newark. In the study carried out by the

[16] Ibid.

[17] Ibid., p. 131. In Detroit, among the sample of people who reported that they had participated in the riots, over 61 percent were between the ages of 15 and 24, and over 86 percent were between 15 and 35. See ibid., p. 129.

[18] See Campbell and Schuman, note 10 above, pp. 27-28.

[19] *Kerner Commission Report*, p. 133.

Survey Research Center in fifteen cities, the question was put in this way: "If a young Negro works hard enough, do you think he or she can usually get ahead in this country in spite of prejudice and discrimination, or that he doesn't have much chance no matter how hard he works?" Overwhelming numbers thought that black people who worked hard enough could make their way, but the responses seemed to vary most importantly with education. Among men in their 20's or 30's, for example, the conviction that ability would be recognized was held by 93 percent of the college graduates, as compared with 68 percent of those with only grade school education.[20] There were no notable differences by age among those who had finished high school or gone beyond that in their education; but among those who had failed to complete high school, the authors noted that "younger men are more willing to attribute lack of success to prejudice and discrimination than are the older men."[21]

These findings are worth keeping in mind if we would come to a more measured sense of the problem of employment and of the places where dissatisfaction was likely to be centered. As the studies indicate, the sense of grievance was concentrated rather strongly among the young—among the people who had less experience in the job market—and as it happens, the participants in the riots were also drawn disproportionately from the young. More young people perceived racial barriers to their progress, and more young people participated in the riots, but it does not follow, as a matter of necessity, that young people participated in the riots *because* they saw that act as a means of responding to discrimination they had encountered in their own experience. Still less, of course, does it confirm the truth of the perception that it was racial discrimination, more than anything else, which had diminished the prospects of these young people. If they were viewed soberly as a lot, their education and skills were likely as yet to be rather limited. But quite apart from the matter of skills, they may have borne as a whole those traits and tempers of the very young that make them less attractive to employers than older people who may be more matured and "settled."

[20] See Campbell and Schuman, note 10 above, pp. 27-28. See also Gary Marx, *Protest and Prejudice* (New York: Harper and Row, 1969; originally published in 1967), p. 24.

[21] Campbell and Schuman, note 10 above, p. 27. The authors went on to note also that "the teenage male group in this instance . . . is even more inclined to see failure to get ahead as caused by racial injustice. Among women, younger people at all levels of education are more inclined to blame the system for failure to get ahead."

As far as the rioters were concerned, the evidence on education was rather equivocal. A greater proportion of the rioters than the uninvolved had some high school education (in Detroit, 93 percent for the rioters as against 72.1 percent for the nonrioters; in Newark, 98.1 percent of the rioters compared to 85.7 percent of the non-rioters).[22] That seems to fall in line with what we have come to expect by now: that activists tend to be recruited from those with more, rather than less, education, and often, too, from those who are relatively better off. The very poor and the least educated tend to lack either the confidence or the skill to take the initiative, and they are often the most intimidated, the ones who fear that they have the most to lose. But from the evidence we have of the riots in Detroit and Newark, the majority of rioters failed to finish high school, and there was a greater representation of people with college education among the counter-rioters—that is, among the people who became active in the community to bring the violence to a stop.[23] The Kerner Commission made some point of the fact that 22 percent of the counter-rioters attended college, compared with 14 percent of the rioters. But then it was also true that more of the rioters had gone to college (and even graduate school) than the nonrioters. In this respect the overall differences in education were even more pronounced between the rioters and the "uninvolved" than they were between the rioters and the counter-rioters.[24] Of course, one would not usually expect to find many doctors or lawyers participating in a riot, but it was probably misleading to suggest, as the staff of the Kerner Commission did, that a high level of education was likely to "prevent" rioting.[25]

If the riots came about as the result of poverty, it would be hard to explain why they occurred just when they did, at a time when blacks were making their most rapid progress in recent history. In 1962, 300,000 blacks, or about one-third of the blacks unemployed, were out of a job for 15 weeks or more. By 1967, the number of long-term unemployed had been reduced significantly to an average of 100,000 (or about one-sixth of the total black unemployment). That was about the same proportion of long-term unemployment as existed among whites. There was an important increase in this period in the employment of blacks in industries that offered the best conditions of pay, advancement, and security. In the separate fields, for example, of education, public administration, and the manufacture of durable goods, black employment grew by a third

---

[22] *Kerner Commission Report*, p. 132.　　　[23] Ibid.
[24] Ibid., pp. 132, 174.　　　[25] Ibid.

or more. Taking all these industries together, the number of blacks employed grew from 1.3 million in 1962 to 2.1 million in 1967, an advance of nearly 60 percent, compared with an increase of 25 percent among whites.[26]

The percentage of blacks in white collar jobs rose from 4.0 percent in 1962 to 5.4 percent in 1967. Blacks still fell short in this separate field of the benchmark figure of 10.8 percent, which was the proportion they represented in the total work force. But as Claire Hodge pointed out, it was significant nevertheless that, within this five-year period, blacks moved about a fifth of the distance that they would have to go in order to reach their "expected" level of 10.8 percent.[27] In the areas of medicine and health, and in clerical occupations, blacks moved about two-fifths of the way toward that mark of 10.8 percent. In the skilled crafts they moved almost a quarter of the way, and in teaching they made up nearly half the distance in these five years.[28]

By 1970 the Bureau of the Census would find that, outside the South, there was no appreciable difference in income between white and black families containing both husbands and wives, where the head of the family was under 35 years old. In fact, for young families outside the South in which the husband and the wife both worked, the incomes of blacks were higher than those of whites. Where the head of the household was under 35, the earnings of black families were 104 percent of those of their white counterparts.[29] In families where the head of the household was under 25, the differences were even more pronounced at times in favor of blacks. This relation has been reproduced now in successive annual surveys, so that it is clear that the approximate equality of blacks and whites in this group is not due merely to some error in sampling.

[26] Claire C. Hodge, "The Negro Job Situation: Has It Improved?" *Monthly Labor Review*, Vol. 92, no. 1 (January 1969), pp. 20-28, at 20 and 21.

[27] Ibid., p. 21. That is to say, if there were no special bars to the entrance of blacks, and blacks showed no special favoritism or aversion to these kinds of occupations, it would be "expected" that blacks would gravitate to these jobs roughly in proportion to their numbers in the population at large—assuming, as one increasingly can here, that there is a sufficient number of blacks who have the education and the skills that are necessary for these positions.

[28] Ibid., p. 22. Hodge noted that the greatest lag occurred in managerial and sales positions, where blacks moved less than 5 percent of the distance they had to cover.

[29] U.S. Bureau of the Census, *Current Population Reports*, Special Studies, "Differences Between Income of White and Negro Families by Work Experience of Wife and Region: 1970, 1969, and 1959," Series P-23, No. 39, December 1971. See also Daniel P. Moynihan, "The Schism in Black America," *The Public Interest* (Spring 1972), pp. 3-24.

Of course, the pattern overall has not been unqualified. For young husbands and wives (those under 35) in the North and West, with only the husband working, the earnings of black families in 1970 were only 76 percent of those of their white counterparts. Among black households headed by a woman, there was no gain at all in relation to whites over the decade of the sixties. The number of these households went from 400,000 in 1960 to about 800,000 in the last census, and more than 53 percent of these families fell below the poverty line.[30] This increase in the number of households headed by women occurred in white households as well: in 1971, in the central cities of metropolitan districts, 27.6 percent of the white households were headed by women, compared with 39.3 percent for blacks.[31] It is not, then, a problem that concerns blacks exclusively, though it has been a relatively greater problem among the black population. Even so, this cannot obscure the fact that the trends have been dominantly and consistently in the direction of improvement. "If [the trends] persist," as Daniel Moynihan has said, "if the present income equality of these young black/white families holds up as they grow older, one of the fundamental correlates of race in the United States—inferior earning power—will disappear."[32]

It is possible, of course, to fall back and argue that here, as in many other "revolutionary" situations, it is not poverty in some absolute sense that is decisive so much as "relative deprivation," the dissatisfaction of those who have been aroused to new wants by a rapid, material improvement in the condition of their lives. But in any event, that is an explanation rather than a justification, and the evidence would be too meager or inconsistent in this case to support that kind of conclusion. And yet even if the explanation were apt, it would hardly tell us what to do. Would we infer, for example, that the best measure to pursue in averting riots would be to slow down the progress of blacks in employment and education?

It may not be possible to offer a satisfying account of the riots by considering the variations in employment, income, and education among the rioters, but that still does not rule out other possibilities of a "political" explanation. The situation may simply point toward political interpretations of a rather different kind, which would not depend any longer on the faults of the social order

[30] See *The New York Times*, February 12, 1971, p. 1; Moynihan, note 29 above, p. 10-11.

[31] See Moynihan, p. 9. [32] Ibid., p. 11.

itself. There was, for example, the emergence of a new political consciousness among blacks, which was approaching its peak of militancy even as the material conditions of blacks had become dramatically better. This new militancy was more likely due to the political trends of the previous twenty years and the growing assertiveness of the black community. Those trends would include the increase in black political strength with the migration of blacks to the northern cities; the impetus of the civil rights movement, particularly as it was spurred on by decisions of the courts on racial segregation; and finally, the acceleration of reform in the Kennedy-Johnson years.

That is one hypothesis. Another kind of political explanation may center on the riots as precedents, and on the efforts that have been made to legitimize the riots by portraying them as a form of political protest. Through the power of example, one riot may make it easier, then, to have another, and that is particularly the case if the riots have been endowed with a larger meaning and made the objects of "understanding" to respectable opinion. Ideas themselves have consequences, and in this area, as James Q. Wilson has pointed out, the spread of violence has probably been affected by the growing acceptance of violence itself as a political act that is no longer seen as unjustified in America. To the extent, of course, that the degree of violence has been affected by ideas of this kind, the "solution" to the problem lies less in our social policy than in the things that we, as a people, teach about the conditions under which violence can be justified in a constitutional order.

3. RIOTERS, MILITANTS, AND CIVIL ASSOCIATIONS

But let us consider for the moment that we might have been dealing, in the riots, with a self-conscious group of activists, who were taking their political struggle into a new phase. There is some evidence in the report of the Kerner Commission that the rioters did have positive images of blacks as a group, and that they did affect some rather strong feelings of racial pride. In Detroit, 48.6 percent of the self-reported rioters in the sample said they thought blacks were more dependable than whites. That view was shared by only 22.4 percent of the sample who had not participated in the rioting. And in Newark the figures were remarkably close to the same level: 45.0 percent of the rioters thought blacks were more dependable, compared with 27.8 percent of those who had not been involved.[33] According to the survey in Newark, the rioters preferred the term "black" to "Negro," and they were slightly more likely than the uninvolved to feel that all blacks should study African history and languages.[34]

On the other hand, it was also true that the rioters exhibited the strongest antiwhite attitudes. Over 72 percent of them admitted that they sometimes harbored feelings of hatred toward whites, compared to 50 percent of those who had not taken part in the riots. That would not, on its face, seem very surprising, especially in the light of the other findings; but I mention it here because it runs strikingly counter to the portrait of the black militant that was presented several years ago in Gary Marx's *Protest and Prejudice.*[35] In that study, the most militant blacks were also the most tolerant in the sense of showing less antiwhite and less anti-Semitic feeling. Those findings were very important to Marx's contention that militancy among blacks was a responsible, enlightened, constructive activism. To be fired up about one's own rights did not dispose one, then, to deny rights to others; and to firm up solidarity within one's own group, one did not have to play on the targets of group hatred. Cohesion could be established within a group quite as well by cultivating the sentiments of just principle.

The black militants in Marx's study had higher incomes and more education, on the average, than other groups in the sample; but they also had more experience in organizational activity in the civil rights movement. That experience in civic organizations was important, because it seemed to give these people practice in what Tocqueville called "the art of associating together." Less than a quarter of them expressed views that were receptive to violence— a higher proportion than appeared among those who were classified as "conservatives" in Marx's study, but considerably lower than

[33] *Kerner Commission Report*, pp. 133, 176. These differences were statistically significant at the .001 level in Detroit and at the .05 level in Newark. That is to say, the differences between the two groups were sufficiently great on this question that the probability was less than one in a thousand in the case of Detroit (and less than five in a hundred in the case of Newark) that the differences could have arisen by chance or by some quirk in the sampling process.

[34] More than 52 percent of the rioters preferred "black," compared with slightly more than 33 percent of the nonrioters—a difference that was again statistically significant (p<.025). A shade more of the nonrioters preferred "Negro" to "black." The differences again were statistically significant (p<.025). See ibid., pp. 133, 176.

[35] Gary Marx, *Protest and Prejudice* (New York: Harper and Row, 1969; originally published in 1967).

was found among the lower-class sympathizers of the Black Nationalist movement.[36] Those blacks in the study who were more
inclined to violence were more inclined, also, to have a negative
"self-image" of blacks as a group. And so anyone who was guided
by Marx's findings would have been led to expect that the vanguard
of black activists was largely averse to political enterprises that
involved the use of violence. It could be surmised, in addition, that
those who were more willing to use violence had no real claim to
represent the black community: they were the least informed about
the problems of the community, they were the least identified with
other blacks, and they were the least likely to have absorbed a sense
of the interests of the community through a commitment to civic
work.

Anyone who subscribed to Marx's analysis would have been
skeptical of the view that the rioters were political activists in any
sense. On the other hand, if there was something plausible in the
celebration of the rioters as revolutionaries, Marx's account of the
black militant would have to be revised in a fundamental way. The
deeper importance of Marx's study, and the source of its larger
reassurance, was that it seemed to confirm the old Tocquevillian
theory of citizenship: those who took part in civic affairs had the
chance to do far more than acquire knowledge about the state of
the public business. They had the chance also to grow more civil.
As they worked in concert they would learn how to reconcile their
interests with those of others, and as they sought the assent of a
larger group they would learn, too, how to act for an interest larger
than their own. As Tocqueville put it,

> [Men] cannot belong to [political associations] for any length
> of time without finding out how order is maintained among
> a large number of men and by what contrivance they are made
> to advance, harmoniously and methodically, to the same ob-
> ject. Thus they learn to surrender their own will to that of all
> the rest and to make their own exertions subordinate to the
> common impulse. . . . Political associations may therefore be
> considered as large free schools, where all the members of the
> community go to learn the general theory of association.[37]

[36] Ibid., p. 115. This is not to say, however, that the figure of "one quarter" who
were willing to accept violence is altogether reassuring.

[37] Tocqueville, *Democracy in America* (New York: Vintage, 1954) Vol. II, Bk. II,
ch. VII, "Relation of Civil to Political Associations," pp. 124-25.

It was not a matter of teaching obedience to the group in any crude sense; the value of association, rather, was that it offered the kind of exercise that could cultivate the highest part of human nature, the capacity for morals itself. As a citizen participated in political associations, he had to face the complaints and interests of people in particular cases and come to a judgment as to what justice required in regard to them. But he could not face the question of justice in any concrete instance without being led outward to the principles that defined the nature of justice more generally. In that way, politics became more than a school of "association"; it became also, as the classics understood, a school of "morals." John Stuart Mill came closer to this understanding when he offered, in effect, a restatement of Tocqueville and wrote of "the moral part of the instruction afforded by the participation of the private citizen . . . in public functions":

> He is called upon, while so engaged, to weigh interests not his own; to be guided, in case of conflicting claims, by another rule than his private partialities; to apply, at every turn, principles and maxims which have for their reason of existence the common good . . .
>
> Where this school of public spirit does not exist, scarcely any sense is entertained that private persons, in no eminent social situation, owe any duties to society, except to obey the laws and submit to the government. There is no unselfish sentiment of identification with the public. Every thought or feeling, either of interest or of duty, is absorbed in the individudal and in the family. The man never thinks of any collective interest, of any objects to be pursued jointly with others, but only in competition with them, and in some measure at their expense. A neighbor, not being an ally or an associate, since he is never engaged in any common undertaking for joint benefit, is therefore only a rival. Thus even private morality suffers, while public is actually extinct.[38]

There was implicit in this view, of course, a rather definite understanding of a moral structure. There was the sense of a ranking or hierarchy among faculties and traits and even ways of life, a sense of the things that were in principle better or worse, and of

---

[38] John Stuart Mill, *Considerations on Representative Government*, ch. III (Indianapolis: Bobbs Merrill, 1958), pp. 54-55.

the features that defined goodness in men and communities. It was understood, for example, that the knowledge of right and wrong was higher than the absence of moral reflection; that the capacity for morals was indeed higher than that capacity for mere physical force which human beings shared with other animals; that a person who took an interest in the welfare of others was a better person than one who was entirely selfish; and that a person who respected some law beyond his own self-interest was far better than one who respected no law beyond his own appetites. The promise of political association at its highest reaches was that men could become more lawful in their reflexes, more moral in their character. But it went almost without saying that men could become more civilized and humane in this way only if their associations were founded and preserved with an understanding of just principles. It could hardly be expected that participation itself, in any kind of association, would be bound to produce good men, regardless of the ends and character of the association. No one would have assumed, for example, that an association of robbers would cultivate in its members a deep commitment to lawfulness and a sense of the things that belong, justly, to others. It was always possible to have "good" associations and still end up with bad men, but there was a better chance of teaching good lessons, and cultivating good citizens, if the association managed to plant within its members an understanding of those premises of morals and law on which their own rights were founded.

From this perspective—the traditional perspective—it could be readily understood why blacks who participated in civic organizations also showed a strong sense of moderation and a respect for the rights of other groups. These people might simply have absorbed the lessons taught in the school of citizenship. And so Gary Marx could observe, after listing the characteristics of the militants, that, "to reverse Yeats, it could almost be said that the best are filled with passionate intensity while the worst lack all concern."[39]

Yet it came out in the survey of Newark after the riots that the rioters were far more likely to have participated in a civil rights group than the people who had not taken part in the riot. And by their own account the rioters engaged more frequently in discussions about the rights of blacks than the nonrioters did.[40] Would that suggest that a different type of militant is emerging now and

[39] Marx, note 35 above, p. 206.
[40] The differences in both cases were statistically significant. See the *Kerner Commission Report*, p. 178.

that the earlier description offered by Marx no longer holds? Might it suggest, with more severity, that there was something defective in the lessons that were being taught in black civic groups—that somehow these groups had lost the sense they possessed earlier of those premises of lawfulness in which their own rights were grounded?

My own guess is that Marx's analysis is probably still closer to the truth, and for that reason it would be hard to view the rioters very plausibly as a new variety of political militant. It seems highly unlikely, based on the evidence at hand, that the rioters were drawn from people who were involved in a substantial way, in positions of responsibility, with the civic life of the black community. That may help to explain many other things, including their lack of tolerance for whites and their willingness to use violence. And since the rioters were lacking in these moral parts of the makeup of a citizen, there is reason to suspect that they were missing other parts as well—most notably, a genuine commitment to the community and its interests.

The surveys carried out among the rioters did not get at these matters directly. They provided only snatches of indirect evidence, but the clues here are very suggestive nonetheless, and they start to show up as one begins to consider where the rioters differed most markedly from the rest of the community. The main differences that appeared immediately were in sex and age. Over 61 percent of the rioters in Detroit were male, compared to less than 44 percent of the nonrioters, and that discrepancy tended to hold for other cities as well. Women apparently did not become involved until the later stages of any riot, and they were not arrested in numbers that were at all commensurate with their actual presence. In 21 cities surveyed by the Kerner Commission, males accounted for 89.3 percent of the total number of people arrested, a situation, as the Commission said, that "probably reflected either selectivity in the arrest process or less dramatic, less provocative riot behavior by women."[41]

The rioters were also drawn disproportionately from the young. In Detroit, as I noted earlier, over 61 percent of the rioters were between the ages of 15 and 24, while in comparison, less than 23 percent of the nonrioters fell into that age group.[42] But apart from

[41] Ibid., pp. 130, 173.

[42] Ibid., pp. 129, 172. The arrest records for 16 cities showed that people between the ages of 15 and 24 formed only 52.5 percent of the arrestees—which would seem to suggest that people of this age were also much better runners.

sex and age, what seemed to characterize the rioters most strongly were their unattached circumstances. Only some 28 percent of the rioters were married, compared with 44 percent among those who had not been involved, and according to the survey in Newark, the rioters were more than twice as likely to have been divorced or separated (14.2 percent of them fell into that category, compared with 6.4 percent of the nonrioters).[43] At the same time, it is worth noticing here, against the background of all that has been heard about the effects of broken homes, that the rioters were no more likely than the nonrioters to have come from homes which lacked the presence of an adult male.[44]

The evidence suggests, then, that the rioters were predominantly young and free-floating, without many obligations to family (or, one suspects, to other groups of a civic nature) that might have acted as an incentive to restraint or discipline. They were precisely the kind of people who were apt to be found, more than others, in spontaneous, explosive outbursts, without a stable leadership, and without a clear political focus. And just as there may be doubts about their ties of obligation to family and civic organizations, there may be questions about the depth of their commitment to their own community. In the Newark survey, for example, the rioters were nearly as hostile toward middle-class blacks as they were toward whites. They were far more likely than the nonrioters to believe that blacks who made more money thought they were better than other blacks, and that blacks who made a lot of money were just as bad as whites.[45] If any lessons can be extracted from

[43] If one considers the differences overall in marital standing, the level of significance in the survey was p<.10. That is to say, there was less than one chance in ten that the differences between the two populations (the rioters and the nonrioters) in these characteristics (marriage, separation, divorce) were a result merely of "chance" or accident in the sampling process. It is customary to look for a probability of less than .05 before one claims statistical significance; but statistical significance is not always a measure, of course, of "true" significance, and there may be some interest in reporting differences that fall short of that level.

[44] Kerner Commission Report, p. 130. Twenty-five-and-a-half percent of the rioters had come from families of this kind, compared with 23 percent of those who had not been involved in the riots—a difference that was not statistically significant. See p. 173.

[45] Ibid., pp. 134, 176. An alternative interpretation, of course, is that the rioters had a more accurate view of the nature of class divisions within the black community, and in this sense they might have represented an advanced political consciousness, more distant from parochial loyalties. That does not seem, on its face, very likely, and one would find further cause for suspicion in the evidence showing the hostility of the rioters toward whites. On the other hand, this questioning of their commitment

the way in which people acted in the riots, it may be instructive to recall, too, that in Detroit, the sign "soul brother" on places of business did not act as a special talisman which could afford any protection. The rioters, in their evenhandedness, struck at establishments owned by blacks as well as those owned by whites.[46]

In one survey taken after the riots in Harlem, residents of the Bedford-Stuyvesant area of Brooklyn were asked to characterize the rioters. The dominant responses were along these lines: 30 percent, the largest bloc, characterized the participants as hoodlums, delinquents, or criminals; 21 percent described them simply as young people or teenagers; 13 percent said they were composed of the unemployed, dropouts, and idlers. *Only 5 percent described the rioters as the poor and deprived*, and it is also clear that the rioters were not looked upon as leaders in the community.[47]

All things considered, it would be a strain, I think, to argue that these riots were a form of political rebellion, carried out by politically conscious and directed groups who were committed to the community and animated by a sense of community ends. That is not to say that the evidence reveals nothing of political import. It is not without significance when many blacks feel a strong resentment against whites for the wrongs of the past; when they distrust institutions that are governed by whites; and when they show a readiness to countenance the use of violence, even if they are not inclined to use violence themselves. Nor would the evidence fail to highlight certain predictable sources of trouble that deserve to be treated. For one thing, it would recall the old truth that when there is a large reservoir of idle, unemployed young men with few commitments to family or, for that matter, to any other groups with

---

to other blacks may be set off in part—but only in part—against the evidence alluded to earlier, that the rioters, far more than the uninvolved, thought blacks were more dependable than whites (48.6 percent for the rioters, against 22.4 percent for the nonrioters). Rioters were far more likely to believe also that blacks were "nicer" than whites (61.0 percent of the rioters held that view, as opposed to 36.3 percent of the uninvolved). But that finding is easily misinterpreted. The nonrioters were hardly more disposed to regard whites as "nicer"; it is just that a majority of the uninvolved were more inclined to believe that all peoples, in this respect, were "about the same." See ibid., p. 176.

[46] Ibid., p. 88. As the Kerner Commission added, "Looters paid no attention to residents who shouted at them and called their actions senseless. An epidemic of excitement had swept over the persons on the street."

[47] See Joe R. Feagin and Paul B. Sheatsley, "Ghetto Resident Appraisals of a Riot," *Public Opinion Quarterly*, Vol. 32, no. 3 (Fall 1968), pp. 352-62, at 357-58. Cf. Edward Banfield, "Rioting Mainly for Fun and Profit," in *The Unheavenly City* (Boston: Little, Brown, 1970), ch. 9.

constructive ends, the potential for uncivil acts of all kinds may be very great.

The question needs to be raised, of course, as to why there were so many unemployed youths between the ages of 18 and 22 when the economy was running at full capacity in the mid-60's and there were many jobs going unfilled. In addition there were, at the time, a number of federal and state programs concentrating on the problems of unemployment among the young. And yet there was only a dim sense then as to how much it was really worth to a young man in his late teens to take a job at the rate of pay that his skills could command. It has become more evident recently that the prospect of employment may not be as inviting to the young as we have been inclined to assume, precisely because it does involve a full-time commitment to the discipline and obligation of work at a time when young people may be reluctant to accept that kind of commitment. One of the fruits of a more generous welfare system is that it may remove the prod of necessity which compelled the young in an earlier time to take on the obligations of employment. It is clear that the decision on work will be affected by the nature of the alternatives, and as the claims of necessity become less insistent, the range of alternatives may become wider. Those alternatives may also embrace the chance simply for more leisure, for more free time to spend cultivating the pastimes of the young. They may also include part-time work in illegal trades (in selling drugs, for example, or running numbers) where the work is far more lucrative and free of taxes.

These interpretations took on more plausibility for Edwin Harwood as he surveyed some programs of the Labor Department that sought to deal with the problems of employment among youth, and he considered the question of why these programs had not been more successful in raising employment among young people. Harwood was moved at one point to observe that unemployed black youths between the ages of 18 and 22 may appreciate this stage of release from the obligation of earning a living, and they may prefer to use these years, as they are used in part by other people of their age who are in college, as a time when they can taste different experiences and consider different styles of life without taking on the responsibilities of a family and a full-time job.[48]

[48] Edwin Harwood, "A Tale of Two Ghettos," *The Public Interest* (Fall 1969), pp. 78-87. What was left unasked here, also, was startling but comprehensible. It is only against the background of the last decade in American education that an American professor could leave unchallenged the assumption that attending college for four years may be the functional equivalent of hanging around on street corners.

Just how far this is true, or how much of the problem of unemployment it accounts for, is hard to say. A substantial portion of unemployment among youth evidently results from a legislated minimum wage, which has the effect of pricing many young people out of the market (along with certain jobs, like "soda jerking," which were performed in the past largely by teenagers).[49] The same effect may be achieved by union regulations and licensing laws, and it may even be accomplished at times by programs designed to provide more jobs directly through the government. As Arthur Laffer has pointed out, a massive program of federal spending may compel the government to increase the taxes that employers pay on each employee, and with that step, the government raises the cost of keeping additional workers.[50] There is a considerable inventory, then, of forces that raise unemployment among teenagers, and it should be clear by now, after a heavy investment in public service jobs, that the problem will not be dissolved simply by measures to provide more jobs through the government or to use more astute methods of "retraining" young people.

Those are issues, however, that are the proper concern of public policy, and it is important to preserve the sense that what is being dealt with here are, in fact, enduring problems of public policy. There are many good reasons for seeking full employment and higher levels of education, quite apart from any relation they may have to reducing the risk of riots—a relation that is rather tenuous in any event. The Kerner Commission was no doubt trying to prod the country into doing good things by pointing out the threat of future riots; but there was considerable danger in approaching the problem in that way, as though it *were* largely a matter of avoiding riots. For one thing, that perspective would force a shift away from the firmer ground of other reasons we would have for preferring to raise levels of education and the standard of living. Those reasons would be drawn, of course, from the moral premises that underlie a constitutional order, and they would remind us, if we ever needed reminding, that knowledge must be higher, in principle, than ignorance; that education must be preferable to the absence of learning; and that the higher reaches for human experience may be rendered more practicable by a higher standard of living.

[49] See Edward Banfield, note 47 above, pp. 282-83, and see generally chs. 5 and 6; also, *The Wall Street Journal*, February 6, 1968, p. 1; and Yale Brozen, "The Effect of Statutory Minimum Wage Increases on Teen-Age Unemployment," *The Journal of Law and Economics*, Vol. 12 (April 1969), pp. 109-22.

[50] See Arthur B. Laffer, "The Iniquitous 'Wedge,'" *The Wall Street Journal*, July 28, 1976, p. 12.

But when we move away from these firm grounds of principle we may encourage people to believe that the main rationale for certain measures of social policy is to reduce the potential for violence. That strategy may succeed only in persuading people that the prospect of civil violence is indeed a very live and urgent problem. From that point they may go on to conclude that the problem does deserve a response in public policy, but not the response that the Kerner Commission had in mind. One such response may be, as it has been, to come forward with a program of heavier investment in the equipment and training of the police.[51]

It is not inconceivable that programs of this kind may be effective in reducing crime, and to the extent that some of this reduction occurs in the black community, it may even be pertinent to some of the tensions that surrounded the riots.[52] But these programs seem no more likely than anything else to affect the incidence of rioting. In the long run the investment in the police may be helpful, but in the short term there may be some disquieting side effects in a situation in which the black community is pictured, from within and without, as poised on the edge of violence. The overall scene would have to encompass those housewives in the suburbs of Detroit who began practicing with handguns, and those people who became even more determined to resist the integration of their public schools and the entrance of black families into their neighborhoods. If attention is diverted from the substantive questions of social policy, if the debate is covered over instead by the creation of a mythology surrounding the urban riots, we should not be astonished if we wind up with policies that are largely irrelevant, if not actually distorting, for our public life—and with a public opinion that has not been educated to the temper of supporting anything better.

[51] After the riot in Newark the police invested $300,000 in bulletproof helmets, antisniper rifles, armored cars, and "all the tear gas we could ever need." One observer wrote in April 1968 that "all across the country, cities have laid in vast supplies of anti-riot hardware. Chicago spent $168,000 on three helicopters to serve as airborne command posts during riots, and to survey rooftops for caches of bricks, bottles, and concrete blocks. New York City bought 5,000 riot helmets at a cost of $100,000. In Virginia, the state police ordered six armored cars costing $30,000 each. . . ." Harold H. Martin, "The Fires of Summer," *The Saturday Evening Post*, April 20, 1968, p. 28, quoted in Button, note 4 above, pp. 126-27.

[52] One of the areas in which technical improvement has had a noticeable effect on the police has been in the reduction of the time lag between the reception of a call and their arrival on the scene; and there has been a wide concern in black communities that the police do not respond very quickly to alarms in their neighborhoods. See Campbell and Schuman, note 10 above, p. 42.

VI

THE SOURCES OF DISORDER: KENNETH CLARK AND THE PROBLEM OF THE GHETTO

I considered in the last chapter one view in which the urban riots were seen as the product of certain underlying conditions of poverty and discrimination. Another view finds the sources of disorder, not in such discrete characteristics as poverty or the relative lack of education, but in a larger complex or system of pathology that is formed by the conditions of "ghetto" life in the black areas. In this perspective, the social maladies come about when blacks of all classes are thrown together and confined to a designated area of the city by a wall of social convention, supported quite often by official acquiescence. The ghetto is at once a magnet and a receiving point for new migrants to the city; for that reason it is likely to retain a strong lower class flavor and to display, rather persistently, all those features that have become marks of a lower-class culture: high rates of violent crime, drug addiction, venereal disease, and the breakdown of families.

In recent years no scholar has spoken with more public visibility on the dynamics of the ghetto and the crises of black life in the cities than Kenneth Clark. Nor has any black scholar seen his researches deployed more prominently in advancing the movement for black rights.[1] *Dark Ghetto*[2] has probably been Clark's most

[1] Clark was launched on a large public stage almost twenty-five years ago, when he was called in as an expert witness in the litigation surrounding *Brown* v. *Board of Education*. When the Supreme Court handed down its decision in that notable case it claimed that its judgment was supported by "modern authority" in the field of psychology; and where the Court found this authority most importantly was in a statement that Clark had drafted for the judges on behalf of himself and other social scientists. However, the only piece of research by Clark that stood behind his reports was a project he had carried out with his wife—the famous "doll experiments," which I will discuss at length in Chapter IX. See Kenneth and Mamie Clark, "Emotional Factors in Racial Identification and Preference in Negro Children," *Journal of Negro Education*, Vol. 19 (1950), pp. 341-50; and their "Racial Identification and Preference in Negro Children," *Readings in Social Psychology*, ed. T. M. Newcomb and E. L. Hartley (1947). These studies have been treated in a critical way by Edmond Cahn, "Jurisprudence," 30 *N.Y.U. L. Rev.* 150 (1950), and by

celebrated book, and in that work he has sought to state, in a concentrated way, the import of his studies of the black community and his reflections on the sources of its problems. According to Clark, *Dark Ghetto* also served as a blueprint of sorts for the people who designed the "war on poverty" in the cities.[3]

And yet, one finds in this work a marked ambivalence on the question of whether we are faced, in the ghetto, with something that is really a political problem after all, in the sense of a problem that admits of a solution through the community and its public policy. In the end there may even be some doubt as to whether Clark is willing to regard the main difficulties in the ghetto as real "problems": when he has been pressed to the point of decision, he has affected a certain reluctance to make judgments and condemn as "wrong" many of those conventions (such as illegitimacy) that make up the character of life in the ghetto. The ambivalence that Clark has shown, in principle, on questions of this kind has affected in a profound way the adequacy of the analysis he has provided of the predicaments of the black community. It is for that reason that I raise here "the problem" that Kenneth Clark exemplifies as a social scientist who has aspired to reach, with his science, to questions about the highest things, but who has also been convinced, as a social scientist, that the principles of moral judgment are beyond the things one can really "know." The burden of my argument is that we would arrive at a rather different factual understanding of the ghetto if we were to make a more demanding effort than Clark has made so far to take matters of moral judgment seriously and to sort out the questions of principle that bear on the task of judgment.

1. PATHOLOGIES AND RESPONSIBILITIES

As we move toward a judgment over questions of public policy, it makes an important difference whether the problems we are addressing arise, on the one hand, from the weaknesses of individuals or from the moral code of a group, or whether those problems find their origin, on the other hand, in the structure of the society and the economy. It makes a difference, of course, to the kinds of

Ernest van den Haag, "Social Science Testimony in the Desegregation Cases," 6 *Villanova L. Rev.* 69 (1960).

[2] (New York: Harper and Row, 1965).

[3] The claim is made in *Pathos of Power* (New York: Harper and Row, 1974), pp. 158-59.

policies that are relevent to the problem, to say nothing of the question of whether any given "problem" happens to lend itself to treatment through the measures of public law. Clark himself showed his awareness of this issue. After he had reflected seriously on the matter, he came to the conclusion that many of the "pathologies" he found in the ghetto could be attributed simply to the natures of individuals:

> One has to accept the fact [he wrote] that under the best social conditions man can devise, some persons will probably be criminal, some will be indigent and seek to exploit others, some will be passive, withdrawn, or lazy for reasons no one fully understands. Some possible reasons are distorted familial relations, inadequate physical constitution, defective nervous system, and a complexity of other factors *that are not primarily related to community pathology. The present lack of scientific understanding cannot, however, be used to justify continuing social oppression.*[4]

Clark had noted earlier that it is often difficult (and it may be said, more properly, unwarranted) to make the transition between aggregate conditions in the community and the defects or pathologies of individuals.[5] But in that event, one would have to be even more cautious before one assumes, as Clark does, that the "pathologies" he charts are in fact the results of "social oppression." The problems themselves (or at least their symptoms) stand out rather sharply; but the larger question of their cause does not become much clearer as Clark moves on through the catalogue of social ills. Clark professes his belief at one point that the pattern of "venereal disease, illegitimacy, and family instability" could be broken if society offered greater means for the male in the ghetto to prove his manhood by sustaining a family. In that way, he suggested, it might be possible to reduce the incidence of transient sexual relations and the casual breakdown of families that become marks of virility and male power.[6] And who is to say that an argument of that kind does not contain some truth? But then the question that must be asked is: Why should the breakdown of families have continued apace and even increased in the 1960's when blacks were making notable gains in employment and mobility, and when the means of sustaining a family had improved

---

[4] Ibid., p. 110. Emphasis added.
[5] See ibid., p. 82.   [6] See ibid., p. 74.

considerably? Why should families break down even in those places where the welfare laws continued to provide grants for the family when the head of the household was unemployed? Under those circumstances the welfare laws did not provide an incentive for husbands to leave, and the disintegration of families could not have been attributed mainly to the government.

What would have to be asked in this vein about the breakdown of families would have to be asked in a similar way about most of the other signs of "pathology" that Clark cited. At the time he was writing, the rates of illegitimacy and venereal disease in Harlem, for example, far exceeded those in the rest of the city. As Clark noted, the rate of venereal disease was more than six times the rate for New York City as a whole—110.3 cases for every 10,000 people in Harlem under the age of 21, compared to 17.2 cases for every 10,000 young people in the city as a whole.[7] Clearly, it would be hard to explain those figures as a function of changes in the level of unemployment, and it is evident, too, that the issue cannot be reduced to a matter of "hygiene," as Clark rather preciously puts it.[8]

Harlem was well ahead of the rest of the city, also, in the rate of homicide and juvenile delinquency, and it led all the other areas of the city in the rate of admission to state mental hospitals.[9] The figures on homicide and delinquency all seemed to fit in well with the notion of a lower-class culture where the tendency to violence ran high. About half of all homicides occur among intimates, rather than among strangers, and nothing bears out quite as vividly the sense of social disintegration as the evidence which shows the most sudden and catastrophic ruptures in the places where the ties of trust and obligation ought to be the strongest.[10] The tensions of lower-class life might account for part of these higher levels of vio-

[7] Ibid., p. 87.   [8] See ibid., p. 88.

[9] Ibid., pp. 82-86. Clark noted that the suicide rate, a classic sign of social "disintegration," was actually lower in Harlem than in wealthier sections of the city. It was apparently, in his view, another one of those privileges appropriated by the rich.

[10] Around the time that Clark was writing, the FBI reported that, in 1963, 31 percent of the willful killings in the country occurred within the family (and more than half of them involved one spouse killing another). Outside the family, 17 percent of the killings apparently arose form "lovers' quarrels." If one adds to all of this the killings that took place in the heat of arguments among friends, the number of murders among intimates would represent a majority of the willful homicides. See Federal Bureau of Investigation, *Uniform Crime Reports—1963* (Washington: Department of Justice, 1964), pp. 6-7.

lence, and it has been suggested also that some portion might be explained by the Southern heritage of American blacks. The incidence of violence has traditionally been higher in the South, and so it is conceivable that the level of violence among blacks in the North may be affected in part by a culture that has been projected from the South.[11] In the case of New York the figures might be higher also as a function of the higher crime rate in the city, with more people keeping guns in their homes. Still, having said all of that, the black sections of New York, or in the nation more generally, have accounted for a much higher proportion of murders than one would expect on the basis of the fraction they represent of the total population. In the nation as a whole, blacks constitute about 13 percent of the population, but they have accounted for more than half of the murders (either as victims or assailants). At the time Clark wrote, blacks constituted 53.9 percent of the murder victims in the country (and 56.8 percent of those arrested for murder).[12]

As Clark conceded by the end of his book, it is not easy to find the roots of these "multiple pathologies" in the inner city. It is clear that they do not lie primarily in employment, and in fact, as Clark said, in a rather pivotal admission, even "if all of its residents were employed it would not materially alter the pathology of the community." Nor, he said, do the roots of the problem lie in the frustrations of bad housing. Housing may indeed heighten morale, but still, he argued, it does not necessarily affect the more fundamental conditions of economic standing, broken homes, and lowered aspirations.[13]

It is not entirely clear, then, that the ghetto is the source of these so-called pathologies; it is possible that the connection between the

[11] If we take the figures, again, from the time Clark was writing, the murder rate in the South was 7.7 per 100,000 population for 1964—more than twice the rate of the Northeast, which was 3.4, and higher even than the "frontier" West, which was 3.9. The rate in New York City was 6.1 per 100,000, and that level was exceeded easily by Atlanta, with 11.2, and Birmingham, with 12.1. Federal Bureau of Investigation, *Uniform Crime Reports—1964* (Washington: Department of Justice, 1965), pp. 50, 52, 70, 80.

[12] See ibid., pp. 104, 114. This does not necessarily mean, of course, that blacks did in fact represent more than half of the assailants. Over a quarter of the people arrested for murder were acquitted of the crime or had the charges dismissed. But even with the possibility of bias in the enforcement of the law, it is apparent that blacks did constitute a disproportionate number of the assailants in these cases, just as they constituted a disproportionate share of the victims.

[13] Clark, *Dark Ghetto*, p. 106.

ghetto and the pathologies may be one of correlation rather than cause and effect. Those who avoid the "pathologies," or those who rise above them, tend to leave the ghetto when they get the chance. The ones who remain, or the ones who take their places, are the ones who continue to display the characteristics of the lower-class syndrome. Clark himself noted that between 1950 and 1960 the population of central Harlem fell by nearly 27,000, a decline of about 10 percent. He tended to attribute the exodus to urban renewal, but he pointed out nevertheless that it was the families with both parents in the home that were more likely to move. The heaviest losses were among those people in the age group of 21 to 44, the group that was probably also more productive and mobile and more likely to take part in civic affairs. And so Clark concluded that central Harlem lost a large segment of its "actual or potential leadership."[14]

The question is, should they have left? If one were convinced that the ghetto was an inescapable source of pathologies, there should have been no hesitation in urging these people to leave when they could. If one had counseled them to stay, one would have implied that the ghetto was indeed workable, that it could be the scene of a creditable civic life, and that it was not even, fairly speaking, a "ghetto," in the sense of a place where people are forced to live because they have no other choice.[15]

Clark intimated that the middle classes ought to stay, but his reasons must remain, in the circumstances, rather uncertain,[16] and it does make a difference here as to what those reasons are. If the

[14] *Youth in the Ghetto* (New York: Harlem Youth Opportunities Unlimited, Inc., 1964), pp. 120-22.

[15] Brian Berry has shown, in this vein, how the "dual housing market" broke down in Chicago in the 1960's and early 1970's as a result almost entirely of the expansion of new housing. A large number of new units in the housing stock set off a chain of moves, which in turn opened up large blocks of good housing for blacks of middle and lower incomes. About 128,000 units were transferred from whites to blacks, with an increase of home ownership among blacks that vastly exceeded the number of new units that were constructed. (The net increase here was 28,000.) Beyond that, roughly 63,000 black families were able to move into better housing from units that were eventually demolished. By 1970 the housing stock in the so-called "ghetto" areas of Chicago was marked by large numbers of vacant units, which came to about 18,000 units in all. See Brian Berry, "Ghetto Expansion and Single-Family Housing Prices: Chicago, 1968-72," *Journal of Urban Economics*, Vol. 3 (1976), pp. 397-423, at 417. For some accounts from the experience of urban renewal in Boston, see Edward C. Banfield, *The Unheavenly City* (Boston: Little, Brown, and Co., 1970), pp. 80-81.

[16] See *Dark Ghetto*, p. 107.

middle classes were to stay, their function, very clearly, would be to teach: they would hold up to the community, through the force of personal example, a kind of life that is not only better in itself, but that is also more likely to generate the habits of obligation and discipline that may bring people out of poverty. To urge the middle classes to stay and teach would be to affirm, in effect, the superior dignity or moral worth of that way of life which has been identified (rightly or wrongly) as "middle class."

But that is an understanding which Clark seemed to find too embarrassing or too impolitic to admit. Understandably, he was not anxious to condemn even a small part of the black community or suggest that the fault really ran to the core of its moral codes; but whatever the motive, his inclination was to hold back in a posture of detachment. Instead of commending the character of middle-class life, he observed that middle-class communities simply had different pathologies of their own—more "alienation," perhaps, and suicide, and different forms of crime (e.g., "white collar crime"); and he professed to be uncommitted on the question of whether one set of pathologies was really any better or worse than the other. Clark put the question, rhetorically, of why blacks should exchange the pathologies of the ghetto for the pathologies, say, of the suburb. "Because," he answered, "the middle-class culture, whatever its frustrations, still remains the norm for personal achievement of the 'good life,' " and the choice of one culture over another involves "moral decisions [that] each individual has the right to make for himself, whether he choose well or ill."[17] In the last analysis, it is nothing more than a question of personal taste or consumer's choice. At best it is a matter of aligning oneself with the conventions that seem to be necessary for success in this society. As Clark has written in another place, the values and standards of the middle class "may be worth having and are saleable in the larger society, which is dominated by the middle class."[18] And there, one gathers, is the long and short of it.

In the slack of this kind of detachment, a clever man may begin to discover one or two saving points in any number of things that have borne, perhaps all too unevenly in the past, the reproach of common opinion. Clark suggests, for example, that there is something to be said at the margins even for illegitimacy for the sake of understanding it a bit better:

[17] Ibid., p. 108.

[18] Kenneth Clark and Jeannette Hopkins, *A Relevant War Against Poverty* (New York: Harper and Row, 1969), p. 53.

In the ghetto, the meaning of the illegitimate child is not ultimate disgrace. . . . The girl loses only some of her already-
limited options by having an illegitimate child; she is not going
to make a 'better marriage' or improve her economic and social
status either way. On the contrary, a child is a symbol of the
fact that she is a woman, and she may gain from having something of her own. . . . [There is a] desperate yearning of the
young for acceptance and identity, the need to be meaningful
to someone else even for a moment without implication of a
pledge of undying fealty and forgiveness.[19]

Against the mitigating tones of this portrait, there comes to mind
very crisply one of the interviews taped with residents of Harlem
and reproduced in *Youth in the Ghetto*:

Now some guys that walk around and say, man, well I knocked
this chick up, and now I'm putting her on the welfare, and I
knocked this chick up and now I'm putting *her* on the welfare.
You know, some of these guys, there's a name for them, they
call them the home-relief pets, you know, the home-relief pets,
and all he does is goes around whenever the check date comes
up he goes around, you know, and he gets so much money
from each one of the women, and he shortens the money.
[Man, about 27 years of age.][20]

No one who has reviewed Clark's writings can be left with many
doubts on the matter of his feelings, overall, about illegitimacy. He
would have the problem dissolved, and he would count a reduction
in the rate of illegitimacy as one clear sign of improvement in the
condition of the black community. But at some point one's un-
weighted feelings will simply not be good enough. When it becomes
evident that problems like illegitimacy and drug addiction will not
yield to the application of social welfare measures alone, our willingness to consider other measures of public policy will depend on
the gravity with which we regard these problems as real "problems." The call for a remedy, after all, implies a wrong to be
corrected, and it is a matter of some consequence, then, that as
Clark comes to the point of judgment over policy, he also weakens
in his surety that there is anything, really, in problems like illegitimacy that strictly deserves condemnation. And so, in *Youth in the
Ghetto*, Clark and his colleagues finally came to the judgment that,
while many of these "pathologies" were serious, they were not

[19] *Dark Ghetto*, pp. 72-73.   [20] *Youth in the Ghetto*, pp. 332-33.

serious *enough* to warrant any special emphasis in a remedial policy. It was their estimate that an emphasis on " 'building a better life' for the unhappy young people in question . . . is more likely to accomplish desired ends than too narrow a concern with the [problem at hand], be it gang fighting, drug use, or unwed motherhood."[21]

Similarly, when Clark came to concede that the source of pathologies in the ghetto did not lie primarily in unemployment, he made a shift also in the form of his argument. He no longer argued that problems like drug addiction should be treated through broad social policies designed to get at the foundations of the problem. He contended, rather, that it was futile to deal with problems of this kind through the general formulas of the law or through public policies that acted upon people in the aggregate.[22] The accent was placed now on the natures and frailties of individuals. It was Clark's assumption, however, that these were frailties of a psychological, rather than a moral, nature. They arose from a want of sufficient "ego" strength (rather than from any simple weakness of character), and their proper cure lay in therapy rather than in any regimen of legal restraint—or moral teaching. Clark preferred to attack the problem, as he said, through the counseling of individuals or the building of "egos," rather than with public measures that worked through the laws and carried the hint of coercive action.

The dilemma that afflicted Clark could be put in this way: his inclination was to argue for the presence of deeper social causes, and for the need of vaster efforts on the part of the government, so long as the plea seemed to lead toward a larger commitment by the government to support projects for "social welfare." Apparently the attraction of the argument was not to be found merely in the creation of more programs (though the programs did have the additional virtue of creating more jobs for psychologists and social workers). What seemed to be even more important about the existence of public measures was that they marked an assumption, in part, of public responsibility. They could be taken, in some quarters, as a concession that the main responsibility for the "pathologies" of individuals really lay with the larger society. But this attraction to public measures on a grand scale represented, as I say, only one side of Clark. On the other side, his impulse was to resist the intervention of the government. That disposition took hold when the issue in question no longer seemed to be one of insufficient

[21] Ibid., p. 356.   [22] See Clark in *Dark Ghetto*, p. 107.

spending on "social" programs, but the lack of success on the part of the government in combating the crimes of individuals.

This kind of "flexibility" may be handy at times, but in this instance it led Clark to evade some notable truths that he himself had once grasped. As Clark recognized, problems such as the epidemic of drug use or the instability of families could acquire a momentum of their own, and they could persist even in the face of rising employment. In fact, the relation to unemployment could be the reverse of what has often been expected: it may be rather hard to induce a young man who is unskilled to accept a legitimate job paying about $100 a week when he can make far more than that selling drugs on the street. Once again, Clark did not have very far to look for some fairly vivid testimony. In one of the interviews reported in *Youth in the Ghetto*, a "warlord" in one of the few active fighting gangs was asked why he did not "go downtown and get a job." He laughed at the man who asked the question and said:

> Oh, come on. Get off that crap. I make $40 or $50 a day selling marijuana. You want me to go down to the garment district and push one of those trucks through the street and at the end of the week take home $40 or $50 if I'm lucky? Come off it. They don't have animals doing what you want me to do. . . . I'm better than an animal, but nobody protects me. Go away, mister, I got to look out for myself.[23]

It is a reflection of the times that we have come to need economists to "prove" to us, with arcane formulas and statistical correlations, that potential criminals are indeed influenced by the relative costs and benefits involved, in choosing illegitimate over legitimate occupations.[24] And yet, in all of Clark's writings on the ghetto it would be hard to find a suggestion that law enforcement may ever have even a marginal effect on some of those problems that concern him. Clark's inclination on these matters was brought out rather clearly on the question of heroin. In *Youth in the Ghetto* he and

---

[23] *Youth in the Ghetto*, pp. 16-17.

[24] See, for example, on this point, Isaac Ehrlich, "The Deterrent Effect of Criminal Law Enforcement," *The Journal of Legal Studies*, Vol. 1, no. 2 (June 1972), pp. 259-76, especially 260. Mr. Ehrlich finds empirical support for a rather venerable conclusion: viz., that "even if those who violate certain laws differ systematically in various respects from those who abide by the same law, the former, like the latter, do respond to incentives: the opportunities (costs and gains) available to them in legitimate and illegitimate pursuits."

his collaborators spoke sharply of the "degradation" that went along with addiction to hard drugs. But apart from recommendations for psychological counseling and some hints of vigilante action in the neighborhoods, the authors strongly preferred the possibility of legalizing the use of heroin and morphine. They thought that the removal of legal penalties would reduce some of the excitement that made these drugs attractive, and they hoped that the problems of crime might recede if one did away with the laws that "created" the crimes in the first place.

By this stratagem, of course, one could easily "solve" the problems of crime that surround prostitution, the numbers racket, and a variety of other local industries that feed into underground networks. But we have an ample fund of evidence by now in matters ranging from gambling and abortion to the regulation of heroin in other countries, and we know enough at least to suggest that the use of heroin will not decline under a program of legalization. Nor, for that matter, will the structure of illegal operations disappear. The general tendency of legalization is to encourage an expansion of the practice that was formerly constrained—in large part simply because the legal restrictions have been removed, but also because the moral inhibitions have been swept aside from things that were previously regarded as forms of "vice." These activities are likely to expand then far beyond their present level, until they consume a larger portion of the resources of the community and draw off people and investment from other callings. The question for anyone who would offer this policy of legalization is: how would one regard the prospect of that expansion? Would it be, in general, a good or bad thing for the black community if, thirty years from now, it continued to have a disproportionately small share of skilled workers, doctors, and lawyers, and a disproportionately large share of pimps, prostitutes, and numbers runners? Even if the standard of living had gone up markedly, would one be willing to say also that things had "improved" in the black community?

If that was a matter which Clark was reluctant to judge, it nevertheless raised a question that had to be faced daily, in a more personal way, by people in the black community who had choices to make about their own lives. And it is a question, too, that lies within the power of the government to affect. By putting its weight on one side rather than the other, the community does have the power to make legitimate occupations more attractive and the illegitimate more costly. The question, for us, for Clark, is whether that distinction ought to matter. I will have occasion later to say something more about the grounds on which we can look again at the things we have traditionally called "vices," and still regard them, with justification, as "vices." For the moment it may be said that for most people, including most people in the black community, the difference between legitimate and illegitimate activities still seems to be taken seriously. It is taken seriously because there is something in the activities themselves that inspires a wariness rooted in experience, and which suggests, in sum, that the difference between the legitimate and the illegitimate is founded on something more than convention.

2. EDUCATION AND POWER STRUCTURES: CLARK'S POLITICAL TEACHING

It was no accident that Clark moved directly from the question of "pathologies" to the issue of education. As he discovered himself, his analysis had to move to a concentration on the character and motives of individuals, and it was education that seemed to be most important in accounting for the success of some individuals in leaving the ghetto. But in addition, it was the issue of education that carried Clark into his "political" argument and raised the most intriguing questions about the ultimate teaching of his work.

Despite the fact that education holds an important place in Clark's analysis, the subject was given a rather odd gloss in *Dark Ghetto*. For one thing, there was no reflection about the ends of education, even though Clark has been moved on numerous occasions to address himself to the moral responsibilities of scholarship and the connection between education and citizenship.[25] It seemed to be assumed in *Dark Ghetto* that the purpose of the schools was to equip children with the technical skills they would need in order to get along in a modern economy, and to achieve that task in a manner that would give all groups, essentially, an equal chance of success. But even with that limited sense of the mission of the schools, the argument was strangely elliptical, and one suspects that there was a purpose behind Clark's reticence. His conclusion, briefly put, was that "integrated" education was necessary to "good" education.[26] The judgments that led to the conclusion must have been, for him, rather melancholy, for Clark apparently came to believe quite deeply that a good education for

[25] See Clark, for example, in *Pathos of Power*, chs. 2 and 6.
[26] Clark, *Dark Ghetto*, p. 150.

black children depended on the presence of whites in the same classroom.

To be sure, Clark offered a gesture or two of assurance that there were techniques, known to professionals, which were bound to raise achievement in the schools, and presumably they would work regardless of whether the schools were integrated by race. He professed to be satisfied, for example, that "crash reading programs" worked, and that something like the "Hawthorne" device could bring results: that is, the performance of children would improve if their teachers showed an intense degree of interest in them, and if, in some cases, the children were gently deceived into believing that they were part of an "advanced" group.[27] There was, of course, the question of how teachers could sustain the intensity of interest over the years, or how they could keep conning slow children into believing they were geniuses.[28] Whether Clark actually believed all of this, it is hard to say. But even if he took it in whole, it was clear that these schemes could play, at best, only a secondary part in relation to the one thing that really was vital for education—and that, in his judgment, was racial integration.

If integration was the key, what stood in the way then of achieving it and bringing about a radical improvement in the performance of black children in the schools? The answer, in Clark's view, was the white middle classes. They opposed plans for the busing of children and the arrangement of racial balance in the schools, and when pressed on the issue, they deserted the central cities. In that way, they undercut the possibilities for integrated education, but they also deprived the city of tax resources that could be spent, in

[27] The "Hawthorne" experiments come from Fritz J. Roethlisberger and William J. Dickson, *Management and the Worker* (Cambridge: Harvard University Press, 1939). They refer to studies carried out at the Western Electric plant in Chicago, in which the researchers found that a group of female workers were increasing their productivity in response to virtually any change they introduced, even changes of a retrogressive nature—removing benches, shortening breaks, reducing the wattage in the light bulbs. The conclusion of the researchers was that the women kept working with greater energy because someone was taking an interest in them and their problems. And thus was born the field of Human Relations and Plant Psychology.

[28] On the other hand, there is some evidence that supports what has always been suspected as a matter of common sense: that even children from the poorest neighborhoods can be taught to read at their "grade level" if one provides rather intense drills in language and reading, and if teachers are willing to work uncommonly hard at the problem. See, on this matter, J. A. Fuerst, "Report from Chicago: A Program that Works," *The Public Interest* (Spring 1976), pp. 59-69.

part, on the problems of the black areas. The question of the white middle class raised the question, really, of how to act politically: How do political men justify their policies to those who are disposed to disagree? How do they earn the assent of their opponents; how do they elicit their obligation to obey? For Clark, the problem of dealing with the resistance of whites tested his understanding of the way in which politics moves and the way in which political power ought to be used.

Clark's first response, interestingly enough, had an elitist or authoritarian tinge. "[T]he economic princes of power," he said—the men he saw as the real "power elite" in any community—"can no longer take their cues from those marginal middle class whites whose immediate anxieties do not necessarily coincide with their own long-term interests or with the good of society as a whole."[29] That is to say, the answer was to stop worrying about the anxieties of the white middle classes and simply impose a solution upon them. The problem, though, as Clark realized almost immediately, is that in city politics the disaffected may have more than one way of resisting. If the authorities refuse to confront their objections and seek their assent, the resistant middle classes, black as well as white, may simply "vote with their feet" and leave for the suburbs.

The reservations of the public simply had to be faced—or some clever device had to be found for getting around them. Two alternatives stood out strongly to Clark in coping with the problem. First, one could deal in a straightforward way with the objections to busing and "racial balance" and perhaps even acknowledge, in a spirit of candor among equals, that many of the objections were reasonable. An effort could have been made then to allay the misgivings or seek out a ground of compromise: from Clark's perspective it might have been useful to consider, for example, just what kinds of integration people were willing to accept. Or it would have been revealing to learn that whites were willing to pay more in taxes in order to spend more on schools and programs that would benefit blacks.[30]

[29] Clark, *Dark Ghetto*, p. 152.

[30] The Survey Research Center found that there was a considerable balance of support among whites for this additional taxing and spending as well as for schemes of integration in which a minority of blacks might be taken into schools that were predominantly white. For example, 78 percent of the whites in the sample thought that the government ought to spend more money on the poorer schools in order to bring them up to the level of the better schools, and 53 percent were willing to have their own taxes increased by 10 percent if that were necessary to cover the cost. See Angus Campbell and Howard Schuman, *Racial Attitudes in Fifteen American Cities*

Second, and alternatively, one might simply find a better way of *imposing* a solution on the middle classes. One could try dealing with the powerful men behind the scenes, not men in politics but in business—the covert elites (as Clark thought) who really pulled the strings in any city.

As to the first approach—facing the objections of the public— Clark did seem to consider that alternative for a while. He remarked very early in his discussion on education that the core of the problem lay in the legitimate fears of white parents that integrated education would also mean poor education.[31] When stated in that way the motives of whites seemed at least to be decent, rather than malicious, and the problem could be addressed, as Clark said, simply by dispelling the fears about blacks and education. The most direct assurance, of course, was to show that blacks, when left to themselves, could in fact produce superior schools.

That was a game response, which seemed to accept for the moment a certain burden of proof for the black community, but accept it in a spirit of self-confidence. And yet, for some reason, that disposition was overcome when Clark finally came down on the side of the second alternative—dealing with the "economic princes of power." It is hard to avoid the inference that Clark moved away from the first approach because he did not have the confidence, in the end, that the black community could really shoulder that burden of proof. That is, when it came down to a hard choice, he apparently did believe, as he had said earlier, that racial integration was necessary to any good education. As a corollary of that judgment Clark must have feared that blacks could not match the level of the white schools, even if the same amount of money were spent. That has an uncomfortable sound today, and it should have been embarrassing even in the early 1960's. Strictly speaking, it did not require any special kind of empirical evidence to disprove that assumption, apart, of course, from the "evidence" showing that blacks shared the same faculties possessed by other human beings. Still, if there was a wish to see evidence in regard to schools, that evidence was not wanting. There were, after all, the examples of institutions such as Dunbar High School in Washington, Frederick Douglass in Baltimore, or St. Augustine in New Orleans. Those schools were virtually all black in composition; they routinely lacked the kinds of facilities and amenities that are associated with "good" high schools

---

(Ann Arbor: Institute for Social Research, 1968), p. 37, and see generally, pp. 29-38.

[31] *Dark Ghetto*, p. 150.

today; and yet they were persistently successful in preparing black students who would go on to distinguished careers in the professions.[32]

That part of the black experience, however, was not to be noticed in the 1950's or early 1960's, because it implicitly raised a challenge to the reigning orthodoxy of the time: viz., that an "integrated" education was necessary to a good education. And as a result, in large measure, of the public teaching of Kenneth Clark, an "integrated" education was understood to mean the presence of blacks and whites in the same schools according to some specified mix or ratio, although no one could say precisely just which ratio was "correct." That was a notably different standard from the one that found the offense of segregation in the practice of assigning students to schools on the basis of race with the purpose of keeping them apart. Clark has been up and down on this matter himself over the years, but although he has embraced schemes that run counter to integration (e.g., the "community control" of the schools) he has retained an attachment to the notion of an "integrated education" that runs beyond any justification he has been able to offer.[33]

Because of that sentiment perhaps, or because he simply felt impatient at the thought of seeking the consent of the white middle classes, his inclination was to deal with the problem of public resistance by taking the more elitist or authoritarian approach. He found his solution in the exercise of power of a manipulative kind, and he came to it in a rather ingenuous way. "In New York," he declared, "a conference of top business leaders like David Rockefeller, John Whitney, Robert Dowling could assume responsibility for deciding what must be done with the city's public educational system if the stability and viability of the metropolis are to be assured."[34] These words were written before the bitter school strikes of the late sixties in New York, when education became a highly politicized issue and Albert Shanker of the teachers' union became a household word. Still, it is hard to understand how anyone as familiar with the city as Kenneth Clark seemed to be would have credited David Rockefeller at the time with the power to impose

[32] See Thomas Sowell, "Patterns of Black Excellence," *The Public Interest* (Spring 1976), pp. 26-58, and his earlier piece, "Black Excellence: The Case of Dunbar High School," *The Public Interest* (Spring 1974), pp. 3-21.

[33] Clark's twists and turns on this question were traced more closely in my piece, "The Problem of Kenneth Clark," in *Commentary* (November 1974), pp. 37-46, at 38-43.

[34] *Dark Ghetto*, p. 153.

a policy in education against the resistance, say, of the bureaucracy that administered the system or the professionals who worked in the classrooms. That is to say nothing, of course, of the political leadership of the city, or of the leverage held by the electorate itself in a period of rising political activism. Perhaps it was because education had not yet emerged as the political issue it became in the late 1960's that there might have appeared to be a lot of "slack" in the system, an ample measure or room in which leaders could take the initiative without much opposition from the public.[35] Clark may have been expecting, in this way, that leaders could count on a certain insulation in making decisions on education; but on the other hand, if the resistance to integration ran as deeply as he thought, it could not have been expected realistically that the whole business could have been handled over drinks at the City Club.

Instead of facing the task of reconciling interests in a divided community, Clark sought to escape the problem by positing the existence of a hidden elite in the business community that really controlled the levers of power in the city. Whether cities in the United States are in fact generally governed in that way is a question that must be addressed at some point in any assessment of Clark's analysis, and I will take it up more directly in a later chapter. For the present, though, it is worth noting again the direction of Clark's argument. It ascended, one might say, from education to power structures and to the question of how political power ought properly to be exercised. Clark had already disclosed in part the kind of manipulation he was willing to accept in the exercise of authority for the sake of ends he regarded as good; and as he moved on through his analysis of power structures in the black community, he raised the issue again about the way in which power ought to be exercised and about the kinds of people who are fitted to govern. But the question was put this time in a manner that came considerably closer to himself.

To be clear on the point, Clark did not come forth with a real mapping of the structure of power in black areas or of the places in which that power structure meshes with the centers of power in the larger city. What Clark offered instead was a portrait of the black community filled with a variety of political actors and groups, but with no evident structure. Still, that portrait did capture a certain truth, for what stood out to Clark as the main problem was

[35] One notable sign of the times in this respect was that Banfield and Wilson's classic book, *City Politics*, published in 1963, contained no separate chapter devoted to education or its politics in the city.

the task of building a sense of civic cohesion. The black community has suffered within itself, and in its relations with outsiders, through its inability to cohere in support of its own civic organizations. This problem has been far more than a matter of mechanics or even money. The community has not been notably successful in cultivating what Tocqueville called the "art of associating together." And its difficulty has arisen precisely from the fact that it has not been able to foster a common understanding about the proper terms of principle on which those associations ought to be formed. There has been a serious question in recent years about the moral perspectives or the sense of ends to which the black community is willing to commit itself. But even when the community was less divided in its moral understandings, it was plagued by an infirmity of commitment, a pervasive unwillingness to tax itself to support its own civic leadership.

James Q. Wilson once provided a telling comparison on this point. In the 1920's the Jewish population in Chicago numbered around 285,000, and since it contained many immigrant families it was by no means a population that was uniformly wealthy. And yet in 1923 that community was able to raise $2.5 million for Jewish charities, and two years later it managed to oversubscribe a drive for $4 million. In contrast, the NAACP in 1954-1955 was able to elicit only $50,000 from a black population in Chicago of 750,000 (i.e., a population three times as large as the Jewish population in the 1920's).[36] Clearly, differences in wealth could not have accounted for differences of this magnitude. There was obviously enough money in the black community to yield far more than what was raised by the NAACP. The problem facing the leadership of black organizations is that money tends to be channeled into individual consumption more than anything else, and the habit was not formed in the community to impose levies on itself for its own civic purposes. No one has voiced these criticisms with more severity than black leaders themselves, and the theme of complaint can be traced back even to the period before the Civil War when free blacks still had before them the task of ending slavery. Frederick Douglass wrote in 1848:

> [I]t is a shame that we, who are enduring wrongs far more grievous than any other portion of the great family of man, are comparatively idle and indifferent about our welfare. We confess, with the deepest mortification, that out of the five

[36] James Q. Wilson, *Negro Politics* (Glencoe: The Free Press, 1960), p. 325.

hundred thousand free colored people in this country, not more than two thousand can be supposed to take any special interest in measures for our own elevation; and probably not more than fifteen hundred take, read and pay for an anti-slavery paper. We say this in sorrow, not in anger. It cannot be said that we are too poor to patronize our own press to any greater extent than we now do; for in popular demonstrations of odd-fellowship, free-masonry and the like, we expend annually from ten to twelve thousand dollars. If we put forth a call for a National Convention, for the purpose of considering our wrongs, and asserting our rights, and adopting measures for our mutual elevation and the emancipation of our enslaved fellow-countrymen, we shall bring together about *fifty*; but if we call a grand celebration of odd-fellowship, or free-masonry, we shall assemble, as was the case a few days ago in New York, from *four to five thousand*—the expense of which alone would be from seventeen to twenty thousand dollars, a sum sufficient to maintain four or five efficient presses, devoted to our elevation and improvement.[37]

Echoes of the same complaint can be found today among black civic leaders and their white allies.[38] What Kenneth Clark came to realize was that, even with all the talk of a "white power structure," there was unexploited power available in the system, and it went unexploited largely because the black community could not overcome the jealousies and divisions that undermined its discipline. As Clark saw it, there was still too much suspicion of the black person who set himself apart in any way, and that suspicion made it very difficult to mobilize the community in a disciplined, organizational way behind a stable corps of leaders. (Bringing crowds out into the street every now and then, or inducing children to boycott school for a day were not quite the same thing.) But when it was expressed in this way, the problem of power was translated into something of a higher order: it became the task of shaping the character of the community by establishing the legitimacy of a certain kind of leadership.

It was a familiar understanding in classic thought that leaders

[37] Frederick Douglass, "What are the Colored People Doing for Themselves?" (July 14, 1848), in Herbert J. Storing, ed., *What Country Have I?: Political Writings by Black Americans* (New York: St. Martin's Press, 1970), pp. 41-46, at 42. Emphasis in the original.

[38] James Q. Wilson has collected a number of commentaries on this theme in *Negro Politics*, note 36 above, pp. 158-59.

would embody the qualities that were held up for emulation in the community. These people were elevated, after all, to positions of authority over the whole society. They were given, at once, the highest visibility and the most decisive political weight, and so they could not help but stand out as models of the kinds of people who were publicly esteemed, the kinds of people who were thought to deserve the highest legal power in the community. Inescapably, then, they held out examples in public of the traits of character that the community regarded as "authoritative" in a deeper sense. For that reason the act of establishing the legitimacy of a new leadership may be equivalent to an act of *founding*. It entails nothing less than the act of establishing the moral bases of a new order, for it involves, at its root, an effort to form the opinions of the community about the traits of character and the "way of life" that ought to be regarded as superior.

3. Toward a New Founding? The Social Scientist as Leader

It was apparently with an understanding of that kind that Clark came to make the case for the "social scientist" as a political leader in the community. The connection to himself, of course, was too obvious to be missed, and he went on to reveal a part of his own experience that might have led him to make this case, as it were, for himself. He recalled involvement at an earlier time with what had been referred to as "the Group," a small collection of educated blacks who were prominent in government and the professions. They were brought together by their common interest in politics and the affairs of the black community, but after a while they began to lose heart over their own lack of influence. Their morale began to ebb until, finally, one gathers, they simply drifted apart.[39] At some point, however, it surely must have occurred to these men that their own legitimacy had to be suspect. They were not, after all, like most blacks in their education, their professions, or their styles of life, and so they did not really represent the community in any simple descriptive sense. It might have been argued, however, that they had a claim to represent the community in a rather different sense—as the kind of men whom people in the community should most wish to be like, or the kind of men who were most qualified to guide the community in its public life. But if that were

[39] See *Dark Ghetto*, pp. 186-88.

the claim, the case had to be made: the task for the erstwhile members of "the Group" was to plant within their community a critical esteem for that life of which they themselves were examples. It was with this problem in mind, apparently, that Clark came to offer his brief for the social scientist as leader.

Two grounds of argument stand out most strikingly in Clark's writings, and it made a serious difference as to which ground of argument he finally settled on in making his case. In the first line of argument, the case for the social scientist was bound up with what he called the "strategy of truth." By that he meant the systematic analysis of social problems by trained professionals, people who could make use of their knowledge to clarify the facts about our problems, and in clarifying the facts, sharpen the recognition of our public duties. In Clark's words, "the search for truth, while impotent without implementation in action, undergirds every other strategy in behalf of constructive social change. None could proceed toward democratic ends without it."[40] If this argument were taken at its best level, it might be read to mean that politics is in fact better—it is a higher kind of politics—when it proceeds through the discipline of giving reasons. This view may affirm the old understanding that, in a regime based on natural equality, the exercise of power does not carry its own justification. Those who would govern others have an obligation to establish the justice of what they are doing, and the highest claim then to govern goes to those who are most likely to act wisely, with a concern for the principled grounds of their public acts.

There is a second argument, though, that threads through Clark's writings. In *A Relevant War on Poverty*, he and his colleague recalled a "poor people's convention" held in Washington in 1966, which broke down into a carnival of meanness and disorder. Sargent Shriver walked out, saying that he would not "participate in a riot," and Roy Wilkins called it a spectacle of "self-degrading bad taste and language."[41] The authors thought, however, that the judgment was too harsh, and they suggested in a gentler way that "the language of the poor and their representatives is likely to be more direct, blunt, and accusatory. The etiquette of indirection, circumlocution, or equivocation does not seem to operate for the poor in their communications with officials." They went on to advise that "the poor's lack of ability to make contact with power

[40] Ibid., p. 221.
[41] *A Relevant War on Poverty*, p. 195.

sources dictates, however, their need for surrogates. . . ."[42] Now it may well be that the higher reaches of business and government contain, in increasing numbers, men who respond more readily to the vocabulary of social science and who tend to nod in a knowing way when someone speaks of "systems," "inputs," and "options." But the simple fact of the matter may be, as Clark has suggested elsewhere, that white leaders in business and government (men such as David Rockefeller or John Whitney) would much prefer to deal with people like themselves—responsible, cultivated, educated men—rather than with the grosser variety of streetcorner militants. They may prefer to deal, in short, with men like Kenneth Clark.

In the first of these arguments, the power of the social scientist as leader would be predicated on his ability to offer reasons that are understandable to the people he would represent. In the second, his authority would rest on personal qualities that are not accessible to the community at large and that cannot be shared. As to which of these understandings was the one that finally moved Clark, we are left to make our own inference. To embrace the first argument, he could not be neutral on the question of whether the politics of giving reasons, or the way of life represented by the scholar, was in fact a higher kind of politics or a better way of life. He could hardly be detached on that question any more than he could be neutral on the matter of whether "middle-class" life was in principle superior to the character of lower-class life. But Clark's disposition in these issues he has already made known, and he has disclosed also his estimate of how much, in politics, the art of giving reasons is really worth. Looking back on the decision of the Supreme Court in *Brown* v. *Board of Education*, he wrote that the knowledge and advice of the social scientist were probably sought in "inverse relation" to the significance of the problems raised by any particular issue and the importance of the political interests that they touched. It was his judgment in the end that "the acceptance or rejection of [the] facts, knowledge, advice [of the social scientist] is determined by the degree to which these are compatible with the prevailing power-determined point of view."[43] That was, all things considered, a strange reflection on the *Brown* case, which was scarcely trivial in the political interests that it touched. It was a strange reflection, that is, unless Clark really had believed even then what he was inclined to assert now: that reasons did not in fact have much

[42] Ibid., pp. 196, 198.
[43] Kenneth Clark, *Prejudice and Your Child* (Boston: Beacon Press; revised edition, 1963), p. 208.

independent weight in politics. In that event, it could only be presumed that the task of the social scientist was to dress up in a more academic form the decisions that men in authority, including men in judicial authority, were compelled to make as a result of other forces.

But apart from the cynicism that Clark affected in public as a brand of "realism," one suspects that it was the first of the arguments on leadership that he would prefer after all; or at least one would wish that to be the case. For in that first understanding, the distance between the leaders and the community would in principle have been bridged. The scholar as leader would indeed have represented something of what the community aspired to be, and to that extent he would have taught something through his personal example that the community wished to be taught. Beyond that, he would have fulfilled the conditions of his legitimacy when he did the very things he was supposed to do well: when he was articulate and reflective in defining the ends of the community; when he gave reasons that were not merely good enough to get through the political day, but reasons that a community of worldly and mature people could credit. He would have reminded us then also that leaders satisfy the discipline of leadership in a republic when they can "give an account" of themselves, when they can justify their decisions and their authority to the community they would presume to lead, and in that way face the test of truth themselves.

TWO

EDUCATION

VII

EQUITY AND COMITY IN
THE SCHOOLS

Kenneth Clark's argument about the ghetto advanced to the question of education, and from there it ascended, as I have argued, to the question of power structures. It moved from the schools to the "school system," and the management of the schools was bound up in turn with the legal and political structures that governed the city as a whole. It is my intention, in the chapters that follow, to pursue the threads that lead out in this way from Clark's analysis. I will consider a number of questions about the principles that may govern the public schools, and I will move to that point at which the management of the schools merges with those structures of power that envelop the entire city. The argument at its further reaches would take in the question of political machines; the leverage of public employees in politics; and the policies on housing and integration which may affect in a serious way the composition of the community and the prospects for party organizations. At the same time one will find in these chapters extensions of many of the principles that were established in the earlier sections on civility and the law. The purpose here, once again, is to draw out some of the implications of those "first principles" as one moves through the problems of policy that arise in the city.

1. A Son of Harvard in the Schools of Boston

Apart from the management of public schools, the question of education would include matters like the performance of children in the classroom or the problem of integration and busing. These are the kinds of questions that must be assayed, in most cases, in aggregate measures; and when questions are reckoned in this way, on larger scales, there may be some advantage in coming to them first through the medium of a concrete, personal case.

In the late 1960's Jonathan Kozol drew a large, sympathetic audience with his book, *Death at an Early Age*,[1] which offered a

---

[1] *Death at an Early Age* (Boston: Houghton Mifflin, 1967); my references will be to the popular, Bantam Books edition (1967).

narrative of his experience as a young teacher in the Boston school system. Kozol worked in Roxbury, in a rather rundown school that was largely black, and his verdict on his colleagues and superiors could be read in the subtitle of his memoir: "The Destruction of the Hearts and Minds of Negro Children in the Boston Public Schools." The picture he painted was a pathetic one of buildings in a state of drabness and disrepair, and of teachers and administrators who ground the students into numbness with their materials and their regimens and their inculcation of a singsong morality.

In Kozol's school there were desks with their tops ripped off, portable blackboards that came crashing down, and in general the building had a forbidding aspect that was more suitable to a workhouse than a school. There were often not enough books to go around, and even when there were, the books themselves were at best irrelevant to the circumstances of the black children, and at worst, offensive to blacks as a race. Even if one did not happen to believe that these arrangements would affect the morale and performance of children in the school, they were important to Kozol for what they seemed to reveal about the attitudes of the authorities. These circumstances seemed to indicate the place held by the children and their families in the estimation of those people who managed the public schools: a central administration that was not anxious to repair the broken windows or redecorate the school was an administration, also, that did not care (it seemed) to provide crossing guards or policemen for the streets. The whole thing went hand in hand with a system where corporal punishment was still used extensively with a rattan; where teachers and administrators consistently underrated the capacities of black children; and where the aims of education seemed to be focused, in their one common point, on the aim of rendering the children submissive.

That the children had to be rendered obedient in part, that some sense of order had to be established in their classroom and their lives, is something Kozol never denies. But the preservation of order, he quite properly thought, was not inconsistent with a certain humaneness, or with an effort to appeal to the children with materials that were more resonant with their own lives. He recalls the time he brought a book of Langston Hughes's poetry to class. The children immediately noticed that there was a black face on the dust jacket, and they were anxious right away to learn more about Hughes himself. After Kozol read some poems from the book, the children began to come up one by one to borrow the volume overnight. That was true even of the "slowest" readers, and after a while many of the children, in their own fascination, committed sections of the book to memory. The story could be retold in a number of different instances, but the point is that it was all quite compatible—did one ever doubt it?—with the preservation of order in the classroom. Beyond that, this enticement to learning could be accomplished with a group of students who were rather below the average.

But if that was the case, there is a temptation to say that "the problem" in the schools was essentially one of finding sensitive teachers with a deft touch. Kozol never doubted for a moment that teachers made a difference; and yet the thread running through his book was that the problems in the schools reflected a larger negligence or malevolence, and that they were bound up with the conditions of a "segregated" education. In that perspective Kozol's own firing comes to stand as a case in point. His dismissal is presented to the reader with no hint of preparation, as a jarring but natural incident in the system. The firing of Kozol is not only the dramatic culmination of the book, but a lesson of some importance—viz., that certain school systems simply will not seek or retain good teachers. Or, if they do retain them, these systems will gradually bend them, through their established routines, until they become functionaries who are more compatible with the character of the system itself.

And yet there is a matter here of sorting out the strands. There are, in Kozol's account, many crosscurrents of feelings and observations, but one is left with the question of whether the essential problem in education stems from institutions or from persons. Does the success of children in the schools depend more on their own natures and abilities, or on the character and stability of their families, or does it depend, on the other hand, on certain forces emanating from the "system"? The "system," could have been understood here to involve any one of several things. It could have referred to the educational bureaucracy—to the character of the administration or to the problems that are inherent in administering a system equitably across a community of widely different ethnic and religious groups. Or the "system" could conceivably have included the political system—the political setting in which the board of education operates; the procedures by which people are selected to run the educational establishment; and the way in which political leadership may shape the ends and character of public education.

Kozol, of course, would have been the last to claim that he looked at the problem with the strictness of a philosopher, and he might have argued also that what he regarded as "success" in education might not be reducible to the measures used by social scientists. But philosophers are not the only ones who are obliged to set forth their arguments precisely; and one need not be a social scientist in order to be concerned about the kinds of evidence that may be pertinent in judging a case. The ends of education are not entirely ineffable, and if they can be expressed, they can in part, at least, be measured. We would not expect standardized tests to measure the depth of wisdom that may be imparted by our civilization or even to gauge the fullness of that competence which can be cultivated in schools. But if it is tenable to insist that schools are indeed capable of conveying knowledge, it is not unreasonable to take some modest soundings now and then in order to see what the students have learned. It is not clear that we would use these methods for the purposes of selecting a brain surgeon or filling a professorial chair in eighteenth-century literature. But for certain limited purposes (for example, in measuring some essential skills of literacy) these tests may tell us one or two useful things that are still related, after all, to the basic mission of the schools.

It was certainly open to Kozol to argue that the conveying of knowledge and the cultivation of discipline are only a small part of what education is about, and that the real end of education is to create "humane" people. That is an unexceptionable point, and it is supported by a venerable tradition. But that tradition carried with it also a sense of the parts of human nature that were higher and lower and which defined, then, the things that were more or less distinctly "humane." The traditional understanding of education discriminated, in other words, between the attributes that defined better or worse human beings; and for all of Kozol's pleadings for a "humane" education, the one thing he declined to offer was a judgment on the things that marked the difference between a "good" and a "bad" man.

As for the efforts of his colleagues to supply the rudiments of that teaching—and supply it, to be sure, in an overly precious and bumbling way—he had nothing but contempt. What they were trying to do, he said, was impose upon the children "a concoction of pretty shopworn middle-class ideas." Those were mainly, he added, "the values of a parched and parochial and rather grim and beaten lower middle-class."[2] That ethic was being pressed, in his judgment, against a "very substantial and by no means barren

[2] Ibid., p. 81.

lower-class culture," which he was reluctant to say should be replaced by a collection of "shopworn middle-class ideas." Whether the values he had in mind were nothing more than the values of a "middle class" is a question I cannot take up at this moment, but to see the problem in that way—to stand outside a social class and set its values, rather knowingly, in their proper place—is already to affirm a sense of one's own class superiority. But exactly what ethic Kozol holds up is something he does not tell us, and what is missing from the story, of course, is the question of whether the children he has taught have turned out to be yet, in any real sense, *better*.

In the *Gorgias* Plato has Socrates twit those Sophists who claimed to be teachers of goodness and yet often ended up accusing their pupils of wronging them by withholding their fees. "And what can be more illogical," asks Socrates, "than this claim that . . . men who have been stripped of injustice by their teacher . . . should act unjustly."[3] If Kozol claims to have taught his students to be more humane, someone may be churlish enough one day to ask for the evidence. They may even wish to see one or two "good men" who have been produced by his tutelage. But if the claims here are slightly more prosaic, if they deal with the success of children in achieving competencies, then it is entirely proper to consider the empirical evidence that is available on the subject. For it is thoroughly warranted to consider just how much of the problem lies, as Kozol believed, with the things that schools failed to provide, and how much of it stands outside the power of the schools to correct.

2. DISTRIBUTIVE JUSTICE IN THE SCHOOLS: SOME EMPIRICAL FINDINGS

Kozol was no doubt right in believing that schools and teachers made a difference. For most of the skills that children learn in mathematics, science and, in some respects, even language, they learn in school, and that is especially the case for lower-class children. Surely, too, it makes a difference as to whether students have books and laboratories and working supplies. Beyond that, it seems plausible on its face that the design and amenities of a school may have an effect on the morale of teachers as well as students. But having said all that, the question is whether the diffusion of schools

[3] *Gorgias*, 519c.

and facilities in this country has not in fact already proceeded to the point of eliminating most of the important differences that might result from disparities between schools. That wide disparities still exist, as, for example, between the schools of Scarsdale or Winnetka, on the one hand, and the schools of Cicero and Newark, on the other, is not to be doubted. And yet if we take the schools over the whole country, or if we compare them by region, the schools in which most blacks find themselves are not, altogether, so strikingly different from the schools of most whites, from the point of view at least of basic expenditures and amenities.

In a reanalysis, for example, of the data in the famous Coleman Report,[4] David Armor put together an index of "school facilities" that contained 26 items. The list included such things as the age of buildings and textbooks; the size of libraries; the availability of speech therapists and remedial teachers; special classes for both slow and rapid learners; the backgrounds of principals; and the tenure and turnover of teachers. Depending on the number of items that were present, the score for each school could fall between 0 and 26. With data from 1,562 elementary schools, or 95 percent of the schools in the sample, Armor found that for the country as a whole, with no control for regions, the "black schools" had a mean score on the index of 12.2. The "white schools," in comparison, had a score of 12.7. The sample was divided among seven regions, and then again by "metropolitan" and "nonmetropolitan" sections. It was found that, in four of six comparisons by metropolitan area,[5] black schools showed slightly higher mean index scores, while in the four nonmetropolitan regions where comparisons were possible (Mid-Atlantic, Great Lakes, South, and Southwest), white schools showed higher mean scores.[6]

This discrepancy between the metropolitan and the nonmetropolitan regions seemed to provide the most striking difference in the comparisons. Across the different regions, of course, the dis-

---

[4] James S. Coleman et al., *Equality of Educational Opportunity* (Washington: U.S. Government Printing Office, 1966).

[5] There were too few schools in the seventh region, New England, to permit a comparison between metropolitan and nonmetropolitan areas.

[6] The differences ranged from 0.2 in the Mid-Atlantic region (a mean index score of 13.2 for the white schools, compared with 13.0 for the black schools) to 2.7 in the Great Lakes area (10.6 for the whites, against 7.9 for the blacks). David Armor, "School and Family Effects on Black and White Achievement: A Reexamination of the USOE Data," in Frederick Mosteller and Daniel P. Moynihan, eds., *On Equality of Educational Opportunity* (New York: Random House, 1972), pp. 168-229, at 187.

parities by race could be magnified. The scores would range, for
example, from a high of 15.9 in the index figures for white schools
in the metropolitan Pacific area to a low of .7.9 for black schools
in the nonmetropolitan area of the Great Lakes and 8.9 in the
nonmetropolitan South. But in the Pacific metropolitan region, the
black schools had a score of 15.7 (that is, a difference of only 0.2
from the white schools), and the white schools in the nonmetropolitan South had a mean of 9.8 (only .9 higher than the black
schools). The figures suggested then overall that nonmetropolitan
areas had much lower scores than metropolitan areas, and to the
extent that more blacks were in regions with the lowest mean scores,
they were likely to be that much worse off nationally. *But within
the separate regions, the differences between black and white
schools were simply not statistically significant.*[7]

The differences between black and white schools were not nearly
as great as the disparities that showed up among the regions. Those
differences had become in fact so insubstantial statistically that one
could virtually rule out any contention that black schools in the
country were being systematically shortchanged. Several years of
federal aid to education, and the policies of the Kennedy-Johnson
administrations, had produced some effect, after all, on the amount
of money spent on black schools.

In gauging the rate of expenditure per pupil on the schools,
Armor took the salaries of teachers as a representative measure.
The salaries of teachers account for more than half the expenditure
on the schools, and the correlation with overall expenditures per
pupil has been thought to be rather high.[8] As Armor found, the

---

[7] Armor notes, for example, that, within the nine areas defined by region and size,
the difference in the mean scores between black and white schools seldom approached one half of a standard deviation. Without getting into a formal statement
of what a "standard deviation" is or how it is computed, it may be enough to say
that the standard deviation is a measure of the degree of dispersion around a mean.
It so happens that one standard deviation unit to either side of a mean would mark
off that area in which about 68 percent of the cases would fall. And so, for example,
a standard deviation of 3.7 in the index scores for all the schools in the sample
would mean that 68 percent of the schools had scores that fell within a range of 3.7
units to either side of the mean (12.6)—which is to say, within a range of 8.9 to
16.3. The larger the standard deviation, the wider the range in which 68 percent
of the sample is arrayed—and so the greater the degree of dispersion around the
mean. A distance of about two standard deviations from the mean would take in
approximately 95 percent of the cases, and it is this degree of difference that most
professionals take as the minimum measure of statistical significance.

[8] Christopher Jencks has estimated that the correlation is probably around the
level of 0.7 to 0.8. (A figure of 1.0 would mark a perfect positive correlation, and

results again were fairly mixed. In the Mid-Atlantic area, black schools had a mean expenditure per pupil of $258, which fell below the average of $284 in the white schools. In the nonmetropolitan South, black schools averaged $163 per pupil, which was $9 less than the white schools. And yet, as Armor also noted, in six of the ten comparisons the black schools had the higher average. (The largest difference, $44, occurred in the Southwest nonmetropolitan area.) It has to be borne in mind, though, that the differences, again, amount to only a small fraction of the standard deviation,[9] which means that the "lead" of the black schools in these areas could be a mere accident in the sample. Another sample might just as well produce a small edge for white schools.[10] But if the lead of the black schools is uncertain, the uncertainty is a measure of the fact that the differences, as they show up here, are not very significant statistically.[11]

To judge the quality of teachers, an index of six items was devised that covered their background and preparation. The survey took notice of formal degrees and graduate work, but it considered also whether teachers had majored, in college, in one of the liberal arts or the sciences rather than education. In addition, the survey sought to include teaching experience and the degree of professional involvement (as seen, for example, in efforts to keep up with professional journals). It was, again, a gross instrument, since there was no easy way of comparing the quality of the educations received by the teachers, and the measure was, of course, blind to those special personal qualities—to warmth or persuasiveness or even simple clarity—that made some people better or worse teachers. Still, the index was responsive to some of the most obvious public criteria that are used as minimal tests by administrators in the assessment and recruitment of faculties. By these tests, the mean score of black schools was slightly higher over the nation than the score of white schools (3.1 to 2.8). Within the separate regions, again the results were mixed. Only four areas showed differences

---

−1.0 a perfect negative correlation.) For Jencks's comment, see his "The Coleman Report and the Conventional Wisdom," in Mosteller and Moynihan, note 6 above, pp. 69-115, at 91.

[9] See note 7 above.   [10] See Armor, note 6 above, pp. 193-95.

[11] Using the same data but concentrating on Northern urban schools, Jencks found that the difference between black and white schools in expenditure per pupil was less than $5 (and by that he seemed to mean the difference in the mean expenditures). He also found that the difference in expenditure between the schools serving lower- and middle-class children was only $1. See Jencks, note 8 above, p. 91.

that were large enough to approach one standard deviation (.6), and in all four it was the black schools that had the higher averages.[12]

It was found, though, that two of the four regions were the South and Southwest, and that most of the teachers in these schools were black. There were some grounds to suspect then that the preparation of these black teachers (probably in all-black Southern colleges) might not really have been comparable to the preparation of teachers in the North. The suspicion deepened somewhat when a test of verbal achievement among the teachers reversed the position of the black schools. The standard deviation among black schools was more than twice that of white schools in the aggregate (which is to say, the range of variability was much wider among the black schools), and in all ten comparisons within the regions black schools fell below white schools in their mean scores.[13]

And so once again the evidence is equivocal: as for those formal badges that professional educators seem universally to demand, black schools will be compelled to gather them no less than white schools. The funds they have for attracting teachers are about equal to the funds available to white schools, particularly in the metropolitan areas of the North. Still, the market will not yield to them teachers of the same caliber that is available elsewhere. For that to occur, there have to be motivations and incentives on the part of whites that cannot easily be generated by boards of education. And in the South, where the problem is most severe, it would probably be hard to move toward parity very quickly through the integration of staffs without displacing large numbers of black teachers and in that way, perhaps, creating even further hardships.

Kozol was intensely persuaded of the importance of newer books, which could appeal to black children with a fresher and, possibly, more sensitive format. But Christopher Jencks found, when he reviewed figures on the urban schools in the North, that the access of children to books was only marginally affected by race and class. Both black and poor children were just a bit more likely to be in schools without a library or a librarian. But even so, there was a somewhat larger number of books available to the average black child than to the average white child, and as far as anything could be learned from the evidence, the distribution of newer books was, again, unrelated to race and class.

What is more to the point, neither libraries nor textbooks had

[12] Armor, p. 188.   [13] Ibid., pp. 190, 192.

any consistent relation to the performance of children as measured by standard tests in reading, mathematics, and verbal ability. In fact, schools that reported "enough" textbooks were likely to fall farther below the norm in "verbal ability" scores than they were likely to rise above it. And a school that kept its textbooks a year longer than another school was likely to score somewhat higher than a school that was more up-to-date. In any event, the differences were not very substantial. As Jencks put it, the disparities in performance were "so uniformly trivial" that it would be tempting to discount them entirely except for the one point they do suggest: that students with more access to books tend consistently to do worse on verbal achievement tests. The findings might herald some crisis for the publishers of American books, but the more likely explanation, as Jencks suggests, is that schools with children falling below the norm in reading ability are likely to invest more heavily in new libraries and textbooks.[14] Whatever can be said about the conditions that prevailed in Kozol's school, it would be hard to argue that black students in general are cut off from the books they need in order to achieve the national norm in reading.

On balance, the reconsideration of the evidence in the Coleman Report has tended to confirm the lines of the main findings: very little of the variance in the achievement of children in schools can be explained by arrangements in the schools themselves (e.g., facilities, curricula, teachers). A far more substantial amount of the variance can be explained by factors "outside" the school—most notably, the family backgrounds and the social composition of the student body. This is not to say, of course, that there was a complete absence of disagreement among the scholars who reconsidered the Coleman study. John Kain and Eric Hanushek argued, among other things, that through incomplete data and a misplaced preference for methods of multiple regression, the Coleman study was biased in the direction of overstating the effects of family and social background while understating the effects of the schools themselves. They also raised the tenable point (which no one, however, had denied) that the Coleman Report suffered as a result of its concentration on aggregates (e.g., on the mean scores of all children within a school), rather than on the performances of individual students. In that vein, as they observed, the study was weakened by the absence of "longitudinal" data, which could trace the same children over time. Lacking that kind of information, the Coleman group

[14] Jencks, p. 95.

fell back to making inferences about the progression from the first to the sixth grade simply by comparing the records of first- and sixth-graders.[15]

Fortunately the statistical findings of social science are irrelevant to any public policy that involves the assignment of students by law to particular schools. In this, as in other instances, the law must establish a foundation of principle that is quite independent of any findings that are merely contingent and statistical. (On this point I will have more to say later.) Citizens with a passing interest could be content then to let the statisticians settle the disputes within their own house before attaching too much importance to their findings in our public policy. For the present, those findings hold some interest because they show the wide disparity that prevails in the level of achievement of students, both *within* and between schools, both within and between racial groups. As I will show in awhile, they also reveal what is radically flawed in any effort to use the findings of the social sciences as the bases for policies on integration and busing. Therefore, whether Kain and Hanushek are more right than Jencks and Armor does not ultimately matter very much in settling the grounds of the law in relation to race and education. The marshaling of evidence on either side may help us discover what is important to the performance of black children in the schools, though even on that score there is reason to believe that some traditional and common-sense understandings—for example, on the benefit of discipline and commitment and a will to learn— may be quite as relevant as anything we are likely to discover with the help of regression equations.[16]

But in the meantime it may be worth noting, in response to Kain and Hanushek, that there is another study, which managed to trace the same group of children over a period of three years, and its results were virtually the same as the findings in the Coleman Report.[17] As Marshall Smith has written recently, the reconsideration of the data in the Coleman study has, if anything, strengthened the

[15] See Hanushek and Kain, "On the Value of *Equality of Educational Opportunity* as a Guide to Public Policy," in Mosteller and Moynihan, note 6 above, pp. 116-45, at 137.

[16] See, for example, Thomas Sowell, "Patterns of Black Excellence," *The Public Interest* (Spring 1976), pp. 26-58.

[17] See Mabel Purl and Judith Dawson, "The Effect of Integration on the Achievement of Elementary Pupils" (Riverside, California School District, March 1969), reprinted in U.S. Senate, Select Committee on Equal Educational Opportunity, *Hearings* (Washington: U.S. Government Printing Office, 1971), Part 9B, pp. 4834-72.

original findings in the Report: even without controls for other variables, facilities and curricula explain less than 2 percent of the total variance in verbal achievement scores for sixth and ninth grade children. For twelfth graders these factors still account for no more than 3 to 5 percent of the variance. When controls are added for other variables, the unique contribution made by facilities and curricula (that is to say, the amount of variance they explain that is not accounted for by other factors) remains at less than 2 percent in all instances.[18]

The Coleman group were not able to correlate the backgrounds of individual students with their scores on achievement tests, and so the data on family backgrounds have been understood more accurately as reflections of the local neighborhood or community. Still, something might be learned by considering the profile of family characteristics that describes each separate school. There were a number of measures that stood out as important: the proportion of students who had both parents living at home; the proportion of fathers who were in white-collar occupations; and the education of both parents. Finally, the study group added another index, called "household items," which was supposed to offer a rough sense of the standard of living of the family. The list included major household appliances, along with an automobile and telephone, and it extended also to such items as a dictionary, an encyclopedia, and a daily newspaper.

In all of these measures the mean index scores of black schools fell below the scores of white schools, and the differences were especially noticeable in the stability of families and the number of fathers in white-collar jobs. For the nation as a whole, white schools had an average of 80 percent of their children having both parents living at home. In the case of blacks, the average was 55 percent, and within the separate regions, the differences between white and black schools in this respect was often as large as one and two standard deviations.[19] As far as parental occupations were concerned, white schools in the nation showed 31 percent of the students with fathers in white-collar jobs. The comparable national figure for black schools was 16 percent, and the differences re-

[18] Marshall Smith, "*Equality of Educational Opportunity*: The Basic Findings Reconsidered," in Mosteller and Moynihan, note 6 above, pp. 230-321, at 283-84.

[19] Armor, note 6 above, p. 204. The standard deviation for black schools nationally was 14 percent—which meant, for example, that two-thirds of the black schools in the nation fell into a range on this measure of 14 percent above or below the mean, i.e., in a range of 41 to 69 percent.

mained consistent (though sometimes smaller) within the separate regions.[20]

And yet, the evidence suggested that there was very little correlation between either family structure or white-collar backgrounds and the level of achievement of black students in standardized verbal tests.[21] It turned out that, of all the variables, the number of "household items" and the education of the parents were the strongest correlates of achievement for both races. For white schools, the percentage of white-collar fathers proved to be a somewhat stronger factor than it was among blacks, and there were certain variations here between the North and the South. In the North, for black and white schools alike, the correlations between the achievement of students and the attributes of the schools were described by David Armor as "practically insignificant." But in the South those correlations were stronger, particularly in the case of black schools. Over the nation as a whole, the attributes of the schools did account for slightly more of the variance in the achievement of black students, and the strongest variable here was the verbal achievement of teachers (as measured on a standard test), which yielded a correlation of .46.[22]

This was not as high, however, as the level attained by many other variables, and David Armor sought to bring more perspective to the problem by testing the variables together in a multiple regression analysis. With that method, it is possible to test the effect of one variable while holding the others constant, and there is the chance also to gauge just which collection of variables accounts for the larger portion of the variance. In a test of sixth graders, Armor found that a model of nine variables was able to account for more than 80 percent of the variation among the schools in average achievement.[23] But, in turn, most of that variation could be ex-

---

[20] Ibid., p. 206.

[21] The correlations were only .14 and .16, respectively. See ibid., p. 214.

[22] Ibid., pp. 214-215. It ought to be noted, though, that in statistical terms the amount of variance that any factor accounts for is equal to the square of the correlation. And so, while the correlation with the verbal achievement of teachers was higher than the correlations with other attributes of the schools, one has to be aware that it would still have accounted for only about 21 percent of the variance, and even that figure diminished when the analysis of this factor was brought into a larger analysis of multiple regression.

[23] The nine variables were (in their abbreviated form): family structure, white-collar professions, household items, education of parents, verbal achievement of teachers, background of teachers, salaries, facilities, and the percentage of blacks in the school. See ibid., p. 215.

plained by three factors: household items (with a correlation of .34), the education of parents (.18), and the percentage of black students in the school (−.35).[24] Against those correlations, the strongest factor in the schools was the verbal achievement of teachers, which had a coefficient of only .08. The gains were only slight and they did not touch all children, but black students promised to do better in schools with a white majority, where the proportion of blacks stayed within a range of 1 to 25 percent. At that level, too, there was only an insignificant decrease in the scores of whites, so that it appeared to be the "best" ratio for both races.

In predominantly white schools, white students showed higher scores, on the average, than the black students, and the differences exceeded one standard deviation. The situation became reversed in schools where blacks made up 65 percent or more of the student body. It was the black students who then scored more highly than the whites. But that had more to do, apparently, with the different social backgrounds of whites who were in predominantly black schools,[25] and the point is that in no case did the average score of blacks in black schools exceed the performance of blacks in schools where the number of blacks was in the range of 1 to 25 percent.[26] From the evidence that is available, it is clear that black schools are far behind white schools in verbal test scores. In most instances, the differences approach or exceed two standard deviations in the national figures, which means that a white school, if it has a score at the national average, will be higher than 95 percent of the black schools.[27]

And yet the students who had the highest scores on these tests were often in the same schools as the students who had the poorer performances. Christopher Jencks points out, for example, that the range of variation within the typical elementary school in the urban North was about 90 percent of the range for the urban North as a whole. In fact, the range of variation that existed in the mean scores of the different schools was less than half of the range that was evident among individual students.[28] Even if it were possible then to eliminate the differences between schools in their mean scores, Jencks has estimated that the variance in test scores among individual students would be reduced by only about 16 to 22 percent. But if the differences between schools remained the same, and if one could somehow remove the disparities *within* the schools,

[24] Ibid.   [25] Ibid., p. 226.   [26] Ibid., p. 197.

[27] See David Armor on this point, ibid., pp. 199, 202-203.

[28] Jencks, note 8 above, p. 86.

one could remove at the same time about 78 to 84 percent of the variation in the achievement scores of the students. As Jencks observes, "In the long run it seems that our primary problem is not the disparity between Harlem and Scarsdale but the disparity between the top and the bottom of the class in both Harlem and Scarsdale."[29]

But just how those differences can be reduced is, of course, the open question. Even in those integrated schools where blacks perform best, their scores in tests continue to lag significantly behind the scores of white students, and the differences, in the aggregate, are often as much as two standard deviations. Those differences seem to be bound up largely with the family backgrounds of the black children and with the fact that they are still less well off on the average than most of the white students in the same school. But to the extent that is true, the higher performance of black children in integrated schools may be due less to integration than to the fact that they are likely to be of a different class background than black students who have remained in a mainly black school. If the disparities in performance are tied up most importantly with the material circumstances of the families,[30] the situation may yield over time to those measures or trends that improve the material condition of black households. In that event, however, the performance of black children in verbal ability tests may stand out as the reflection, rather than the cause, of social improvement. But if the disparities between black and white students has less to do with wealth, and more to do with the kinds of motivation and discipline that are cultivated in their families, the sources of improvement would seem to lie most importantly in the hands of the families themselves.

In either case, the findings would not settle comfortably with the judgments of Kozol. If he favored the integration of the schools, it was out of the conviction, apparently, that only integration would insure to black children the supplies and services they needed: the white community could not shortchange black children in that case without shortchanging its own children as well. It was never a part of his understanding, though, that integration was necessary because there might have been something lacking in the perspectives of lower-class people, or because middle-class children might have been able to impart attitudes to lower-class children that were not provided to them in their own families or culture. In fact, Kozol

---

[29] Ibid.   [30] Armor, note 6 above, p. 226.

reacted rather stiffly when it was suggested to him once that the problem of education was in some measure beyond the control of schools, that it might be bound up with the moral character of family life. That these opinions would issue from that "parochial and rather grim and beaten lower middle class" was not, after all, so surprising. But that he should hear the same thing one day from "an educated man who went on regular trips to Europe and had placed his own child in a sophisticated little French school" was something he could not abide with the same temper.[31] Here, as in other instances, the young man of sensitivity could be strangely insensitive to the moral understanding and the intentions of those people he identified with the "shop-worn middle class." The fitting irony was that they, with all the overlay of their artlessness, with their tendency toward piety and exaggeration, probably saw the issue far more clearly than he.

3. The School as a "Public" Institution

That is not to say, though, that Kozol's experience failed to touch on problems of a more "systemic" or institutional nature. The most dramatic case in point was the culminating incident of the book, when Kozol read to his class some "unauthorized" poetry of Langston Hughes. A complaint was brought by an angry white parent, and Kozol was fired for departing from the established curriculum. The incident did reveal something about the nature of the school system as an institution; but the lesson it taught was not, very likely, the lesson that Kozol would have drawn.

Kozol naturally found no harm in reading to his students poetry that was not in their regular texts, and the children particularly liked a poem by Langston Hughes, called "Ballad of the Landlord." At the request of some of the students, Kozol made mimeographed copies of the poem. It is not clear whether the poem was "assigned" to the class, but it was apparently distributed to everyone, and several children, on their own, chose to take it home and memorize it. Sometime later Kozol was called to the office of the principal, where he was confronted by the father of one of the white children in the class. The father, Kozol was moved to point out, was a policeman, and he had taken offense at the poem by Langston Hughes. Precisely why he was offended is never explained. It is not clear, for example, whether the father detected in the poem a theme

[31] See Kozol, note 1 above, p. 141.

of hostility toward whites, or whether he thought there was an attempt to cast the police in a poor light as the agents of injustice (as the protectors, in this case, of the landlord). Then, too, he might have found in the piece a certain sympathy toward the use of violence, or he might simply have foreshadowed the judgment reached by the Board of Education: viz., that the writing set a mood of defiance toward authority. (The protagonist in the poem was evicted, and when he resisted in anger, the full weight of the law came down on the side of the landlord.)[32]

But whatever there was about it, the poem was being waved now in Kozol's face. This was not the first time, apparently, that Kozol had departed from the official Course of Study. The parent recalled that Kozol had once forced his son to read a book about the United Nations and its Human Rights Commission (which Kozol thought he mistook for a "civil rights" pamphlet). According to Kozol, the principal broke in at this point and offered her own view that there was nothing really wrong with the United Nations. It is too bad that the principal was not moved also to consider, with the parent, the merits of the poem by Langston Hughes and the case that might have been made for using it in the class. But what seemed to tell in this case was the pattern of Kozol's abrasive relationship with the local community, and he was now, finally, let go. The question, though, is: What was exemplified in this confrontation? What did it reveal about the nature of the system itself?

It is tempting to say, in the first instance, that the incident offered a classic example of bureaucratic rigidity—the brittle adherence to the prescribed Course of Study and the firing of a teacher when he did nothing more than use a poem or reading that was not on the approved list. That may seem plausible on the surface, but I think the issue really ran more deeply than that, and the account of bureaucratic rigidity or uninventiveness would not fully square with other things that were known about the Boston school system. By the conventional measures of innovation—the willingness to experiment with new materials and programs—the Board of Education in Boston had shown itself to be as willing as any other group of professionals to try out all the latest gimmicks in the field. But what is more to the point here, it did adopt books written by black authors, including some books with poems by Langston Hughes, *though not the particular poem that was used by Kozol.*

It was not entirely an accident that the poem selected by Kozol

[32] Ibid., pp. 229, 236.

was not included in the official curriculum; nor was it unforesee-able that it might elicit the protest of a parent. "Ballad of the Land-lord" could probably have been incorporated in the Course of Study with little disturbance, but it was not like most of the other poetry that was likely to be found in school assignments, and that, indeed, was why Kozol chose it. The poem struck out in one or two ways that might well have provoked some serious questions or res-ervations. Among the themes I have already mentioned, there was the note of resistance and threat when the protagonist faced the landlord and rose to the confrontation:

> . . . You talking high and mighty
> Talk on—till you get through;
> You ain't gonna be able to say a word
> If I land my fist on you.

There were some people who might have been alarmed by the note of violence here, no matter how muted it may have been, and it was arguable that there was, in this poem, a more sympathetic view of violence than was usually presented under the aegis of the Boston public schools. It was part of Kozol's purpose, after all, to choose a poem with some bite, and as he himself commented, it was im-portant "not to try to pick a poem that [was] innocuous."[33]

Of course, the passage need not have been unhinging to sophis-ticated people, but a public school system usually serves a public of rather varying sensibilities. When it comes to matters of style and tone it is not so hopelessly retrograde to believe that the cur-riculum of the schools ought to respect even some of the tenderer feelings in the local community and accommodate itself in certain ways to the decent shades of local opinion. In the last analysis, this was what the dispute with Kozol was about. Kozol proved offen-sive, as a teacher, to a parent who was bound up in the community of the school—and Kozol proved offensive, it must be said, on grounds that were not really arbitrary or unreasoned. Instead of being the response of a closed bureaucracy, the firing of Kozol marked a high degree of "responsiveness" to local opinion on the part of the educational bureaucracy. And for the Board of Edu-cation *as an institution*, that responsiveness was tied in very im-portantly with the preservation of the Standard Course of Study.

The action of the school system reflected an institution that was working in a highly vulnerable, public arena. To order the affairs

[33] Ibid., p. 196.

of a public school system stretching over a large city was not like administering an imperial province. As a public body, the educational bureaucracy had to work under the discipline of public consent. The education it offered had to be founded on principles that were broadly acceptable to the public that supported it. That constituency was broken down, however, into many parts which seemed to be defined most decisively by religion, race, and national origin. The city presented a virtual landscape of different ethics, and the task of the educational system was to span those divisions with an ethic of its own. Of course there was enough in the business of education itself, in the task of conveying knowledge and cultivating competence, to provide a proper ground of meeting. But the political setting of the schools also offered encouragement for them to avoid sectarian conflicts and place the emphases, in their teaching, on the principles that defined a common citizenship.

And yet it was also true that the building of citizens could not be seen in a wholly ecumenical way. A popular government could not simply be indifferent to the habits and moral codes of any immigrant group, and at different moments the schools had to be understood by the men and women who ran them as great schools of democracy in a deeper sense. They were places that would transform the culture of immigrant groups and make the children of the newcomers into the children of a republican regime. But of course, as that vision was acted out, it managed to produce its own characteristic excesses. Anglo-Saxon Protestant schoolmasters, determined to "Americanize" the new Irish and German immigrants, could be tempted to use the authority of the classroom to ridicule their "Romanism."[34] In a similar vein, gentile teachers and administrators could argue that it was, after all, "a Christian country," and they would insist on having all children, even the children of Jews and nonbelievers, participate in public prayers and sing hymns with the name of Christ. More recently, in Newark, a comparable problem flared up when it was decided that, in some schools where blacks were in a majority, black nationalist flags would be placed in the classroom. For some white parents, however, this display of symbols was quite jarring—as jarring as it would have been, say,

---

[34] Catholics could object, at the same time, to the anti-Catholic tone of certain instruction in the public schools and to the absence of a "Christian" perspective in those parts of the curriculum that bore on moral education. For an account of these conflicts in the 1840's in New York City, see Diane Ravitch, *The Great School Wars* (New York: Basic Books, 1974), chs. 3-5.

for Jewish parents if the schools had installed crucifixes on the walls. The same thing that made the symbols important to the black parents made them equally unsettling for the whites, and after an impassioned series of protests, the flags were finally removed.

It is because the public schools are so preeminently "public" institutions that it has become vital to offer some assurance to the public, in all its variety of small, vulnerable communities, that the public schools will not be used as instruments for a sectarian purpose. It has been important to assure parents in this respect that teachers will not use the classroom as a sanctuary for imposing their religious or political beliefs on the children.

Thomas Eisenstadt tried to convey essentially the same point when he replied in public for the Board of Education in the case of Kozol's firing. The flexibility of the schools, said Eisenstadt, "should not allow for a teacher to implant in the minds of young children any and all ideas . . . Without any restrictions, what guarantees would parents have that their children were not being taught that Adolf Hitler and Nazism were right for Germany and beneficial to mankind?"[35] Kozol as Goebbels? Not very likely, and Eisenstadt himself was clearly in no danger of confusing the two. But the dilemma was indeed the same. There are many urbane men who could not set forth in a convincing way the reasons for excluding a totalitarian party from the political arena or proscribing the teaching of Nazism in the public schools. A compelling argument can indeed be made for measures of this kind, but the best arguments that have been presented in the past have required the skills of the most accomplished writers and political theorists.[36] As a mercy to us all, we have prudently refrained from assigning to professional educators the responsibility for framing these delicate arguments in public.

It is not that defensible principles of censorship do not exist or that they cannot be applied in a sensible way. The point, rather, is that there is little in the training of professional educators today that prepares them for this enterprise, and they would be the last ones to claim any expertise for the undertaking. But to recognize that fact is to recognize, at the same time, that there are good reasons behind the conventions that have evolved on this matter. Teachers and administrators may not be able to articulate principles or judge cases with the analytic dash of a professor of philosophy.

[35] Reprinted in Kozol, note 1 above, at p. 230.
[36] A notable example can be found in Harry Jaffa, *Equality and Liberty* (New York: Oxford University Press, 1965), ch. 8.

But they do have enough sense to recognize material that takes a benign view of crime and violence, or which is defamatory of certain ethnic and religious groups.

After that, our species has had the collective wit to contrive things in such a way that the administrators of school systems can avoid the vexing problems of adjudication by resorting to a simple bureaucratic expedient: rather than pronounce on the legitimacy or illegitimacy of certain works of literature, the administrators may simply "adopt" a fairly commodious, but fixed curriculum. The schools may have a healthy range of choice, but the Board of Education may discreetly choose not to add to the curriculum books that are patently offensive, or that are too close, perhaps, to the zone of the objectionable to warrant the risk of offense. The books are not taken off the shelves of local libraries and bookstores. Students and teachers, as private individuals, suffer no inhibition in their access to these works. But the books are not presented to the public under the sponsorship of the Board of Education. If teachers depart from the established curriculum in a significant way, if they take advantage of their situations in order to promote their own sectarian views, then the Board of Education will not be placed in the position of explaining why one particular sectarian view is that much less tolerable than another. The offensive teacher can be dismissed in that case for the more neutral "administrative" reason of "departing from the established curriculum."

Whether the firing was in fact justified in the particular case of Kozol is unclear on the evidence at hand. Mr. Eisenstadt claimed, in his letter for the Board, that this incident was merely one in a whole series of incidents, and that Kozol had given offense on other occasions by the nature of his departures from the Course of Study. It is apparent also that the dismissal was significantly affected by Kozol's uneasy relations with the principal and other teachers, and it is arguable that these abrasions arose quite as much from the insensitivity of Kozol as from any offenses that were chargeable to his colleagues.

Even with these problems, however, it is hard to see why the public schools of Boston would have been improved overall by the removal of a teacher like Kozol. But regardless of the judgment that might be reached on the merits of the case, it is worth getting clear on the precise factors that accounted for his being fired. As I have suggested, Kozol's troubles could not have been laid to a simple resistance within the schools to innovation; nor could they have been attributed to an aversion on the part of the authorities toward black writers. I think it would have to be recognized finally that Kozol's firing arose out of the peculiar situation that envelops the school system as a *public* institution. The procedures that eventually led to dismissal had their rationale, in principle, in a certain respect for the sensitivities of parents, and in the frank concession to parents of a kind of political weight or "standing" when it came to protecting the interests of their own children.

Whether one regards the firing of Kozol as a good or bad thing may depend then in large part on one's disposition toward the "community control" of the schools. If one happens to believe that the management of the schools should be highly sensitive to opinion in the local community, and if one is convinced that hostile parents should have a measure of power in cashiering teachers whom they regard (with some reason) as offensive, then the dismissal of Kozol would have to be understood as a regrettable, but plausible, incident in the working of this system. There is some irony in the fact that many people who favored Kozol were quite vigorous also in supporting the movement for more "community control." But in any event, wherever one's sympathies lie, it is worth considering in a more demanding way the argument that might be made for "community control" of public schools. And it is to that phase of the problem that the next chapter turns.

VIII

THE THEORY AND PRACTICE OF "COMMUNITY CONTROL"

Taking stock of the argument again, one would be led in either of two directions, depending on the judgment one reached in the case of Kozol.

(1) One may think that what happened to Kozol was a bad thing—that teachers generally deserve more insulation and freedom, which may often mean freedom to teach lessons in class that fly in the face of opinion in the local community. In that event one would recognize the importance of certain standards of "due process" for teachers. But the enforcement of those standards would seem to have the best prospect of success if authority in the schools could be vested in a distant and impersonal institution, which did not have to be overly responsive to pressures exerted at the local level. That is to say, anyone who takes the issue of due process seriously is likely to favor the authority of a strong central administration rather than the authority of a local board, which may succumb more easily to the dominant forces in the neighborhood. But if local school boards were deprived of the power to discipline teachers or to remove them "at pleasure," they would lose a large measure of their freedom to mold the content of education and bend the schools more closely to their own character.

And so, if a local board seeks to evade the procedural rules that inhibit its freedom, the move is likely to be very threatening to teachers, for their interests are bound up with the arrangement of legal restraints on the board. This was the matter at issue in New York City in 1968 in the controversy that surrounded the school district in Ocean Hill-Brownsville. The governing board of the district sought to achieve a quick coup in which it would effectively seize a kind of power over the schools that it had not been granted in law. The board ordered the removal of nineteen teachers and supervisors without seeking the approval of the central Board of Education, and without providing hearings or any statement of formal charges. (Under the law, it was bound to follow these procedures if it were acting officially to "terminate" the assignment of a teacher.) The nineteen teachers and administrators were dismissed, according to the board, because they had been opposed to the demonstration project in Ocean Hill-Brownsville and because they had sought in various ways to sabotage the experiment. Before the crisis was over, the city of New York experienced the full fire power of the teachers' union. The dispute in this one district eventually brought on a strike by the teachers in the entire system, with the result that almost every school in the city was closed for about five weeks. But on the main issue that triggered the strike, the leadership of the union had seen the matter with full clarity. The governing board in the district had affirmed its intention to "write our own rules," and in doing that, it crossed a rather clear line of principle. It created precedents for the arbitrary dismissal of teachers, and if these acts had been indulged, they would have led inescapably to the erosion of any sense of due process and "constitutional" restraints in the governance of the schools.[1]

(2) In a second and alternative view, one may think that what happened to Kozol was by and large a good thing: that parents *should* have the right to get a teacher fired, and that teachers should in fact be made responsive to currents of opinion in the local community. When Kozol was told by an official of the Board of Education that the complaint of a parent was usually sufficient grounds for dismissal, the story was received with some bitterness and surprise by a group of black parents.[2] Those parents had apparently pressed complaints of their own about the treatment of their children, but the teachers, in these cases, had not been dismissed. Indeed, the argument was frequently heard in New York City that, with decentralization or "community control," black parents might finally achieve the privilege that white parents already enjoyed: the privilege of having their views treated with such concern that any

---

[1] The case is recounted in detail in Diane Ravitch, *The Great School Wars* (New York: Basic Books, 1974), chs. 32 and 33. Ravitch has succeeded in unraveling the maze of events here and conveying the intentions of the governing board in their ultimate form: "by removing the nineteen [teachers] the governing board hoped to establish the unilateral power to transfer personnel out of the district, an authority which was just as valuable as the power to fire them. There was always the possibility, given a vacillating Board of Education and a cowed union, that the local board might prevail by virtue of a fait accompli. One press release from the governing board stated bluntly that '*if these transfers were made, it would demonstrate control of the school by the elected local Governing Board.*' " (Page 356; italics in the press release.)

[2] Jonathan Kozol, *Death at an Early Age* (New York: Bantam Books, 1967), p. 203.

teacher they found offensive would be transferred to another school.

The argument for "community control" has been that members of the local community should be able to secure the kind of education they want for their own children. There is nothing radically new about this kind of desire, since it must be implicit in the decisions that are made quite often to send children to private, rather than public, schools. What was notably new about the argument as it came up in the debate on decentralization was the meaning it held in the context of a public school system: a faction in the black community would make use of the means and authority of a public system and yet they would be freed from the restraints and objections of other people in the city as they sought to improve the performance of black children with a curriculum of a more distinct, racial character. It was hoped that the efforts of black students could be stimulated in a new way by a curriculum that contained a stronger flavoring of separatism. There would be a new emphasis on black history and literature, on the symbols of the black past and the current movements toward a new political assertiveness. In short, this new education would play heavily on the theme of racial pride by stressing persistently the things that made blacks different from others.

For someone who was steeped in the spirit of the old civic education, there was something, of course, unmistakably sectarian about this scheme. The old civic education might have been more solemn and insistent than urbane people could bear, but at least it was firmly grounded in its understanding, and it emphasized the right things. It held out the sense of a common citizenship and common standards of the public good, and it tried to avoid as much as possible the cultivation of divisive themes. But the emphases now would be placed rather differently, and it was only to be expected that this new sectarianism would be no more subtle than the old sectarianism in conveying its themes to children.

1. Schools, Sectarianism, and the Interests of Citizens

What was apparently beyond reckoning was the possibility that ordinary citizens might object to this new sectarianism in the same way in which they may object today to the use of the public schools to support religious education. Just to be clear on the point, I am not suggesting that we would be faced here in most cases with the teaching of things that were in principle wrong (and in a fundamental sense, therefore, illegitimate). If that were the case, we would not be raising the question of whether the teaching ought to be permitted in the *public* schools, but in any schools at all. The principles that define right and wrong are indifferent to the distinctions that separate the public from the private: we would grant no establishment a license to instruct students in the "principles" of prostitution or pickpocketing, regardless of whether the tutelage took place in private or public schools. But as I have also tried to suggest, the principles that define the wrong of racialism and Nazism are quite as necessary and compelling as any principle that defines the wrong of pickpocketing. And so if we discovered sectarian academies that schooled their pupils in racial hatred, or in other things that were illegitimate, we would be justified in doing far more than withdrawing the support of public funds. We would be justified in removing the charter or closing down the school until the offensive practices had been ended.

If the regimen of "community control" brought schools that were dedicated to instruction in racial hostility, there would be strong grounds for refusing to constitute schools on these terms. But we are not likely to be faced so directly with the prospect of a curriculum that is patently unwholesome. There are many forms of teaching that are legitimate in themselves, but which may be inappropriate for the public schools. If there is nothing illegitimate, say, about Christianity, there can be nothing illegitimate about offering instruction in Christianity, or offering instruction on secular subjects in rooms that contain the symbols of Christianity. And yet it may be inappropriate and wrong to have a cross on the wall of a public school, if the cross is taken as a symbol of the official commitments of the school.

What is ultimately at issue here is the kind of education that is suitable to a republic, because a republic is not strictly founded on a religious or ethnic principle. It was understood by the men who framed the Declaration of Independence that a republican government is founded on certain "self-evident" truths that must be accessible to human beings as human beings, quite apart from their religions or their ethnic cultures.[3] But it is legitimate then to insist that education in a republic be constituted on the same premises, that it foster an awareness of those principles of lawful government

[3] Walter Berns has developed this point (in a slightly different way) in regard to religion and the founding principles of the American republic. See *The First Amendment and the Future of American Democracy* (New York: Basic Books, 1976), ch. 1. The question that may be raised is whether, in all strictness, the same point must be made in regard to other republics as well.

that do not depend on religion or ethnicity for their understanding. For that reason a heavy burden of proof would have to be carried by anyone who would impart a sectarian character to public education and break down the teaching of a common citizenship.

In the same vein, the dispute that flared up over the "community control" of the schools revealed a serious division among the public over the principles that ought to govern public education. The parents who were disaffected might not have been in a position to stage a legal challenge, but they were free to press their objections in other ways which could remake the political framework in which the schools were placed. For one thing, they might have demanded that "decentralization" be applied with its full logic to include fiscal autonomy as well. There was nothing strikingly new, after all, about the notion of "local control" of the schools; that had been the established arrangement in America since the beginnings of a public school system. What was different about the argument for "community control" was the assertion of a claim to govern the schools, divorced from the main responsibility for supporting the schools fiscally. That anomaly rendered these schemes of "community control" uniquely vulnerable to the complaints of those who were being compelled now to support a system of education they found deeply offensive. The slogan of "neighborhood control of the schools" could be met by a demand, in the same cast, for the control by the neighborhood of its own financial resources. In that event, the taxes paid by residents of middle-class areas could not be funneled off by a central administration and redistributed to the poorer sections of the city. The losers, of course, would be the poorer districts in the city.

As a second point of response, the citizens in opposition might have taken a more radical step and sought to remove the management of education from the public domain. What they might have sought to do, in effect, was return to the situation that existed before the expansion of the public school system in the nineteenth century; and that possibility was not really fanciful. In New York City, for example, the enrollment in the private schools has been sustained since the early part of this century, and in 1970 over a quarter of all students were in private academies.[4] Parochial schools showed a capacity to offer education at a lower cost than the public schools and with results that usually surpassed those of the public schools. It is not entirely clear that tutelage in the parochial schools

[4] See Ravitch, note 1 above, p. 405.

was really better. It is very likely that the private schools were able to gain an advantage through their own selectivity: those who were in the schools had probably chosen to go, and they had parents who were sufficiently committed to the private schools that they were willing to pay fees beyond their taxes for the sake of keeping their children in these schools. In addition, these private academies may have profited from the freedom to preserve an institution with a rather definite moral or religious perspective, without the need to make the curriculum acceptable to a broader public. In any event, this trend toward the private schools might have accelerated until a substantial portion of parents had placed their children outside the public schools, and they might have been able to join then in defeating bond issues and taxes that would have forced them to continue supporting the public system. Failing in that, they might simply have left for the suburbs. Or they might have thrown their political weight to the support of one of the "voucher plans" that have been proposed for the schools since the early 1960's. In these schemes the government would give parents vouchers that could be spent only on education, and the parents would be free to decide just which kind of school they preferred for their children—public, private, Catholic, black, racially mixed, or virtually any school of legitimate description.[5] The aim is not only to widen the field of choice, but to give parents an added measure of influence over the schools.

In any case, these proposals would imply a new reluctance on the part of some whites to be joined any longer with black militants in a relation of community as far as education is concerned. They would signify, in effect, a new will to have public authority recede from the management of education. For the objecting citizens it would be a move to reclaim the privileges of personal choice and

[5] The first important proposal for a voucher plan was made by Milton Friedman in *Capitalism and Freedom* (Chicago: University of Chicago Press, 1960), ch. 6 (Friedman's proposal on education originally appeared in 1955). Another version was put forward in the early 1970's by Christopher Jencks, and in the current spirit of *liberal* policy it contained, of course, many more restrictions. For one thing—and quite tenably—schools that received vouchers would not be permitted to discriminate on the basis of race in their admission of students. But in certain cases, also, Jencks's plan would have compelled schools to forego standards of selection and choose about half of their students on a random basis, through the use of a lottery. See Jencks's proposal as it was presented in U.S. Senate, Select Committee on Equal Educational Opportunity, *Hearings* (Washington: U.S. Government Printing Office, 1971), Part 22, pp. 10971-982, especially 10974-979.

to withdraw the polity from its dominant role in the shaping and governance of education.

It is one of the paradoxes of our own day that a move of this kind by parents to reclaim their freedom of choice would probably be resisted by many liberals or libertarians—by the same people, in other words, who would strongly defend the freedom of a Beauharnais to purvey his defamatory pamphlets under the protection of the First Amendment.[6] The incongruities may become embarrassing as we compare in this way the kinds of purposes that are seen by libertarians as sufficiently decent and legitimate to justify freedom, and the purposes that are considered so offensive and injurious that they must be restricted through the use of public authority. In the scale of libertarian values as they are interpreted today, we may be faced then with this inversion: the purposes of a Beauharnais would be placed on a higher plane of legitimacy than the purposes of those people who would simply wish to avoid complicity in a regimen of education that was arguably sectarian. For in the libertarian perspective it is not Beauharnais who ought to be restrained by the law; the restraints in this case would be applied, rather, to those parents who would wish to withdraw from the agencies of government the principal authority to manage the education of their children.

The libertarians have argued that, before the freedom of speech may be restricted, it is necessary to show a direct and immediate connection between the speech and the occurrence of material injuries. But if that is the preeminent test, it is only fitting that the same test be applied to the restraint of personal freedom in other areas as well. The analogy would create no unnatural burden for conventional libertarians; they are the offspring of modern jurisprudence, and any view of the law and public policy would become comprehensible to them only after it was cast as a concern, at its base, for the relief of a material injury. In this particular case the argument would probably be made that the black community would suffer in a material way if the dissenting parents were allowed to reclaim their personal freedom, for the policy of "community control" would be undercut and the system of public funding for the schools might be weakened. But if this is indeed the form of the argument, those who make it ought to live more strictly by its terms, and the terms ought to be made more explicit: what injuries

---

[6] See Chapter II.

would in fact arise for the black community if the dissenting parents reclaimed their freedom of choice?

2. "Community Control" and the Schools: The Range of Argument

In trying to make the case, it would simply not suffice to argue, as a first line of attack, that if everyone acted on this precedent and withdrew his support for public schools, the schools would be deprived of funds and the education of poor children would suffer. That argument will not do in this instance, because the opponents of "community control" may not be at all reluctant to support a system of public schools. What they object to is the presence of a new sectarianism which has been added to the equation, and which forms no necessary part of the original mandate to establish a system of public schools.

The argument would have to become considerably finer then, and it would have to provide a more precise justification for the particular kind of education that would be offered in these schools. The most important argument that has been put forward, of course, is that these new schools, administered in the local community, will succeed where the central boards of education have failed most dramatically. It was thought that they might arrest the relative decline in the performance of children in the public schools, as measured, for example, in the results of standard reading tests. Until very recently, each succeeding year would find in the central cities larger proportions of children falling under the average score in the statewide tests. That trend seemed on its face to be a function of the increasing dominance of lower-class children in the public schools in the inner city, as the middle-class children withdrew to the suburbs or to the private schools. And yet, the trend in the scores has been taken as an unquestionable sign that the schools have not "worked," a conviction that has not been noticeably shaken by the fact that the pattern of decline continued in New York City even after the program of "decentralization" went into effect.

But putting that vexing point to the side, the argument has been that the schools under "community control" may succeed more easily in exciting the interest and effort of students from poor black and Puerto Rican families. For these people the traditional local school may appear as the outpost of an alien system controlled by a distant white establishment. To the parents the school may seem impenetrable, while to the students the system seems to impose a curriculum that must be acceptable, in its main ingredients, to the larger community in the city. In the argument for "community control" these two themes have been connected. The promise of improving the performance of the children in the schools has been bound up with the prospect of enlarging the political competence of the parents and the community. These prospects have been seen to depend in turn on the possibility of removing decisions on education, not merely from the central administration, but from the sphere of "administration" itself, where they are treated as matters of management. The decisions would be placed instead in the hands of local governing boards and community meetings, where they would be brought into the arena of a public politics. And once there, the disputes and abrasions of politics would lay open to the public the political premises that have been implicit in education all along. The schools would become more sensitive to their political setting, and they would become especially responsive to the things that local parents want. What those parents seek most of all is the education of their children, and through the power they are capable of flexing under these new arrangements they may be in a better position, one might say, to concentrate the minds of the administrators.

But if one pauses here and takes these arguments in order, it would be hard to stake the case for "community control" on the promise of improving the performance of children in the schools. There has been enough experience by now with black suburbs and schools controlled by black communities, and the control of a black community seems to make little difference in itself to the educational achievement of the students. Even if it were true that under the conditions of "community control" a school district could wrest more money for itself, it is not at all clear that the money would be spent on facilities (in the form of new books, say, or equipment) rather than on patronage in the form of jobs. And even if the money were spent on facilities, it has already become apparent from the data in the Coleman Report that the amenities in the schools have little bearing on the progress of the students as measured in standard tests.[7]

If there is a case to be made for "community control" it is more likely to rest on a political, rather than an educational, argument.

---

[7] See Chapter VII, Section 2, "Distributive Justice in the Schools: Some Empirical Findings."

From a political perspective the aim of community control would be to end the crisis of legitimacy that has been afflicting the public schools; and if that problem could be overcome, it is entirely possible that some improvement would be found after a while in the performance of the students. But if there *were* an improvement, it is not likely to have come about because parents finally had the political clout to force the schools to do things that they were previously failing to do. The improvement would have come, rather, because the political weight of the parents had been brought in to support the authority and the mission of the schools. That is to say, the "political" solution is one that would work ultimately upon the children by shoring up respect for the schools, and by supporting the discipline that is essential to learning.[8]

There is another variant of the political argument, in which the aim once again is to act upon the children, but to act upon them through their parents. In this view, the object would be to heighten the interest taken by the parents in the work of their children by drawing the parents into the political life of the school and enlarging their sense of civic competence. The argument, in other words, would follow the understanding of civic participation that was set forth most notably by Tocqueville and Mill. In that older understanding, the end of civic participation was not the exercise of "power" in some crude sense; in fact, it often involved the decision to hold oneself back and abstain from the effort to exercise influence. Nor was the end, in any immediate sense, that of improving the community as a whole, since it could never be assumed that the participation of just any citizen would be bound to augment the wisdom and soundness of public policy. The aim, rather, and simply, was to improve the individual himself by "civilizing" him: he would learn how to reconcile his interests with those of others; he would become practiced in honoring some interest other than his own; and he would acquire the discipline of giving reasons when he sought to commit others to his ends. As he came to face the question of what public policy ought to provide in treating the interests of one person or another, he would be drawn outward to the standards that defined what was just or unjust. And as he faced the problem of what was in general just or unjust, he necessarily

[8] As Christopher Jencks has remarked in a somewhat different context, "the best index of a school's success or failure [in preparing students for advancement in life] may not be reading scores but the number of rocks thrown through its windows in an average month." "A Reappraisal of the Most Controversial Educational Document of Our Time," *The New York Times Magazine*, August 10, 1969, p. 44.

raised the question of what was good or bad, just or unjust in regard to himself. It was in that sense that politics became a school of ethics, and Mill could write of "the moral part of the instruction afforded by the participation of the private citizen, if even rarely, in public functions."[9]

When it came to public assemblies, participation did not provide a license for the citizen either to act out his "opinions" as law or to make use of power for whatever ends he would. As Mill put it,

> Entire exclusion from a voice in the common concerns is one thing, the concession to others of a more potential voice, on the ground of greater capacity for the management of joint interests, is another. The two things are not merely different, they are incommensurable. Everyone has a right to feel insulted by being made a nobody and stamped as of no account at all. No one but a fool, and only a fool of peculiar description, feels offended by the acknowledgement that there are others whose opinion, and even whose wish, is entitled to a greater amount of consideration than his. To have no voice in what are partly his own concerns is a thing which nobody willingly submits to; but when what is partly his concern is also partly another's, and he feels the other to understand the subject better than himself, that the other's opinion should be counted for more than his own accords with his expectations. . . . It is only necessary that this superior influence should be assigned on grounds which he can comprehend, and of which he is able to perceive the justice.[10]

When the argument is framed in this way, the understanding of "community control" may be thoroughly recast. The ingredients of "power" and "control" are muted, and the enterprise is no longer seen as a matter of wresting control and imposing one's own will. The aim of the policy is not to give people power so much as to give them a means of instruction and improvement. And by acting in this manner on the character of the parents, community control may help bring about the kinds of changes in their family lives that seem to be more important than anything else in accounting for the performance of children in the public schools.

If we did in fact follow that older understanding of participation which is associated with Tocqueville and Mill, the main emphasis

[9] John Stuart Mill, *Considerations on Representative Government* (Indianapolis: Bobbs-Merrill, 1958), p. 54.

[10] Ibid., pp. 136-37.

would be placed on duties rather than rights. The culture of "demands" would be overborne by a more persistent awareness of the proper limits and constraints on the things that may be demanded. That overall sense of the scheme would remind us that we come to the matter of "community participation" only in a constitutional framework, which implies some restraints on arbitrariness in the management of the schools and some standards of "due process" for the people who work in them. It would recall to us once again that here, as in the past, the arrangement of local control by a homogeneous community does not find its characteristic expression in the impulse to freedom and the opening of "options"; it expresses itself, rather, in the search for a community ethic and the firming of social discipline.

On those terms, one might be able to accept the case for "community control," although it would place a greater burden on the classic argument by Tocqueville and Mill than that argument was ever meant to carry. And while the case for community control depends for its plausibility on the best things being true, it contains no provision for the worst things—and no presentiment of what the worst things, under this arrangement, might be.

It was never expected, in the classic understanding, that participation would transform everyone in the community, for not everyone would have the interest to come forward and take part. The effects of participation might well be felt in the community at large, and occasionally people might be lifted out of their own private concerns to find new powers in themselves and new lives as public figures. But for the most part we would tend to suspect, on the basis of what we have known for a long while, that the people who took an active part were rather different to begin with from those who did not. They and their children probably had, from the outset, a more intense feeling of engagement that was already present in the family.

It was never assumed in the past that political participation was *guaranteed* to make men better. The kind of person one became through politics would depend in large part on the kind of person one already was and the kind of character that was manifested in the fabric of one's judgments. Good men could grow corrupt, modest men could find new sources of strength. And those who cultivated wickedness as an end would be, through it all, ineffaceably, wicked. The long and the short of it was that politics was good when it was practiced by good men and bad when it became a vehicle for bad men; and if the strains of politics tore men apart, it could be anything but a "civilizing" experience. (In certain times, in communities that are tensely divided, politics can worsen those divisions, bring conflicts to a head, and drive society to a point of pervasive and debilitating violence. Politics has not had a particularly healing or uplifting effect on Lebanon and Northern Ireland, and there are moments, as in the lives of these countries, where it may be in the interests of everyone to replace the turbulence of a public politics with the salve of a bureaucratic calm.)

It is not always the case then that political activism and participation will increase cohesion in the local community, and even if they did, it does not follow that any cohesion they developed would be good for the larger community. It is possible to unite the local community, for example, by organizing the residents to resist the sale of homes to black families. Remarkable cohesion has been achieved, after all, in bands of thieves and in the fraternity of lynch mobs. Whether unity is good or bad, whether it is welcome or unwelcome, depends on whether it is directed at good ends and founded on just principles. And so the case cannot be made, say, for black nationalist schools by suggesting simply that they promise to raise the "cohesion" of the local community. That is particularly true if there is some reason to suspect that the cohesion would be fashioned out of an animosity that is likely to weaken, in the long run, the prospects of civility and of the kind of political regime that depends, more than others, on civility.

3. The Arguments Considered: "Community Control" and the Experience in New York

In point of fact, however, the prospects for cohesion are rather poor. The lesson was learned rather well in the poverty program that one of the best ways to tear communities apart is to create a new supply of patronage very suddenly in the form of jobs and money and then invite a group of poor people to divide it.[11] As the new school districts in New York came to be seen as fresh sources of patronage, it was only to be expected that the same kinds of conflict would take place. The districts were to have a large measure of freedom from the procedures and controls of the central board

[11] The point was made to me by a congressman from the Bronx, who saw relations between blacks and Puerto Ricans deteriorate in his district; and the same observation was recorded publicly by Herman Badillo, who was the president of the Bronx in the late 1960's. See Daniel P. Moynihan, *Maximum Feasible Misunderstanding* (New York: Free Press, 1969), p. 139.

of education, and that opened the possibilities for some creative use of discretionary spending. There were, after all, contracts to be let for maintenance, and there were substantial numbers of jobs to be filled in teaching and administration. To put the matter gently, these possibilities for patronage have not been overlooked. At their best, they might have encouraged political organizations to form in black areas for the sake of gaining control of that patronage; and as these organizations came into their own, they might have been able to act as forces of cohesion within the neighborhoods. At their worst, however, these new stocks of patronage threatened to foster violence in the community and set one faction against another in a crude grab for power.

At the same time, the conditions of election under community control promised to make the governing boards vulnerable to a takeover by any group with a minimum of discipline and with an organization already established. There has been a good fund of experience by now with "off year" elections, and especially "off year" elections for special governing bodies such as park district boards and sanitation commissions. There is enough known at least to say that the turnout of voters will usually be a small fraction of what it is in general elections, in which offices are at stake at the state or federal levels. Strong local machines like the Byrd organization in Virginia or the Cook County organization in Chicago long ago learned the importance of holding their key elections in off years, when the electorate will not be swollen by the larger number of voters that are brought to the polls in contests over the presidency or the governorship. The experience of the elections under "community control" in New York was probably best foreshadowed in the elections that took place to community boards under the "war on poverty." The turnout of eligible voters for the poverty boards rarely reached as much as 15 percent, while in some places (for example, Los Angeles in one election) the turnout was 0.7 percent.[12] In one poverty district in the Bronx that was not really untypical, the polls were open one day in 1969 from nine o'clock in the morning; the first voter did not show up until three o'clock in the afternoon; and that voter, as it turned out, was one of the candidates!

What happens in these elections is that the turnout is usually confined to those who have a keen interest in the contest, either because they care most intensely about the issues or because they

[12] Ibid., p. 137.

have a direct material stake in the outcome. Referenda over spending issues are more likely to be lost, for example, in off-year elections, because the taxpayers who are opposed to further spending will turn out in firm numbers, and they may make up a disproportionate share of the electorate.[13] In the venerable tradition of municipal politics, the universe of those with a "direct material stake" in the outcome has included, most notably, patronage workers, their families, and their collateral dependents (to say nothing, of course, of their creditors).

It should not be surprising then that when it comes to elections to school boards under "community control," it is the teachers' union that may have the strongest incentive to defend its interests. Ironically, the conflict over "community control" was focused, in New York, on the teachers themselves, as exemplars of interests that were likely to be adverse to those of the people in the local community. And yet, when the regimen of "community control" got underway, the advantage did in fact pass to groups like the United Federation of Teachers or the Catholic Church—to the groups, that is, which had the strongest organizations in the district or the greatest potential for cohesion. The culmination of this logic was probably seen most dramatically in the special election that was held in District 1, on the Lower East Side of New York, in May 1974. A closely fought contest brought a "record" turnout at the polls of 30 percent (the usual turnout, as one might have expected, was around 15 percent). In that restricted poll, a ticket of candidates supported by the United Federation of Teachers managed to win a majority over a faction called Por Los Niños, which was composed predominantly of Puerto Ricans.[14] In the absence of political parties that could provide their own labels, as well as a larger blend of interests, the political leverage moved to the side of the teachers and the union.

But when strong political machines decided to enter the new politics of the schools, the arrangements of "community control" were clearly vulnerable to a takeover. The new "decentralization" law in New York went into effect on July 1, 1970, and within a matter of months the district that included the Ocean Hill-Brownsville area had been taken over by the political organization under

[13] See Harlan Hahn, "Correlates of Public Sentiments About War: Local Referenda on the Vietnam Issue," *American Political Science Review*, Vol. 64, no. 4 (December 1970), pp. 1186-98.

[14] *The New York Times*, May 22, 1974, p. 25.

the leadership of Samuel Wright, a black Assemblyman. The eight schools that made up the Ocean Hill-Brownsville demonstration district were absorbed into a larger district of twenty-four schools, and a new local board was elected, which turned out to be hostile to the remaining members of the old board. By the end of the first school year the new leadership had succeeded in removing all but one of the principals who had been appointed by Rhody McCoy, the former administrator in the district.[15]

In some districts in New York City the participation of members of the community has gone forward as though the scheme had been prescribed by John Stuart Mill.[16] Even though the citizens may claim certain formal powers through their participation in boards and public meetings, they seem to be willing to be guided by the professionals in the schools, with an interest, first, in learning something more about the subject on which they must act. For some critics, the arrangement has tipped too far in that direction. The local boards may have become mere appendages to the administration in certain cases, so that the net result of "community control" has been to bolster the authority of the professionals who run the schools. In some areas the governing boards have brought new people into public roles, including many not likely to have come forward in the past to hold public office, and a good number of them have performed with a creditable competence. But most of these success stories have been in middle-class areas, where the people who served on the boards were quite often men and women in the professions. And where a district has been composed of

[15] *The New York Times*, August 9, 1971, pp. 1, 14. The succession that took place here might have reflected the differences that often existed between the militancy of the governing boards in their early stages and the more conservative tone of opinion in the black communities. Surveys of black communities have shown rather dominant strands of support for an ethic of personal responsibility and work—and a strong preference also for traditional forms of leadership, such as that of the NAACP and Roy Wilkins, rather than the more recent varieties of militants and nationalists. See Gary Marx, *Protest and Prejudice* (New York: Harper and Brothers, 1967), pp. 25-27; Angus Campbell and Howard Schuman, *Racial Attitudes in Fifteen American Cities* (Ann Arbor: Institute for Social Research, 1968), pp. 5, 15-26, 47-61. At the time of the debate over decentralization in New York City, a survey by Louis Harris showed that most parents were opposed to the plans for decentralization. Interestingly enough, most parents thought that teachers would do a better job under decentralization; and yet contrary to the arguments made for "community control," most parents, black as well as white, professed to be indifferent to the race of the people who taught their children. Most of them also thought that the teachers were doing a good job. See *The New York Times*, January 30, 1969, p. 22.

[16] Note 9 above.

people of this description it is likely that the children would have performed fairly well in the schools anyway.

A rather different story emerges, however, in other parts of the city, and once again the Ocean Hill-Brownsville district in Brooklyn may provide a good case in point. The control of the new school district was seen by some observers as the decisive factor in establishing the dominance of Samuel Wright's organization. If Wright could actually build an organization that would lend cohesion to the local community and help direct it toward decent ends, the plan for decentralization might bring some measure of good to the community after all, even if it has little to do with education. The evidence so far, though, has not been very reassuring. The tone of things in the area was conveyed rather vividly by an account, in *The New York Times*, of an effort to remove the superintendent of the district. The superintendent had been at odds with Wright, and Wright had been charged with misusing federal funds. The misuse might have arisen quite as plausibly through confusion as through design, but whether the charges were valid or not, the incident revealed the manner in which Wright had managed to incorporate the management of the schools into his conglomerate of enterprises. As the superintendent complained, her duties were progressively stripped away, and most functions were transferred to an agency called the Community Education Center. The Center comprised a number of educational programs that took place outside the schools, and which were supported by $2.6 million in state funds. The hiring of paraprofessionals and aides for the schools was given over to a screening committee, and the supervision of spending was assigned to an accountant. The management of the schools became locked then in a local complex of organization that the superintendent no longer had the power to control. As the superintendent testified, "I couldn't even get a pencil unless I went to him [the accountant]. . . . Even my personal secretary was hired by someone else."

Everything was centralized in the Community Educational Center, and the Center in turn was under the effective control of Samuel Wright. The Center had a budget of $2.5 million; it disposed directly of 600 jobs; and apart from that it was able to exert influence over the filling of jobs elsewhere. For stakes of this kind local politics soon became an intensely serious—and violent—business; and during the course of events a member of the school board was shot. Whether the shooting arose out of a dispute in the schools was not entirely clear, but the incident nevertheless tended to enlarge the tension that surrounded the schools. Public meetings of the school board broke out into brawls, and on one notorious occasion the vice-chairman of the board of the community corporation was beaten as he attempted to take the microphone away from Samuel Wright. The board member, Tito Velez, was struck down by a man who was listed as an employee of the Community Education Center, and who was apparently one of Wright's retainers.[17]

From the perspective of Tocqueville and Mill, the evidence was quite sufficient to suggest that participation, in this one place at least, had proved morally corrosive rather than civilizing. Peace would either settle on the community through the dominance of Samuel Wright, or politics would continue in its turbulent form with a divisive effect on the community. In an area already afflicted with a high rate of personal violence, the politicizing of the schools merely created new divisions or brought old quarrels past the edge of violence. What all of this had to do with education was rather hard to see. But whatever could possibly have been gained in the schools surely must have been outweighed by the lessons taught every week by the public struggles among the adults to "dispose" of the business of the schools.

And yet even that construction may be too finely tempered, for there is some reason to believe that the students were affected rather directly by the political turmoil that surrounded the schools. It was hard to believe that the scheme of "community control" would really improve learning, and it seemed likely, in any case, that certain allowances would have to be made in the first year or so while the students and teachers were settling into the new arrangements. But even with all of these allowances, some startling results came out of the Ocean Hill-Brownsville area, where one of the first three experimental districts had been set up in 1967 with the support of the Ford Foundation. The Ocean Hill-Brownsville district was in the center of the conflict over "community control," and it managed to endure as an arena of political combat even after its first administrator, Rhody McCoy, had departed from the scene. For the first three years the governing board resisted any effort to administer a standardized test to the pupils under its control, which would have made it possible to compare scores across the districts in the city. In the fourth year (in the spring of 1971) the district

[17] The account of the brawl, as well as the story of the district superintendent, can be found in *The New York Times*, March 24, 1971, pp. 1, 47.

lines had been redrawn, the governing board had been reconstituted, and it became possible for the first time to administer a standardized test.

The results, in sum, were rather sobering. Not only had there been no visible improvement among the students, but the scores on the tests were actually lower in the aggregate than the scores that had been obtained from the same schools in 1967, before the "experiment" had begun. As Diane Ravitch noted, "Every school in the district reported poor reading scores—as compared with other schools in the city, with other schools in the borough of Brooklyn, and even with other ghetto schools." The school with the highest score in the district was an elementary school, which had only 24.5 percent of its students reading on or above grade level. Junior High School 271 fell into place one slot above the lowest school in Brooklyn, with only 5.5 percent of its students reading on or above grade level. The eighth grade at JHS 271 was more than three years behind the reading norm at its level; and yet no school in the Ocean Hill-Brownsville area had achieved a higher score than this school in 1967.[18]

Of course, not all of the students were the same in this comparison of aggregates over an interval of four years. And it is possible that the scores could have been affected overall by changes in the class composition of the school. Still, it hardly seems likely that the population of the school or the class composition of the neighborhood had changed so drastically in those four years; and even if one were inclined to believe that the problem really lay outside the schools, there was something telling in the fact that these schools produced rates of absenteeism that ran far beyond the rates in other parts of the city.[19] Perhaps the figures that are available here should be compared with the same schools in other years, and with schools having students of the same background. Yet, it is hard to avoid the impression that the wave of strikes and counterstrikes left habits among the students that would not easily fade. The question one cannot help asking is whether these habits were ultimately at odds with the discipline of education—whether, in shaking children in their attachment to the schools, in furnishing them with a facile,

[18] See Diane Ravitch, "Community Control Revisited," *Commentary* (February 1972), pp. 69-74, at 74. By this time, however, the erstwhile administrator of the school district (and the founder of the new order) had fled to safety in the School of Education at the University of Massachusetts, where he apparently found lasting happiness as an inmate.

[19] Ibid., p. 74.

"political" excuse for missing their classes, the political attack on the schools may in fact have weakened the students in their disposition to accept the regimen of learning.

All things taken together, then, it would be hard to make a compelling case for the "community control" of the schools as that scheme has been understood in our recent politics. And the flaws in the case were apparent to many observers well before the experience of "community control" offered a record of evidence. The arrangement cannot be expected to improve the education of children, and it may even make matters worse. It cannot be relied on to enlarge the political participation of the community or to animate people in the most decent way, toward the most salutary ends. For a number of reasons, which I have already mentioned, it may even have a malign effect on the political community by degrading the conditions of civility and lawfulness. It would be quite untenable, therefore, to suggest that poor people, and especially poor people who are black, would suffer any material injury if the scheme of "community control" were not put into effect. And for that reason it would be hard to resist the claims of those citizens who would wish to be free from the compulsion to support a form of education that they regard (with some reason) as sectarian and destructive.

4. THE SCHOOLS AND THE STRUCTURE OF POLITICS IN THE CITY

I have argued that the response to the firing of Kozol would lead to one of two conclusions about the governance of education: (1) one might wish to insulate the schools somewhat more from the pressures and controls of local opinion; or (2) one might prefer in the end to remove schools entirely from the management of public authority because there seems to be little agreement any longer on the principles that ought to govern public education. Extremes, of course, are best avoided by prudence, and without a sense of practical wisdom and moderation no institutional arrangements will ultimately be very satisfactory. In that spirit, one wonders if there are any practical arrangements that might help to insulate the schools from the less enlightened demands of local opinion, while at the same time avoiding the creation of a closed bureaucracy.

There is one incident in Kozol's story that suggests the beginning of an answer. It may also tell something more about the political structures in which educational systems are set. As Kozol recalled, Mrs. Louise Day Hicks announced one day, for the Boston School

Committee, that six new positions would be added to the central administration at a cost of over $100,000. Administrators at the highest levels in the system were scheduled to receive substantial increases in salary—so substantial, as it turned out, that even the assistant superintendents would be earning more than the Mayor of Boston. It was announced at the same time that the budget would be "balanced": to cover the cost of these new steps, Mrs. Hicks reported that $1 million would be taken from the account for alteration and repairs.[20]

Kozol himself was critical of the decision, but it bears noticing that he was not the only prominent "figure" who assailed this decision in public. Mayor John Collins also expressed his anger to the press, condemning the School Committee for being so "extraordinarily open-handed with taxpayers' money." He thought that salary increases of $4,000 were excessive, and he professed to be "appalled" by this "lavish" use of public funds. "I always thought," he remarked, "that elected representatives were responsible to all citizens of Boston, all taxpayers and also to those with children who go to our schools."[21]

But why this disagreement between Mr. Collins and Mrs. Hicks? Was it merely a difference in judgment, or was it a difference in perspective that was related in some way to the constituencies that these two people represented, and perhaps also to the routes by which they came to public office? Mrs. Hicks, like Mayor Collins, was elected at-large in the city, in an election that did not contain party labels. The fact that Mrs. Hicks was elected, rather than appointed, apparently caused her to view herself as a public figure with a constituency of her own to cultivate. The inclination to see herself in that way was reinforced, also, by the conditions under which she was elected. Mrs. Hicks and Mr. Collins were elected in the same city, presumably by the same electorate, and yet there were still slight but telling differences. The most important was that the electorate was able to vote separately on the members of the School Committee, and for that reason it was possible to remove the issue of education from other electoral choices. The voters in Boston would not be faced, for example, with the kind of dilemma that would arise later for the followers of George Wallace in choosing between the Democratic and Republican parties. From what we know of the Wallace voters they were drawn to some of the "pop-

[20] Kozol, note 2 above, pp. 144-46.
[21] Quoted ibid., p. 145.

ulistic" strands in the character of the Democratic party, but at the same time they were put off by the dominant commitments of the Democrats on matters of race. If the Wallace voters had given preeminence to their concerns over race, they would have been moved to support the Republican party; and yet they profoundly distrusted the Republicans in the management of the economy, and the migration to the Republicans might have involved a severe jolt to their psyches. One of the wholesome features, though, of a system with only two or three major parties, is that it persistently compels voters to confront this kind of perplexity. As the saying goes more technically, the electoral system "aggregates" issues. It presents ensembles or packages of issues to the electorate, instead of encouraging the individual voter to pick one issue out of the rest and vote his gut preferences.

The voter may still decide to give a more decisive weight to one issue among the others (e.g., the economy, race, or military policy), but when the choices have been collected for him in larger ensembles he chooses with a greater awareness of the costs, and that makes a considerable difference. The Wallace voter who decided finally to vote Democratic on the issue of the economy knew that he would be helping to bring to power an administration that would be highly sensitive to the demands of blacks. To vote Democratic under these circumstances probably reflected a consciousness on the part of this voter that the issues of "class" that might have connected him with blacks were more important at the moment than the issues (e.g., busing) that separated him from blacks. In a case like this, the coalition formed at the polls may turn out to be more than a statistical creation. It may leave its impression in the consciousness of the voters themselves; in some way, in fact, it may change people in their private, as well as their public, lives. But these effects, let me say again, are more likely to occur when the electoral system works to complicate the question for the voters by forcing them to choose among larger and, we hope, more "principled" packages of issues.

That useful tension, however, was not present for the voters of Boston as far as the issue of education was concerned. The electoral system allowed the question of the schools to be isolated, rather than bringing it into a larger ensemble of interests. A traditional Democrat in Boston could vote for liberals in the nation, the state, and even the city at large; but if he were somewhat more conservative on the issue of the schools, he could convey his special judgment about that one question through his voting in the election to the school board. For in politics one can be sure that if a constituency is there and the means become available to appeal to it, candidates will not be wanting who come forward and appeal to that electorate. In the case of Boston the voters were asked to elect a school board by voting for several candidates on a long list, and that arrangement probably had the effect of bringing to the board members who were more than usually divided from one another. The electoral scheme allowed the possibility of "bullet" voting— that is, voting for only one or two favorite candidates, rather than using all votes one may cast and taking the risk of adding votes to the other candidates. In a situation of that kind, a minority with emphatic views stands a better chance of electing someone to the school committee who reflects its perspectives.

Those were, more or less, the rules that defined the election in which Mrs. Hicks had risen to public office. For the mayor, on the other hand, the situation was rather different. He too ran "at large" in a nonpartisan election, but if no candidate secured a majority on the first ballot, a runoff was held between the two top candidates. The alignments of the voters were usually far more fluid under these conditions than in elections in which party labels were present to provide cues to the voters. Still, the result of the second ballot was to force candidates to seek out the same kinds of broader alliances that come into being in contests between the parties. John Collins, as a Democrat, had the support of conservative Democrats, and he probably had more Republican support than a Democrat might ordinarily receive in a straight partisan contest. But in the nature of things he was likely to be far more responsive than Mrs. Hicks to the interests of blacks in the schools. It seems highly doubtful, then, that if the school board were appointed by the mayor, Mr. Collins would have chosen to appoint someone like Mrs. Hicks.

That is not to say that Collins would have appointed only liberals to the school committee. On the contrary, it is reasonable to expect that he would have made some effort to mirror the range of opinions in the community, and he probably would have appointed one or two people *like* Mrs. Hicks, who had deep reservations about policies of integration and busing. But it is unlikely that even the more conservative members he appointed would have been in the same cast as Mrs. Hicks. They might have been separated from the other members of the board by their dispositions on policy, but they would have been connected with their colleagues in other ways, by the ties they had formed through political parties, the unions, the business community, or through the mayor who appointed them all. In Chicago under Richard Daley, in New Haven under Richard Lee, the mayor would appoint blacks to the boards of education along with Irishmen, Italians, Poles, and Jews. These people would often see themselves as the spokesmen for their groups, and yet they would be connected to one another through the mayor or the governing party, and they could feel a strong responsibility to reconcile the interests that divided them.[22] As a result, the school boards in these cities could satisfy a combination of needs. They could assure different groups that their interests would be consulted, but at the same time they would be sensitive to the interests of the political leadership and the larger concerns that it represented in the community.

Similar stories could be told of a number of other places and they would be examples of the more exacting prudence that seems to be supplied best by people who have real aptitude as political leaders. The process is rarely understood in its better light, but it is, in the most practical terms, a matter of rendering more justice to different groups in the city than any one of them would be likely to render to the others if it were left to its own preferences. The problem in Boston was that there was probably too much direct, undisciplined influence by the community over public education. That defect showed in the use of separate, nonpartisan elections, and in the absence of certain mediating devices, such as political leaders or political parties, which could have offered some constructive help in the direction of the schools.

This sense of the matter was borne out several years ago in a study of eight large cities in the North and West by Robert Crain and James Vanecko.[23] Crain and Vanecko surveyed the relations between school boards and the political leadership in the handling of desegregation, and they of course considered in their total scheme of things the structure of city politics. Their sample covered the

[22] In relation to New Haven see Robert Dahl, *Who Governs?* (New Haven: Yale University Press, 1961), ch. 11; for Chicago a recent account may be found in Paul E. Peterson, *School Politics Chicago Style* (Chicago: University of Chicago Press, 1976), ch. 4. In Chicago the Mayor faced the added discipline of having to deal with an advisory commission on nominations and enticing the commission to offer him the kinds of appointments that he wished to make. For examples of some of the finessing that took place under these arrangements, see pp. 96-102.

[23] See their "Elite Influence in School Desegregation," in James Q. Wilson, ed., *City Politics and Public Policy* (New York: John Wiley and Sons, 1968), pp. 127-48; and see also the larger study from which this material was drawn, Robert L. Crain et al., *The Politics of School Desegregation* (New York: Doubleday, 1969; Chicago: Aldine, 1968).

"strong mayor" form of government, as well as governments characterized by a strong city council; they included cities with partisan as well as nonpartisan elections; and they took account of the presence or absence of strong political parties. Finally, they considered the backgrounds of the people who made up the boards of education and the methods by which they were selected. Without collapsing all of their findings into one or two items, what they found was that the most "liberal" or accommodating school boards had these characteristics: they were appointed, rather than elected; they were made up disproportionately of corporate businessmen and members of the civic or social elite (rather than the political leadership); and they had their greatest strength in cities that happened to contain strong parties or political machines. It was characteristic of these cities, too, that they had a large working-class population (the traditional base for political machines); a strong and active upper class; and a fairly weak middle class.[24]

It was mainly through appointment rather than election that members of old families or the corporate elite could hope to gain places of authority on the school board in a city dominated by working people and a party machine. But at the same time, the party leadership was able to provide the kind of support and insulation that a school board needed in carrying out policies of a controversial nature, which ran the risk of stirring up resistance in the city.

For their own part the mayors of cities have often found it useful, or even necessary, politically, to have "apolitical," "blue ribbon" school boards, composed of the most respectable citizens. In Chicago, in the mid-1940's, a series of scandals showed that the schools were still tied in with the ward organizations as they had been at an earlier time, when many of the teachers were incorporated in the patronage system.[25] The scandals apparently had some effect on the decision of the incumbent mayor not to seek another term, and it became clear thereafter to the leaders of the Democratic organization that it was politically necessary to preserve a certain distance from the management of the schools. To that end a new arrangement was contrived, in which the mayor would appoint members to the school board from a list of candidates drawn up

[24] See, for example, Crain and Vanecko, "Elite Influence in School Desegregation," pp. 144-45.

[25] For a reflection of the politics of the schools in an earlier period in Chicago, see Jane Addams's memoir, *Twenty Years at Hull House* (New York: Macmillan, 1935), pp. 328-34.

by an informal congress of civic groups. Strong and clever mayors have not been without influence on the groups that form this congress or even on the kinds of nominations that are eventually made. But this regimen of selection has been a powerful support for the convention of "professionalism" in the administration of the schools, and it seems to account, more than anything else, for the kind of influence that has been exerted in the school board by reformers. That influence has also been markedly out of proportion to the strength that reformers can claim in the overall politics of Chicago.

For the political leadership this "nonpolitical" arrangement offers the chance, at convenient times, to back away from the troubles of the school board. When it is a matter of obtaining higher salaries for teachers and bringing an end to a strike in the schools, the mayor may be quite willing to intervene and use his strength for the sake of aiding the teachers. (In that instance he would also be helping a union that is tied in with organized labor in the city. He would then be able to use the political strength of his organization to pry more money out of the legislature and pass the costs of the settlement on to the state.)[26] On the other hand, when the policy at issue is the busing of black students into white neighborhoods, the political leadership has been quite content to stand back and invoke the maxim of "keeping politics out of the schools." And so in 1967, when the superintendent of schools offered a plan for busing, Mayor Daley was asked by a reporter whether he would support the policy. Daley could answer then, with the wisdom of his craft, "Do you want the schools brought back into politics?"[27]

As for the interests, therefore, of political leaders, the arrangement of appointed, "nonpartisan" boards is about as good, politically, as it might well be. But then what of the interests of corporate

[26] This pattern of operation became strained late in 1979 when the accounting system of the Board of Education was found to be in disarray. The untangling of the accounts uncovered a massive deficit, which finally prevented the Board from issuing paychecks to the teachers. The financial problem of the schools was then compounded by the political weakness of Mayor Jane Byrne, who could not command the kind of leverage that Mayor Daley had been able to exercise with the state legislature and the unions. But it is doubtful that even Daley could have finessed this financial crisis and escaped the embarrassment of a strike by the teachers.

[27] As Milton Rakove observed, "It was clear what the mayor was doing. He was going to run [the superintendent] up the flag pole and let him wave up there before he involved himself in such a controversial issue." Milton Rakove, *Don't Make No Waves—Don't Back No Losers* (Bloomington: University of Indiana Press, 1975), p. 67. See also Peterson, note 22 above, pp. 159-61, 190, 202.

businessmen? For them it might be said that they have an interest in the stability and success of the schools that is not likely to be shared to the same degree by any individual owner of a small business. Corporate businessmen employ larger numbers of people, with a higher than average turnover, and it becomes a matter of some concern to them that there be a reservoir of skilled and literate workers in the city. For that reason they cannot be indifferent to the question of whether the schools are doing a tolerably decent job in rendering their students competent. By temperament and interest also, they seem to be alarmed by the spectacle of disruptive conflict in the schools; and in the cities studied by Crain and Vanecko these businessmen were inclined to accommodate the demands of dissident blacks rather than force a confrontation. Seen in their worst light the businessmen may suffer from an infirm sense of principle and a misplaced aversion to "making a scene." Regarded in their best light they may simply display the arts of practiced and prudent men.

In any event, it has been found that corporate executives are more likely to be active in the civic affairs of the city in which they live than the city in which they merely work.[28] As Crain and Vanecko discovered, there were less likely to be liberal, acquiescent school boards in cities from which these corporate businessmen had departed in large numbers for the suburbs. As a practical matter, even men and women with a strong civic consciousness may find it hard to stay in the city if other people like themselves are generally unwilling to live there. Some effort would have to be made then to encourage these businessmen, as a social class, to remain in the city. What that means, for example, in a place like New York, is the preservation of those amenities that have meant so much to urbane people in the past and kept them living in the city rather than the suburbs. It means Carnegie Hall and the Met, Saks and Bloomingdale's, the extraordinary restaurants and fine, small shops, and the ambience of places like Fifth Avenue and the East 80's. It takes a certain commitment, in tax policies as well as other resources, to preserve these amenities and make the city enduringly attractive to sophisticated people.[29] But in the long run, the commitment of the urbane and the rich to the city would make

[28] Crain and Vanecko, note 23 above, pp. 140, 146-47.

[29] On this point see Roger Starr, "The Decline and Decline of New York," *The New York Times Magazine*, November 21, 1971, pp. 31ff.; and cf. F. A. Hayek, *The Constitution of Liberty* (Chicago: University of Chicago Press, 1960), ch. 8, especially sections 5-8.

a profound difference, and not least of all to the poor. For the continued presence of the wealthy goes hand in hand with the continued presence of the enterprises in which they work and the industries that spring up to cater to their tastes. These people may put the stamp of civility on a landscape that might otherwise be merely the site of an aggregation of dwellings and businesses, and, if the political culture permits, they may also give the city the benefit of a more enlightened civic leadership.

The vision that takes form here overall is not, then, without its irony. It would in fact be rather uncongenial to those who have insisted in recent years that the only way to save the cities and improve the schools is to break down the old political structures (and especially the political machines), wrest education away from the local businessmen or "capitalists," and turn the schools over to "the people" in the local neighborhoods. Quite apart from everything we have seen that is problematic in this persuasion, our experience on all of these items points in a wholly different direction. By and large, the Jonathan Kozols of the world are more likely to find a congenial home in those cities where the party machines are alive, and where the tone of the community is still affected by the noticeable presence, not merely of businessmen, but of corporate businessmen and the kinds of services that make the city attractive to them. On balance, the Kozols are likely to be more comfortable also in places where the influence of local opinion in the management of the schools is tempered by the workings of other institutions, which have no less a stake in the performance of the schools and an even stronger interest in preserving the possibilities for education as a public undertaking. These are not, of course, the characteristics that are universally esteemed today in the cities. But many Ph.D.'s who are now gracing pastoral scenes in the academy received most of their formal education in cities of this description, and we may all have reason to regret someday that we did not esteem those communities more than we have. For in view of the alternatives we have seen in this country, they may offer the best politics in which a man of understanding can still take part.

IX

SEGREGATION, BUSING, AND
THE IDEA OF LAW

Since the time Jonathan Kozol wrote, the issue of education that has become dominant in Boston, and suddenly eclipsed nearly everything else, is of course the issue of busing. That question has become a bitter and divisive one in many other cities as well, and it has surpassed, in its import, the question of "community control." As one would expect, many of the same people who supported "community control" in different cities have also been the most adamant in refusing to consider any retreat by the federal courts from their orders on busing. Yet those orders have been promulgated in the face of persisting evidence that the vast majority of blacks as well as whites are opposed to the busing of their children for the sake of achieving "racial balance" in the schools. If there seemed to be something unacceptable in the notion of having the schools run by a central bureaucracy, the governance of the schools would be displaced even further from the hands of citizens when it was transferred to the federal courts.

And in Boston that was essentially what occurred. Decisions about budgets and staffing and the assignment of students were taken over by Judge Arthur Garrity of the Federal District Court, who became in effect the unelected superintendent of the Boston public schools. The administration of Mayor Kevin White was virtually compelled to provide an extraordinary outlay of additional spending on police and security for the sake of enforcing the orders that Judge Garrity handed down.[1] In order to cover the increase in expenses, the administration finally had to raise the property tax, and so an additional squeeze was applied to the diminishing number of middle-class families that still remained in the city. In November 1976, it was reported that 20,000 white students had been withdrawn from the Boston school system since Judge Garrity's initial decision in *Morgan* v. *Hennigan*[2] in 1974. In November 1973, white students constituted more than two-thirds of

[1] See *The New York Times*, May 18, 1976, p. 17.
[2] 379 F. Supp. 410 (1974).

the population of the public schools in Boston, but as a result of these recent migrations white students now make up less than half of the population in the public schools.[3]

Once again, in the name of "integration," a federal court finds itself pursuing policies that may actually bring about more separation between the races in the schools and in the patterns of residential settlement. The result in the case of Boston may be to encourage the movement of whites to the suburbs, to reduce the tax base of a city whose base had already been rather narrow, and to put Boston on the path of becoming a black enclave in the metropolitan area.

But of course none of these consequences would be relevant if the orders of the courts on busing represented measures that flowed inescapably from the very idea of constitutional government and from the principles that underlie the case against racial segregation. The problem, however, is that the recent decisions on busing do not flow logically from the earlier decisions of the courts in the segregation cases. Indeed, it could be shown that the decisions on busing are incompatible at their root with the firmest principles that must underlie the decision reached in *Brown* v. *Board of Education*.[4] I should add, however, that nothing I say here would imply any defense of the school board in Boston. It is evident from the record that the board did take conscious steps to avoid any significant mingling of blacks and whites in the public schools, and to the extent that public officials made conscious use of "race" in assigning students to schools, the school board must come under censure. But even if the Board of Education in Boston were justly open to reproach, that itself would not establish the suitability of busing as a remedy. And even if it could be shown that orders on busing were likely to succeed in compelling blacks and whites to attend the same schools in fixed ratios, nothing in that success

---

[3] *Washington Post*, November 10, 1976, p. A23. Diane Ravitch noted recently that, of the twenty-nine largest school districts in the nation, only eight still had a majority of white pupils in the schools. The eight were: Milwaukee, Jacksonville, Columbus, Indianapolis, San Diego, Seattle, Nashville, and Pittsburgh, In all of these cities there were controversies over desegregation, but in only a few of them did the courts order busing for the sake of achieving a racial balance in the schools. On the question of "white flight" from compulsory busing and racial balance, see Diane Ravitch, "The 'White Flight' Controversy," *The Public Interest* (Spring 1978), pp. 135-49, especially pp. 145-57; Christine H. Rossell, "School Desegregation and White Flight," *Political Science Quarterly* (Winter 1975), pp. 674-95; and the exchange between Ravitch and Rossell in *The Public Interest* (Fall 1978), pp. 109-13.

[4] 347 U.S. 483 (1954).

would establish that there is any principled foundation for these measures: there would still not be a principled ground for ordering any particular black or white student to a school on the basis of his race. Nor would there be a ground on which to show that one ratio of "integration" is any more valid or authoritative than another.

In fact, a large measure of the confusion over the question of busing arises from the uncertainty that has existed from the very beginning over the meaning and ends of "integration." That confusion was reflected most notably in the difficulties that the Supreme Court itself had in settling the grounds for its decision in *Brown* v. *Board of Education*. The problem in the *Brown* case was that the Court seriously confounded questions of "injury" and principle in judging the nature of the wrong that was involved in segregation. The Court was abetted in this misadventure by the testimony of social scientists, and since that time the courts have shown a reliance on the social sciences that can only be considered disturbing. For it is in the nature of the social sciences that their findings are merely statistical and contingent: what social science "knows" are patterns of averages and aggregates within "confidence intervals," bounded by circumstances that may be highly mutable. This does not mean that the findings of social science are not worth knowing; the question, rather, is whether findings that are based on correlations and aggregates can ever supply a proper basis in the law for ordering the conduct (or restricting the freedom) of any person in particular. I had occasion earlier to recall Kant's teaching on this point: viz., that any commands which aspire to the moral standing of "law" must be grounded in truths that are categorical, rather than propositions that are contingent and changing.[5] Before we would be justified in imposing laws on other people, we would be obliged to establish, as the ground of our action, propositions that hold true as a matter of necessity for others as well as ourselves. As Kant suggested, propositions of that kind must be extracted from the concept of morals itself or from the nature of that creature which has the capacity for moral judgments. I tried to show earlier that the wrong of racial defamation is rooted, in this way, in the concept of morals itself, and for that reason it must be "wrong" so long as we preserve in our language the understanding of "right" and

[5] See Chapter II, pp. 47-48, and the citations to Kant in notes 53 and 54. Also, see Thomas Reid, "First Principles of Contingent Truths," in his *Essays on the Intellectual Powers of Man* (Cambridge: MIT Press 1969; originally published in 1785), pp. 614-43.

"wrong." In that sense, the wrong of racial defamation is founded on a categorical proposition which holds true as a matter of necessity, and its validity as a proposition cannot possibly be affected by the vagaries of experience or the rearrangements of circumstance.

There is a radical difference between propositions of this kind and propositions on the order of, "If Saks Fifth Avenue moves into the neighborhood, the whole neighborhood will prosper." That proposition may be true; but then again it may not be. Whether it is true or not will be dependent or *contingent* on a number of other events. As we shall see shortly, the problem for our jurisprudence is that, over the past forty years, the argument against racial discrimination has been cast in the form of contingent propositions—propositions in the form, "If Saks Fifth Avenue moves into the neighborhood, the whole neighborhood will prosper."[6] As we shall also see, it has required at times a rare legal genius—to say nothing of a certain touch of fatuity—to translate the issues of any case into terms that could fit this formula. But the exercise has been wholly needless: it could be shown that the wrong of racial discrimination, like the wrong of racial defamation, is grounded in a principle that arises from the idea of morals itself. If our jurists had understood years ago the difference between a principle and an empirical prediction, if they had been clear from the beginning about the principle that was engaged in the cases on segregation, they could have spared us the confusion and the portentous silliness they have produced over the years as they have contrived racial formulas of one kind or another in matters ranging from busing to "affirmative action."

As it turns out, the same grounds of principle that establish the wrongness of segregation would make it necessary to reject the policies of busing and "affirmative action," or any of the other policies that seek to arrange benefits and restrict personal freedom on the basis of race. If we can turn away from the distractions of these policies, we may be freed to turn our attention to the proper ends of civil rights, including a number of possibilities that may previously have gone unnoticed. For once we come to recognize more precisely the principles that underlie a policy on civil rights, we may come to appreciate just how far those principles actually reach.

[6] For a fuller statement of this argument see my piece, "Bakke: The Legal Profession in Crisis," *The American Spectator* (February 1978), pp. 5-8.

1. THE SEGREGATION CASES AND
THE QUESTION OF "INJURIES"

When the Supreme Court came to its judgment in *Brown* v. *Board of Education*, it called back its landmark decision of 1896 in *Plessy* v. *Ferguson*;[7] and in four separate references it made clear that the earlier decision was being abandoned. At least as far as public education was concerned, the Court declared that "the doctrine of 'separate but equal' has no place."[8] It appeared that, as far as the Court itself was concerned, the doctrine had no place, for that matter, anywhere else in the public domain. And yet here, as in other instances, what the Court chose to leave unsaid was far more notable: in spite of the very precise and self-conscious references to the *Plessy* case, the Court made no mention of the first Justice Harlan. Nothing revealed more surely than that singular omission the decision that the Court had made *not* to found its judgment in *Brown* on that classic opinion by Justice Harlan in dissent. The *Plessy* case had involved an ordinance in Louisiana that all railroads carrying passengers within the state should provide "equal but separate accommodations for the white and colored races," either by providing two or more coaches or by setting up partitions within the coaches. In an opinion by Justice Brown, the Court upheld the statute as a regulation that was not unreasonable at the time as an effort to deal with two populations which were in many ways alien and hostile to one another, and to provide for the "public peace and good order."[9]

But the question of unreasonableness, of course, was bound up with the sense of whether any principle was being offended, and for Harlan a separation of the races ordained by law was offensive in a way that was wholly removed from the matter of those separations that were brought about by private aversions. There was a distinction that Harlan wished to preserve between social and civil equality[10]—between those discriminations that people observed in their private lives, and those disabilities they were willing to impose on others through the instrument of the law. Privately and socially, the races did not stand at that moment in a condition of equality in the United States. "The white race," said Harlan, "deems itself to be the dominant race in this country. And so it is, in prestige, in achievements, in education, in wealth, and in power."

[7] 163 U.S. 537 (1896).
[9] 163 U.S. at 550.

[8] 347 U.S. at 495.
[10] Ibid., at 559.

But the question of civil equality, equality in the law, was another matter:[11]

> [I]n view of the Constitution [wrote Harlan], in the eye of the law, there is in this country no superior, dominant, ruling class of citizens. There is no caste here. Our Constitution is color-blind, and neither knows nor tolerates classes among citizens. . . . The arbitrary separation of citizens, on the basis of race, while they are on a public highway, is a badge of servitude wholly inconsistent with the civil freedom and the equality before the law established by the Constitution. It cannot be justified upon any legal grounds.

In Harlan's understanding, the separation of the races by law placed the stamp of inferiority on a whole class of citizens, or at least it had that effect when it was animated by a clear intent to disparage, when the separation was embodied in "unfriendly legislation."[12] On the surface, Harlan's language seemed to come close to the accents of the modern Court when it declared in *Brown* that "separate educational facilities are inherently unequal," and that "to separate [black children] from others of similar age and qualifications solely because of their race generates a feeling of inferiority as to their status in the community that may affect their hearts and minds in a way unlikely ever to be undone."[13] But these words in the opinion of the Court did not precisely reflect Harlan's understanding. Or at least the Court was not willing to commit itself simply to the line of argument set forth by Harlan, because, it appears, the Court thought it had gotten hold of something far more compelling—the testimony of "modern authority" in "psychological knowledge."[14] At any rate, the apparent decision of the Court to turn away from Harlan—to avoid quoting him or even mentioning his name—was a clear indication that the Court had decided not to settle this case on the ground of Harlan's opinion in *Plessy* but along the lines of a different argument, which it had been developing over several years. It preferred to attach the decision in *Brown* to a train of cases that had begun in 1938 with *Missouri ex rel. Gaines* v. *Canada*,[15] and which had been continued most recently by *Sweatt* v. *Painter*[16] and *McLaurin* v. *Oklahoma*.[17]

[11] 163 U.S., 559, 562.   [12] Ibid., 556.

[13] 347 U.S. at 495, 494.   [14] Ibid., at 494.

[15] 305 U.S. 337 (1938).   [16] 339 U.S. 629 (1950).

[17] 339 U.S. 637 (1950); see also *Sipuel* v. *University of Oklahoma*, 332 U.S. 631 (1938).

In all of these cases the Court worked within the terms of the "separate but equal doctrine": its disposition was not to raise the question, in *principle*, about the justification for separating people on the basis of race. Its approach, rather, was to test the strict accuracy of the claim that separate facilities were rendering "equal" services. The design of its argument, as it became evident retrospectively, was to challenge the doctrine of separation *empirically* rather than philosophically—to show, in a variety of separate cases, that segregated conditions could never in fact be equal. In *Missouri ex rel. Gaines* v. *Canada*, Missouri had refused to admit blacks to the law school supported by the state. Instead, the state offered to pay "reasonable" tuition fees for any of its black citizens who could gain admission to law schools in adjacent states where segregation was not practiced. The Court struck down this arrangement and argued that Missouri was attempting to evade its responsibilities to provide equal treatment through the law: in furnishing a law school for whites only, the state was establishing privileges for white students that it was denying to blacks solely on account of their race.[18] Skipped over in this web of reasoning was the question, *What if the law schools in neighboring states were in fact superior to the law school at the University of Missouri?* Was it possible that blacks were given access, on account of their race, to a legal education that was better and more costly than that which was available to whites at the expense of the state?

In response to the ruling in the *Gaines* case, a number of states began to provide separate law schools and graduate facilities for black students. In *Sweatt* v. *Painter*, Sweatt had applied to the law school at the University of Texas and he had been rejected simply because he was black. The next year, the state set up a separate law school for blacks, but Sweatt refused to attend. In upholding Sweatt's claim, the Court became very precise in ticking off the features by which it would measure the equality of those facilities that were offered to blacks. As Chief Justice Vinson took care to point out in his opinion for the Court, the University of Texas Law School had sixteen full-time and three part-time professors, some of whom had a national reputation. It had a student body of 850 and a library with over 65,000 volumes. It had a law review, facilities for a moot court, and scholarship funds. Beyond that, its alumni held important places in the local practice of law and the public life of the state. In contrast, the law school for blacks was

---

[18] 305 U.S. at 342-43, 349.

to have no independent faculty; it would have four professors borrowed from the faculty of the University of Texas Law School; it would have a library of 10,000 volumes (most of which had not arrived), and it was, at that moment, without a librarian and without accreditation. In the meantime, a new law school had been opened at the Texas State University for Negroes, and that law school had five professors, twenty-three students, and one alumnus who had become a member of the Texas bar.[19]

"It is difficult to believe," wrote Vinson, "that one who had a free choice between these law schools would consider the question close."[20] Hovering over all these figures was the sense of those qualities, as Vinson said, "which are incapable of objective measurement but which make for greatness in a law school. Such qualities, to name but a few, include reputation of the faculty, experience of the administration, position and influence of the alumni, standing in the community, traditions and prestige."[21] Besides, as Vinson noted, no one would wish to study law in an "academic vacuum": blacks could study law in Texas only in a school that excluded from its student body that race from which the most influential members of the bar would be drawn.[22] It did not strictly follow, however, that the mere presence of blacks and whites in the same school could be guaranteed to provide the black student with the social intimacies and the personal connections that would be useful later in a career in law. The argument rested then on nothing more than a collection of *contingent* propositions of the most problematic kind. But no one on the Court was disposed to question these assumptions, and Vinson was content to find, in the diminished possibilities for student fellowship, a deprivation that foretold, *by necessity*, the want of material equality.

The Court found a rather similar kind of problem engaged in the *McLaurin* case, which was decided on the same day. There, a black student had been admitted to a graduate program in education at the University of Oklahoma, but by the provision of the legislature the instruction had to be provided in these cases on a "segregated basis": McLaurin was compelled, for example, to sit apart from the class in an anteroom adjoining the classroom; to work at a designated desk in the mezzanine of the library, but not to use the regular reading room; and to sit at a specified table by himself in the cafeteria.[23] In a formal sense, then, he did have access to the

---

[19] 339 U.S. at 632-33. [20] Ibid., at 634. [21] Ibid.
[22] Ibid. [23] 339 U.S. at 640.

library and to other facilities for study, and of course he could receive the instruction that was offered in the classroom (though he could not readily participate in any discussions in class). But these arrangements were still insufficient for the Court. Once again, the objection was not that there was something *in principle* questionable about the notion of separating people on the basis of their race, something that on the face of things called out for justification. The objection, rather, was that the restrictions placed on McLaurin deprived him of "effective graduate instruction." As Chief Justice Vinson wrote, these restrictions would "impair and inhibit his ability to study, to engage in discussions and exchange views with other students, and in general, to learn his profession."[24]

But whether, as an empirical matter, the absence of discussions would impair the ability of McLaurin to learn his profession or to cultivate his mind would have to depend—one is almost embarrassed to point out—on the quality of the minds that he encountered. (It is doubtful, say, that Thomas More would have found his own mind improved if he had been miraculously delivered from his solitude in the Tower of London and preserved for discussions with students at some graduate school of education.) But beyond that, if we were really considering the adequacy of the empirical argument here, it was not even evident that these clumsy arrangements of segregation would prevent, as Vinson said, the "intellectual commingling" of students of different races. As far as one knew, no legal barrier prevented students from talking outside of classes or even from meeting in the interstices of the cafeteria. There is no doubt, of course, that the state sought to discourage that kind of intercourse and to establish barriers, based on race, to an intimacy or acceptance that might have taken place privately on its own terms. But if the arrangement was to be challenged, it would have been better to challenge it by addressing the justification in principle for separation rather than linking that separation to the prospect of substantive injuries that were speculative in nature—injuries that did not flow as a matter of logical necessity from the fact of separation, and which were therefore open to the insistence, in any particular case, that the injury be demonstrated. All of these burdens and infirmities were built into the very nature of this "empirical" argument, and the contingent propositions, that the Court chose to employ, and they were carried over then into *Brown* v. *Board of Education*.

[24] Ibid., at 641.

Whatever the presumptions of an earlier age, the Court in *Brown* professed to be convinced that segregation itself was the source of substantive injuries, and, for that reason, it concluded that "separate educational facilities are inherently unequal."[25] The Court was not fully precise, though, on the nature of the injuries that it purported to find in this case, and it was not clear that the injuries were confined solely to the capacities of black children for education. As Chief Justice Warren presented the argument for the Court, the injuries could have been conceived in two separate ways. First, there was the sense of a diffuse, psychological harm, which did not have anything to do, necessarily, with education, but which *could* affect education, along with many areas of one's personal life. This is what the Court seemed to have in mind when it wrote, in that passage I quoted earlier, that "to separate [black children] from others of similar age and qualifications solely because of their race generates a feeling of inferiority as to their status in the community that may affect their hearts and minds in a way unlikely ever to be undone."[26]

A second possible kind of injury had a closer relation to education, and here the Court chose to speak indirectly by quoting from a lower court in Kansas:[27]

> Segregation of white and colored children in public schools has a detrimental effect upon the colored children. The impact is greater when it has the sanction of the law; for the policy of separating the races is usually interpreted as denoting the inferiority of the negro group. A sense of inferiority affects the motivation of a child to learn. Segregation with the sanction of law, therefore, has a tendency to retard the educational and mental development of negro children and to deprive them of some of the benefits they would receive in a racial[ly] integrated school system.

On a close reading, this passage from the lower court might have lent itself to two different constructions: the source of the injury might have lain in the sense of inferiority that was impressed on black children when the state imposed a system of segregation with the "sanction of law." On the other hand, the court might have been arguing that blacks were being deprived of some substantive thing, some benefit that would flow to them if they had access to an "integrated school system." It is the latter proposition that comes

---

[25] 347 U.S. at 495.   [26] Ibid., at 494.   [27] Ibid.

closer to the understanding that has been drawn more generally from *Brown*, and it presupposed two further points. It assumes, first, that we can in fact know the approximate balance among the races (50-50? 60-40? 70-30?) that would constitute an "integrated" school—i.e., a school sufficiently integrated that it would avert the putative injuries which are suffered by black children in segregated settings. Once we define the problem as the Court defined it here, it is not sufficient any longer to say that a school avoids the practice of segregation if it simply refrains from assigning pupils to school on the basis of race for the purpose of preserving separate black and white schools. By that measure, a school system may avoid policies of segregation, and yet the students could arrange themselves, through their own private decisions, in schools that are almost entirely black or white. The argument of the Court here, however, is that "integration" commands the actual presence of blacks and whites in the same schools, and commands them in sufficient numbers to avoid injuries to black students. As a second point, the *Brown* decision assumed that we can indeed specify the nature of the injury sustained by black students as a result of going to school without the presence of whites. But *this* proposition, as we have learned over the last twenty years, is no easy matter to prove.

In any event, with all of its burdens of argument, this is the understanding that the Court finally supported, the same understanding that guided its decisions in *McLaurin* and *Sweatt*: viz., that black students were being injured in a material way as a result of being deprived of the presence of white schoolmates. It was for this "finding" that the Court claimed the support of "modern authority" in "psychological knowledge"; and what the justices drew on here most importantly was a short, summary report that had been drafted for the Court by Kenneth Clark, the psychologist, and two of his colleagues. The report was derived mainly from a paper that Clark had written a few years earlier for a White House conference on children.[28] But that document, in turn, was largely another survey of the literature in the field. As far as original research went, there was only one project of Clark's own undertaking that was mentioned in the body of the report, but that work, brief as it was, became the pivot on which the argument turned.

[28] "Effect of Prejudice and Discrimination on Personality Development," prepared for the Mid-Century White House Conference on Children and Youth (1950); revised and reprinted in *Prejudice and Your Child* (Boston: Beacon Press, 1955 and 1963).

There is no need for an extended discussion here of Clark's work, since it has been considered in detail elsewhere in a critical vein.[29] It may be sufficient to describe very briefly the design of his experiments and recall the main points he extracted from the research. The principal study that figured in Clark's report had been published in two separate pieces by Clark and his wife. The Clarks focused on a sample composed entirely of black children who ranged in age between three and seven. A little more than half of them were in segregated nursery and grammar schools in Arkansas, while the remainder were in racially mixed schools in Springfield, Massachusetts. In one part of the study, the children were given four dolls that were identical in every respect except that two were brown with black hair, while two were white with yellow hair. After it was established that the children were indeed aware that the dolls were meant to represent different races, the children were told to choose the doll they liked to play with or liked best; the one that was a "nice" doll or a "nice" color; the one that looked "bad"; the one that looked like a Negro child; and the one that looked like themselves. In the second part of the study the children were given a set of line drawings that included a boy and a girl, along with a leaf, an apple, an orange, and a mouse. There was an initial test to determine whether the children had an accurate sense of color, and then they were asked to color the boy or girl the color that they themselves were. Finally, on a fresh set of drawings, the children were asked to color them the color they liked little boys or girls to be.

Without reviewing the findings in all their detail, it may be enough to say that they described, most importantly, a certain aversion on the part of the black children toward the condition of being black. Overall, 67 percent of the children preferred to play with the white dolls; 59 percent thought the white doll was the "nice" one; and 59 percent thought the colored doll looked "bad."[30] These preferences tended to drop off gradually as one advanced among the cohorts by age, and so among the seven-year-olds there were as many children who favored the colored as favored the white dolls.

But within the geographic regions represented in the sample, the differences began to sharpen. A larger majority of the children in

[29] See Arkes, "The Problem of Kenneth Clark," *Commentary* (November 1974), pp. 37-46.

[30] Kenneth and Mamie Clark, "Racial Identification and Preference in Negro Children," in T. M. Newcomb and E. L. Hartley, eds., *Readings in Social Psychology* (New York: H. Holt, 1947), pp. 173-74.

the North tended to favor the white dolls (72 percent, as opposed to 62 percent in the South); but, while even the children in the South were inclined toward the white dolls, they were much less disposed at the same time to reject the colored ones. (Seventy-one percent of the Northern children thought that the colored doll looked "bad," while only 49 percent of the Southern children shared that view.)[31] The differences were even more pronounced when it came to the coloring tests. When they were asked to fill in the drawing with the color they preferred little boys or girls to be, 70 percent of the Southern children showed a preference for brown, while only 36 percent of the children in the North expressed that preference. Forty-four percent of the Northern children conveyed a preference for white, while that choice was registered by only a quarter of the children in the South.[32]

When the children were asked about their reasons for rejecting the colored doll, two of the children in the South remarked, " 'cause he is a nigger." Many of the children were evasive in their answers, and in some cases they were clearly strained by the prospect of defining their racial character and connecting themselves, explicitly, to a color. As the Clarks reported, "two children ran out of the testing room, inconsolable, convulsed in tears." In the Northern group, a seven-year-old with light skin tried to explain that he was actually white, but that he had become very suntanned in the summer. This gesture merely confirmed, though, for the Clarks, the things that the boy already knew. By the age of five, they concluded, most black children could not escape a realistic sense of their own racial character, and they had absorbed the notion that to be colored in America was a mark of inferior status.[33]

But then what exactly had these studies established? There was the need, said the Clarks, for "a definite mental hygiene" and a program of education that would "relieve children of the tremendous burden of feelings of inadequacy and inferiority."[34] There was no mention here of the integration of the schools as the remedy for the problem disclosed by the study, and the omission was not inadvertent. What the study suggested most strongly was that black children esteemed themselves less for their blackness; and, in that

[31] Ibid., 174, 177.

[32] Kenneth and Mamie Clark, "Emotional Factors in Racial Identification and Preference in Negro Children," *Journal of Negro Education*, Vol. 19 (1950), pp. 341-50, at 346.

[33] Ibid., at 348; Clark, note 30 above, at 178.

[34] Clark, note 32 above, at 350.

want of esteem, that sense of being stamped instantly with a lesser worth, one may indeed find a certain burden or injury, especially for younger children. But in all strictness, the Clarks had not established in their own study that the schools were the principal or even an important source of those things in the society that instilled in black children an awareness of inferior standing; they had not shown that these attitudes of the black children were in any way related to disabilities in learning; and clearly they had not demonstrated that the injuries were likely to be redressed through the racial integration of the schools. In fact, if the injury were shown in the tendency of black children to reject their blackness, then it was the children in the *North*, in the less segregated settings, who had exhibited these injuries to the greatest degree.

There was a striking discrepancy then between the thesis that the Court had been arguing in *Brown* and the evidence that had allegedly supported it. Of course, one need not have taken Kenneth Clark's work as the last, or the only, word on the subject. It was open to others to conduct studies that might confirm the argument or demonstrate that certain levels of integration are in fact more beneficial than others. The most notable effort in this direction came with the Coleman Report and with the reanalysis of the Coleman data that was carried out at Harvard.[35] I had reason earlier to review some of the most important findings in these studies.[36] and it may be enough here to recall only one or two of the points that bear most decisively on the question at hand.

The Coleman study seemed at first glance to lend some support to the case for racial integration in the schools. For it was found in the study that the main differences among schools—in facilities, books, or even in the teachers themselves—accounted for very little of the disparity between those students who did well and those who did poorly. What seemed to be more important in accounting for these differences was the social composition of the student body, and three measures, in particular, stood out from the others: the education of the parents, the standard of living of the family, and—rather tellingly—the percentage of black students in the school. But among these measures, the first two produced a positive correlation with the average scores among schools on standardized tests, while the third one, the percentage of black students, produced a negative correlation. That is to say, the larger the proportion of black stu-

[35] See Frederick Mosteller and Daniel P. Moynihan, eds., *On Equality of Educational Opportunity* (New York: Random House, 1972).

[36] See Chapter VII, Section 2, "Distributive Justice in the Schools: Some Empirical Findings."

dents in any school, the lower generally were the average scores of the students. To put the matter more exactly, the melancholy conclusion from the data was that black students were likely to do better, in the aggregate, in a school with a white majority, where the proportion of black students did not exceed 25 percent.[37]

Still, there were some points of caution that had to be considered. When the study was undertaken for the Coleman Report, only about 13 percent of black students in the sample could be found in schools in this "optimal" range (where the proportion of black students did not exceed 25 percent). There is some reason to suspect that the social standing of these black students might have been somewhat higher than those of blacks in predominantly black schools. In the converse situation, white students who were in predominantly black schools tended to fall below the blacks on measures of social standing, and they were generally below the black students, also, in their test scores.[38] The upshot may be that the variations in performance have more to do with the social standing and the attitudes of the students than with special effects that are generated by a racial "mix" of 75-25.

It is necessary to recall that the black children in these predominantly white schools did not perform at as high a level, for the most part, as the white students (perhaps because they still lagged behind white students in the "middle-class" attributes of their families). In fact, as I reported earlier, the black students were generally far behind: the differences between the averages of the two groups were often as much as two standard deviations.[39] In other words, even under the conditions of integration that were supposedly the best, the schools did not efface the important disparities, in the aggregate, between black and white students, and they did not bring about an equality of achievement, on the average, between the two groups. Of course, the discussion here is cast in terms of aggregates, and that may conceal the fact that many individual black students performed beyond the level of individual white students. But at the same time, the aggregate character of the findings should warn us about the problematic nature of deploying them as the basis for anything that would call itself "law."

That is to say, a serious question could be raised about the adequacy of any such statistical correlations as the basis for overriding the personal freedom of anyone in particular by assigning him to

[37] See David Armor, "School and Family Effects on Black and White Achievement: A Reexamination of the USOE Data," in Mosteller and Moynihan, note 35 above, pp. 197, 215.

[38] Ibid., p. 226.   [39] Ibid., pp. 199, 203.

a designated school. If he happens to be a black student, all we could tell him is that this is a school where black students, on the average, are likely to score higher than the black students in a predominantly black school. Whether he himself would show an improvement as a result of being placed there, we could not know. All we could say is that, on the basis of the studies we have had so far, a racial mix of 75 percent white and 25 percent black can account for about 9 percent of the variation in the test scores of students. The question is whether these odds are sufficiently great to justify compulsion in assigning a student to a school that he prefers not to attend. Are there any demonstrable injuries that will be averted if this scheme of compulsion is forgone? Are the interests at stake here sufficiently real or substantial that they outweigh other interests reflected in the choice of a school—for example, the interest in sending children to school nearer to home, where the parents may have some prospect of involving themselves in the life of the school? But even more to the point, the question is whether such empirical and contingent findings can ever replace those moral axioms that ought to be adduced as the ground of action before we place citizens under the compulsion of law.

It could hardly improve matters to suggest that integration in the schools holds out the promise of "education" of another kind: perhaps not the cultivation of competence in the formal disciplines of learning, but the acquisition at least of a certain worldliness through an exposure to different races. In the groove of this kind of argument, it is rather easy, also, to merge with the so-called "contact" hypothesis, which enjoyed for many years an engaging credulity among sophisticated people that was largely free from any obsessive reliance on the merits of the argument: to wit, that the more people came to know one another, the more they would come to like one another. This revelation was buoyed up for a long while by a host of convenient sociological studies. More recently, however, there have been other studies that have restored, for academic audiences, the common sense of the matter, which is usually accessible to most people with experience in the world: that whether people actually come to like one another as they come to see more of one another depends most decisively on the terms on which their meeting takes place—whether they meet, for example, in collaboration for good ends, or whether they meet as victims and assailants; and it depends, then, on whether they happen to be, as individuals, particularly worthy of being liked.[40] It is doubtful that the expe-

---

[40] David Armor reported on one study, written in 1972, which found that "those

rience of integration in South Boston, attended as it has been with reciprocal and persisting violence, has in any way enlarged the goodness of the community. Even in a more liberal community, such as Berkeley, some recent testimony suggests that, in spite of a firm policy of busing and integration, blacks and whites (and Chicanos and Orientals) have managed to isolate themselves in their own groups and pastimes. It appears, also, that they have avoided even an elementary commerce in the common affairs of the schools (such as elections to student government: a black student in Berkeley High School won election as president when the white students refused to vote).[41] One may deplore these tendencies toward isolation, except that the motives for this drawing in are not always malicious or ungenerous. One may have a certain sympathy, for example, for the black parents who would prefer to have their children in a school that is predominantly black, where there may be a firmer accent placed on the history and achievements of black people. A preference of that kind is no more inscrutable than the preference of certain Catholic parents that the education of their children should be attended by explicit religious and moral teaching from a Catholic perspective. There can be nothing illegitimate in the disposition of these parents toward an education that cultivates the sense of a more particular ethic, so long as that ethic is not incompatible with the principles that underlie a common citizenship. And would it not be damning to suggest that a school composed almost entirely of black children is in itself pathological, or that it must retard, by its very nature, the capacity of black children to learn? No policy based on such assumptions could survive critical examination, nor could it be grounded in anything approximating the status of a principle of law.

2. RACE, MORALS, AND THE IDEA OF LAW

Yet the Court, in the *Brown* case, did glimpse at least the outlines of a real principle. In the passage that the Court had quoted from

---

students who had direct classroom contact with bused black students showed *less* support for the busing program than those without direct contact. In fact, the kind of students who were generally the most supportive [of the program on busing]— the middle-class, high-achieving students—showed the largest decline in support as a result of contact with bused black students." Armor, "The Evidence on Busing," *The Public Interest* (Summer 1972), pp. 103-104.

[41] Nathan Glazer, "Is Busing Necessary," *Commentary* (March 1972), pp. 39, 51; also, *Hearings before the Select Committee of the Senate on Equal Educational Opportunity*, 92nd Cong., 1st Sess., Pt. 9A, 4058ff. (1971).

the lower court in Kansas there could be found this separable theme: that "the impact [of segregation] is greater when it has the sanction of the law; for the policy of separating the races is usually interpreted as denoting the inferiority of the Negro group."[42] For a number of reasons it tends to be overlooked now that, in the brief presented to the Court by Kenneth Clark and the social scientists, the explicit emphasis was placed on this very same point: Clark and his colleagues did not claim to document the injuries done to black students or to establish the degree of integration that was likely to avert those injuries. They professed to speak only in relation to segregation that "results from or is supported by the action of any official body or agency representing some branch of government."[43] It was one thing if private citizens brought about a pattern of racial separation through a host of private, uncoordinated acts; but it was far worse when the state took up that practice of exclusion, raised it to the level of principle, and then held it up to the public with the force of law. What all of this recalled, of course, was the spirit of Justice Harlan's argument in dissent in the *Plessy* case, that "in view of the Constitution, in the eye of the law, there is in this country no superior . . . class of citizens. . . . Our Constitution is color-blind."

But apart from the summoning force of these lines, Harlan never explained the principle which entailed the conclusion that the law must be colorblind. He was undoubtedly right when he argued in *Plessy* that the separation of the races in railway carriages "proceed[ed] on the ground that colored citizens are so inferior and degraded that they cannot be allowed to sit in public coaches occupied by white citizens."[44] And it was indeed wrong, as Harlan said, to place a whole class of citizens in an inferior rank. But in the tradition of political and constitutional theory that Justice Harlan shared, it was quite legitimate to place a whole class of people in a lower position simply by denying them admission to the privileges of citizenship. For his own part, Harlan was quite willing himself to make these discriminations, but what is more, he made it clear in his opinion in the *Plessy* case that *he was willing to found these discriminations explicitly on race*. At one point in his opinion, Harlan had the occasion to mention the Chinese, and he said, "There is a race so different from our own that we do not permit

42 347 U.S. at 494.
43 "The Effects of Segregation and the Consequences of Desegregation: A Social Science Statement," reprinted in Clark, note 28 above, pp. 166, 167.
44 163 U.S. at 560.

those belonging to it to become citizens of the United States. Persons belonging to it are, with few exceptions, absolutely excluded from our country."[45] But one could not accept the use of race as a ground of principle in making these kinds of discriminations in regard to citizenship without implying, at the same time, that it might be legitimate to use race as the basis for other discriminations, among citizens as well.

Harlan's comments on the Chinese cannot be easily dismissed as a personal aberration, for he was willing on other occasions to join the majority of the Court in cases that dealt rather illiberally with Chinese aliens.[46] In these instances, he noticeably held back from joining the dissenters in the kinds of judgments that typically moved him to opposition when they were directed toward blacks and Indians.[47] Just how he was able to reconcile these conflicting lines in his jurisprudence I cannot say, but his comments on the Chinese are sufficient to raise serious doubts about the grounds on which Harlan ultimately understood that the separation of the race by law must be in principle a wrong. It is doubtful that Harlan would have found it unreasonable if, instead of separating people by race, the state of Louisiana and the railroads had provided that convicted criminals who were on the way to prison would have to ride in a separate compartment. The principle that is finally involved in cases like *Plessy* and *Brown* is the same principle that was engaged in the defamation of racial groups; and its recognition would begin, I think, with a sense of the things that distinguish "groups" such as "convicted criminals" from groups such as "blacks." The only kinds of classes that may, with justice, be disparaged in the law, or placed in a position of lesser privilege, are classes defined by the performance of specific criminal acts or by the presence of common disabilities (e.g., mental incompetents). At rare moments certain religious groups may come close to that first category (as, for example, if they engaged in the practice of burning a widow on the funeral pyre of her dead husband) although our tendency would probably be to ban the practice rather than the sect. In general, however, it may be said that aggregates such as racial, religious, or nationality groups cannot be among those classes that the law may single out for special punishment or restriction. And the reason, once again, is that we cannot attribute to these groups, as corporate

[45] 163 U.S. at 561.

[46] See, e.g., *Fong Yue Ting* v. *United States*, 139 U.S. 698 (1893).

[47] In relation to Indians, see, for example, Harlan's dissenting opinion in *Elk* v. *Wilkins*, 112 U.S. 94, at 110-23 (1894).

entities, a tendency toward criminality or immorality, as though the group exerted some unfailing deterministic control over the moral practice of each member. One would have to assume, in this perspective, a determinism of behavior that is so thorough and unshakable that the individual could not detach himself at any moment from the ethic of the group, that he could not hold himself back on occasion and reach a judgment of right and wrong that diverges from the dominant code within the group.

As I argued earlier, this notion of group determinism would withdraw from human beings that attribute of moral autonomy which is the distinct mark of human nature and the premise of law itself. For without the assumption of some essential moral autonomy on the part of individuals, there could be no place for the concepts of jurisprudence and citizenship. Jurisprudence must assume that individuals can be held responsible for their own acts, and this assumption would hardly be warranted if human beings did not have sufficient autonomy to form their own acts and reach judgments over matters of right and wrong.[48] If they lacked that capacity, they could not be admitted to the office of citizenship, for they could surely make no claim to take part in reaching judgments about the gravest matters.

The problem therefore with policies of racial segregation is that they rest on premises that must be inconsistent at their root with the concept of morals itself and the foundation of all legal rights. If those policies are not wrong, nothing can be wrong, for there can be no such notions as "right" and "wrong" to which individuals can be held responsible. For that reason it is not necessary to show any ancillary "injury" that flows from segregation; nor does it require any series of empirical experiments to show that segregation is wrong. The wrongness inheres simply in the principle that animates the act.

Whether the problem at hand is racial discrimination or the defamation of racial groups, there is a willingness to create disabilities for individuals, not on the basis of their own merits, but on the strength of certain characteristics that they are presumed to share with a racial aggregate. It is assumed that if we simply knew the racial or ethnic group to which a person is connected, we would know something also about his prospects for being a good neighbor, perhaps, or a good employee or citizen. And so if we find that the rate of violent crime is in fact higher in black neighborhoods, we

[48] See, again, Chapter II, pp. 48-49.

may conclude that the risk of violent crime rises as the proportion of blacks in the neighborhood increases. Those calculations may in fact be tenable in the aggregate, but, as I remarked earlier, it would be a manifest injustice to assume, on the basis of aggregate data, that the black man who wishes to move in next door is likely to be a criminal. What we know about the characteristics of blacks in the aggregate cannot be the basis for anything we do of moral consequence in relation to any black person in particular. To assume otherwise, we would have to overturn the notion of morals itself and reject the premises that are implicit in the very idea of law. It is these reasons, I think, which finally establish the ground of principle on which the holding in the *Brown* case must be settled; and they explain that sense of the matter, which seems now to have become so widely diffused, that there is, in the principle of separation by race, the essence of injustice.

Once one is clear about the nature of the controlling principle, many other things begin to fall into place, and there may be a means of avoiding many of the confusions that have distracted the courts over the years in their efforts to apply the logic of the *Brown* case. It would make a profound difference, for example, to recognize that the "wrong" involved in racial discrimination is contained in the principle itself, and that the question of a material injury is not only rather speculative and problematic, but largely irrelevant to the point of law. The explicit separation of students by race would hardly be rendered more defensible by any showing that the students are "happier" or that their academic performance has even improved as a result of the segregation. Such contingent, empirical findings have no bearing, one may say, on the principle of the case. There is a serious confusion, then, when the case against segregation is made to rest on the promise of some other, material benefits that a policy of integration will bring. No such benefits can possibly be implicit in the notion of ending segregation; no such benefits have been demonstrated over the last twenty-five years, nor, in the nature of things, can they ever be.

The search for the material injuries of segregation has led to ritual acts of vacuity on the part of lawyers and judges, as they have sought to justify the extension of the law to cover instances of discrimination in places other than the public schools. It is no sign of a sound profession when its practitioners show a persistent willingness to delude themselves, and the law may become disordered in a fundamental way when it comes to accept a notable disparity between the legal grounds on which it decides a class of cases and the grounds on which the injuries in these cases are indeed judged to be "wrongs." And so when it came to the matter of barring discrimination in places of public accommodation, the argument offered by the government in the highest tribunal did not rest upon any wrong in principle that was implicit in the act of discrimination. Nor did it rest finally on any material injury that was visited upon black people. Instead, the argument was shaped to fit the contorted formulas that have become rituals under the Commerce Clause: The problem was not so much that blacks were discouraged from traveling in interstate commerce because they were deterred by conventions of discrimination; the problem, rather, was that, if blacks *were* discouraged in this way, the effect would be to reduce the total volume of trade that was available to restaurants, inns, and other places of public accommodation. In turn, that shortfall of trade would reduce the amount of orders that these businesses would place with other businesses (for food, linens, furniture, or any number of other things) and so the effect would be to depress even further the level of trade and, presumably, the standard of living.[49] In the eyes of the law then, the problem with discrimination in places of public accommodation did not lie in any injustice that was done to black people, but in the interference it might produce in the interstate flow of meat!

It might be pointed out, with some irreverence, that when the argument is made to rest on an empirical prediction, rather than a necessary principle, it may be overcome by means that are quite as divorced from the conditions of justice. In this instance, if the argument is taken on its own terms, the justification of the law would dissolve if the racists in the country simply decided to eat more meat or do more traveling.

The question of how the government would reach places of public accommodation is a separate matter from the question of, "Where precisely does the wrong of the case lie?" If we could get clear on the principle involved in these cases of racial discrimination, we would discover that the principle is capable of having a much wider application than any doctrine which was actually set down in the *Brown* case. We would be able to explain then, far more persuasively, just how the Court could extend itself from *Brown* and the problem of education to the point where it could reach public inns, restaurants, and swimming pools. By analogy, once we are clear

---

[49] See *Katzenbach* v. *McClung*, 379 U.S. 294, at 381-82 (1964).

on the principle that accounts for the rate at which a ball moves
down an inclined plane, it becomes virtually irrelevant as to whether
the plane is blue or yellow, whether it is made out of plastic or
wood, or whether it is located near an interstate highway. Once
we understand the principle that defines the nature of the wrong
in cases of racial discrimination, there is no need to fashion a
separate rule for every instance in which the same principle manages
to manifest itself.

With that recognition we would have a basis for moving beyond
the distractions of busing or "racial balance" and identifying
wrongs that have only barely been perceived—and which have
found no place in our current laws. In the case, for example, of
racial discrimination in employment, we would have the grounds
on which to identify the presence of a wrong even in companies
with fewer than fifteen employees that might not have much effect
on interstate commerce.[50] What we would come to recognize, in
other words, is that the nature of the wrong would be more important than the size of the establishment or the extent of its operations. From the standpoint of what public law may properly
reach, it is conceivable that it may cover the proprietor of a hotdog
stand, who has no discernible effect on interstate commerce, while
it may tenably leave untouched any private discriminations that
take place in the homes of Henry Ford or David Rockefeller, where
the numbers of people could be far larger and the "influence" on
interstate commerce could be far more pronounced.

And so the understanding I am holding out here of the principle
in the *Brown* case would be able to reach many cases of discrimination that have not been reached before (or which have not been
reached as clearly). At the same time, though, this understanding
would draw us back in a number of other instances where the rule
in *Brown* has not only been applied erroneously, but where the

---

[50] These were the terms of limitation that were employed in the Equal Employment
Opportunity Act of 1972 in an effort to define—not, ultimately, in a very satisfying
way—the principled bounds to the coverage of the Act. An "employer" subject to
the Act was defined as "a person engaged in an industry affecting commerce who
has fifteen or more employees for each working day in each of twenty or more
calendar weeks in the current or preceding calendar year." 42 U.S.C.A. Sec. 2000e.
The number had been fixed in an earlier Act at twenty-five employees, and with
these guidelines the courts have held in different places that the Salvation Army is
an "industry affecting commerce" within the meaning of the Act, but that the statute
does not apply to a package liquor store with less than twenty-five employees.
McClure v. *Salvation Army*, 460 F. 2d 553 (1972); *Coon* v. *Tingle*, 277 F. Supp.
304 (1967).

extension has to be inconsistent with the basic principle that comes out of the *Brown* case. The example that stands out most conspicuously in this respect is the understanding of "desegregation" and busing in the schools.

3. RACIAL BALANCING AND BUSING: THE UNDOING OF A PRINCIPLE

In the understanding I have set forth here, the nature of the offense in *Brown* was the assignment of students to schools explicitly on the basis of race. The offense would be removed, very simply, by discontinuing the system of racial assignment. Aside from that, there would be no principled grounds for saying that any particular ratio of blacks to whites in any school makes a school more "integrated" and less offensive in the eyes of the law. Once a school board had removed the public hand of discrimination, parents and students would be free to choose schools in any practicable way they could, and the manner in which the races are distributed overall in the schools would be a matter largely of indifference as far as the law is concerned. For it would be legitimate for black parents, if they wished, to send their children to schools that were predominantly black, or to prefer schools within walking distance of their homes. (It may be recalled that, in the *Brown* case, it was the black children who were forced to be bused out of their neighborhoods so that they could attend a school that was confined legally to blacks. The white children had the privilege of going to schools within their own neighborhoods; the black children had the "privilege" of having their transportation expenses picked up by the state.)[51] That is not to say that it should be a matter of indifference to society if there are racial concentrations in housing that are brought about by racial discrimination. It is to say, rather, that the conventions which work toward the separation of the races in housing deserve to be attacked on their own terms, in the places where they exist. The burden of social policy in these other areas should not be borne by the schools, especially when there is no basis for saying that any given distribution of blacks and whites in the schools is better or worse in principle than any other.

As I have already shown, the only data that would furnish anything resembling a guideline on integration are the findings that come out of the Coleman study, and those findings would prescribe

[51] *Brown* v. *Board of Education*, 98 F. Supp. 797, 798 (1951).

a proportion of blacks in each school that does not rise about 25 percent. But as I have argued, there is something in the very nature of those findings that renders them invalid, in a strict sense, as the source of a standard in the law. And yet if it is assumed for a moment that the findings in the Coleman study suggest the levels of integration that are "optimal," they could not possibly be the guidelines that the courts have had in mind when they have ordered a racial balance in the schools that approximates the ratio of blacks to whites in the local community as a whole. That formula, when applied in New York City, would establish in each school a white minority of about 33 percent. If credence were given to the Coleman Report, the results of this "racial balancing" would not be very salutary as far as education is concerned, and the most likely outcome of a plan of this kind would be to force an even larger movement to the private schools or the suburbs.

In order to understand what it is that the courts have had in mind with the orders on busing and racial balance, it is necessary to begin with a sense of the predicament that the courts found themselves in as they sought to carry out what they thought to be the imperatives arising out of the *Brown* case. The decision in *Brown* might have been understood, as I have said, in a very simple way, to mean that local school boards may not assign students to schools on the basis of race. In this reading of the decision, a system of neighborhood assignment may suggest itself, quite plausibly, as a method of assignment that is racially "neutral." And if it were understood at the outset that the precise number of blacks and whites in any school is not especially critical, the system of neighborhood assignment would commend itself as the most likely and workable solution.[52] But it was not fully clear to the judges that the proportions of blacks and whites in each school were largely irrelevant. Beyond that, the persisting imbalances among the schools began to draw the attention of the courts to those instances in which the system of assignment within the neighborhoods bore the traces of a lingering intent to distribute students, as much as possible, on the basis of race: the lines that defined the neighborhood zones were drawn by some school boards in such a way as to coincide with the division between black and white settlements

---

[52] See, e.g., *Green* v. *New Kent County*, 391 U.S. 430 (1968), where there seemed to be an absence of residential segregation, and so the Supreme Court thought that a system of neighborhood assignment or "geographic zoning" was likely to produce a racially neutral distribution of students.

in the city.[53] The courts would intervene and order the school boards to draw new zones, which could not be identified by race.[54] But then the courts found reason to believe that the new lines were taken as official signposts or markers, which would set off movements of white families until the school districts coincided once again with neighborhoods defined by race. And so even when a school board committed itself to a neutral system of assignment within the neighborhoods, those clear public guidelines provided an incentive for families to arrange themselves in such a way that the distribution of students among schools was still determined largely by race.[55]

Faced with this prospect, the courts began to insist that, in making decisions on new construction, a school board had an obligation to build new schools in certain "in-between" areas at the edge of racial settlements, where there might be a chance of pulling in a more heterogeneous student body. In Pontiac, Michigan, the school board came under the censure of the courts for building schools within the established zones in order to accommodate the overflow of students in black and white schools without disturbing the racial character of any district. When a black school became overcrowded once in the mid-fifties, the board built another one in the black neighborhood to catch the overflow. At the same time, a white school in the northern part of the city had an excess capacity, but no black students were assigned there. In the judgment of the federal district court, school boards could be held responsible now for acts of omission: the tendency to hold back from efforts to promote "more" integration would be taken as the sign of an intention to preserve "segregation." "When the power to act is available," said the court, "failure to take the necessary steps so as to negate or

[53] See *Davis* v. *School District of Pontiac*, 309 F. Supp. 734, 741 (1970); *Brewer* v. *School Board of Norfolk*, 397 F. 2d 37 (1968); *Sloan* v. *10th School District of Wilson County*, 433 F. 2d 487 (1970); *U.S.* v. *Board of Education, Independent School District No. 1*, 429 F. 2d 1253 (1970); *U.S.* v. *School District 151 of Cook County*, 404 F. 2d 1125 (1968); *Spangler* v. *Pasadena Board of Education*, 311 F. Supp. 501 (1970).

[54] See *Swann* v. *Charlotte-Mecklenburg*, 402 U.S. 1, 27-28 (1971); *Bradley* v. *Richmond*, 338 F. Supp. 67, 74-76 (1972); also, *Davis* v. *Board of School Commissioners of Mobile*, 402 U.S. 33 (1971); *U.S.* v. *Board of School Commissioners of Indianapolis*, 332 F. Supp. 655 (1971); *Haney* v. *Sevier Co.*, 410 F. 2d 920 (1969) (a black school board seeking to preserve an all-black school district); *Yarbrough* v. *Hubert-West Memphis School District*, 329 F. Supp. 1059 (1971).

[55] See *Swann*, note 54 above, at 20-21.

alleviate a situation which is harmful is a wrong as is the taking of affirmative steps to advance the situation."[56]

The problem, though, was that these efforts to build school districts around people, as it were, and lure them into integration could be seen rather quickly for what they were, and they, too, threatened to launch movements of population. Under these circumstances, a local school board might have been forgiven if it took a more modest view of its own mandates and decided that it did not have, after all, a license to set off movements of population and alter the residential landscape of the community. For their own part, the courts found, in a sobering way, that, despite their persisting efforts, the ends of integration, or what they thought were the ends prescribed in the *Brown* case, continued to elude them. One prop after another would be knocked out from under the "dual school system," but the judges came to see a "dual system" in any place where there were large concentrations of blacks and whites in separate schools; and when the matter was viewed with that kind of lens the "dual system" seemed to be standing very much as it stood earlier. Of course, the experience could have been taken as a warrant for raising some hard questions about the ends of the law or the standards of the courts. But in the absence of that kind of reflection, the judges seemed to be driven finally to bypass all of the barriers that were being cast up by a combination of law, social convention, and simple administrative ingenuity. Instead of tinkering with a succession of "neutral" schemes of assignment that turned out to produce very little mingling of the races, they would cut through the problem more directly: they would simply assign pupils to schools *in the very proportions in which they would be distributed by race if the forces that directed students to different schools were thoroughly "colorblind" in nature.* Hence the decision to "balance" schools by race: to assign students to the schools by race in proportions that would reflect the ratio of blacks to whites in the local community.[57]

What the courts had decided to do, in effect, was to order the results that would have occurred if the students were assigned to

---

[56] *Davis*, note 53 above, 734-41.

[57] *Swann* v. *Charlotte-Mecklenburg*, 306 F. Supp. 1299, 1312 (1969). This part of the judgment of the district court was approved by the Supreme Court in *Swann*, note 54 above, at 23-25, but even more importantly, see the judgment of the Court in "Swann II," *North Carolina State Board of Education* v. *Swann*, 402 U.S. 43, 45-46 (1971).

schools in a "random" way. In simple random sampling, each individual in a population has an equal chance of being selected, and, as the method would be applied to the schools, it would mean that each individual in the pool of students in the city would have an equal probability of being selected for any particular school (depending, of course, on its size), anywhere in the city. The process would banish race completely as a relevant feature of selection, along with every other attribute that would make individuals in the pool distinguishable from one another (e.g., religion, hair color, athletic abilities). As a result, students would be distributed among the separate schools by race in proportions that were roughly equivalent to their proportions in the city as a whole. And so, if the ratio of whites to blacks overall in the school system were something like 60-40, and students were assigned in a random way, the results would be a division in each school that was roughly 60-40. (There could be some slight departures—59-41 or even 55-45—but most schools would be rather close to 60-40.)

The process would be faultlessly, quintessentially impersonal. It would be the ultimate guarantee of impartial selection, and it would be suited to the end it was supposed to serve: not the assignment of students in a fixed proportion to meet some formula for an "optimal" racial balance, but the guarantee that students were being assigned to schools in a manner that had absolutely nothing to do with race. If the judges had known something about statistics, they might have ordered a system of random assignment and said nothing about racial quotas. Instead of fixing the proportions of the races in each school, they could have declared merely that they were ordering a system of assignment that was wholly colorblind and that they would abide by the racial distributions that were produced in any school by that method.

But if the judges had been clear and explicit in this way about what they were doing, and if they really had ordered a system of random assignment, then they would have brought out even more explicitly the things that were most problematic about their ends. Randomness may be the essence of impartiality, but in popular understanding it is also identified rather widely with arbitrariness; and as it would be applied in assigning students, randomness would indeed have the aspect of arbitrariness. For with a system of random selection the assignment of students to schools would be divorced from any governing educational purpose, except, of course, that of integration itself (but without any sense of what "integration" strictly means, or why this pattern of assignment would constitute "integration"). The surrender to randomness, the willingness to assign students helter-skelter throughout a city without any clear educational purpose could not help but be regarded with alarm if parents happened to take the matter of schools seriously. The objections, of course, would be justified, and they would be rendered even more substantial if the parents did in fact have plausible reasons for preferring one school, with a special curriculum or character, to another.

But just what those other interests are that would be excluded in this scheme would become more apparent as one began to work out the practical arrangements of the system. If students really had an equal chance of winding up in any school in the city, that would mean, in the case of cities like Los Angeles, Detroit, or Chicago, that a student could spend as much as an hour and a half or two hours traveling *one way* across the city to school. Nor could the situation be eased in any way through an arrangement in which school buses would collect students at designated points. With the strict use of random selection it is highly unlikely that two students living next door to one another would be selected for the same school, and it is entirely conceivable that they could be assigned to schools at different ends of the city. That means that students would be on their own, as it were, to make their way by public transportation, perhaps into neighborhoods that may be a bit dangerous, and the chances are that they would be going in most cases without that added support which comes from making the journey to a new school with friends from one's own neighborhood.

Exactly how old children would have to be before parents would be willing to countenance this kind of regimen for them is a question that would mark the limits of acceptance for a perfectly colorblind system, even if there were no other serious drawbacks. If for no other reason, though, than the logistics of transportation, some concession would have to be made to a principle of neighborhood or regional organization (that is, some narrower geographic limits within the city). But it becomes necessary also to include the personal needs that become important to integration, such as the benefit, for young people, of being joined by a group of friends when they enter a strange school. When considerations of this kind are taken into account, it becomes clear that a system of random assignment would be thoroughly unworkable, and that randomness, as a principle, deserves to be subordinated to other concerns which might be quite as legitimate as integration. There is the concern, for example, to encourage parents to take an interest in the schools (something that is far less likely to occur when the school is an hour or two away, rather than in the neighborhood). There is a valid interest in preserving the schools with slightly different curricula and specialties (as in a good technical high school or a school with more cultivated offerings in music and the arts). There may be a value in having schools that are responsive to certain cultural themes in the neighborhood (as in black culture or Jewish studies or, as the matter came up recently in one neighborhood in Boston, instruction in Greek). Or there may be an interest simply in having the children closer to home in case of sickness.

In short, there are many good reasons for moving away from strict randomness in the assignment of students to schools, and yet any movement away from strict randomness must imply a movement away from colorblindness as a principle. Once the courts agree to start reassigning students, but only within more circumscribed regions of the city—or in a way that manages to preserve a Latin School or a special High School of Science—then they have moved decisively away from any scheme of assignment that could, in truth, be called "colorblind." Whatever integration might occur then in the schools will not have come about as a result of a neutral, colorblind system. It will have come about only because the courts have now fallen into the practice of doing the very thing that defined the nature of the offense in *Brown* v. *Board of Education*: assigning students to schools explicitly on the basis of race.[58]

Of course, the use of racial assignment by the courts would not reflect the same invidious intent that was present when students were assigned by race in order to preserve segregation. But the courts would partake of the same fallacy that defined the wrongness of racial assignment when it was used by the segregationists; and in their tendency to affirm, in a backhanded way, the premises of racial determinism, we may find the essential evil in what the courts are doing. For once again the law would be fixing the status of individuals, not on the basis of their own actions, but on the basis of the things that are known or assumed about groups. Since "whiteness" is associated, in the aggregate, with higher income and

[58] Lino Graglia has charted, in its precise and maddening detail, the path by which the courts made their way from rules of racial neutrality to racial discrimination—from the ending of racial assignment to the imposition of racial quotas, without the benefit of supporting principles. He shows, at the same time, just how blithe—and thoughtless—the judges were as they cast aside the explicit prohibitions of the Civil Rights Act of 1964 in order to mandate racial "balancing." Lino A. Graglia, *Disaster by Decree* (Ithaca: Cornell University Press, 1976).

higher scores in school, it is assumed that blacks will improve in the aggregate when they are mingled in large numbers with whites. Or, there is the variation that has been heard often in recent years as part of the argument for "affirmative action": that the presence of black students will actually improve the education of whites, by exposing them to the perspectives of an impoverished or deprived class.[59] But of course it cannot be assumed that, if we merely know a student is black, we know also that he comes from an impoverished family, that he has the ability to articulate a perspective, and that he will actually talk with white students.[60] Again, we are asked to make inferences about the character of people merely on the basis of race. But this time we are asked to assume that, if we know a person is black, we know also that he is likely to be a good person, who is likely to have a *benign* effect on his surroundings.

In that respect there is nothing *in principle* that separates the courts (or the proponents of "reverse discrimination") from the racialists, old and new: both sides purport to draw moral inferences about individuals on the basis of what is known in the aggregate about the conditions of their racial group. The two differ only on the question of who has made the most plausible inference from the aggregate data. But if the issue stands on that ground alone, the data, after all, may point in a number of directions. And if it is defensible to assign students to schools by race on the strength of the correlations and the aggregate data in the Coleman Report, it becomes even more plausible and compelling for the racialist to argue in these terms:

> The aggregate data show that the crime rate is generally higher in black neighborhoods. Therefore, the larger the number of

[59] This line of argument was picked up, in part, by Mr. Justice Powell in his opinion for the court in *University of California v. Bakke*, 57 L. Ed. 750 (1978), at 785-86 (Section IV, D).

[60] Nor can it be assumed that he himself or his family has suffered an injury in the past. For that reason the argument I have been offering here must be inconsistent at its foundation with any scheme of "reverse discrimination" or collective "reparations" for racial groups. In any literal understanding of justice, it is only the people who suffer harms who have a claim to compensation. To bestow benefits in a broad way on groups defined by race, sex, or class is to move the process ever farther from the notion of measuring the deserts of individuals and from the strict requirements of equity. A policy which seeks to settle "reparations" on groups of this kind must be incompatible with the ground of principle that defines the wrong of racial discrimination—and the defamation of racial groups (see Chapter II). A notable instance of an argument for "reparations" can be found in Owen Fiss, "Groups and the Equal Protection Clause," *Philosophy and Public Affairs*, Vol. 5 (1976), pp. 107ff.

blacks in the area, the higher the crime rate will be. Of course, that doesn't mean that any particular black person will be a criminal. But the statistics are sufficiently clear in the aggregate that we may be justified in turning certain students away on the basis of race now for the sake of achieving a larger good in the aggregate. For if it is plausible to believe that a student will be able to convey to other students the sense of his culture in the ghetto, it is quite as plausible to argue that he will also carry with him many of the looser conventions about theft and crime that prevail in the ghetto.

The issue presented to us in these terms would be, as I say, an "empirical" question only, and if it were to be resolved on the basis of statistical correlations, the verdict rendered by social science is apt to support the racialists quite as often as the proponents of integration. In fact, it could be shown on the basis of aggregate data that single males in America are threatened with a far more substantial injury in remaining single than blacks or whites are faced with in attending schools that are not "integrated." George Gilder has reported, for example, that bachelors are twenty-two times more likely than married men to be committed to hospitals for mental disease (and ten times more likely to suffer chronic diseases of all kinds); that single men have nearly double the mortality rate of married men and three times the mortality rate of single women; that divorced men are three times more likely than divorced women to commit suicide or die by murder, and they are six times more likely to die of heart disease.[61] The evidence of the aggregate data here is far more compelling than anything which has been produced so far in all of the studies of integration in the United States. And yet no one would think for a moment of using these findings as the foundation of a policy in the law to save single men from these injuries by assigning any one of them, in particular, to a bride. The notion is no less bizarre of using the findings of social science as a basis for ordering any particular student on a bus and assigning him to a school to fit a ratio of the races. The lesson that must be absorbed is that this whole mode of reasoning from aggregates to law is in point of principle inadmissible. The social sciences may tell us much about the conditions of our lives, but the findings of these disciplines cannot claim that force of necessity which attaches to real "principles." They cannot take the

[61] George Gilder, "In Defense of Monogamy," *Commentary* (November 1974), pp. 31-36, at 32.

place of those moral axioms which must be present, as a foundation, before the freedom of any person may be restricted in the name of "law."

For well over a decade surveys have revealed that a majority of white Americans, in the South as well as the North, have favored the equal treatment of the races in public facilities. But majorities of blacks as well as whites have been opposed enduringly to the use of busing to achieve "racial balance in the schools."[62] For reasons that seem to be accessible to ordinary citizens in a way they have not been to federal judges, most people in this country apparently see, in the orders on busing and racial balance, the hand of arbitrariness. Once again, as in the past, we are faced with a situation in which men seized with zeal rather than true moral judgment are willing to pursue their enthusiasms even at the cost of obscuring those principles on which civil freedom rests. Whether they are judges issuing orders on busing to a local community or public men who will acquiesce in anything done by the courts in the name of "progress," they threaten to bring us far—they *have* brought us far—from that sense Plato had of the law as "the appointment of understanding."

[62] A Gallup survey published in September 1973 showed that only about 9 percent of the blacks in the national sample and 4 percent of the whites favored the use of busing to bring about integration. *The New York Times*, September 9, 1973, p. 55.

THREE

POWER STRUCTURES

X

POWER STRUCTURES
IN THE CITY

When Kenneth Clark grew melancholy over the prospects for integrating the schools in New York he revealed, in a flash of pique, his outlook on the ways of the world and the arrangements of power in New York City. The resistance of the white middle classes might be overcome after all if "the economic princes of power," as he called them—the men who really made the decisions—would simply care enough to take the lead and settle the matter of the schools. "The real decisions," he wrote, "can only be made by those who have the most to lose from social decay. . . . In New York, a conference of top business leaders like David Rockefeller, John Whitney, Robert Dowling could assume responsibility for deciding what must be done with the city's public educational system if the stability and viability of the metropolis are to be assured."[1]

Scarcely three years after these words were written, the organization of the public schools became a bitter and divisive issue in the politics of New York City, and it managed to touch all parts of the community. But even before the schools became a live issue in the late 1960's, anyone with a passing knowledge of cities should have been skeptical of Clark's account. For if Clark were taken at his word, it was possible to carry through the most serious decisions on the governance of the schools and the assignment of students without reckoning the civic weight of parents, teachers, principals, and the media, to say nothing of those who professed to be political leaders. Of course this is exactly what the courts have done recently in Boston, with effects on the civic life of the community that have not been altogether wholesome. And yet it was beyond belief that the public schools could have been reordered on a massive scale at the direction mainly of businessmen behind the scenes who did not possess the least trappings of authority. Even at the time Clark wrote, the question could have been raised as to whether his view of power in New York City was in fact very realistic.

But if we put aside for a moment the precise content of Clark's

[1] Kenneth Clark, *Dark Ghetto* (New York: Harper and Row, 1965), pp. 152-53.

visions, the incident nevertheless reflected his understanding that the question of the schools merges with the question of power structures in the city. It is necessary to move beyond the management of the schools to the larger political setting in which the problems of the schools are dealt with. And indeed, that was the direction in which it was necessary to move as one worked through the problem of Jonathan Kozol and the schools in Boston. As I came to argue, some of the more notable oddities that marked the administration of the schools there could be traced in good part to the way in which the school committee was assembled, and to the differences that separated members of the school board from the mayor of the city. My purpose in the next three chapters is to continue on the path I began earlier of pursuing the threads that emerged from Clark's analysis. I will try to explore, in the next two chapters, some of the more important questions that might be raised about the matter of "power structures" and the political integration of the cities. From that point I will move, in the following chapter, to the question of housing. For the character of housing, and the policies that govern its distribution, will affect in a very direct way the composition of the community and the foundation of political organization within the city.

1. Who Governs?
The Dispute Over "Community Power"

The question of "community power structures" has spawned by now a rather bulky literature. On the whole it is not a literature that particularly nourishes the mind, and it has absorbed the efforts of grown-up men and women in a manner that is vastly out of proportion to any points of lasting import that have been extracted from these researches. To put it charitably, these studies have not exactly made an enduring contribution to the history of philosophy.

As with any other subject, the question of "community power structures" has generated its proper share of "schools," and there has been no want of scholars who have come forward to stake out a special place for themselves, with their own shadings and refinements. As far as I can see, however, most of the monographs on this subject have arranged themselves on one side or another in a field that has been defined by two polar alternatives, two different views of the nature of power structures, which have been associated with Floyd Hunter[2] and Robert Dahl.[3] With one refinement or

[2] See his *Community Power Structure* (Chapel Hill: University of North Carolina Press, 1953), especially pp. 81-82, 102, 161ff.

another, the people who come closer to Hunter are more persuaded to the view that most cities, most of the time, are governed by a fairly cohesive power elite, which is not confined to the positions of official authority in the city. In fact, it is held in this school that the major levers of power are held largely by men outside the government. To be more exact, they are likely to rest with men of substance in business, who may be in a position to control the economy of the city. The elite shows its true nature as an elite through its ability to influence in a decisive way almost any question of importance that arises for the community, whether it concerns the schools or urban renewal or the war on poverty. The elite is not constrained, then, in its influence either by the limits of its own technical competence or by the power that may be exerted by countervailing groups with interests of their own.

On the other hand, the writers who have aligned themselves with Robert Dahl have seen a far more variegated set of relations in the structures of power in the cities. They have sought to estimate the distribution of influence in a community by looking at concrete cases in which interests were in conflict and decisions had to be made; and what they have discovered in those instances is that the configurations of the powerful change from one issue to the next, depending on the interests and the skills that are engaged. It may come as no surprise that teachers and administrators in the school

---

[3] A number of Dahl's works bear on this question, but the book that was directed more precisely to the issue of power structures in local communities was *Who Governs?* (New Haven: Yale University Press, 1961). I should mention, however, that there are many other estimable and engaging books on the question of politics in local communities even though they were not exactly directed to the issue in dispute between Dahl and Hunter. Indeed, that is probably why they remain estimable and engaging. Among the more estimable titles here would be Edward Banfield's *Political Influence* (New York: Free Press, 1961), Banfield and Myerson's *Politics, Planning, and the Public Interest* (New York: Free Press, 1955), Wallace Sayre and Herbert Kaufman's *Governing New York* (New York: Russell Sage, 1960), and Theodore Lowi's *At the Pleasure of the Mayor* (New Haven: Yale University Press, 1964). This list would not even touch upon many valuable works, such as the books done by the late Harold Gosnell, which may illuminate local politics without seeking to graph the distribution of power or chart the patterns of influence across the fields of public policy. I am assuming here, also, that the study of so-called "nondecisions"—the attempt to explain why certain decisions do not get made—would fall into the orbit of the dispute between Dahl and Hunter. One may see, on this subject, Peter Bachrach and Morton S. Baratz, "The Two Faces of Power," *American Political Science Review*, Vol. 56 (1962), pp. 947-52, and Matthew Crenson, *The Unpolitics of Air Pollution* (Baltimore: Johns Hopkins University Press, 1971). A long bibliography on "community power" has been compiled by Willis D. Hawley and Frederick Wirt under the title of *The Search for Community Power* (Englewood Cliffs, N.J.: Prentice-Hall, 1968).

system are likely to count more heavily in making decisions on the schools than in setting the policies for the city on housing or urban renewal. Instead of a single, cohesive elite, Dahl and his followers have found a variety or "plurality" of elites—but with one notable exception: there are a number of people who may be present as a common element in all the spheres, and that element turns out, in the end, to be the political leadership of the city. It is not insignificant that these people are invested, after all, with legal authority. As leaders in a public, competitive politics, they are also likely to have cultivated a certain skill in connecting groups and interests and developing a more "generalized" power, which can be used then to some effect on a variety of issues.

The academics who come closer to Dahl's perspective on the structures of power have become known, for obvious reasons, as the "pluralists." They have not sought to deny that some people in the city have more power than others, but they have been more sanguine than their opponents in assuming that the absence of cohesion among the influential is enough to ease the dangers of "domination" by an elite and render control by the public more likely. They have assumed that the elite is penetrable and porous or generally open to the demands of the public, and they find ample evidence to suggest that the incentives at work in a competitive politics will make leaders highly responsive to the felt interests of the majority. Those people who have been reserved about the "pluralists" have been reserved also about this optimism over the prospects for popular control. The implicit assumption, however, which these people have shared with the pluralists is that the main purpose of democratic government is in fact to insure the control of the public over its leaders. And yet in the traditional understanding, the highest test of a democratic government is not whether the people "control" the government, but whether the people exercise their power justly and reasonably. That means, as Lincoln understood, that the first responsibility of free people is to come to an understanding of the principles on which their own freedom rests. And if they can arrive at that understanding, they will come to recognize also the things that they may not decently demand in the name of their own sovereign power.[4]

But with minor variations, most studies can be found, as I say, on one side or the other of the division marked by Hunter and

[4] See, in this vein, Harry Jaffa, *Crisis of the House Divided* (New York: Doubleday, 1959), pp. 302-307, 330-46.

Dahl. They have argued over such questions as whether the power structures of Schenectedy and Cucamonga are really more like that of the Atlanta studied by Hunter, or whether they are closer to the New Haven portrayed by Dahl. The accretion of knowledge they represent has been tantamount to the filling in of the places after the decimal point. What is apparently beyond their consideration is that, at different times, the same city may resemble both Atlanta and New Haven. The difference between the two cities as they were pictured in the 1950's and 1960's may be the difference between political development and decay as it has been illuminated in the literature on comparative politics.[5] That is to say, the most important differences between cities may turn on the question of whether a certain integrity or autonomy has been preserved in the political institutions of the city, or whether the main political forces (for example, the political parties, or the mayor) have simply become, in different places, the tools of business or the unions, or of people who are dominant elsewhere in the society (perhaps even in that circle known as "society").

I will come back to this point in a while, for it is the decisive end, I think, to which the problem of "power structures" must eventually lead. It would also emerge almost naturally, with only an additional step or two, out of the body of Dahl's work; and for that reason it is worth taking a moment to look a bit more closely at the foundation of Dahl's argument. Neither Dahl's book nor Hunter's was meant to apply, respectively, only to New Haven or Atlanta. Both writers claimed a more general validity for their accounts, and the cities they studied were to stand as representations of a more common reality. But if these two works were to be understood as alternatives to one another, how could one judge their separate claims to truth? Even if it were supposed that they were fair accounts, on their own terms, of New Haven and Atlanta, their claims to a more general application could be judged only by considering the foundation from which the conclusions were drawn: were the findings rooted in either case, in conditions or structures that were likely to be found more widely in the United States? But since "power structures" are not fashioned in a mechanical way—since they are the products of moral understandings and personal commitments, as well as of political management—

[5] See, for example, Samuel P. Huntington, *Political Order in Changing Societies* (New Haven: Yale University Press, 1968), and David Rappoport, "Rome: The Case of the Corrupt State Reconsidered," *Political Studies*, No. 16 (October 1968), pp. 411-32.

it cannot be assumed that these structures will be preserved more easily with the advance of time and the growth of the economy. All of these considerations found a reflection at one point or another in Dahl's analysis.

Dahl's argument about the growing pluralism of power structures was grounded, in the first instance, in the structures and tendencies of a modern economy. An economy characterized by an advanced technology would be marked by increased complexity in the division of labor. As Max Weber anticipated, the ethic of "rational-technical" organization would be extended progressively to each sphere of social life; but as more areas of life became "organized" and bureaucratic, they would also grow more separable. As specialization advanced, the professions would become more distant from one another as a result of their own, accumulated experiences and the cultivation of their own techniques. Young men and women would go to "law school" for three years rather than "reading at law" while they were working in a law office; and after steeping themselves in the law as a career, they would find it harder to break away suddenly to study medicine and enter the medical profession. But these separations, which would become commonplace in the economy, would find their expression on a larger scale in the disassociation of whole social spheres. There was a time, as Dahl records, in the New Haven of the eighteenth century, when the families who were the most prestigious socially were also the most prominent in business and the professions, and they were most likely to be dominant also in the polity.[6] Power of all kinds seemed to depend on the same coin, and the same old-line Yankee and Congregationalist families who enjoyed high social standing had no trouble in transferring that position to the law and commerce and the control of political office. The structure of power was in fact very concentrated; it might be said, in the current vernacular, that there was a "superimposition" of hierarchies, a state of affairs in which the possession of place or authority in one sphere fairly well determined a comparable standing in other spheres as well.

But that situation gradually came apart in the nineteenth century with the growth of population, the advent of immigrants of different religions and class standing, and, perhaps most important of all, the extension of the franchise to people without property. Before long, the old families of New Haven were simply outnumbered in a "mass" electorate, and it became impossible to preserve their power in the polity without the acquiescence of the immigrant

[6] See Dahl, *Who Governs?*, chs. 2, 7, and 20.

Catholics. It was only to be expected, sooner or later, that the old elite would be displaced in politics by men of a new type, who bore a closer resemblance to the class that filled out the electorate. As the immigrant groups rose in turn to power, they made use of the levers of patronage to open up jobs in the schools and the civil service, and politics became then, in their hands, a route of advancement into white-collar jobs.

In fact, politics became, altogether, a more autonomous activity, for the route of advancement in politics was quite separable now from the routes of advancement in other spheres. Of course, money and social position could still count in politics, but clearly they were no longer enough. The possession of a distinguished name or an upper-class accent could be a liability as well as an asset, as candidates went out to solicit among the multitude. Politics worked through a currency of its own based on numbers; it had its own logic, its own internal requirements. The skills that would be required in collecting numbers, in attracting support and knitting together the interests of discrete groups, did not necessarily flow from social standing or the possession of wealth.

In sum, the functional specialization that became evident in other spheres became evident in politics as well. The art of the politician is not precisely identical to the arts that are cultivated in other professions, even though the need to be politic, to say nothing of being just, is arguably present in all other occupations. Even in fields other than politics there is a need to cultivate the discipline of judgment and the art of exercising authority; and the cultivation of this competence brings some healthy complications of its own to the business of making decisions in a city. There is likely to be a specialization of interests and skills as the focus shifts from one profession or subject to another, and that process of selection will make a difference for the other elites with whom a political leadership will be compelled to deal. It is only to be expected, for example, that in issues arising over the schools there will be a particularly intense interest on the part of teachers, principals, and the administrators in the central board of education. In regard to policies governing the schools (including, of course, the matter of salaries) these people would bring to the issues the concentrated attention of their self-interest; but they would bring also the special claims of their expertise. And what can be said in this respect of the "education establishment" could also be said about merchants, bankers, real estate agencies, and unions, depending on the case at hand.

Of course, interests may not always be so narrowly encompassed.

For real estate agencies, the state of the housing market may be affected significantly by the condition of the schools and by the sudden introduction of policies such as busing. Businessmen may have to take account of the strength of the schools and the state of the housing market before they make their own commitments in the city. And since almost all of these interests could make a serious difference in the lives of political leaders (the people who have a stake in running the city as a whole) it is not beyond imagining that those who govern the city will have a strong incentive to worry about more of these issues at once.

Political leaders are likely to make their presence felt in almost all important questions of policy that affect the city, but they would be unwise and imprudent if they did not rely to some degree on the competence of other professionals in their own fields. In a modern economy and a competitive politics, the "interdependence" of elites becomes inescapable. That implies, as it ought, a certain sharing of power in different spheres, without denying in any way the distinct authority of people in government or the perspectives that they, more than others, are likely to represent.

As Dahl observes, there is a movement here toward the "dispersion" of political resources. That dispersion may be rendered all the more apparent in certain places, where the different elites in the city are drawn from different strata of the society, with rather different backgrounds in their educations, professions, and social standing. In the New Haven studied by Dahl, the so-called "subleaders" who were active in issues of urban redevelopment were drawn from business and the professions; they were almost certain to have attended college; they earned salaries that were well above the average in the community; and they lived in the most exclusive neighborhoods. In contrast, the subleaders involved in the field of education were drawn from more "middling" backgrounds. Their salaries, of course, were more modest than those of people in business, and while they owned homes in areas that were above average, they were not in the "best" neighborhoods. Still, they had more formal education than the subleaders involved in the management of the political parties, and they were more likely to come from middle-class backgrounds (with fathers who were small businessmen or white-collar workers). The most pronounced differences showed up in the comparison between the first two groups and the subleaders who were involved in political nominations. As Dahl observed, only the most negligible portion of the subleaders in education and urban development were clerks, technicians, or wage earners. But 42 percent of the subleaders in politics fell into those categories. These people were less likely to have gone to college; they were more likely to be Catholic; and they were drawn in larger numbers from immigrant families, with fathers who did manual work. Their homes were rented or owned in "average" neighborhoods, and their incomes were not very different from those of people in the working class. As Dahl summed it up, the subleader in politics "might strike many people as the epitome of the average man."[7]

At the same time, the dispersion of political resources was likely to be enhanced by the dispersion of economic power as well. As Dahl noted in regard to New Haven, the largest firm in the city (Olin Mathieson Chemical) employed only about 7 percent of the working population. The next three firms in size (the Railroad, the Telephone Company, and Yale University) each employed about 5 percent.[8] In fifth place among the employers was the city itself. As far as Olin Mathieson was concerned, its political activities, as Dahl said, "did not even make a ripple on the surface of New Haven's politics." No single private firm enjoyed the kind of dominant position that was held, say, by Kodak in Rochester or Prudential in Newark, and their interests were too disparate for them to develop, in combination, the kind of political leverage that they separately lacked.

As Madison foretold in the Federalist #10, a dispersion of power of this kind would make it that much more difficult for any single faction or interest to gain power over the whole. But the further consequence of this dispersion is to make the political leadership more autonomous. There is simply no need, under these conditions, for political leaders to make themselves dependent on any one social force (such as a corporation or a union). In fact, it would be hazardous for politicians to make themselves overly dependent on a restricted clientele in this situation. The dispersion of power allows a political leadership a measure of insulation to cultivate its independence, and as it does that it cultivates interests of its own that are not fully reducible to the interests of all those associations and enterprises that make up the city. As the political leadership develops these separate interests and perspectives, it acquires a certain integrity and autonomy as a leadership. Samuel Huntington got at the logic of this relationship in his writing on political development and decay, and he is worth quoting at length:

---

[7] Ibid., pp. 174-78, especially pp. 176 and 178.   [8] Ibid., p. 250.

Political institutionalization, in the sense of autonomy, means the development of political organizations and procedures which are not simply expressions of the interests of particular social groups. A political organization which is the instrument of a social group—family, clan, class—lacks autonomy and institutionalization. If the state, in the traditional Marxist claim, is really the 'executive committee of the bourgeoise,' then it is not much of an institution. A judiciary is independent to the extent that it adheres to distinctly judicial norms and to the extent that its perspectives and behavior are independent of those of other political institutions and social groupings. As with the judiciary, the autonomy of political institutions is measured by the extent to which they have their own interests and values distinguishable from those of other social forces. As with the judiciary, the autonomy of political institutions is likely to be the result of competition among social forces. A political party, for instance, which expresses the interests of only one group in society—whether labor, business, or farmers—is less autonomous than one which articulates and aggregates the interests of several social groups. The latter type of party has a clearly defined existence apart from particular social forces. So also with legislatures, executives, and bureaucracies. . . . Political organizations and procedures that lack autonomy are, in common parlance, said to be corrupt.[9]

No one would have accused Mayor Daley in Chicago of being nothing more than the instrument of the business community. Thanks to the formidable Democratic organization in Cook County, Daley had a basis of power that was quite independent of the business community. For that matter, the organization made the mayor independent of the unions or any other interest groups in the city. He did not need them to be elected, and none of them, singly or in combination, could have mustered enough power to defeat the party organization in any free election. For that reason, none of them was in a position to exercise any special leverage in the administration of the city in order to promote its own interests. What Daley did for business or the unions, he did because he thought it served the interests of the city or the party or himself, and the special alchemy of party government is that it may produce a benign confounding of those interests. Daley identified his per-

[9] Huntington, *Political Order in Changing Societies*, pp. 20-21.

sonal interests with the interests of the party; he fused the interest of the party with the interests of the city; and he clearly loved his city.

Madison warned us once, in an exercise of prudence at its highest level, that when we establish political orders we ought to contrive things in such a way that "the interests of the man" are connected with "the rights of the place." We know that when we speak of a "body" politic we speak, of course, in a metaphor, for in no real sense can a population of millions be fused into a "body corporate." And yet we persist in taking seriously the notion of the political community as a moral association or as a corporate entity founded on the principles of justice. But the only way in which a community of many parts can achieve the character of a body politic is if it fosters the sense within itself that the community, as a political association, has an identity and character of its own that makes it more than a mere aggregate of its members. The discovery of the political community depends on the possibility of recognizing certain "public interests" residing in the community as a whole and which may be quite separate from the sum of the private interests in the community.

But those perspectives on the public good have a better chance of being discovered if there is a class of political leaders in the community that has an interest in discovering them. For reasons too lengthy to explore at this moment, polities are not apt to be governed by people with the understanding and disinterest of philosophers. It is therefore likely in any event that the judgments made by public men will be alloyed with self-interest, and the question then, in the spirit of Madison, is whether their personal concerns can be connected in a more wholesome way to the interests of their institutions. In the absence of true philosophers who can govern, the good of the public domain is more likely to be secured by people who have a lively sense of the interests they hold distinctly as "political" men. Where that sense is insufficiently cultivated, or where the sources of support for political parties are weak, a political leadership may be far more vulnerable to being taken over by social forces (for example, in business, in the unions, or in the public bureaucracy itself) that are directed almost entirely toward their own "private" interests. If leaders can preserve their autonomy then as "public" leaders in a regime of law, they can help to resist the corruption of politics in the classic (and the deepest) sense: they can resist the tendency to pervert or corrupt the nature of politics from an activity that is essentially public in its methods and its ends, into an activity governed by private criteria, in the service of private ends.

The classic difference between a decent and a corrupted polity may turn, therefore, on the preservation of autonomy for political leaders in a constitutional order. And that, I think, is what is ultimately at issue in the differences between Hunter and Dahl on the question of power structures. In Atlanta political power was largely taken over by people outside of politics. Public officialdom was relatively weak, and as a function of that weakness power gravitated to a collection of men who were prominent in business and the professions, and who were connected to one another socially. Even if it were true, of course, that public policy had been directed in Atlanta to the needs of business or economic growth, it would not have followed that the benefits of that policy would have been confined only to a very few. A small number may indeed become very rich, but they may become rich through a policy of growth whose benefits may be diffused rather widely through the population. If one compared Atlanta to New Haven for the vibrancy of life and the breadth of opportunity, Atlanta would probably be far more appealing than New Haven—which is to say, that it would not bear any obvious signs of a city that had not been governed in the "public interest" even before liberal mayors came to power in the late 1950's and 1960's. Still, there is something immanently suspicious in an arrangement in which a city is essentially governed by a collection of notables outside the sphere of official responsibility. Under conditions of that kind, the dangers of corruption in the classic sense are enlarged, and people can hardly be blamed for suspecting that public authority is being exploited for the interests of those who are closer to the levers of power.

2. The Dispute Superseded: The Recognition of Political Development and Decay

The question then is: why did the nominal political leadership in Atlanta lack the strength and autonomy that can be found in the leadership of other cities? There is no reason to suppose that the economy of Atlanta was any less a "modern" economy than the economy of New Haven. The division of labor was surely as complex in the one as in the other, and it is hard to believe that the effects of functional specialization were somehow retarded in Atlanta in comparison to New Haven. These attributes of the economy may indeed provide conditions that encourage more insulation and independence for the political leadership. But clearly these aspects of the economy cannot be decisive in themselves. The plain fact of the matter is that the autonomy and integrity of political leaders may be wholly independent of economic development. A political leadership may grow corrupt and feeble; a government of law may begin to break down; a constitutional government may atrophy into a despotism; and all of these things may occur even as the standard of living in a country rises markedly.

The point hardly comes as a surprise to anyone. But if it occasions no surprise, one wonders why this minor insight has not been applied to the question of power structures in the local community. It would tell us, for example, that it is largely idle to argue over the question of whether most cities in the United States are likely to come closer to a "pluralist" or an "elitist" structure of power. Certain conditions in a modern society and economy may dispose cities to be more like the New Haven of the 1950's than the Atlanta studied by Hunter, but nothing in these conditions can guarantee one result rather than another. The autonomy of political institutions can be eroded as well as established; and whether that autonomy is preserved or dissipated may depend most importantly on the moral judgments and qualities of political leaders themselves.

A formidable enterprise such as a great ruling party cannot be preserved by people who have the mentality of bosses in a criminal syndicate. In a competitive politics, where popular support does have to be garnered, there is a need for prudence as well as firmness if an organization is to be preserved. But prudence, at its highest level, must proceed from an awareness of principle, and so the discipline of leadership cannot be divorced from the task of setting the ends of public policy and establishing the terms of principle on which interests can be reconciled in a just way. Successful organizations, like the Democratic Party in Chicago, have shown considerable suppleness in their ability to reach out and bring into the party people who were well outside the mold of party functionaries. Before Richard Daley became the chairman of the Cook County organization, his predecessors managed to contribute Adlai Stevenson and Paul Douglas to the politics of the nation. While those two luminaries were bestowed on the nation, they were also kept out of Chicago (and out of the way of the local leadership). But the party was still able to draw to itself the constituency that was attracted to Stevenson and Douglas. Mayor Daley, for his own part, was able to take into the organization liberals on the order of Marshall Korshak and Abner Mikva, and he was even able to reach an accommodation with a group like the Woodlawn Organization, which had been at odds with City Hall over issues of housing and urban renewal. Of course Daley did not move toward an accommodation with the Woodlawn Organization until that group had been able to show, in a local referendum, that it did have a certain following in the community. However, the Woodlawn Organization was never able to demonstrate that it could beat the Democratic machine in a local election, and that singular defect had to establish some limits to its claims. Daley was quite right in his refusal to grant to this private group the license to control an operation like the Model Cities program in Woodlawn. But he was able to incorporate the group into the workings of a number of programs, and he could be sure at least that his patronage would not be used to build up an organization that otherwise had no support in the local community.[10]

There is far more then to the exercise of prudence than a disposition to compromise. The leadership could not have brought the Woodlawn Organization closer to the party if it were thought that the aims of that organization could not be reconciled with the aims of the leaders or with the interests of other sections of the party. As far as the party was concerned, there was a certain principled tension that was simply inherent in the enterprise of building a coalition in a public politics. A political party, in these circumstances, cannot be all things to all men, because it cannot appeal to all interests at the same time. What it does in its public policies, or what it offers in its public statements, cannot avoid attracting some groups and repelling others. If certain neighborhood groups, say, were opposed to an extension of public housing projects into middle-class areas, they might be highly suspicious of a leadership that was promising not to concentrate more public housing in lower-class "ghettos." That is to say, individuals and groups are more likely to stay in a party coalition if they are persuaded that their interests do indeed mesh, in some comprehensible way, with the interests of other members of the coalition.

It should become clear, then, that the enterprise of building and preserving a political party can never be reduced to a mechanistic task; for it requires nothing less than the wisdom and discipline of statesmanship. Nor is it any wonder that the autonomy of parties

[10] See John Hall Fish, *Black Power/White Control* (Princeton: Princeton University Press, 1973), pp. 51, 63, 72, 85, 96, 114, 182-83, 276, 281, and 296.

has been a fragile thing, or that parties have managed to become moribund in certain states and cities even while their national branch has been winning control of the White House. The autonomy and strength of parties may be lost in different places through the mistakes and corrupt judgments of leaders, whether or not they have the asset of a strong party organization. Parties can be weakened by the loss of popular support if they guess wrong about any candidate or issue (as the Populists, in 1896, guessed wrong in backing William Jennings Bryan). They can be undercut when their leaders fall into scandal (just as the Republican Party was hurt severely by Watergate, even while the stance of the party on taxes and public spending was becoming more and more popular with the electorate). Finally, a leadership may surrender its autonomy when it becomes overly dependent on a single patron or clientele, or when it is simply bought out altogether. More than one city in this country has had a government that was merely the agent, in politics, of the local Mafia. In other places city governments have been taken over, in effect, by a dominant local business, or political leaders have been content to take their cues from figures in local industry who have played a large part in their rise to office. At times the local "industry" may even be another political party: in many wards of Chicago the Republican Party is mainly a paper organization, and its workers are apparently on the payroll of the Democratic machine.[11] These "Republicans" may enjoy some of the public notice of politics (to say nothing of a bit of spare cash), while at the same time they avoid the risks and responsibilities of competition.

In the rest of the state outside of Chicago the Republicans have been, of course, more of a real party. For many years, though, the party was under the strong influence of Col. Robert McCormick, the publisher of the *Chicago Tribune*. The *Tribune* had the largest circulation in the Midwest; it was clearly the single most important newspaper in the state; and McCormick possessed, as a result, an extraordinary fund of resources in finance and the media. Just what the relation was in the 1940's between McCormick and the Republican leadership of the state is illustrated in an incident that was witnessed by Win Stracke, the folk singer. In an interview with Studs Terkel, Stracke recalled the time in the late 1930's when he used to sing in the Choir of the Air on radio station WGN. The

[11] See Milton Rakove, *Don't Make No Waves—Don't Back No Losers* (Bloomington: University of Indiana Press, 1975), pp. 162-78, especially 167, 168, 174, 175, 176.

station was owned by the *Chicago Tribune*, and the performances of the choir took place in the Tribune Building. Ten minutes of the program were set aside for a short talk by McCormick, who would discourse on such subjects as the defense of Detroit against the Canadians. One evening McCormick was sitting on the aisle, and as Stracke recalled the scene:

> Next to [McCormick] was his wife, next to her was his Great Dane, and next to the Great Dane was . . . Governor Dwight Green. When the Colonel began his speech, the dog started to snuffle loudly. The Colonel's wife reached over into the Governor's breast pocket, took out his handkerchief and held it over the dog's muzzle. After the talk, she just reached over, put it back in the Governor's pocket.[12]

When the Administration of Theodore Roosevelt pursued the prosecution of the Northern Securities case it taught a dramatic lesson in public: that the Republican Party was not simply the tool of corporate businesses and that the interests of the party, as a governing party, could not be reduced to the interests of the railroads. The same theme was expressed for the Conservative Party in Britain when Anthony Eden declared at a conference of the Party in 1947 that "we are not the party of unbridled, brutal capitalism . . . we are not the political children of the laissez-faire school."[13] Apart from cases of plain venality, the autonomy of a political leadership may be gained or lost depending on their own wisdom and luck. With the right conditions, the task may be less difficult in some places than others. In Chicago, the successors of Mayor Daley will find it easier to preserve their autonomy as a political leadership as a result of the strength that has been established in the party over two generations. But even that strength is no ultimate guarantee: the party machine may come apart if the new leadership is not as successful as the old in keeping all of its constituent groups together; if the black "subsidiary" of the machine decides to strike out on its own; and if, in the fragmentation that results, a "reform" movement gains a foothold in the electorate.[14]

---

[12] Stracke, interviewed in Studs Terkel's *Hard Times* (New York: Pantheon Books, 1970), pp. 186-87.

[13] Quoted in Samuel Beer, *British Politics in the Collectivist Age* (New York: Alfred A. Knopf, 1967), p. 271.

[14] Since these words were written they have been borne out in part by the defeat of Michael Bilandic in the mayoral primary in Chicago in 1979. Bilandic had succeeded to the mayoralty after the death of Richard Daley in December 1976, and he was running for a full term with the backing of the redoubtable Cook County

The autonomy of the political leadership is persistently open to enhancement or atrophy, and in the case of Atlanta as it was portrayed by Floyd Hunter, it seems clear that this leadership simply lacked the essential attributes of autonomy. The question, again, is: what rendered the political leadership so weak in Atlanta in relation to other forces and groups in the city? The political leaders seemed to be decent enough as men, and so one wonders just what *conditions* in Atlanta might have made it harder for them to establish their autonomy.[15] For some reason there is a tendency to neglect the fact that Dahl himself drew attention to the strength of party organization as an important part of the overall scheme he described in New Haven. It seems odd, in retrospect, that in all the disputes which have raged over the differences between Dahl and Hunter, there has been very little consideration of the structure of the *party system* as a factor that might have affected in a significant way the political differences between Atlanta and New Haven. Atlanta in the 1940's and 1950's was still embedded, after all, in the one-party framework of the South. As V. O. Key showed in his classic study, *Southern Politics*,[16] the consequence of the one-party structure was not to eliminate conflict in politics, for the competition could often be intense, the electorate highly divided, and the rhetoric quite hyperbolic. The main result of the one-party structure was that it made it vastly more difficult to preserve stable party organizations, and that state of affairs had a rather pronounced effect on the character of politics in the South.

Democratic Organization. The defections from Bilandic and the regular organization seemed to come from all parts of the constituency of the party, but it appears that the losses resulted mainly from an aversion to Bilandic himself and his clumsy attempts to manage politically a natural disaster that could not be managed well— viz., the snows that paralyzed Chicago during the winter of 1978-1979. Bilandic was defeated, however, by Jane Byrne, who had worked for Mayor Daley, and who was herself a seasoned member of the Democratic organization. She quickly received the support of the organization after her victory in the primary, and since she has been in office she has seemed more disposed to preserve the machine than to dismember it. But what the experience confirms, altogether, is just how much the strength of the machine has depended all along on the support it manages to gather through administrative competence and political deftness.

[15] It has been argued in a more recent study that the state of affairs in Atlanta today resembles more closely the kind of political arrangement that was described by Dahl in New Haven. Indeed, there seems good reason to suspect that Dahl's account was closer to the mark in Atlanta even at the time Hunter was writing. See M. Kent Jennings, *Community Influentials* (New York: Free Press, 1964), especially chs. 7, 8, and 10.

[16] *Southern Politics* (New York: Alfred A. Knopf, 1949).

Under the conditions of the one-party system, the real electoral contests were fought out within the Democratic primaries, and as the old saying went, victory in the primaries was "tantamount" to election. There was a time in the 1950's when congressmen in the South actually faced more competition for reelection than their counterparts in the North, but the competition took place entirely within the Democratic primary.[17] The arrangements were comparable to the formats that have appeared elsewhere under a "non-partisan" system. Candidates were listed on the ballots as individuals, without the addition of party labels. But party labels can make a decided difference for many voters, and the absence of those labels may have a serious filtering effect on the electorate. It is highly unlikely that all potential voters will know something about the career, the views, and the character of every candidate on the ballot, but we know from a variety of surveys that the parties are associated in the minds of voters with rather different dispositions on public policy, which derive from certain *principled* differences about the proper ends of government. Voters have a rough, but accurate, sense of the perspectives that separate Democrats from Republicans, and if they do not know much in detail about any candidate, they may still make a faintly rational choice on a more general level by voting for the party rather than the person. In that sense party labels on the ballot act as cues for many voters in ordering their choices *and stabilizing the principled pattern of their voting from one election to the next.*

In the absence of party labels, the voters have the burden of collecting a larger measure of information on their own in order to detect the kinds of patterned differences that usually characterize contests between the parties. Without labels, attention must be focused elsewhere. It may be focused on specific issues, or it may fasten on a number of other things that help to distinguish the candidates as individuals. Those items may, of course, include the character and personality of the candidates, but also their race or religion or even their place of residence. In primaries and nonpartisan elections there is likely to be a skewing of the vote to reflect

[17] V. O. Key, for example, collected figures for all congressional seats won by the Democrats in the four elections of the 1950's (1952-1958). He found that one-fifth of the nominations outside the South were made without a challenge in the primary; but no primary in the South went uncontested. In only half of the primaries outside the South did the winner receive less than 60 percent of the vote; and yet 94 percent of the nominees in the South had to be content with that kind of margin. Key, *Politics, Parties, and Pressure Groups* (New York: Crowell, 1964; fifth edition), p. 448, n. 14.

what is called the "friends and neighbors" effect. If the voters are not aware of party divisions or of differences on the issues, they may be more likely to gravitate to candidates who are simply better "known" to them personally, and the candidates who are better known are often the ones who have lived in their own communities.

And so, as Key pointed out once, two liberals running in Alabama in two successive elections less than two months apart were not able to draw on the same constituency. The votes for either one of them were concentrated first near the home counties of the candidates, and the rest of the vote showed no clear pattern. The same county that could give 54.5 percent of its vote to Jim Folsom when he was running for the governorship could give only 5.4 percent of its vote several weeks later to John Sparkman when the latter was running for the Senate.[18] Both men were liberals, but the attributes that connected them were blocked from view in this framework, which provided no direct means of representing those similarities in outlook (as would have been done, for example, if a common party label had been printed alongside their names on the ballot).

Voters were conditioned to be sensitive, rather, to the characteristics that were readily evident on the surface in discriminating among the candidates. And when noticeable differences were wanting, candidates would not be loath to conjure some up. A premium was placed at times on the crudest devices for capturing attention, from the use of hillbilly bands to the cultivation of zany styles and eccentricities, in order to sharpen, for the voters, their awareness of the candidates. As a result, candidates could succeed quite often simply through their adroitness in making themselves visible, and the critical point here is that people could become "known" for reasons that had little to do with politics. William Lee ("Pass the Biscuits") O'Daniel could succeed extravagantly in Texas because he had become known to millions in the state through a radio show he sponsored, which combined hillbilly music with fundamentalist sermons.[19] Others became known through a prominent family name, and still others became conspicuous through the possession of money, which gave them in turn the means of making themselves known.

In this scheme of things people could float to the top in politics for thoroughly *apolitical* reasons. There was often little patterning

---

[18] Key, *Southern Politics*, p. 48.
[19] For the stirring account of O'Daniel, see ibid., pp. 265-71.

to the vote, as voters shifted widely from one election to the next in response to some display or sideshow, and the electorate would light upon one candidate or issue as the day would offer. The result was that it became far more difficult to sustain a stable coalition of voters based on programs and principles. That is not to say that it was entirely impossible to produce stable alignments of this kind in the one-party framework. The advent of Huey Long and his organization had a polarizing effect on politics in Louisiana, and the division of the electorate there often displayed the kind of stability that was more commonly found in party contests in the North.[20] It is also the case that a strong party organization can deliver its vote in a steady way and win elections, even in political "primaries," when there are no labels on the ballot.[21] But then, party organizations have been strong in primaries largely because of the cohesion they have been forced to cultivate in competitive party contests. It is worth recalling, in this respect, that the discipline which became the hallmark of urban political machines was developed in the nineteenth century, before the advent of political primaries. If politics took place persistently in a one-party framework, it would be very difficult to produce cohesive organizations with a stable following in the electorate.

In the meantime, the absence of those organizations would make a serious difference to the structure of politics in the long run. For reasons that cannot be explored fully in this space, the absence of stable parties is likely to exert a gentle discouragement to voting, particularly among the poor and the less educated (who may not

[20] See ibid., ch. 8, especially pp. 168-79.

[21] David Greenstone and Paul Peterson once sought to gauge the strength of party organizations in different cities by considering the extent to which the parties were able to dominate primary contests for seats in the lower house of the state legislature. Considering all the seats that were at stake in Chicago between 1958 and 1964, they found that in 77.5 percent of the cases the candidates of the Cook County organization won with no opposition. In only 8 percent of the cases did the opposition candidates get more than 20 percent of the vote. These findings might be offset by the fact that in Los Angeles, where the party organizations were rather weak, 51.7 percent of the contests were still won without opposition. Greenstone and Peterson took it as an hypothesis that where the party organization was more formidable it would discourage opposition. The differences that appear in their data do reflect the relative strength of the Democratic organization in Chicago; but the growing advantage in favor of incumbency may make it harder to treat the absence of opposition as a telling sign in itself of the strength of the party. See Greenstone and Peterson, "Reformers, Machines, and the War on Poverty," in James Q. Wilson, ed., *City Politics and Public Policy* (New York: John Wiley, 1968), pp. 267-92, at 279-80.

have the inclination or the skill to inform themselves in the way that this scheme without stable parties would require). Whether that is ultimately a good or a bad thing cannot be said in the abstract. What may be more pertinent here, though, is the effect of this structure on the mode of entrance into politics and the skills that become relevant to a political career. For the young person starting out in politics it makes a considerable difference whether he must plunge in on his own or whether he has the prospect of attaching himself to an ongoing organization. If the novice decides to work his way up through the party, he would be able at some date to draw on the breadth of support that attaches to the organization. He would receive the benefits of that discipline by which the party seeks to turn out as much support for the black and Puerto Rican at the bottom of the ticket as for the Irishman who may be at the head of the slate.

Of course, the young politician could not rise through the party without absorbing obligations and incorporating in himself something of the character of the party. There may be advantages at times in "breaking in at the top," without the need to work through an organization, but that possibility is not open to everyone. Mayor Daley probably overstated the point when he remarked that a politics of party organizations is necessary for people who are not rich. Still, there was no small measure of truth in his observation. To break into politics on one's own in a large city would require a fairly substantial amount of money for advertising, and if aspiring politicians do not have the money, they need at least the capacity to raise it. The problem may be even more severe if a candidate is running for the city council, let us say, in a city without legislative districts, where all the councilmen run "at large." In that event the candidate would have to run in the city as a whole, even in sections where he may be completely unknown. He may come to need more expensive advertising through television or publications, and even if he can afford it, there is still the danger that the member of a minority group may find his candidacy overwhelmed in the larger electorate of the city.

The choices here break down into alternatives that are rather clear in their outlines. Leaders may rise in politics through a process of apprenticeship in political parties, where they may become practiced, as Burke said, in the discipline of honoring interests other than their own. They may also break in with a dramatic play on issues, but they are more likely to be successful in that case when they are buoyed up by additional assets—social position, perhaps, or a famous name or a prominent place in business. To phrase the matter another way, it might be said that the absence of a distinct political route to office puts the accent on a different set of attributes in getting ahead—personal connections, social standing, money— and those attributes are not evenly distributed in the population as a whole. When politics takes place, then, in a one-party (or a no-party) framework, when it is attended, as it was in Atlanta, by lingering restrictions on the voting of blacks, it should come as no surprise if power seems to flow to a collection of social notables and businessmen.[22] For these people simply have within their hands the resources that become vastly more decisive in a politics of this kind.

3. THE GOVERNING PARTY AND THE AUTONOMY OF THE POLITICAL COMMUNITY

I began this book by alluding to the *functional* view of the city that has become dominant in our own day. In this perspective the city has been seen as a dense and permanent settlement with a heterogeneous population and a high degree of specialization in the division of labor.[23] This functional specialization in the provision of services springs from the initial separation between residence and work, and it becomes the cardinal feature that defines the character of the city: it accounts for the nature of a settlement that has a tendency to enlarge the diversity of services (and of the people it draws to perform them); to place an accent on functional, impersonal relations; to foster a sense of social distance and disengagement and a certain freedom from surveillance; and to create, withal, a climate in which conventions lose their stringency and moral codes are softened.

But in contrast with this view, I have held out, in these chapters, an older perspective, in which the city was understood in the first instance as a moral association or a political community. In that older understanding, the end of the city was to cultivate a sense of morals and justice in its members, and the very meaning of morals called forth, by its logic, the existence of law and authority. Through

[22] The same point was recognized by Jennings in his more recent study of Atlanta: i.e., that the political strength of the business community was in large part a function of the weakness of the political parties. See his *Community Influentials*, p. 166.

[23] See Louis Wirth's classic essay, "Urbanism as a Way of Life," in Albert Reiss and Paul Hatt, eds., *Cities and Society* (Glencoe: The Free Press, 1957), pp. 46-63. This essay was originally published in 1938.

the use of the laws the community would articulate its character as a polity and it would hold out a sense of the ends or principles that the community as a whole was obliged to respect. On the question of power structures these two perspectives on the city may come together (although, as we shall see, the tension between them will not be effaced). The progress of specialization may render different functions and professions more distinct from one another, and along with everything else it may bring a certain distinctness as well to the function of political leadership in the society. With the advance of functional specialization there may be an enlargement also in the diversity of interests in the community. As Madison anticipated, the greater the number of contending interests, the harder it is for any single group or interest to dominate the political leadership. Functional specialization may provide, then, the conditions that encourage autonomy in political leaders, and it may go on to encourage the development of those organizations which distinctly support the function of political leadership. In short, it may produce political parties. With the presence of politicians who have interests of their own as political leaders, and with the advent of parties that can support the independence of a civic leadership, the city may gain the blessing of institutions that are in a position to represent the *autonomy* of the community as a *political community*.

On the other hand, we know also that the maturation of the economy and the growth of functional specialization do not guarantee the development of autonomy in the political leadership. Political parties are wholly capable of growing corrupt and losing their autonomy even as a community prospers. And prosperous communities are more likely to produce "middle-class reform" movements, which may undercut the political parties even further through such reforms as "nonpartisan" elections, the extension of civil service coverage, and the removal of patronage.[24]

[24] On the other side, however, liberal reformers may also seek the enlargement of public services in the welfare field. Those services in turn would furnish possibilities for patronage and political services on a scale that was hardly dreamed of by the practitioners of the "old" politics. Even party leaders with less than average wit have been able to find new opportunities in providing aid and counsel to people who are trying to get on welfare or who are trying to obtain something more for themselves of the services that burgeoned under the Great Society. Since most government benefits are conditioned by rules and regulations, young lawyers who hope to advance through the local party may be called on to provide free legal aid, in effect, for the clients of the party. See, for example, Rakove, note 11 above, pp. 118, 120, 123.

In the meantime, the development of a modern economy brings an increasing tendency toward "organization" in other enterprises and occupations. As Marx understood, organization may bring people to a new level of consciousness about their interests, not least because it may produce a specialized set of leaders with a stake in pointing out to the members the particular interests they share as a group. As a result, one can expect to find among certain groups a heightened awareness of threats to their interests, and one can reasonably expect a sharpening of public conflict. All of this assumes, of course, that these trends of modernity are at work in the society described by Madison in the Federalist #10, where groups have the liberty to press their contending interests in public. In regimes in which that liberty does not exist, or in which groups lack autonomy in relation to the government, conflict may still take place, but it will take place largely within the halls of a ruling bureaucracy. It will not happen in such a way that the conflict works to support a regime of public dispute and competition: it will not produce the turbulence of a republican politics, and neither will it produce the abrasions and incivilities, the marks of divisiveness and disintegration, that Madison recognized as the characteristic flaws of a regime of freedom. In other words, we are not likely to find bridge-tenders in the Soviet Union backing up their demands for wages by lifting all the bridges and preventing people from getting to work. This scene describes one of the commonplace villainies in New York City, and one that is likely to be overlooked in a catalogue that includes shutdowns by the operators of elevators and the staging of strikes in the mental hospitals.

The somber recognition here is that modernity may bring a sharpening of conflict, but it will not necessarily bring a strengthening of those political institutions that represent the wider interests of the community. We have had ample experience by now in the ways by which strong political parties may induce contending groups to moderate their interests or reconcile their demands for the sake of avoiding injury to the community and embarrassment to the party. These contributions of the parties have never been so evident as in the present day, when we have been faced with the disappearance of many of the old city machines. At the same time, strong parties still survive in cities like Chicago, and by the contrast they form with their counterparts elsewhere, they bring home to us just what other qualities departed the city with the weakening of the old machines.

In the absence of strong parties that can provide a force of integration, one might say that the functional character of the city is likely to be the source of sharp conflict and division, which could break down the restraints of civility and community and aggravate the main problems that already mark the condition of the cities. What is likely to come about then, as the parties recede, is a politics dominated by the unions of public employees, the bureaucracies in the municipal government, and a variety of other interest groups. The result, as we have already seen, may be a politics more venal than the old politics, and with nothing approaching its flavor.

The question for our own time, therefore, is whether the functional character of the city may come to undermine its character as a political community or a moral association. The same dispositions of mind that make people reluctant to accept some governing principle beyond their own self-interest will make it difficult at the same time to use the authority of the community for the sake of common ends. The pressing need in the cities is to find some means of restoring the distinctiveness and unity of the community itself as a political force. And the instrument most suited to that end is the strong, governing party, which is in danger now of disappearing under the impact of the New Politics and the attack on the Old.

XI

THE "NEW" POLITICS
AND THE OLD

1. THE RECESSION OF THE "MACHINES" AND
THE ADVANCE OF THE UNIONS

In the last ten to fifteen years there has been a noticeable tendency toward the breakdown of civic cohesion in the cities as politics has come to be dominated by the demands and abrasions of public employees. But the trend toward civic disintegration was visible to some observers by the early 1940's, when the cities were at the height of their political power in the nation. In an excellent piece of political conjecture published in 1942 Harold Gosnell wrote:

> The political machines of the future may face a scarcity of patronage to dispense, and the public may face a great body of governmental servants whose participation in politics would be a delicate matter to adjust. Professional party workers may be few, and more and more dependence on voluntary workers and organized groups may result. With an increased class antagonism, the labor unions and the employers' associations may be expected to take up an increased amount of the burden of supporting the parties.[1]

The central link in this construction or hypothesis was the assumption that the old political machines, which found their sustenance in patronage, would begin to recede. They would recede, it was believed, for a variety of reasons, which were bound up in one way or another with the removal of patronage from the agencies of city government; for with the extension of middle-class "reform," more and more positions in municipal government would be placed under the protection of civil service. As the economy grew, and as the society became more securely middle-class, fewer people would come to depend (it was thought) on the prospect of patronage jobs in the local government. Where there was a need for welfare the responsibility would be taken over largely by the

[1] Harold Gosnell, *Grass Roots Politics* (Washington: American Council on Public Affairs, 1942), p. 134.

federal government, and the local machine would lose another one of its traditional means of leverage.[2]

In retrospect many observers were simply too optimistic about the fullness of employment, and they did not quite appreciate the extent to which patronage jobs could still be found attractive, even by people in a modern economy. In that respect, they did not have a realistic sense of the degree to which a society may offer resistance to "modernity," when "modernity" is understood as the progressive extension of bureaucratic rules and organization. In Chicago it has been estimated that the Cook County organization controls anywhere from 25,000 to 30,000 jobs at the city, county, and state levels, and those jobs may be suited to lawyers and professional people as well as to clerks and manual workers. That is to say nothing of the patronage that may be extended, in effect, to certain jobs in private firms that do business on contract with the city. It also overlooks the kind of responsiveness that is often shown to the governing party by large firms that do not have contracts with the city, but which wish to remain, nevertheless, on good terms with the ward committeeman or the political leadership.[3]

But beyond that it has been common to overlook the way in which the modern welfare state has simply multiplied the raw materials available to local machines. There are simply more goods and services available through the government than ever before, and as the government creates a sense of dependence in the population for certain services and transfer payments, it may foster a dependence at the same time on those local machines that are in positions to act as brokers for these benefits.

The survival of strong political machines in places like Chicago and Albany stands as rather good evidence, then, that there is nothing implicit in modernity itself that compels the dissolution of these organizations. In point of fact they *have* disappeared in most cities, but the disappearance probably has less to do with the reduction of patronage than with the cultivation of a certain aversion on the part of middle-class society toward the political culture of a "machine." Machines can find new sources of patronage outside

[2] This explanation for the decline of the old machines was put forward by Edwin O'Connor in his novel, *The Last Hurrah*, and it has been argued by a number of political scientists as well. See Fred I. Greenstein, "Changing Patterns of Urban Party Politics," *Annals of the American Academy of Political Science*, No. 353 (May 1964), pp. 1-13.

[3] See, on this point, Milton Rakove, *Don't Make No Waves—Don't Back No Losers* (Bloomington: Indiana University Press, 1975), pp. 112-13.

the agencies of city government, and so it is possible, in theory, for machines to persist even while public employees become more insulated, under civil service, from the direction of these political organizations. Still, it is important for machines to have a sizable stock of jobs to depend on, and the jobs available to city government would be vital as the base, at least, of any patronage system. It is no accident then that the political machines have become weak at the same time that the coverage of the civil service has been extended, even though, in principle, the two events are separable.

Whether or not these events are related as a matter of cause and effect, they have in fact occurred at the same time, and their correlation has some bearing on the line of conjecture offered by Gosnell. With the weakening of political controls, public employees would find it easier to organize themselves into unions of their own; and with the recession of the old political machines, the organizations of public employees would find an incentive to involve themselves in politics. For the recession of the old machines created a kind of power vacuum, and it had a politicizing effect on other organizations in the cities. Under the conditions of a vacuum of power at the center the political advantage flows to those groups that have organizations "in being." If unions had mailing lists and research staffs, if they had a body of members willing to tax themselves to support the common interests of the group, they had the materials for a cohesive force in politics. Their stake in the politics of the city was direct and obvious. Their own jobs and benefits (including pensions and grievance procedures), their interest in enlarging their autonomy in relation to the political leadership—all of these things would be affected in the most direct way by the power that the unions could flex at the polls. The temptation became strong, therefore, to step into politics as a natural extension of the activities of the unions in pressing the demands of their members. The unions could deploy their mailing lists and recruit their members for "voluntary" precinct work; and if a mayor did not have a strong political party to protect him he could be especially vulnerable to the threat posed by these very cohesive minorities in politics.

In Hartford a Fireman's Party was formed to put pressure on the mayor for the interest of firemen alone; and even where they have not declared themselves as separate parties, unions have shown themselves to be quite artful at the game of politics in manipulating the agencies of government. Once again Hartford is a source of memorable cases. In the mid-1950's the administrative officers of the city negotiated with their unionized workers and arrived at a comprehensive pay plan. The plan was set down in a memorandum of understanding, which was signed by all the parties to the arrangement. But the city administrators were then taken by surprise as the unions representing the police and firemen circumvented the administration and made a pitch to the members of the city council. The unions were able to persuade a majority on the council, and they managed to win scales of pay for themselves that were beyond the levels established in the memorandum of understanding they had accepted earlier. For many years, in fact, the local affiliate of the International Association of Fire Fighters (IAFF) refused to seek official recognition because it would have been required then to bargain only with the city manager. The IAFF wished to preserve the freedom to press its demands on the city council after it had gone as far as it could with the city manager.

But in its relations with public unions the city of Hartford has produced tales that could be rivaled only by Sholem Aleichem's legendary Village of Helm (a village in which no idea was so imbecilic that it could not become public policy). In 1967, the city manager refused a proposal of the IAFF to reduce the work week of the firefighters from 56 to 42 hours. The union stood fast and took its case to the council. One week prior to the municipal elections, the council gave in once again. Reacting with outrage, the city manager pointed out that the new plan would in effect raise the wages of the firefighters by 17 percent: for a long while it would not be possible to put the new arrangements into force by finding enough additional men, and so the current firemen would have to work an extra eight hours a week, which meant, of course, that they would work at overtime pay. The city manager did nothing to help his case, however, when he made this recognition explicit. The effect of this epiphany was merely to inspire the policemen, who demanded a raise of 17 percent for themselves—which the city manager was finally forced to accept. But when the policemen were formally granted this raise, the firefighters were not about to be outdone. In a singular display of chutzpah they insisted on "parity" and won a 17 percent increase for themselves, on top of the gains they had already made.[4]

It did not take many experiences of this kind to convince mayors with any degree of insight that it would be better to have the unions

[4] These baroque tales are recounted by Harry H. Wellington and Ralph K. Winter, Jr. in *The Unions and the Cities* (Washington: Brookings Institution, 1976), pp. 123-24.

with them than against them. As a result, some unions began to take the places that were once held in the city by party organizations. They became, in effect, adjuncts of the mayor's party, and as parts of the dominant machine they were in positions to extract benefits of a more fundamental nature—i.e., the kinds of benefits that would in turn produce more benefits. In 1958 Mayor Robert Wagner introduced the practice of collective bargaining in the civil service of New York City, and that order provided a fillip to the organization of public employees. In 1962 President Kennedy issued Executive Order 10988, which established the practice of collective bargaining for federal employees. The executive order did not permit strikes in the public service, and it did not touch local governments, but as Harry Wellington and Ralph Winter noted, the order served as "the legitimating federal imprimatur on the principle of collective bargaining by public employees."[5] It only remained for the New Frontier and the Great Society to expand the services of governments at all levels in the 1960's, so that the army of public employees would expand even further and the unions would become a truly formidable force in politics. Between 1960 and 1970 employment in state and local government grew from about 6 to 10 million; the corresponding growth in the federal service was from 2.4 million to 2.9 million. In this same period, full-time employment in the government of New York City grew by 43 percent and the membership in civil service unions increased by a factor of four. In 1960 only one-third of the city employees had been members of unions; by 1970 three-quarters of these employees were members of unions and over 90 percent of them were represented by a union for the purpose of collective bargaining.[6]

By 1974 more than 51 percent of the employees in state and local governments would be organized into unions. In contrast, only 29 percent of the workers in private industry were members of unions. These differences in the figures reflect a rather accurate sense of where unions had the chance to exert their greatest leverage and extract the largest gains for themselves. In the private economy the market was in a better position to restrain settlements over wages. Higher costs to the company could lead to higher prices for products, the loss of business to competitors, a decline of jobs in the

[5] Ibid., p. 42.

[6] Raymond Horton, "Economics, Politics, and Collective Bargaining: The Case of New York City," in *Public Employee Unions: A Study of the Crisis in Public Sector Labor Relations* (San Francisco: Institute of Contemporary Studies, 1976), pp. 183-201, at 186.

firm, and even, in some cases, the dissolution of the business itself. Of course, those constraints are not entirely missing in public employment. The resistance of taxpayers may lead to layoffs in the public service, the replacement of labor by machinery, or even the use of private contractors when they are available (as in the case of collecting garbage). But in a highly politicized situation, there may be opposition in the community to a reduction in services (in the way, for example, that parents in New York City once resisted the efforts of the Board of Education to reduce the employment of substitute teachers). In a time of rising revenues (as in the 1960's) the limits of taxation may not be as evident, and in a very large, complex budget it may be very difficult to gauge the long-range consequences of specific wage settlements. (It was revealed also, in New York, that there were artful ways in which the leadership in the city could finagle the budget and even conceal the consequences of their decisions from themselves).

As the economists put it, the demand for many public services is "inelastic." It is not likely to be affected by an increase in cost, and indeed a reduction in supply may bring a significant increase in price. This is most notably the case with certain monopolies or near-monopolies, such as fire protection and policing, and it reminds us just why strikes in the public service may be disruptive and painful. For their own part politicians continue to act on that law ascribed to them by David Hume: they soon discover that it is easier to lay the costs for their present policies on future generations, and the bills will come in (they hope) only after they have moved on to other jobs. As John Lindsay learned with a vengeance in New York City, the most important political pressures in dealing with the unions are short-run in nature. There is the need to avoid the embarrassment of a strike that puts a strain on the public, and there is an interest in avoiding the alienation of a strong union which can make a difference in a close election. As Wellington and Winter observe, "a large part of a mayor's political constituency will . . . press for a quick end to the strike with little concern for the cost of the settlement."[7] That is particularly the case, as they point out, in instances in which the costs of the settlement may be passed on to the state or federal governments. Altogether then, the use of the strike in these circumstances of "public" enterprise gives a considerable advantage to the unions in comparison with other interest groups in the city that cannot force a stoppage of public

[7] Wellington and Winter, note 4 above, p. 25.

services. The consequences of that difference we will see more fully in a moment, but for the present we may simply recognize that, under the conditions of politics in most large cities today, there is a critical disparity in power that separates the public service unions from the mayor and the remaining, run-of-the-mill interest groups.

The result of that disparity has been to alter the structure of party politics in the cities. As Theodore Lowi noted, the new pattern of politics became evident in 1961, with Mayor Wagner's campaign for a third term in New York.[8] As in the past, there was a scrupulous effort to provide an ethnic balance on the ticket. But instead of piecing the ticket together by drawing on people from the different clubhouses or precinct organizations, it was assembled by recruiting men from within the bureaucracy of the city. For president of the City Council Wagner selected Paul Screvene, an Italian who started his career as a garbage man. Screvene had worked his way up the organizational ladder until he had become the head of the sanitation workers and then, under Wagner, commissioner of sanitation. For the position of comptroller Wagner chose the durable Abraham Beame, who had been the director of the budget over several administrations, and had served for a number of years before that as a professional employee of the city.

John Lindsay would repeat the pattern when he ran for reelection in 1969. By that time, of course, he had been given a drubbing by the transportation workers, the sanitationmen, and the teachers' union, and he was determined that peace with the unions would no longer be endangered through any want of liberality on his own part. Lindsay became very acquiescent in his dealings with the unions, and when it came time to assemble his own ticket he followed the course set earlier by Wagner. He drew his candidate for comptroller from the Finance Administration, and he took, as his president of the City Council, an administrator of rank in the police department, who had started off as a policeman on the beat and had worked his way up in the department. Instead of making his way among the political clubhouses in the city, Lindsay went about collecting the endorsements of the Patrolmen's Benevolent Association, the Transport Workers, and the Uniformed Sanitationmen. The latter two had been his adversaries in the beginning of his term, but since Lindsay had absorbed so completely the lessons they had sought to teach, they had a new interest in preserving him in his

[8] Theodore J. Lowi, "Machine Politics—Old and New," *The Public Interest* (Fall 1967), pp. 83-92.

place. Some of these groups would be deployed for work in the precincts, particularly the sanitationmen, who were organized by precinct in their own work, and who were developing a fair reputation as a political force. As Gosnell had anticipated, "professional party workers" might have been fewer, while there was "more and more dependence on voluntary workers and organized groups." But the "voluntary" nature of this precinct work should not have fooled anyone; and clearly it did not mean that these political exertions were unaffected by self-interest. The unions and their members saw their own fortunes at stake in the elections just as much as those workers in the past whose jobs had depended on patronage. By showing their muscle at the polls, they could enlarge the sense of their own importance in the election of the mayor. In that event they would be in a better position to increase their autonomy, preserve (and even expand) the jobs they held, and expect even more liberal settlements with the city in the future. What Marx once said of Louis Bonaparte and his army might have been said equally well about Lindsay and his appendages in the unions: that he was supported by a force "which he had bought with liquor and sausages, and which he had continually to ply with sausage anew."

2. THE POLITICS OF DISINTEGRATION

In this manner bureaucracies in the municipal government came to receive an explicit recognition of the preeminence they now held in the politics of the city. The old political machines may have died off, but as Theodore Lowi has remarked, the cities had come to be ruled in many places by new machines, which were far stronger than their predecessors—and yet less coordinated among themselves, and far less responsive to the public. The "new machines" were of course the bureaucracies, which had become more impermeable to outside groups and less obedient to political direction as they had come under the protection of the civil service. As Lowi has said, the old machines depended on jobs, fraternity, and a centralized system of rewards. The new machines depend less on graft and corruption of a more mundane variety, but they rely on forms of blackmail that range between the subtle and the gross, and they are unified by the common interests of the members in their jobs and their own autonomy. Quite often the leadership in bureaucratic departments is self-perpetuating, and the career line will be wholly internal, with people advancing through the ranks rather than coming into high positions from outside the organization. The leaders may then be as insulated from popular control as any of the old political bosses. But unlike the old political bosses, their loyalty is confined almost exclusively to their own narrow clientele. As Lowi has commented, "No mayor of a modern city has a predictable means of determining whether the bosses of the New Machines—the bureau chiefs and the career commissioners—will be loyal to anything but their agency, its work, and related professional norms."[9]

The consequence is that it is much more difficult these days to impose a unified policy on the separate agencies in the city. Certainly it is far harder than it was at an earlier time, when city employees were dependent for their jobs on the political machines, and the machines could provide a source of centralized direction and authority. But the absence of that unified control is not the only, or even the most telling, way in which a new disintegration has been manifested in the cities. The most corrosive trend for the morale and character of the cities has been the expansion of strikes in the public service. As a result of their new weight, the unions have been able to secure through their political leverage a right to strike that has been denied them in the law. In many, if not most, instances the rationale for the public management of services such as sanitation, police, and transportation has been that a cessation of these services would simply be intolerable for the community. In point of fact, the laws in all the states are still set strongly against strikes in the public service. Even in a liberal state such as Oregon, where a limited right to strike is granted, a provision has been made for the use of injunctions when a strike poses a threat to the public health, safety, or welfare. And in the case of police and firemen, the laws of Oregon prohibit strikes altogether.[10] If there has been a dramatic rise in recent years in the number of strikes in the public service, it would be hard to attribute the increase to any equivocation in the law.

Nor is it likely that this new militancy in the public services can be explained by a deterioration in the conditions and compensation of public employees. Their conditions and their benefits have in fact improved. The increase in the number of strikes has to be connected with the enlargement of the power of the unions in the 1960's, and with the growing acceptance of collective bargaining.

[9] Ibid., p. 87.
[10] See David Lewin, "Collective Bargaining and the Right to Strike," In *Public Employee Unions*, note 6 above, pp. 145-63, at 155.

When Mayor Lindsay began his term as mayor of New York in January 1966, he was met by a strike of the transport workers. That strike seemed to set the tone for things to come, not only in New York but in other places as well. For all we know, the transport workers may have set a dramatic public example which was quickly emulated in New York, and from New York the idea may well have been spread to other cities. In any event, 1966 marked the beginning of a new era of relations with the unions in the public services. Before 1966 work stoppages in the civil services occurred at an average of about 29 per year. But between 1966 and 1974 the number leaped to about 319. Between 1958 and 1965 an average of 3,900 workers were involved in these strikes every year; in the period between 1966 and 1974 that number rose to almost 176,000.

These trends were mirrored also in the figures on workdays lost during the strikes. Before 1958, an average of 26,000 man-days were lost each year by strikes in the public service. Between 1958 and 1965 the number grew to 50,000; but between 1966 and 1974 that figure increased *28 times* to an average of over 1,400,000.[11] The consequences of these strikes ran well beyond the number of man-days lost, and the results could be charted as they moved from very tangible matters of distribution to the erosion of spirit and the wasting of civic decencies in the city.

For one thing, the strikes were a measure of the new power of the unions, and apart from the harm that they were capable of inflicting on the city they could also be highly profitable for the union members. From 1952 to 1966 there had been a rough parity between the average salaries of people in public service and in private industry. (By greater or lesser amounts the people in the public service generally lagged behind.) But starting in 1966 the level of compensation in public service began to advance in relation to private industry, and by 1970 the average pay in the government exceeded that in private industry. By 1973 the difference had widened to the point where employees in the public service were paid an average of 10 percent more than people in private industry.

[11] The number of workers involved in strikes reached its highest level in 1970, while the largest number of man-days were lost in 1968. The figures have been reported by David Lewin in ibid., p. 148. As it turns out, more than half of the total man-days lost in 1974 were lost in education. See U.S. Department of Commerce, Bureau of the Census, *Labor-Management Relations in State and Local Governments: 1974*, State and Local Government Special Studies No. 75 (Washington, Government Printing Office, 1975), p. 6.

Some of the disparities might have been explained by the large number of college graduates in the civil services. But a number of studies have controlled for education, race, and other "variables," and they have suggested, at various times, that 41-44 percent of the difference in salaries remains unexplained, which is to say that it seems to arise only by virtue of the fact that these people are working for the government.

As it turns out, the differences in pay are most pronounced in the comparison between private business and the federal government, and they are likely to be less dramatic at the state and local levels. Nevertheless, there has been a growing trend toward an enlargement of salaries in the public services in comparison with the private sector, and the differences can show up as quite substantial in a number of cities. In the early 1970's, for example, Philadelphia was paying its clerical workers a third more, on the average, than the amount that was paid in private industry; in Houston and Buffalo the pay of the city clerks was a fifth larger. In New York and Newark, the average salaries of maintenance workers were 42 percent larger than those of their counterparts in private business.[12] And this says nothing, of course, of the kinds of salaries and pensions that have been given in New York City to sanitationmen, transport workers, and college teachers. In a reversal of John Kenneth Galbraith's old dictum, we now seem to have, as Daniel Moynihan put it, a case of "public affluence" and "private squalor."

It is not merely that sanitationmen working for the city may be making more than custodians in private establishments. The critical point rather—the point that touches the issue of equity in these arrangements—is that people in the private economy are being taxed to provide a higher standard of compensation and benefits to people doing comparable work in the public service. The comparisons become glaring when it becomes a matter, say, of taxing custodians and gas station attendants in order to support professors at a state university at a level that could not be matched by a private university.

What seems to be overlooked quite often is that people of modest means may be rendered poor ("private squalor" can be produced) through the extractions made by the government in the form of

[12] Stephen H. Perloff, "Comparing Municipal Salaries with Industry and Federal Pay," *Monthly Labor Review* (October 1971), pp. 46-50, quoted in James W. Kuhn, "The Riddle of Inflation—A New Answer," *The Public Interest* (Spring 1972), p. 66, n. 3.

taxes. In the late 1960's and early 1970's the chief mystery for economists was how the economy was able to experience at the same time high unemployment and unabating inflation. It is not exaggerating to say that just a short time earlier reputable economists had considered the prospect virtually inconceivable. Yet in the late 1960's something new occurred. These novel patterns just happened to coincide with the expansion of public charges which was brought about by the enlargement of social programs and by the success of public service unions in pressing their own, advanced claims. Some economists argued that the association was far more than coincidental. James Kuhn pointed out, for example, that, contrary to the expectations at the time, it was not the large corporations and industrial unions that had been leading the inflation. The gains made by workers in manufacturing and transportation (the "corporate, unionized sector of the economy") were exceeded by workers in wholesale and retail trades, *and both groups were outstripped by workers in the public services.*

In fact, the causal connection in the problem of inflation was quite plausibly the reverse of what had been expected. It was the extraordinary gains secured by employees in the public service that made it necessary for workers elsewhere to raise their own demands and spur on the cycle of inflation. As Kuhn commented, "Workers and employees in big industries . . . have sought wage increases to meet the soaring cost of living and to help them pay even higher state and local taxes, both of which were pushed up by the rising price of services."[13] Social security taxes doubled for the average production worker between 1965 and 1970, and that increase offset all or part of the reductions that took place over the same period in federal income taxes. Industrial unions managed to make substantial gains in compensation during this time, and yet these gains were virtually washed away by increases in taxes and prices.[14] Those increases were caused mainly by the enlargement of costs for public and private services, and it is sobering to consider that a large portion of the gain made by employees in the public service derived simply from the political leverage that was held by the unions.

When this recognition surfaced, it produced melancholy effects on many people who had been the partisans in the past of labor organization, for it suddenly became evident that the regime of union power was simply compelling a diversion of resources to the

[13] Kuhn, note 12 above, pp. 65-66.
[14] Ibid., pp. 66-67.

powerful. In an article in the *New Republic* Frances Fox Piven traced the extended consequences of this diversion for the life of the city. The outsized settlements won by the local unions created a strain on the city budgets, and to meet the new commitments the cities had to raise property taxes while they sought to cut back on other services. The public libraries would be reduced in their hours; subway trains would go unrepaired; welfare grants would be trimmed. San Diego, Cleveland, and Washington, D.C. reduced their collections of garbage. Detroit began to close some toilets in the public parks. Kansas City allowed its elms to die rather than draw funds from other programs in an effort to save the trees.[15] Dallas cut back on capital improvements, and there was a disposition in the cities generally to scale down the provisions for museums and the arts. Gradually, but very discernibly, there was an erosion of those amenities that marked a civilized community—or a city, at any rate, with a large enough spirit to live a more robust public life.

But beyond these constrictions in the public life of the city, the demands of the public employees were forcing a diversion of funds from those parts of the budget that supported services for the poor. Piven reported that special appropriations for health and education in ghetto districts had been pared in a number of states. Nine states had made reductions in their Medicaid programs, and at least 19 states had cut back on their welfare benefits. The governing presumption here was that financial commitments to the poor were relatively "soft" when compared to the commitments that arose out of contracts with the municipal unions. The bills for the public services were more insistent and they were supported by a constituency that was far more powerful than the poor.

For the most part, this "transfer" of funds from the poor to the public employees has been inferred from a comparison of the aggregate figures. In some cases, however, the diversion of funds was made quite explicit. In the summer of 1969 the firefighters in Newark staged a strike that lasted for twelve hours. The crisis was resolved when certain "urban aid funds" from the state, which had been earmarked for the poor, were shifted instead to an account for salaries. There they were used to support raises in pay for the firemen and the police.[16]

[15] See Frances Fox Piven, "Cutting Up The City Pie," *New Republic*, February 5, 1972, pp. 17-22, at 22.

[16] *The New York Times*, August 7, 1969, p. 25, cited by Wellington and Winter, note 4 above, p. 27, n. 45.

And yet there was one notable counterpoint to the pattern that Piven described. As she herself noted, the state of affairs she related seemed to be part of a trend that was taking hold in all large cities— *except Chicago*. In contrast to other cities, Chicago had almost no strikes in the public service. The city was solvent; the amenities of an urbane community were being preserved and expanded; and public employees were paid rather well without creating gross disparities between the public and the private sector. Nevertheless, when Piven turned her mind to the source of those maladies she had charted, she placed the blame first, for some reason, on "a fiscal structure that limited the contest [of groups] mainly to benefits paid for by state and local taxes." As she went on to argue, the effect of that arrangement was to confine the political conflict "within the lower and middle strata of American society." For Piven, apparently, the problem could not be solved unless our public policy moved beyond the perimeter of the cities and drew on the tax resources of the whole country. Even that, however, would not be enough unless it included an attack (as she argued) on "the concentrations of individual and corporate wealth in America."[17]

But it was not the wealthy in America, either in families or corporations, who were responsible for the power of unions in local politics. Nor was it they who were causing the middle classes to be taxed more heavily in order to raise salaries in the public service well beyond the comparable levels in private industry. Beyond that, there simply was not enough money in the hands of the wealthy to cover the costs of the public services in the United States. A decision to draw more heavily on the federal government was a decision to draw taxes more heavily from the middle classes, and this resort to federal funding could only have made matters worse. It would have removed whatever restraints were still imposed by the limits of local resources, and it would have confirmed the understanding that was held by the unions: namely, that the disputes over salaries were really contests of power by different claimants on the public treasury.

Neither the fiscal resources of the federal government nor the concentration of wealth is at all relevant to the main structure of the problem. The center of the problem is the political power exercised by the civil service unions, and that power arises from a combination of public ownership (or management) and the institution of free elections. Nothing in that essential structure is likely

[17] Piven, note 15 above, p. 22.

to be altered even by a regime that professed to be "socialist." In fact, a socialist regime that understood socialism to imply the enlargement of the public sector would face many of the same problems that Piven described in the cities. In a larger number of enterprises, disputes over work and pay would be disputes between unions and the government, outside the restraints of the market. Once again the unions would bring to bear the threat of their concentrated force at the polls, and they would put the government under further pressure through their capacity to make life burdensome (if not painful) for the rest of the society. Unless people lose their freedom to press their interests in public, the contest over the distribution of goods will continue, even in a socialist order, and the unions will continue to hold an uncommon political leverage. But Piven was as likely as anyone else to be aware of these things, and all the weighty intimations about the "concentrations of individual and corporate wealth" were probably a camp way of distracting the credulous from a rather simple and more obvious question: Why can't other cities be more like Chicago?

3. THE MACHINES AND THE MORAL INTEGRATION OF THE COMMUNITY

Exactly why things should have been different in Chicago is not so hard to fathom. Until the recent advent of Mayor Jane Byrne, the city had rarely been disrupted by strikes. It did not mortgage its future in order to pay bills to its public employees, because unions had not been able to command as much leverage in Chicago as in other places. They could not hold as much leverage because the political leadership had its own base in the supporters of the Democratic organization, and for that reason the party leadership did not have to be dependent on any single interest group or union. The firefighters and the police in Chicago have had no real prospect of fielding a separate slate of candidates in the city elections and defeating the Democratic organization. They have had no impulse then to emulate the firefighters in Hartford in seeking to enter politics for the sake of blackmailing the political leadership.

The recent series of strikes on the part of the transport workers, the teachers, and the firefighters seem to have as much to do with the combative style of Mayor Byrne as with any strains on the city budget. But the willingness of the public unions to challenge the political leadership with a strike may be a reflection of their own hunch that the party organization has been weakened under the leadership of Mayor Byrne. A weakened party would put each union on its own, to extract whatever advantage it could on the basis of its own strength. A party organization that cannot protect the mayor from these demands is an organization that cannot be depended on any longer to secure the interests of the unions against the claims of their competitors. But if the mayor survives these crises—if she succeeds, for example, in her policy of replacing the firefighters who went on strike—it is likely to be a sign that the structure created by Daley and his predecessors has not in fact been destroyed. If the mayor can resist the unions, it will be in large part because of a lingering conviction among the unions and the public that her political position is likely to be buttressed ultimately by the enduring strength of the party.

The dominance of the party has given a different structure to politics in Chicago, and as a result of that structure the local unions have been dissuaded from taking the course followed by many unions elsewhere. They have been turned away from the temptation to challenge the leadership of the city in overt political contests; they have found an incentive instead to attach themselves to the party and its leadership as allied organizations. For the unions the party can offer a climate of support in their dealings with private firms. It can take a position of benign neutrality in relation to certain strikes by unions in private industry. It can assure that contractors with the city make their proper connections with the unions. It can support the interests of labor at the state and national levels through its delegations in the legislature and in Congress. And beyond that, it may take care also to represent the perspectives of the unions in other places where the interests of the union may be engaged (as, for example, on the Board of Education, which will be guaranteed enduringly a representative from organized labor).

On the other hand, a strong political leadership is not likely to encourage city workers to form themselves into unions. The leadership will often be quite generous in regard to salaries in the city government, but it is unlikely to favor any scheme that would reduce its control over its own apparatus or remove the patronage that it requires to preserve the loyalties (and energies) of its own party workers. When there was a move among the police in Albany to organize a branch of the Patrolmen's Benevolent Association, it was deftly stopped by the chief of police and the O'Connell organization.[18] A campaign in Chicago in the 1960's to increase

[18] James Q. Wilson, *Varieties of Police Behavior* (Cambridge: Harvard University Press, 1968), pp. 241-42.

the number of city workers organized into unions was quickly undercut by Mayor Daley and the party leadership. As of 1974, only 33 percent of city employees in Chicago were organized in unions, the lowest figure in any major city in the United States outside the South. In Boston, the comparable figure was 90 percent, and in Detroit, the capital of industrial unionism, over 93 percent of the city workers were in unions. The political leadership in Chicago has generally been friendly over the years to organized labor, and yet the proportion of union membership in the public service there is slightly lower than it is in Houston (34.7 percent), a city that is located, after all, in a state that has traditionally been averse to unions. (In Dallas, which has nearly the same number of public employees as Houston, no unions of any kind have been established among the public employees.)[19]

In Chicago, the interests of the unions are the objects of persistent sympathy and attentiveness on the part of the political leadership, and through the party the unions gain access to many benefits in the city. But at the same time the unions must be sensitive to the interests of the party (in which they, along with others, have a substantial stake). The demands of the unions must be placed in the larger context of the party organization and the commitments that the party has to other parts of the community. The party may be solicitous about the workingmen in the unions, but it has a critical interest also in seeing that the buses and trains continue to run, and that working people in the city will be able to get to their jobs. What can be said in this vein about the transport system would apply equally well to the operation of the hospitals and the schools, the supply of electricity, the cleaning of streets, and the provision of police and firemen. The aversion to strikes in all these areas does not arise from an intolerance of "disorder." It arises, rather, out of a concrete sense among the leaders in the party of the ways in which people in their wards are injured by the withdrawal of these services. Beyond that, the leaders of the city are seriously affected, as leaders, if the economy suffers under the strains of a strike. Sales may be lost, incomes may be diminished, and the public, in its irritation, may focus its resentment on the politicians themselves.

What the party leadership is compelled then to foster among its allied groups is a sense of restraint. The cardinal assumption is that

---

[19] The figures are taken from a survey of public employment that was conducted by the Bureau of the Census in 1975. I would like to thank Allen Stevens of the Bureau, who furnished me with the figures on the separate cities.

the interests of all groups in the party coalition can be reconciled in some way, and that the interests of any one group can be pressed with vigor only so long as it is bounded by a decent regard for the interests of others. One case recalled by David Greenstone may stand as a paradigm here. It concerned the dispute that arose within the party in Chicago in 1960 over the replacement of Congressman Charles Boyle, who had died in an automobile accident. Boyle had been an active liberal and a favorite of the labor unions, and there was a concern among the unions that his successor be someone of the same cast. The Committee on Political Education (COPE), which was the political arm of organized labor, was drawn to two of the candidates for the nomination. One was a director of labor education at Roosevelt University and the other was a representative in the state legislature. The former, however, was a Unitarian, and his selection would not have furthered the representation of any ethnic or religious group of importance in the district. The second candidate was Jewish and the Democrats already had a Jewish congressman in the adjacent congressional district. But what the party sought, for the sake of ethnic balance, was an Irish Catholic to take the place of the Catholic Boyle.

The Democratic leaders came to settle then on Edward Finnegan, a precinct captain who had worked for years in the organization. Finnegan was a lawyer who could claim to displace at least a respectable weight in the local community. To ask whether he was an "intellectual" or a programmatic "liberal" was to measure him suddenly by a standard that was foreign to his daily habits. He was not, in short, the kind of candidate that the people at COPE had in mind. As the reports had it, they regarded his selection as a "joke" ("an insult to our intelligence"); and they were disposed to look elsewhere.

Around the same time, the Republicans were nominating Theodore Fields, a liberal Jewish civic leader. Fields was a personable fellow, who was taking advanced liberal positions, and actively seeking the support of labor. COPE was drawn very strongly to Fields and it saw a chance, in this contest, to demonstrate something of its own strength. Fields was endorsed then by the local organization of COPE in the twelfth congressional district, but the endorsement had to be ratified by the state organization. Before that approval could be given, however, the party leadership pressed its case at all levels in the COPE hierarchy, and that pleading in turn generated pressures on the district COPE, both from within the party and the labor movement. Finnegan had been a trade union lawyer and a union member, and he could be expected to vote loyally with the party caucus on all issues considered important to labor. On the other hand, Fields might have been a more articulate liberal, but when he arrived in Congress he would have been incorporated in a more conservative, Republican caucus, and that was likely, in the long run, to have some effect. The loss of the seat to the Republicans would have removed a labor vote that was reinforced by party loyalty, and it would have reduced the bargaining power of the Democratic delegation from Chicago. These considerations finally proved telling, and the district organization of COPE was induced to back away from its endorsement of Fields. Finnegan won the election and he went on to be, as expected, a predictable friend of the unions in Congress. As one leader of COPE remarked at the end of Finnegan's first term, he was "a guaranteed vote for progressive legislation. You can't criticize his voting record."[20]

The incident did not, of course, involve the unions of municipal workers. But I cite it because it does, I think, reveal something of the essential relation between the party and its constituent groups; and therefore it bears as well on the relation between the party and the sundry groups in the public service. As David Greenstone observed, the case suggested that the alliance between labor and the Democratic party "rested on considerations far more pervasive than a case-by-case evaluation of individual races."[21] That is, the logic of alliance and commitment made it illegitimate for either the party or labor to make its decision in every case by the narrowest calculus of self-interest. What both sides shared, presumably, was a long-term, principled interest in preserving the party coalition. And that interest implied a willingness to surrender one's own preferences at times out of a respect for the claims of other groups that made up the coalition.

To COPE and the unions the party offered a congressman who could be depended on as a supporter of labor and of the liberal agenda in Congress. What the party asked in return was that the unions accept an Irish Catholic candidate and help the party meet its obligations to other parts of its constituency. This was, in its

[20] Not long after that, the congressional districts were altered. The twelfth district was merged with another area and received a liberal Jewish congressman. Finnegan eventually stepped aside to become a judge.

[21] David Greenstone, *Labor in American Politics* (New York: Knopf, 1969), p. 309; the account of COPE and the problem of Finnegan is drawn from pp. 304-10, 312-13.

essentials, the logic of the situation, and it was the logic that was ultimately honored.

Like the employees in the civil service, COPE came to discover what it meant, in a very concrete moral way, to have its interests bound up with a party that had obligations stretched across the whole community. The mechanics may alter from one case to another, but the logic of the matter is essentially the same. In 1966 Martin Luther King led a civil rights march into Cicero, a white working-class suburb just over the western border of Chicago. He was met there by a barrage of rocks and bottles loosed by the residents of the area, who generally debased themselves in the violence of their reaction. Four years later the Democratic organization of Cook County put across a black candidate for Congress in a district that contained some western precincts of Chicago, along with the sections of Cicero into which King had led his march. Apparently a good number of the whites who were moved to resist King were nevertheless willing to vote for a black candidate as part of their loyalty to the party. If these two populations had to confront one another directly, the result was violence. But if they were spared a confrontation they would separately elect men to office from the same party; and those men would be willing to serve the interests of both groups as a result of the connections they had to one another through the party. As a form of moral integration, it is no mean accomplishment, and there is nothing modest about it: through the mediation of the party, different groups in the city may be induced to render greater justice to one another than they would in fact render if they were left to confront each other face to face. In that very practical way the strong political party may indeed represent a force of moral integration in the city that cannot easily be reproduced by any other institution.

The significance of that kind of integration may be read all too vividly in the experience of those places in which it no longer exists. As the sense of civic obligation has broken down, it has taken with it the modest bonds of civility that can make a profound difference to the character of a city. The example of New York in the late 1960's became stamped on the consciousness of the country, and the problem there could not be reduced merely to the sum of the strikes in the public service. What was far more portentous was the spirit of rapacity that lay behind the stoppages—a brazen willingness to press one's interests to the point of injury to others, a strident refusal, spreading through the citizenry at large, to respect any law beyond one's own demands. The spirit of the city could be read then in a host of little villainies that the citizens of New York perpetrated against one another. What state of mind was present, for example, among the professionals and attendants in mental hospitals who were willing to leave their charges unattended? What did that reflect about their dedication to the good of their patients? What could one say of the operators of elevators or the tenders of bridges who were willing to suspend their services, even when they knew that some people were likely to suffer strokes as a result of their acts? Whatever the precise shape of these dispositions, there is little doubt that this state of affairs may have a pronounced effect on the tone of relations among people and on the character of individuals themselves. In New York these truths became palpable, and they were found alarming even by people who had never counted themselves as beamish idealists. Richard Reeves wrote in *The New York Times*:

> The strikes, slowdowns and threats by teachers, policemen, firemen, Consolidated Edison employees, welfare workers and even students are part of a pattern that is straining the structure of government, of the unions, of society itself.
>
> There is no name yet for the dangerous and destructive game being played in New York—and in many other cities across the nation. Perhaps it is the 'politics of confrontation,' perhaps the 'politics of raw power,' or perhaps, as one bewildered city official said, it is the 'politics of selfishness'—grab everything you can get and the hell with everybody else.[22]

Urbane people might have been willing to acknowledge that Chicago, under Richard Daley, was a city that "worked"; but even the most disinterested admirers of Daley were somehow too diffident to say that the governance of Chicago was also morally superior, in certain ways, to the example held out by New York. They were too aware of the incidents of graft, and they were inclined, along with most people in the country, to equate "morals" with a regimen of saintliness. What they did not understand was that "morals" involve standards of right and wrong that can guide practical decisions, and that they can be manifested in the smallest things— in the ways in which people bring up their children and treat their neighbors, or the manner in which they generally deal with the interests of others. What was overlooked here was the larger pattern of morals that a city exemplifies in the way it governs itself and the

[22] *The New York Times*, December 8, 1968, p. E1.

obligations that citizens accept in their relations with one another. That the structure of politics in the community can make a serious difference to the moral character of a city in this sense may not have been as evident at an earlier time, before the troubles of the cities began to unfold in the 1960's. But literate citizens cannot claim any longer an innocence of experience or a want of instruction. That does nothing to make it easier, of course, to restore the reign of strong party machines in an age when people have become averse to authority and resistant to obligations. Nor does it mean that the solution always lies in the advent of strong political parties. But given a choice between a politics dominated by party organizations and a politics in which the sanitationmen and the police can become political forces, a person of ordinary sensibility should no longer have to pause.

FOUR

HOUSING

XII

BLACK POLITICS AND
THE QUESTION OF HOUSING

1. Black Politicians and White Machines

The kind of "integration" brought about by political parties is not usually an integration characterized by social intimacy. It is an integration that involves, rather, the sharing of purposes, the reconciliation of interests, the pooling of resources to support common ends. It may be a modest form of integration, but it may produce in its own way a wondrous alchemy: a number of white Democrats who fought Martin Luther King, Jr. in Cicero, Illinois find themselves voting a few years later for a black candidate for Congress on the Democratic ticket, or they find themselves voting for white politicians who are connected to blacks through the medium of the political party. Unions that might otherwise close down the public transportation system of a large city hold back from a policy of strikes out of a sense of obligation to the party leadership. As they restrain themselves for the sake of the party, they are led to modify their interests out of a respect for other groups—or even for the public at large—whose interests may be represented in the local party. This may be a rather limited kind of achievement, but there is a noticeable difference between communities that have cultivated these habits of reciprocity and those which have not.

The process of knitting together a stable coalition in politics involves nothing less than the task of reconciling interests in an enduring way. At its best it may be a mode of instructing different groups on the question of what their own, just interests are. In that respect, the task of governing through a political party may lead on to the highest tasks of statesmanship, for the business of the statesman at the peak is to articulate the proper ends that ought to animate a decent society, and then to establish the practical conditions of politics which could support those ends. At the same time the responsibility of the leadership in a lawful regime is to justify its exercise of power, to establish the justification for its policies to those people who will be expected to support them. To a remarkable degree, these different sides of the discipline of governing come together in the business of building a party coalition in a public politics. The interests of disparate groups cannot be connected in a stable way without suggesting something about the larger grounds of principle on which those interests meet. It made a profound difference, for example, that Northern industrialists in the nineteenth century chose to connect their interests to those of the small farmers in the Middle West rather than plantation owners in the South. Their economic interests could have been served quite as usefully by one coalition as the other. But in one case the alliance supported a strong central government and the principles of freedom, while in the other case the industrialists would have been tied in with a regime of slavery.

To convince different groups to stay in coalition is to convince them that the ethic embodied in the party—that peculiar meshing of interests and principles which the party represents—is one that can validly claim their attachment. A party leadership that persuades groups to stay in coalition is a leadership that has essentially succeeded in making itself and its policies acceptable to different sections of the public. But what is equally important, it has helped these various groups in the task of justifying themselves to one another. When whites in South Boston continue voting Democratic, even while they recognize the weight held by blacks in the Democratic Party, they would seem to imply a judgment about the ranking of their interests. They would suggest, in the most decisive way, that the interests which they share with blacks in a Democratic Administration are somehow more important than issues (such as busing) that would separate them from the black leadership. One of those issues, traditionally, has been a concern about unemployment, but if the problem of unemployment eases, the issue of busing could suddenly take on more importance. In that event, white voters in South Boston could end up defecting from the Democrats if they are not satisfied with the efforts made by the national leadership to resolve the issue of busing.

The interests of blacks and whites could indeed be reconciled in the case of busing, but a failure to reconcile them would offer an object lesson of sorts on the consequences that may arise from the refusal of different sections of a party to justify their demands to one another. If black leaders and voters manage to persuade themselves that the commitment to "racial balancing" in the schools flows ineluctably from the principles that underlie *Brown* v. *Board of Education*, they may refuse to accept any accommodation on this matter. The result could be a defection from the party of large numbers of whites, and the consequences could be costly for blacks as well. The defections might have the effect of displacing from the control of the government that party with which most blacks have invested their political interests. Whether that investment has been altogether wise or justified is quite another question. But if we accept for the moment the way in which most blacks have defined their interests in politics, it is sufficient to point out that, by their own measure, the consequences for them would be disastrous if whites were moved, in substantial numbers, to leave the party.

The same thing could be said, of course, on the other side, in relation to whites who have identified their interests with the success of the Democratic Party. By their own reckoning, they too would stand to lose if they refused to take any steps to make their objections understandable and reasonable to blacks, and if they brought about, through their intransigence, the unraveling of the party. There is a temptation to say, therefore, that the process of preserving a party coalition carries its own sanctions. Those people who refuse to accept the discipline of offering justifications to other groups in the coalition may see the coalition come apart, and they themselves may suffer the consequence of falling out of power along with the remaining members of the alliance. The moral, in short, is that those who will not make their interests reasonable to others may lose their license to exercise political power.

The logic of a party system may foster a connection, in that case, between propriety and self-interest, between the obligations that attend the exercise of power and the material gains that are often sought through the uses of politics. The lesson has a special point to all groups that happen to be less than a majority, which is to say, all groups that stand in need of allies if they would gain access to political power and govern with consent. It should go without saying that the proposition applies with equal force to blacks, even in those places in which they constitute a much larger portion of the population than they do in the nation as a whole. For some inscrutable reason the question came to be argued with agitation in the late 1960's and early 1970's as to whether blacks should seek to take power on their own or whether they should seek out coalitions with white allies. The question was thoroughly silly as far as the national government was concerned, but it was scarcely more plausible even in places like Newark, where blacks formed a majority of the population.

Just before the election of Kenneth Gibson in Newark as the first black mayor, it was said, in a flight of hyperbole, that Newark was on the threshold of a "black government." And yet what could have been meant by a "black government"? Was there suddenly a mandate for black officials to rule without the slightest interference from institutions and forces outside the black community? Were the courts no longer open? Were the state and federal governments in suspension? Had Newark become a separate republic? The most important business enterprises in Newark were not in the hands of blacks. What would have stopped them from transferring their establishments elsewhere if the political climate became insufferable and the level of taxation tended to inhibit growth? It was hard to imagine just what tax resources would be available to a "black government" that had not been available to a "white government," if it were presumed that the maladies affecting Newark could be relieved mainly by more public spending and taxation. If it were a matter, on the other hand, of generating growth in the economy of Newark by attracting more investment, a black government would have to look toward "white" businesses and investors, and its fiscal policies would have to be rendered acceptable to those people who do not typically invest by rolling dice.

In point of fact, there has never been a serious question in this country as to whether blacks would exercise power on their own or in coalition. Even where blacks made up the universe of officialdom, the exercise of power in a constitutional order meant that black officials would have to be dependent, and properly so, on many voters, officials, and businessmen who were not black. That elementary fact of life has been accessible to almost all black politicians, and it helps to explain why most of them have been disposed to moderation, even at a time when the rhetoric of black power seemed to be dominant in the black community. A number of black mayors (for example, Thomas Bradley in Los Angeles, Matthew Carter in Montclair, New Jersey) managed to win in cities that were predominantly white. And even in Newark, Kenneth Gibson was measurably helped in his first election when he won 20 percent of the white vote in a racially polarized contest.[1]

In one recent study in New Jersey, 87 percent of black officials who were sampled *disagreed* with the proposition that "black elected officials put the interests of the black community ahead of those of the entire city."[2] However, that does not stop black pol-

[1] See Leonard A. Cole, *Blacks in Power* (Princeton: Princeton University Press, 1976), pp. 70-72, 76.

[2] Ibid., pp. 113-14. On the other hand, 45 percent of the white officials who were sampled, and 27 percent of the black citizens in the survey, thought that black officials did favor the interests of blacks.

iticians from claiming at the same time that they are somehow more "responsive" to the interests of blacks than white politicians have traditionally been. Still, black politicians seem to have been affected by their very positions with a marked infusion of prudence. To the extent that blacks need politics at all to enlarge their prospects, they will be dependent on resources controlled by whites, both in politics and the economy, and black politicians have been quick to grasp that understanding. Some of the most formidable leaders in the black community have been men who came to power as the leaders of black contingents, or even black "subsidiaries," within political machines that were headed by whites.

It is the measure of the shallowness of current perceptions that, in the rhetorical infatuation with "black power," the political power of blacks has been equated with the number of black mayors or officials, rather than with the actual influence held by black politicians. There are other important grounds on which it would be desirable to have a larger number of black officials. People in positions of public authority may become models for emulation, and it may be salutary in the United States, for blacks as well as whites, if people could see black men and women in positions of official authority. But that is quite a separate matter from the question, say, of whether blacks have been "without power" in Chicago because they have not been able to dominate the Cook County organization, or because they have not been in a position yet to elect a black mayor. By any strict test, few politicians of any color in this country have had the kind of power that was exercised by Congressman William Dawson in Chicago. Until his death in 1970 Dawson was the preeminent black figure in the Cook County organization and the head, in effect, of the black subsidiary of the machine. When he shifted to the Democratic Party in the 1930's he gained the "franchise" of the regular organization. Through the machine he obtained access to a fund of patronage and jobs, and with the help of that patronage he built one of the most disciplined black political organizations in the country.

The strength of the black contingent would become indispensable to the machine as the years passed. When Richard Daley ran for his sixth term as mayor, blacks constituted about a third of the population of Chicago, and according to some estimates he managed to get about half of his vote from blacks when he faced his Republican opponent. As the machine grew more dependent on its black contingent the claims of the black leaders were enhanced, and there was a larger flow of jobs and services into the wards that were under Dawson's leadership. As black politicians began to control a greater fund of resources, they began to experience, in turn, an enlargement of their own power in the black community. In this vein, James Q. Wilson recalls the time when an aggressive labor leader took over the presidency of the NAACP in Chicago. For two years he struck a militant posture on questions of race, and criticized some black politicians for failing to take a sufficiently stern, provocative line themselves. Prior to his leadership of the NAACP this man had been active in ward politics on the South Side, both as a candidate and as an organizer of opposition to the machine. When a moderate candidate appeared as an alternative to the militant leader, the machine lent its weight to his side. It took out about 400 new memberships in the NAACP, which it then distributed to precinct captains, patronage workers, and people who were, in one way or another, connected to the machine. And when the elections were held, that corps of new members proceeded to vote out the old leadership.[3] As Wilson commented, "Once the new president was in office, the machine did not attempt to interfere in or direct the course of the NAACP's affairs. The new president was not an agent of the machine; he was only an acceptable alternative to a thoroughly unacceptable leader."[4] Within a year the new president was up for reelection, and when his campaign flagged he called on the political machine once again for help—and once again the machine came to his rescue.[5] This was, for better or worse, a formidable demonstration of "black power," and it has not been reproduced very easily by black politicians in many other communities. A leadership with this kind of strength and discipline may diffuse its influence rather widely until it manages to build a network of ties among businessmen, journalists, ministers, and any other people of consequence in the community.

But the incident also recalls the differences that have separated black politicians from other leaders in the black community, not only in their styles but in their ends as well. The black political leadership in Chicago might have had a more conservative bent because it was itself a part of the establishment, and black leaders did not wish to be the source of disruptions and problems for their white counterparts in the city. (Sometime after the machine had succeeded in restoring a moderate leadership in the NAACP, one black politician observed that "the thing is to keep the pinkos out. . . . Those other people are pretty red.")[6] And yet, in their essential

---

[3] James Q. Wilson, *Negro Politics* (Glencoe: Free Press, 1960), pp. 63-64.
[4] Ibid., p. 64.   [5] Ibid.

interests and inclinations black politicians in Chicago have not been so different from black politicians in other places. The middle-class professionals who have led civic groups like the NAACP have committed themselves to the ends of "integration" in the sense of gaining access for blacks to "goods" and services that were previously restricted to whites. The black politicians certainly share that perspective in part: they too are interested in getting more jobs for blacks in the public services, in jobs that were previously reserved for whites. But black politicians have not taken as their central concern the question of whether blacks may buy homes, for example, in distant white suburbs, or whether blacks are excluded from certain hospitals in white areas.

Power flows to black politicians to the degree that they succeed in organizing the black community in politics, and that task would be made vastly harder if more blacks were dispersed to white neighborhoods. The interests of black politicians lay in concentrating their constituency, and in that respect they are representative of many other people and institutions in the black community. Quite a number of establishments have cultivated a special "black" character as a result of appealing distinctly to a black market. There are black newspapers and insurance companies and, of course, black civic organizations like the NAACP. There are ministers and undertakers, dentists and doctors, who have served a black clientele, and who may have a problem competing in a more integrated setting. In this regard, James Q. Wilson recalled the fate of the Mid-South Chicago Council, which had been organized to deal with problems of blight, largely through a program of strict enforcement of the building codes. The organization faded from the scene after two or three years, and one important reason for its disappearance was that many black members—businessmen, real estate brokers, and property owners—began to have reservations about the enforcement of the building codes. It would have been necessary to close many buildings down when the owners could not afford repairs. People would have been forced out of the area, and businessmen would have found their market contracting. If buildings were torn down and a program of redevelopment got underway, the result might have been to bring in white businesses with firm financial backing, which would only have meant more competition for black businesses.[7]

The disposition of the black political leader is to favor material gains that may have a broad effect in the community, rather than

[6] Ibid.   [7] Ibid., p. 202.

ends that appear largely symbolic and which, in any event, would benefit only a small stratum of blacks. For many years the NAACP was inclined to oppose the construction of new public schools if they were to be located in areas that were heavily black and if it seemed certain then that the schools would be almost entirely black. The problem for the NAACP, however, was that black parents seemed to prefer to have new schools in their own neighborhoods and to have the schools sooner rather than later. As one leader in the NAACP complained, most black parents did not really seem to be interested in changing the boundaries of the school districts for the sake of encouraging integration. "They are interested," he said, "in things like double shifts, getting good teachers, uncrowded classrooms."[8]

The same story could be told in a number of other instances, with subjects like public housing and public hospitals. Once again it would be a question of having *more* public housing or more hospitals built right away, or delaying construction until there was an assurance that the new facilities would be integrated. With the new mood of "black power" in the late 1960's there was a disposition to challenge, with a new irritability, the notion of bartering material gains for the prospect of integration. Since the proponents of integration had never come to an understanding themselves of the *principle* behind integration, it was only to be expected that integration would one day be judged on the basis merely of *utility*. By that measure the policy would be in perpetual danger, and it would come to be regarded, at best, as a means of serving the interests of middle-class blacks, who were the ones most likely to benefit from it. And so Frances Fox Piven and Richard Cloward were moved to point out in the *New Republic* that by 1966 the nation had not managed to build yet the number of units of public housing that were mandated under the Housing Act of 1949. In a sweeping license of interpretation they laid the responsibility for this failure on the passion for integration, which would benefit, they thought, only 10 percent or less of the black population.[9]

Whether their judgments were apt or not, it was a curious turn of affairs in which the views of radical spokesmen for "black power" seemed to coincide now in a number of respects with the perspectives of black politicians. The black politicians did not conceive their ends, of course, in radical terms, and they differed im-

[8] Quoted ibid., p. 187.
[9] See Piven and Cloward, "Desegregated Housing: Who Pays for the Reformers' Ideal?," *New Republic*, December 17, 1966, pp. 17-22.

portantly from the proponents of black power on another point of understanding: they were able to appreciate that the only political power worth having was that power which came through an alliance with whites. There was little profit, after all, for blacks in taking charge of a city from which most whites had fled. If political power were thought to be important for the economic advancement of the black community, it made little sense to take power in such a way that a black leadership was left to preside over a population that was largely poor, with a diminishing tax base. The hard fact of the matter, which seems to be accessible to most black politicians, is that when power can be taken very easily or completely, it may not be worth taking. On this point of revelation, David Greenstone and Paul Peterson came to discover in the war on poverty what should have been apparent all along: when the political parties in a city were so weak, and the power structure so porous, that "representatives of the poor" could virtually come in off the street and gain a share of formal power, that power was not likely to be worth very much. Authority was likely to be dispersed in that case among a large number of people, who could not commit an organization or a constituency. Under those circumstances it would become vastly harder to reconcile the groups in conflict or impose a common policy.

The actual result was a program in which leaders could not act with much authority or effect in distributing jobs and getting projects underway.[10] In comparison, an organization like the Daley machine in Chicago had no trouble in getting its agencies set up for the war on poverty. Through its own skills in organization it could easily establish the structure of an agency; it could fill out the membership on the governing boards; and it could recruit people for jobs, from counselors to janitors, by drawing on its own list of the deserving. The machine provided for the representation of all the important ethnic groups on the governing boards, but those representatives would not be at each other's throats in the way they were, for example, in New York City. These people may have been the representatives of blacks and Puerto Ricans and Poles and Croatians, but they were also tied to one another through the organization, and they had an incentive, through the machine, to reconcile their differences.

[10] David Greenstone and Paul Peterson, "Reformers, Machines, and the War on Poverty," in James Q. Wilson, *City Politics and Public Policy* (New York: John Wiley, 1968), pp. 267-92; and see also their book, *Race and Authority in Urban Politics* (New York: Russell Sage, 1973).

But this success of the Daley machine in dispensing jobs and services—the one thing, after all, which it did best in this world—could be achieved only by adhering to its characteristic modes of operation. The machine would not give a position of importance to anyone who was not known to the organization, either through service or personal connection. And it would not use its patronage in order to promote someone who could not be counted on to respect the paramount interests of the party. Certainly the organization would not yield power to anyone who simply showed up one day and claimed to "speak for" the poor. Experience usually showed, as it did in the war on poverty, that when formal power could be obtained with such little effort, nothing very constructive was likely to be done with it.

The same lesson could be applied to the matter of taking power in the city as a whole. In cities with a substantial presence of whites, blacks cannot win control of the government with any caricatured appeal for "black power." And indeed, in cities of this kind in which blacks have won the mayoralty as, for example, in Los Angeles with Thomas Bradley, they have not run under a program of "black power."[11] The slogan of "black power" may be misunderstood by whites in the same way in which it is inflated by blacks, and the result could be, in certain cases, to accelerate the movement of whites out of the cities and into the suburbs. In some places, the advent of a black administration may simply be a reflection of the fact that most whites have already left; and so rather than marking the threshold of a new vigor for the black community in politics, the event may indicate, on the contrary, that the city is entering a period of hardship and fiscal crisis. By the time what was called a "black government" took over in Newark the city was largely a shambles. To be sure, it had many economic assets, but the city was dilapidated, most of the white population was in the suburbs, and the prospects for investment in the central city were plagued by serious doubts about its future. Under these conditions a municipality may quickly take on the aspect of the "city as reservation," as Norton Long has called it—a place that is occupied to an inordinate degree by people who are living on public welfare, along with the people in the public services who minister to them.[12] The

[11] Blacks constituted only 18 percent of the population in Los Angeles when Bradley was elected, and that figure probably had its own effect in determining the kind of black candidate who could win.

[12] See Norton Long, "The City as Reservation," *The Public Interest* (Fall 1971), pp. 22-38.

emergence of a black leadership under these circumstances may have a certain symbolic value, but in reality it may mark only the ascension of those people who will be privileged to preside over the decline of the city. These men and women will be spending most of their time as supplicants, seeking grants from the state and federal governments (as well as handouts of different kinds from private foundations). Pericles would have been a rather different person as the manager of a vast staff seeking grants from HUD, HEW, and the Ford Foundation, and the practitioners of this new politics will be different in the same measure.

And yet the ascension of Kenneth Gibson in Newark was celebrated as a new age of black power, while the absence of a black from the office of the mayor in Chicago has been taken, on its face, as a sign of the relative subordination of blacks in that city. In fact, as I have suggested, there was probably more substantial power in the hands of black politicians in Chicago—men like William Dawson, Ralph Metcalfe, Wilson Frost, or Joseph Bertrand. These people did not generally brandish the symbols of a black takeover in politics; they simply demonstrated, through their presence and importance, that the black contingent had become one of the main pillars of the Democratic machine. What they secured for themselves was a steady, reliable share in the management of the resources of a solvent city; they held positions of consequence in an organization whose power was projected beyond the local scene to reach Congress and the President as well.

In the aftermath of Richard Daley's death, an effort was made by the black contingent to fill the office of acting mayor with Wilson Frost, who was, at the time, president of the City Council. But when the leadership of the party assembled with its full breadth, the claims of the black contingent were measured in their proper proportion, in an organization and a city that were still mainly nonblack. At any rate, the leadership turned aside for the moment the move to name a black man as mayor. They chose instead Michael Bilandic, who had been the alderman from Daley's home ward and the holder of an important post as chairman of the Finance Committee of the City Council. But Wilson Frost was in turn moved into Bilandic's place as chairman of the Finance Committee, and it was apparent that, even if Chicago were not to select a black mayor in 1977, the strength of blacks in the machine would be respected. There was the possibility for a while that the black contingent would put up a candidate in the special election for mayor and risk the unity of the party in a primary. But for men who had come to absorb the ethic of the machine as the best means of keeping the whole party together and insuring their own power, a move of that kind seemed highly unlikely (and in fact it did not come to pass). The black contingent had become one of the most disciplined sections of the party, and black politicians had drawn the most salutary lesson that any political order may teach: they found that their interests could prosper, their own influence could expand, even as they practiced self-restraint.

Since the death of William Dawson the leadership of the Democratic organization has sought to avoid a situation in which one black leader may concentrate in himself the full power that was available to Dawson. In that minor strategy the leadership seems to have registered its own understanding that the self-restraint of its black contingent would be preserved more easily if it were attended by a clear awareness of the limitations of black power. In the meantime, that code of restraint, which has been cultivated through the party, has worked to sustain the sense of a community that can peacefully accommodate many parts: not a city that is deciding whether it will have a "black government" or even a "white" one, but a place that is seen to exist quite as much for Michigan Avenue as for 47th Street; for the old and wealthy families—for the McCormicks and the Blairs—as well as for newcomers from Mexico; for the substantial middle class of blacks and whites as well as for people on welfare. Indeed, the recognition that comes along with this character of governance in Chicago is that the disappearance of the middle classes could do nothing to enlarge the capacity of the city to generate growth and ameliorate the conditions of the poor.

2. The Flight from the Metropolis and the Search for the City

If Chicago has managed to extend its reputation as a place that is vibrant *and* good, it is the result in large part of this ethic of restraint, which has been preserved in important ways in the character of its political life. Without that governing discipline the city might have fallen into the condition of a racial enclave in the metropolitan area, or perhaps even a reservation for people on "welfare." By this time there can be no excuse for any mistakes about the matter: it is not nature or inertia that preserves cities. The tendencies within American society—the interests of businesses, the preferences of householders—have moved people rather steadily out of the old central cities in the Northeast and the Midwest. Between 1960 and 1970, for example, the central cities in the fifteen largest metropolitan areas lost 836,000 civilian jobs while their suburbs gained 3,086,000.[13] This movement to the suburbs has become so far advanced that some observers have finally urged us to acknowledge in our public policy that some cities, very plainly, may be "dying."[14] In that event, a massive investment in these cities by the federal government might only skew the urban development of the country and waste the money of taxpayers. It may well be true, as it is often said, that the future of this nation is in our cities. But it does not follow from that aphorism that our future is bound up with the old central cities—with Newark, Philadelphia, Boston, Cleveland, and Detroit. In the movement of population in this country, in the new weights of numbers and influence in our politics, Houston has now surpassed Cleveland, Phoenix has overtaken Newark, and the 1980 census will show that Dallas has exceeded Boston in population.

But even apart from regional shifts, there has been a general

---

[13] It has been argued recently by Bennett Harrison that this trend, which has been part of our national life since the early part of this century, may be losing its force. Harrison has argued in a recent analysis that there is no evidence now of any acceleration in the rate at which jobs are being created in the suburbs, and that the number of jobs as a proportion of the labor force has probably increased in the central city since the mid-1960's. See Bennett Harrison, *Urban Economic Development: Suburbanization, Minority Opportunity and the Condition of the Central City* (Washington, D.C.: The Urban Institute, 1974), pp. 7-38.

Harrison's argument may be encouraging. Still, he concedes that his calculations are based on the performance of the economy in the middle and late 1960's, when it was in the midst of a sustained expansion. According to Harrison's own assessment, it requires a tight labor market and a growth rate in the economy of 4 percent per year to make the city more attractive as a location for businesses. During times of recession, when businesses are under greater pressures to cut back on operations that are more costly at the margins, it is the plants in the city that have been cut back to a greater degree in favor of plants in the suburbs. See pp. 24-25. This is not to say, of course, that growth cannot be sustained and that the central cities cannot be rendered more productive. But at the same time it cannot efface the conditions that have made the suburbs more attractive for investment over the past twenty-five years. Nor does it take into account the kinds of policies on spending and taxation which took hold, for example, in New York City in the late 1960's, and which had more than a little to do with the fact that New York lost about 500,000 jobs from the early to the late 1970's.

[14] See William C. Baer, "On the Death of Cities," *The Public Interest* (Fall 1976), pp. 3-19.

move away from settlements of high density. Over 70 percent of the population does live in urban centers, and in that sense it could be said that America is an urban nation. Yet only one person in ten lives in a city with a population over one million, and it has become clear in recent years that the attraction to the city has become weaker rather than stronger. In one study carried out in the mid-60's, the Survey Research Center of the University of Michigan interviewed people in thirty-two metropolitan areas about the kinds of places in which they preferred to live. About 85 percent of the respondents said that they preferred to live in houses designed for single families (and the state of this arrangement as an ideal was underscored by the fact that two-thirds of the people in the sample did not live at the moment in single-family dwellings). Only 15 percent wished to live in the center of town; 25 percent preferred to live farther away from the city; and for four people out of ten even the suburbs were not far enough away (they preferred to live in the countryside).[15]

At about the same time, a Gallup survey found that nearly half of the respondents living in cities of 50,000 or over said that they would like to live somewhere else (a suburb, small town, or farm area), and very few people in the suburbs expressed any wish to move back to the city.[16] By the 1970's the metropolitan areas in the country were actually beginning to show a net loss of population to nonmetropolitan areas. As William Alonso noted, one-sixth of all metropolitan areas lost population in the period 1970-1974, and in 1974 the proportion increased to one-fourth. By 1978 half of the people who were living in metropolitan areas were living in places which were losing population.[17] In this respect, the surveys seem to bear out the observation that the American notion of urban living has never been quite the same as that of Europeans. Even within the old central cities the tendency in America has been to recreate, in the outer sections of these areas, the aspect of a more spacious country life, dominated by the presence of small, independent households—the yeoman farmer, as it were, transferred to the urban setting. In 1960, over 60 percent of the dwelling units in the United States consisted of houses that were owned and occupied by single families, and as Daniel Elazar has pointed out,

[15] See the report in *The Public Interest* (Winter 1969), pp. 131-32.

[16] Cited in Robert Dahl, "The City in the Future of Democracy," *American Political Science Review*, Vol. 61, no. 4 (December 1967), pp. 953-70, at 965.

[17] William Alonso, "Metropolis Without Growth," *The Public Interest* (Fall 1978), pp. 68-86, at 71.

that was essentially comparable to the proportion of small, single-family farms that existed in the United States in 1900.[18]

Some commentators have suggested that the American ethic may actually be "anti-urban" because of the persisting preference for smaller communities with less concentration. But then again, size was not always thought to be the most decisive condition for the things that were most important in the city—not, at least, in the period before cities were seen as little more than great mercantile centers. Nor is it clear that size is so critical any longer for the amenities that many people have found attractive in large cities. It has been estimated, for example, that a library meeting minimum professional standards may be supported with a population base of about 50,000 to 75,000. An art museum may be sustained with a base of 100,000, and the figure may be only somewhat higher for museums of science and history.[19] We know that the support for institutions such as libraries, symphony orchestras, and the theater has usually come from a minority of the middle and upper classes, and there is no reason why some of these institutions cannot be recreated in suburbs of sufficient size, where like-minded people can concentrate their tastes and their purchasing power. In fact, there has been some suggestion in recent studies that the optimal size of an American community may be between 50,000 and 200,000. Apart from water and sewage, an increase in size does not seem to reduce unit costs for most services, and the slight gains in economy that occur in the supply of water and the tending of sewage may be offset very easily by larger expenses in other areas, such as welfare and police.[20]

But in the classic view, and in the view that comes to us in more modern times from Rousseau, the availability of theater tickets is decidedly less important for the city than the possibilities for citi-

[18] The Census of 1900 reported that 64.4 percent of the housing units on farms were occupied by owners, and the Census of 1960 showed that 61.9 percent of the dwelling units in the country were occupied by their owners. See Daniel J. Elazar, "Are We a Nation of Cities?," *The Public Interest* (Summer 1966), pp. 42-58, at 50; and *U.S. Census of Housing, 1960* (Washington: U.S. Government Printing Office, 1963), Vol. 1, p. 1-1.

[19] See Dahl, note 16 above, p. 967.

[20] Ibid., p. 966. There is some evidence, as Dahl notes, that expenditures per capita increase with the size of the city in the United States. In 1960, the mean expenditure for American cities over 150,000 was $123 per capita, compared with $70 per capita for cities in the range of 25,000-50,000. See p. 966. It is arguable, however, that the figures do not discriminate sufficiently for the very largest cities, and that the suburbs were measured here at a very early stage in their development of amenities.

zenship.[21] And that view has not been so remote from the motives that have led many people to leave the cities for the suburbs and smaller communities. A good portion of that movement has been impelled, of course, by the search for better housing and for areas of lower density. But as Nathan Glazer has argued, that movement has also involved motives that reach back ultimately to the concern for community.[22] There has been an evident desire for a simpler and more penetrable form of government, which is not as distant or as hard to deal with as the formidable bureaucracies in the central cities. There has been an aversion to the corruption and manipulation of machine politics, and there has been a concern, also, to create a community with a definition of its own, which can express its character in its public policies. In this perspective, the issue of size is important, and it raises the enduring question of appropriate inclusion or exclusion: who should be included in the community, and who should be excluded, if the community is to preserve its special character?

It would be a grave mistake, then, to interpret these population movements as little more than movements of convenience. Even if they had started out in that way for many people, it was in the nature of things that they would become something more. The decision as to whether to leave the central city (and where precisely to settle in the suburbs) implied a judgment about the kind of people one wished to live with, and the conditions under which one expected to live. It is not so surprising, therefore, that suburban areas have been very sensitive about guarding their control over matters that make a difference to the character of the local community. They have been willing to participate in metropolitan schemes for water, sewage, and transportation, but they have been reluctant to transfer powers over zoning, and they have been especially adamant in clinging to control over education. Even where so-called metropolitan governments have been created in the United States, the suburban areas have usually managed to secure considerable autonomy in the governance and funding of their own schools. In other words, the suburbs have been quite willing to make use of

[21] Nowhere is the point made more forcefully than in Rousseau's famous *Letter to D'Alembert*. For an English translation see Allan Bloom, trans., *Politics and the Arts* (Ithaca: Cornell University Press, 1960).

[22] Glazer, "For White and Black, Community Control is the Issue," *The New York Times Magazine*, April 27, 1969, p. 26ff. For a classic work on the suburbs and their political character, see Robert Wood, *Suburbia* (Boston: Houghton Mifflin, 1958).

metropolitan schemes when they involve simply the provision of technical services, but they have been inclined to resist the creation of any institutions at the metropolitan level which could imply a serious amalgamation of purpose.[23]

Of course, "metropolitan government" has had an enduring appeal to those people in the academy and government who identify "efficiency" with larger units, and who are prepared to find, in the abstract, that the proliferation of small governments is likely to create "irrational," "uncoordinated" policies. These people are also apt to show, in demonstrations that usually surprise no one, that the suburbs and the central city are "economically interdependent." But as Aristotle recognized, the fact that people trade with one another rather extensively does not mean that they care to be brought together in a more solemn association, as citizens in a common polity. Nor does it suggest that it would be good for them to be joined in that way. Local communities have shown on a number of occasions that, given a choice between efficiency and control, they would prefer governments closer to home even if they were a bit more expensive.[24] And quite apart from the advantages that may flow in certain instances from economies of scale, the preference for keeping governments smaller may result quite often in expenditures that are far more disciplined and, by any reckoning, much more efficient.

Most people are likely to be immune, however, from the impulses that grip experts on public administration; and so, if a number of communities have talked themselves into forms of metropolitan government, it can usually be assumed that this change has little to do with any passion, lately conceived, for administrative "coordination." In many cases a more melancholy assessment would probably also be a more accurate one: viz., that schemes for metropolitan government have been more appealing when they have offered a device for neutralizing the political power of blacks, especially in those instances in which blacks have appeared to be on the verge of a political breakthrough in the central city. In that event, the black organizations in the city could be overcome by vesting decisions in a larger board or agency for the metropolitan region. And in that order of things the city could be outvoted by communities in the suburban ring, while the whole arrangement

[23] See Peter Northrop Brown, "The Good City and Metro," Senior Honors Thesis, Department of Political Science, Amherst College, 1968.

[24] See, for example, Robert B. Hawkins, Jr., *Self-Government by District: Myth and Reality* (Stanford: Hoover Institution Press, 1976), especially chs. 2 and 3.

may be buttressed by federal grants for planning, along with federal regulations and procedures. The result may be to reduce even further the range of choice available to public officials, and to hem in political leaders in the inner cities as they try to extend their influence to the suburbs. The discussion of policy in this setting goes forward in a rather specialized, technical idiom, carried on by lawyers with experience in the most rarified callings. Altogether, the complex may simply be too formidable for a layman or a politician to penetrate, and it is not the kind of arena in which black politicians from the inner city are likely to do well.[25]

The movement away from the cities cannot be understood, then, without recognizing that it is in part, at least, a flight from the political authority of the city; and those who have settled in the suburbs are not eager to be linked to the city again, either through devices for regional government or through the decisions, say, of courts to bus children to school across municipal lines.[26] The current in recent years has been in the direction of smaller communities, where there may be a larger possibility for the sharing of public purposes. If public policy becomes unacceptable on any decisive point, there is the prospect of moving to another community; and so the problem of moral discordance may be softened by a combination of freedom of choice and the powers that are still preserved in local communities to define their own character.

The question, though, is whether that freedom of choice is fully available without serious restrictions based on race. The search for small communities with a more definite character has been present among blacks as well as whites, and it has been manifested not only in the search for "community control" in some cities, but in the creation of suburban communities that are predominantly black. Between 1960 and 1970, the number of blacks living in the suburbs rose from 2.2 to 3.7 million.[27] The rate of movement to

[25] For a suggestive piece on this matter see Frances Fox Piven and Richard Cloward, "Black Control of Cities: How the Negroes Will Lose," *New Republic*, October 7, 1967, pp. 15-19.

[26] The impulse to bus children across municipal lines in a compulsory program has been checked for the moment by the Supreme Court in *Milliken* v. *Bradley*, 41 L. Ed. 2d 1069, 1078, 1091, 1095 (1974). But the argument of the majority did not find its firmest ground of principle, and it is entirely possible that the issue may be opened again at a later time.

[27] According to the Census of 1970, there were 3.6 million blacks in the suburbs of metropolitan areas and 13.1 million in the central cities. For whites the balance was reversed: 71.1 million were in the suburbs and 49.4 million were in the central cities.

the suburbs increased dramatically for blacks, from about 20,000 per year in the early 1960's to about 200,000 per year at the end of the decade. A good portion of that movement seems to have occurred in the form of spillover, as blacks moved into suburban areas that were adjacent to black sections of the central city. It would appear, then, that most of the growth in the black population in the suburbs has been concentrated in a relatively few places. Eighty-three percent of the blacks living in the suburbs of Chicago in 1970 were clustered in 15 out of the 237 suburban municipalities.[28] Of course nothing in these figures alone establishes the presence of discrimination, and there has been evidence recently of an important increase in black population in suburbs that are not chiefly black. More will be said on that point in a moment, but the concentration of blacks does raise a question at least as to whether their patterns of settlement are determined largely by the choices and resources of blacks themselves, or whether blacks are restricted from certain areas solely through the test of race.

In the nature of things, no judgment on that point can properly be made on the basis of aggregate figures. The presence of discrimination or injustice can be discovered only where it shows itself in an individual case or in a discrete series of acts. As it happens, there are more than enough cases of that kind to establish that people are in fact excluded from certain housing on the basis of race; and so no matter how limited or extensive the practice may be, there is ample cause for considering just what the argument would be in principle for a public law that bars discriminations based on race.

The question is by no means without its tangles, and the problem may be rendered more difficult by the fact that the law would be addressing, for the most part, discrimination that occurs in a very circumscribed, private context. We would not be dealing here with public accommodations in the form of restaurants or inns that are open to public business. Most of the housing in the United States consists of dwellings that are owned and inhabited by single families. The sale or rental of this housing may proceed through means that are highly public (through the use of advertisements and real estate agencies) but the transactions may go forward also on a more intimate, informal level, without the use of public media. And yet even if public media were used in a highly visible way, nothing in

[28] See Michael N. Danielson, *The Politics of Exclusion* (New York: Columbia University, 1976), p. 9.

that arrangement would be sufficient to convert this property into anything other than private property, held for private use.

Whether the law can reach private decisions on the disposition of private housing is a question that compels the sorting out of many important questions of principle. The essential case for reaching these transactions through public law would be virtually the same in principle whether the public agency happens to be the state, federal, or municipal government. A federal law would raise a number of additional and more refined questions, but for the purpose of addressing the main issue it may be just as easy to focus for the moment on the federal law that is already on the books. That law has the advantage of containing most of the important features that could be found in any legislation on open occupancy. But it also contains certain points of perplexity, certain tensions of principle, which ought not be evaded by anyone who would seek to reach this problem of discrimination through public law.

3. "Open Housing": The First Phase of an Argument

The Fair Housing Act of 1968 made it unlawful to "refuse to sell or rent after the making of a *bona fide* offer, or to refuse to negotiate for the sale or rental of, or otherwise make unavailable or deny, a dwelling to any person because of race, color, religion, or national origin."[29] The law went on to forbid any discrimination against persons in the terms, conditions, or privileges of a sale or rental of a dwelling, or in the provision of any services or facilities that were connected with the housing. Beyond that, the law contained some rather exhaustive prohibitions on the freedom to publish an intention or disposition to engage in discrimination. It was made illegal to:

> make, print, or publish, or cause to be made, printed, or published any notice, statement, or advertisement, with respect to the sale or rental of a dwelling that indicates any preference, limitation, or discrimination based on race, color, religion, or national origin, or any intention to make any such preference, limitation, or discrimination.[30]

There was one turn in the law, though, that added a bit more complexity to the purpose or intention of the Act: for about a year and a half, until December 31, 1969, the law would exempt dwell-

[29] 42 U.S.C.A., Sec. 3601 et seq., at Sec. 3604. [30] Ibid.

ings that were owned and occupied by single families. After that date, the exemption might continue, but only on conditions that once again restricted in a serious way the right of a person to pursue his private choice by making his intentions public. The exemption would be in force only if these houses were rented or sold:

> without the use in any manner of the sales or rental facilities or the sale or rental services of any real estate broker, agent, or salesman, or of such facilities or services of any person in the business of selling or renting dwellings . . . without the publication, posting, or mailing, after notice, of any advertisement or written notice in violation of . . . this title. . . .[31]

The framers of the Act had apparently settled for a compromise, but they created a highly paradoxical situation in the law. They must have appreciated the importance of covering single-family dwellings in the Act, but they were plainly reluctant, also, to extend the reach of public authority to areas of private choice involving the small family holding, as opposed to those acts of private choice that involved the sale or rental of units in large apartment buildings. Why that should be a tenable distinction was a question they decided, for a while, to skirt. They would preserve the right of private choice in disposing of one's own family home (as opposed to the buying and selling of other homes, in a short interval, for the sake of business). But this private choice would be respected only on the condition that any discrimination which occurred should indeed remain private: those who would discriminate could not have the privilege of furthering their private ends through the use of public media. If they were allowed to make free use of advertising and real estate agents, then (the argument might have gone) they would implicate others in their private discriminations, and they would lend the sanction of respectability to a whole pattern of attitudes and behavior that public policy had condemned.

That, roughly put, is what might have been said in justification. Still, it was not entirely convincing, and it did nothing to erase a paradox in the law which raised serious questions of principle. On the one hand, the law declared that certain private acts of discrimination would still be considered legitimate; but on the other hand, it withdrew from individuals the freedom of expression that would form a necessary instrument or extension of their lawful rights. This paradox should have occasioned some grave doubts at least

[31] Ibid., at Sec. 3603.

among those who considered themselves civil libertarians. As one might imagine, however, the American Civil Liberties Union did not exactly rush forward to challenge the law. And yet the issue did not deserve to be decorously ignored, for it presented a serious inconsistency for anyone who might have resisted the use of the law in restraining the speech of Joseph Beauharnais or the American Nazis in their efforts to break down the climate of civility and stir hatred toward racial and religious groups.[32] On the surface of things, it is hard to see why the speech or writing of the homeowner in these cases should stand on a lower plane of dignity in the eyes of the law than the speech of Beauharnais or the Nazis. Surely it could not be argued that the speech of the homeowner would be more injurious or malicious (or even more destructive of the climate of civility in the community). Nor would there be a case, in this instance, in which the speech of the homeowner was an integral part of an unlawful act that produced a material injury. Someone may be deprived of a house by the owner who discriminates (and who advertises his intention to discriminate), but the law itself made clear that this was not an "injury" that it was prepared to recognize or to reach.

I will take up this question more fully in a while, along with the rather dubious argument that the speech of the homeowner is less deserving of protection because it is "commercial"—as though it required merely the taint of a "sale" in order to render a person more offensive in the judgment of the law than Beauharnais or the Nazis. For the moment we may say this: our aversion to discriminatory advertising shares the same ground of principle with the aversion we have cultivated in the past to signs reading, "No Irish Need Apply," "Gentiles Only," or (to recall a sign that was seen not too long ago in Roanoke, Virginia) "No Syrians, Jews, or dogs allowed." Our aversion to these forms of expression is entirely independent of any material injuries they may help to inflict, and indeed our objections would stand even if it were impossible to demonstrate that any material injuries would in fact be caused by these signs. All of which is to say that, if the law can reach this type of advertising, it must have an independent ground of principle, and if we sought to explain the ground of the law, it would be the ground on which we have condemned in the past the defamation of groups.

The matter is worth raising here, even in a preliminary way,

---

[32] See Chapters II and III above.

because it is the source of a tension that may force a decision: those who have resisted the notion of restraints on speech have felt less troubled about the issue when the speech was integral to some other, unlawful act. (In that event they manage to persuade themselves that they are not restricting "pure" speech, but only speech that is connected to a material injury.) The inconsistencies in the law would be dissolved for these people if the law simply rid itself of limitations and went on to cover the sale of all private housing, including homes that are owned and occupied by single families. I think that a case could be made to extend the law in this way to cover all transactions that involve single-family dwellings, no matter how they are advertised. But that case would still have to encounter some serious questions. Most notably, there would be the problem of explaining how these private dwellings, owned and occupied by single families, may come within the reach of the law. And an argument that proceeded on the premises of modern libertarianism would have quite as heavy a burden in defending a law of this broader reach as it would have in defending the more restricted statute that is currently on the books. For the libertarian who would defend the rights of a Beauharnais in the law would be sorely pressed to show how the person who quietly discriminates in the sale or rental of his home can be the source of any more mischief or injury in the community than a Beauharnais could generate. It would require advanced skills of argument to explain just why it is that *this* man deserves to have his freedom restricted in a way that Beauharnais did not. For anyone who insists that a material injury must be imminent before personal freedom can be abridged would have just as hard a time demonstrating the presence of an injury in these cases of housing as he would have had in the case of Beauharnais. If the libertarian argument were applied with the same strictness in all incidents in which personal freedoms were open to restriction, it would rule out most of what has become known as the "liberal" agenda in politics. The law may indeed strike at discrimination in housing, even in cases involving single-family dwellings; but we would discover that the law cannot be used toward these ends while respecting at the same time the premises of modern libertarianism.

The substantive argument for a law on open occupancy would have to move through several tiers of considerations, but the problem may be addressed most clearly if the considerations were brought to a focus on two questions: (1) What precisely is the nature of the injury or the wrong in these cases? (2) On what grounds could the wrongs in these cases be reached by "public authority"?[33] The first of these questions I will take up right now; the second will be reserved for the succeeding chapter.

The question as to where, precisely, the wrongs would lie in cases of discrimination in housing may seem on its face to be fairly simple; and yet, as I tried to show with the issue of busing, this question has been deeply confused by the tendency to confound matters of principle and injury. In that spirit of positivism which prevails in the law, the disposition of lawyers has been to say that the purpose of the law is to deal only with the vindication of material injuries. In matters of civil rights the end of the law, in this perspective, is to gain access for blacks to discrete goods and services that are being denied them on the basis of race. If the question were posed, then, as to what the injury was in these cases on housing, the answer would probably be offered unequivocally that the blacks would be deprived of a substantive thing, namely, the possession of a house.

And yet by any strict reckoning it would generally be hard to show in any individual case that a material injury had taken place—much as we saw, in an earlier chapter, that it was hard to find a material deprivation in cases arising from public accommodations. The fact that a person is turned away from a restaurant because of his race cannot be taken to mean that he is being deprived of food. Quite apart from the question of whether he can obtain groceries, it is entirely possible that he may be served at a restaurant next door or across the street. (And in the case of the celebrated Ollie's Barbecue,[34] blacks had access to food at a takeout counter in the same establishment that refused to seat them in its dining rooms.) If it were plausible to argue that the wrong involved in these cases is the deprivation of food, it would be quite as tenable to argue that a man is being denied food when he is turned away from a restaurant for the want of a necktie. He, too, would not be served with food, but no one has suggested so far that there would be an injury here, much less a deprivation that threatens a constitutional right. As I argued earlier, the sense of whether an injury has been committed does not turn on the denial of goods or services, but on the principle on which the exclusion was based.

In the case of housing, the imputation of a material injury would

---

[33] As I have already suggested, once it is established that these wrongs can be reached by a public authority of some kind—by a government, for example, at the state or local level—the question of whether the federal government can also reach them becomes a far easier (and, one might say, a second-order) question.

[34] 379 U.S. 294 (1964); and see Chapter IX, note 49.

be equally unsatisfying. The fact that a family is turned away from the purchase of one home, or even from a number of homes in succession, cannot in itself be taken to mean that they will be turned away from the next house. For all one knows they may be able to buy a house of comparable (or even better) quality in the same neighborhood at a comparable (or even better) price. What is at issue again is the principle that animates the exclusion, not the material injury which might be visited on the people who are seeking to buy. But if it has been difficult to show the presence of an injury in particular cases, a number of people have sought to circumvent that problem by pointing up the material injuries that occur in the *aggregate*, as a result of a pattern of discrimination. As we shall see, the arguments cast in terms of aggregates and patterns involve special infirmities of their own. Yet even where they touch a plausible issue, it soon becomes apparent there, also, that the issue turns on a question of principle rather than a test of material injuries. One such argument draws the problem in its fullest sweep by considering just how much of the national housing stock is accounted for by single-family dwellings. Another (and, as it turns out, a more apt) argument points to the patterns of exclusion that are still preserved through "restrictive covenants" and the policies of real estate companies, rather than through the uncoordinated acts of individual households.

The argument in the first instance may start from the sense conveyed by Justice White in *Reitman* v. *Mulkey*[35] that housing provides the gateway, as it were, to many other substantial benefits in this society—to schools, jobs, social connections, or simply to more attractive and spacious surroundings, with a lower crime rate. If those gateways were allowed to become closed to blacks, it would mean that disadvantages which had accumulated over generations might be accumulated even further. Just how important the gateways may be would depend on the size of the housing stock to which they control access. The extent of housing owned and occupied by single families in this country may be hard for Europeans to grasp, as indeed it may often be surprising to Americans who have spent most of their lives in urban centers. It can be startling to learn, for example, that 45 percent of all the apartment buildings in the United States in the 1960's were in New York City alone.[36] In the suburbs or in the cities of the South and West the urban

[35] 387 U.S. 369 (1967).
[36] See George Sternlieb, "New York's Housing: A Study in *Immobilisme*," *The Public Interest* (Summer 1969), pp. 123-38, at 128.

landscape looks rather different. At the time Congress was passing the Fair Housing Act, nearly 62 percent of the total dwelling units in the country were homes that were owned and occupied by single families.[37] Some of that 62 percent was accounted for, of course, by black people, but if this kind of housing could escape the coverage of the Act when owners refrained from advertising, the law would be exempting the single most important stock of housing in the country.

The very magnitude of the housing stock involved here is enough to trigger an argument that has been used quite commonly (and all too casually) in the law, especially in arguments that are offered under the Commerce Clause. As it would apply in this case, the argument would run in this way: the separate acts of discrimination may be thoroughly private in nature and, taken by themselves, they may not be the source of any substantial injury. But when the principle of exclusion becomes operative in most communities, when it attains the level of a custom that becomes widely imitated and pervasive, the consequences of racial exclusion move well beyond the point of isolated private acts. The consequences become quite widespread, and there is a common temptation to say then that they become *public* in their significance. At that moment, the argument goes, the transactions that make up this pattern may be open to the regulation of law. And if we are dealing with a pattern that is national in its extent, it may be enough, by the standards that prevail these days in the profession of law, to justify the reach of the federal government under the Commerce Clause.

Of course it takes no small leap of reasoning to suggest that acts which are admittedly private become "public" in their nature simply through cumulation. But that is by no means the sole oddity in this brand of reasoning. This mode of argument has been accepted for so long now as part of the rationalization for federal power that it becomes difficult to get outside it and view the inventory of arguments with a fresh and critical eye. Justice Robert Jackson could hardly be called gullible, and yet he offered one of the classic expressions of this perspective in his opinion in *Wickard v. Filburn*.[38] In that case, the federal government was in the awkward position of enforcing penalties on a farmer for setting a portion of his crops aside for consumption in his own household. But with the inexorable logic of "What if everyone acted in that way?"

[37] By 1970, the figure was 62.9 percent.
[38] 317 U.S. 111 (1942).

the government was able to hypothesize a significant effect on interstate commerce, and Justice Jackson conveyed the point:

> The effect of the statute . . . is to restrict the amount which may be produced for market by producing to meet [one's] own needs. That appellee's own contribution to the demand for wheat may be trivial by itself is not enough to remove him from the scope of federal regulation *where, as here, his contribution, taken together with that of many others similarly situated, is far from trivial.*[39]

In this manner the courts have played a certain havoc with our law (to say nothing of our conventions of moral reasoning) through the misuse of the old question, "What if everybody acted in that way?" The question holds the import of a moral test only as a reflection of what has been called the principle of "generalizability" (or "universalizability"),[40] which is simply another expression, in turn, of the Categorical Imperative as Kant stated it: ". . . I ought never to act except in such a way that I can also will that my maxim [i.e., the maxim underlying the act] should become a universal law."[41] The rudimentary logic of this rule, as a moral test, is that it raises the question of whether a person is acting merely for the sake of the most narrow self-interest or whether his action is in fact drawn from a principle: does the act respond to a rule of action that is arguably valid for anyone in a comparable situation? Does the rule describe, that is, something that is more generally or universally good, and would a person be willing to act upon it even when it runs counter to his immediate interests?

The logic of this moral question is indeed present in the query, "What if everyone acted in the same way?" But that test, as it has

---

[39] Ibid., at 127-28. Emphasis added. For a notably different view, from a mind less tutored in modern jurisprudence, one might consider this passage from Jefferson, "A Summary View of the Rights of British America": "By an act passed in the 5th year of the reign of his late majesty kind George the second, an American subject is forbidden to make a hat for himself of the fur which he has taken perhaps on his own soil; an instance of despotism to which no parallel can be produced in the most arbitrary ages of British history." Saul K. Padover, *The Complete Jefferson* (New York: Sloan and Pearce, 1943), p. 9.

[40] See, for example, Marcus Singer, *Generalization in Ethics* (New York: Knopf, 1960), and R. M. Hare, *Freedom and Reason* (New York: Oxford, 1963), chs. 5 and 6.

[41] Kant, *Groundwork of the Metaphysics of Morals* (New York: Harper and Row, 1964), p. 70, but see also pp. 68, 80-84. By the standard, second edition of Kant's work, the passage I have quoted here appears on page 402.

been used in the law, has been misconstrued, and the misunderstanding has something to do with the transformation of the law in the nineteenth century with the infusion of positivism and utilitarianism. Without tracing the history of the malady, the problem may be seen clearly enough in a glance in the example of John Austin and his classic *Lectures on Jurisprudence*.[42] For Austin the classic notion that there were certain moral truths grounded in nature was just so much hocus-pocus, a bundle of religious sentiments masquerading as law. In his judgment, the true "natural laws" of justice—and the true impress of God in this world—could be found in the natural laws of "utility." The laws of utility were grounded in the most unambiguous needs, and there was nothing subjective or arbitrary about them. Shortsighted men might always be inclined to conceive their interests (or their "utility") in rather hedonistic and selfish terms, but the principle of utility refused to honor just anything that men happened to "like." The understanding of "utility" contained its own discipline, and it forced the expression of wants to a higher plane of principle through the agency of that question, "What if everyone acted in that way?" And so for Austin the clinching argument against murder—the reasoning that finally established the case on a moral plane—was the argument that simply answered the question, "What would it be like if everyone were free to kill?" The answer, for Austin, was that we would have, as a consequence, the war of all against all, and the world would become depopulated.[43] Ridding the world of population surely could not be reckoned a useful thing (it was unambiguously lacking in "utility") and on that basis one could say with confidence that killing was undesirable. That is to say, *killing was judged to be wrong in individual cases only because it was known to be wrong in the aggregate.* For it was only in the aggregate that the wrong of certain acts could be reliably known.

What was conspicuously left out of this construction was that human beings have the capacity to look at particular acts and judge them, on their own merits, to be justified or unjustified, right or wrong. All of that was, for Austin, little more than airy metaphysics; and yet it was his own view, arguably, that was more distant from natural understanding. If an assailant attacks an elderly man on the street and takes his money, it is well within the competence of other men to consider the question of whether there was any provocation or justification for the act. And the absence of a justification would

[42] (Jersey City: Frederick Linn, 1875?), Vol. I (originally published in 1869).
[43] See ibid., Vol. II, pp. 64, 67-69, 72; or, sections 92, 99-106, 114.

be quite sufficient in itself to establish the wrong of the act. It is not necessary to wait for a long series of muggings to take place, or to let the consequences of mugging unfold over a long period, before it becomes possible to pass judgment on the question of whether *this particular act* was right or wrong.

The paradox of Austin's jurisprudence is that it replaced *moral judgment* with the task merely of making empirical estimates or predictions. Instead of reaching judgments on the question of whether any given act could be *justified* or not, the person who renders moral verdicts would reach his decisions by weighing propositions of this kind: if killing were considered acceptable, would most people take advantage of the privilege, and would the consequence be to rid the world of people? If property were unprotected, would the assault on property become nearly universal, and would the world end up then barren of property? As one can see, the chains of reasoning here were highly problematic and contingent—far more problematic, in fact, than the principles that underlie moral judgment, and they were notably deficient then as a moral ground of law.

But then again, this mode of argument represented a decisive shift away from moral reasoning altogether. The revolution in jurisprudence that found its beginnings here involved nothing less than the detachment of jurisprudence from moral philosophy. It goes without saying, of course, that the change has been carried over now into our current habits of mind in the law, and it has become part of the standard equipment (or the operating fallacies) with which many lawyers come to address the question of housing. And yet the specious is not redeemed by age. The line of argument that comes down from Austin deserves to be resisted as a general matter, and therefore it cannot be used as a ground of support for a policy on open housing. It would be necessary to insist, then, on the general point, that *if an act is not wrong in the particular it cannot be wrong in the aggregate*: if the law finds no ground for interference when an owner discriminates on the basis of race in the sale of his home, it has no proper ground of intervention if the experience of this one household is merely replicated many times over. If the act of this first homeowner was not wrong in itself, it surely cannot be rendered worse in any way by the fact that it is copied by other people. In order to reach acts of this kind the law would be compelled finally to address the *principle* on which these acts are based, rather than find the wrongness of these practices in the cumulative pattern of their results.

Someone may wish to argue that there are instances, however, in which acts that cause little or no damage in themselves may cause serious damage in the aggregate. If one person walks on favored grass there may be little consequence; but if his path becomes a track for others the grass may be destroyed. Therefore, the argument goes, it would not be unreasonable to ban walking on the grass. The analogy is made imperfect, though, by a number of considerations, and the main difference would turn again on the principle underlying the act. As Kant taught, we can interpret the correlation of two sensations as a relation of cause and effect only because we are capable of recognizing an underlying principle of causation that connects the two events. That recognition does not arise from experience; the concept of causation is within us, so to speak, almost anterior to experience.

That concept is aptly extended to the material world when there is in fact a relation of cause and effect, which may be immanent in the nature of two events. The concept of "trampling on grass" has a clear connection to the concept of "destroying the grass"; their relation, one may say, is embedded in the principles of their natures. We may find a situation, for example, in which the advent of an ice cream wagon on a town common at noon causes many people to rush across the common to buy ice cream, and the effect over time is to destroy the grass. If we were operating merely on the basis of correlations, we might announce the revelation that it is the arrival of the ice cream truck that causes the grass to be destroyed. If we went on to legislate on the basis of these correlations, we might end up passing an ordinance against the appearance of ice cream trucks on the town common during the lunch hour. But if we tend to hold back from that kind of measure, if our natural inclination is to restrain the stampedes on the grass rather than the visits of the ice cream wagons, it may be precisely because we grasp the difference, at a very elementary level, between causation and correlation.[44]

In that event it should be just as apparent to us that there is no *causal* relation between the denial of a particular house to a person on the basis of race and the inability of that person to find a house. There would be no necessary connection there, any more than there was a connection, on the one hand, between the refusal of a res-

---

[44] On the general problem of causation and "synthetic" propositions, see Kant, for example, in the *Critique of Pure Reason*, Bk. I, ch. II, and Lewis Beck, "Once More Unto the Breach: Kant's Answer to Hume, Again," *Ratio*, Vol. 9, no. 1 (June 1967), pp. 133-37.

taurant to admit a patron without a jacket, and the likelihood, on the other hand, that the patron would starve from a lack of food. Whether blacks will be deprived of housing in the aggregate simply cannot be foretold on the basis of any individual case. What can be addressed, however, is the principle that is implicit in the individual act of discrimination. For if there is something wrong about the prospect of barring blacks, in the aggregate, from housing, *the grounds of our judgment that it is wrong do not become accessible to us only when the cases are aggregated.* Those grounds of moral judgment must be accessible to us, rather, in any single case taken by itself.

4. THE ANALOGY OF RESTRICTIVE COVENANTS: WHAT PRINCIPLE DOES IT SETTLE?

It is strictly necessary then, in moral reasoning, to reject this form of argument from cumulation: viz., that practices which are innocent in themselves may be taken as wrong if they are reproduced on a large scale. On the question of housing, however, there is a second argument on the level of "aggregates," which may be more apt (even though it may not quite succeed in carrying the case). This argument concerns the patterns of exclusion that are preserved through real estate companies and the operation of restrictive covenants. In these cases there are demonstrable acts of discrimination by particular persons and groups, and the discrimination is not confined to private households acting singly, without the presence of coordination.

The tenacity of these practices may be found in their sheer persistence and brazenness even in the face of state and federal law. The techniques for circumventing the law may be seen, in their variety, in the documents and affidavits that have been collected in recent years in the Department of Justice. Not untypical of the lot was a deposition that was filed by one young woman who had been employed by a real estate developer in Wheaton, Maryland. The woman, who was twenty years old and a student at the University of Maryland, worked as a telephone solicitor during the summer of 1969, after the Fair Housing Act had gone into force. She reported that when a person called on the phone and was thought to be black, a card that was normally kept on a client would be thrown away so that he would not be solicited. If the caller was *believed* to be black, the card was marked with a double-X as a signal to other solicitors not to make any further calls. (After the FBI investigated the practices of this company the code was changed, but the policy was not curtailed.) Telephone solicitors would receive bonuses if they succeeded in arranging an interview between a salesman and a prospective buyer, but they would receive no bonus if the persons who were visited turned out to be blacks. Finally, it was revealed that, after a visit from the FBI, a black girl was hired for the office just so that there would be a black employee on the scene when the FBI came back. But the black girl was to be given a special list of names, and the head of the office made it clear to his people who supervised the staff that the girl would be fired a few weeks later "after the heat was off."[45]

The same story could be told, of course, in a number of variations, merely by changing the names and the devices. In the case of the real estate agencies, the willingness to take risks in this way may be explained in good part by their awareness of being in a competitive situation: while the government mandates one rule of action, the people in real estate plead that the clients they are seeking to attract are obdurate in holding to their own customs and preferences. The redoubtable William Levitt once insisted that his firm would be risking suicide if its Levittowns were thrown open to blacks while other developers sold only to whites. As Levitt argued, "most whites prefer not to live in mixed communities. . . . It is not reasonable to expect that any one builder could or should undertake to absorb the entire risk and burden of conducting such a vast social experiment."[46]

Levitt made this remark, of course, years before most of the laws on open occupancy were on the books. Those laws might have served the purpose of assuring the different builders that no one would be allowed to exclude people on the basis of race and that no developer would be hurt then if he sold to blacks. For men in business, however, that assurance had to be discounted by the probability that other builders would nevertheless succeed in finding some way around the laws. Since the housing industry is highly decentralized, and since techniques of evasion are vast in number, the compulsion to steer around the law has been very hard to extinguish. It will persist to some degree at least so long as real estate agencies continue to perceive that their clients are determined to make discriminations on the basis of race in disposing of their

[45] Affidavit of Marian Kay Meyers, October 1, 1969. For a copy of this deposition as well as other affidavits and briefs, I am grateful to Frank Schwelb, chief of the Housing Section, Civil Rights Division, U.S. Department of Justice.
[46] Quoted in Danielson, note 28 above, p. 132.

property. Evidently, the customs and habits of the local community have their effect. And the endurance of these sentiments can be seen in the fact that, almost thirty years after restrictive covenants were declared unenforceable in *Shelley* v. *Kraemer*,[47] they have continued to flourish in other forms.

Before *Shelley* v. *Kraemer* "restrictive covenants" took the form of explicit provisions within contracts which barred the buyer from selling his home at a later date, for example, to a black or Jewish family. Currently, these "covenants" take the shape most often of provisions that forbid the owner to sell or lease the property without the consent of the developer or of an association of homeowners who hold property in the neighborhood. In another variation, the sale or lease of a house may be forbidden to anyone who is not a member of a particular club or association. Perhaps the most common arrangement is one in which the developer or a group of neighbors is given the first option to buy a house in the event that an owner chooses to sell.[48] No reference may be made to either race or religion in these contracts, and so the task of using the law to block such arrangements becomes far more complicated. There would be the problem, then, of disentangling cases of racial exclusion from exclusions based on other grounds which may be quite permissible. For example, a group of art historians may form an association to buy homes in a certain area and preserve its special architectural style. In restricting buyers to their own circle they may be, willy-nilly, excluding blacks, if there are not many blacks among art historians. Whether the intent of the plan is to discriminate against blacks would not be entirely clear. Since the terms of the association would not imply the exclusion of blacks as a matter of necessity, there would be no principled ground on which the courts could invalidate these arrangements on their face. The law would be compelled to work here, as it does in other cases, by demonstrating that a qualified applicant was turned away solely on account of his race.

In the case of real estate agencies we are dealing with a business engaged in transactions with the public, and so the matter in that instance has moved well beyond the point of a private owner exercising the right of choice in disposing of his own property. The restrictive covenants came under attack because they, too, seemed to move to a level of public regulation beyond the private judgments

---

[47] 334 U.S. 1 (1948).

[48] See Paul G. Haskell, "Contractual Devices to Keep 'Undesirables' Out of the Neighborhood," 54 *Cornell L. Rev.* 524 (1969).

of individual owners: the restrictive covenants worked as a kind of zoning regulation enforced by private parties. But instead of zoning for the exclusion of industry or neon lights, the parties in this instance would zone for the exclusion of blacks. In this way a restrictive covenant could partake of the character of "public" regulation in the sense that the owner would be bound by a rule outside his own private preferences. That aspect of restrictive covenants was brought out rather well in *Shelley* v. *Kraemer*: Kraemer sought to prevent the black purchaser from taking possession of the house on the grounds that Fitzgerald, the white owner, had no right under the restrictive covenant to sell the property to blacks. The restrictive covenant worked, in other words, to prevent a willing white vendor from conveying his own property to a willing black buyer.

Chief Justice Vinson sought to embellish this argument by contending even further that the restrictive covenant acquired the force of public law because it was enforced by the courts. The preference of the contracting parties to exclude blacks became, in effect, the purpose of the state as the courts put the full authority of the law behind the enforcement of these covenants. "It is clear," Vinson wrote, "that but for the active intervention of the state courts, supported by the full panoply of state power, [Shelley] would have been free to occupy the [property] in question without restraint."[49] It was also clear, as he said, that these restrictions based on race "could not be squared with the requirements of the Fourteenth Amendment if imposed by state statute or local ordinance."[50]

And yet there was a striking difference between a case of this kind and those instances in which the courts had enforced policies of discrimination in the name of the state, as, for example, when they barred blacks from service on juries. In the case of the restrictive covenants the courts were not enforcing the policy of the state, but the terms of a private contract. And it was one of the properties of a valid contract, after all, that it would have the force of a binding law for the parties, even if they no longer found the terms congenial. In other words, contracting parties were often restrained by contractual rules that did not reflect their own preferences at any moment, and it was not assumed for that reason that the agreement which bound them was the equivalent of a public law. If the restrictive covenants had committed the parties to certain rules of safety in the wiring and construction of their homes, or if

[49] 334 U.S. at 19.   [50] Ibid., at 11.

they had stipulated common standards of architectural design, it is doubtful that there would have been any complaints about these interferences with the right of an owner to arrange his own property.

The Court never questioned restrictions of this kind, and Vinson never challenged the propriety of regulating property for many decent purposes through a system of covenants among private parties.[51] What was at issue in the case, as Vinson noted for the Court, was whether the Constitution inhibited the "judicial enforcement by state courts of restrictive covenants based on race or color."[52] It was only *that* particular class of restrictive covenant which was being called into question, for it raised issues of principle that were not presented in the other uses of this instrument. But if Vinson's holding was limited in that way, it was nevertheless sweeping in its import. What Vinson suggested here was that no action may be undertaken by private parties, through the device of contracts, which the state would not be free to undertake itself if it were acting in its own name. By this reasoning, apparently, the police could not be called in to enforce private rights if the state would have to implicate itself in policies that were in principle wrong. If the argument were taken to its root, it would have meant that people were free to pursue, in their privacy, ends that were different from the ends pursued by the government, but their private right to pursue these ends could not always be supported by the state. And yet the question has often been asked in response to *Shelley* v. *Kraemer*: just what importance can there be in private rights if they cannot be vindicated through the law?

I must confess that, as I have had the occasion over the years to come back to this case, my own reactions have oscillated between puzzlement and incredulity. It is not for nothing that Philip Kurland once referred to *Shelley* v. *Kraemer* as "the Finnegan's Wake of American constitutional law." And yet I think I would have to say now that, with all its bizarre leaps of reasoning, this case has, like Zorba the Greek, a redeeming touch of madness. The doctrine in the case may indeed seem staggering if it were understood to mean that no project may be pursued by citizens privately, with the protection of law, unless it could be undertaken by the government as well. But that is not exactly the rule to be drawn from the case. The federal government, for example, would have no evident justification for undertaking a venture in the pants business, but it

[51] See ibid., at 10. [52] Ibid., at 8.

would take an eccentric reading of *Shelley* v. *Kraemer* to suggest that the law would refuse to enforce the contracts that are made in pursuing this legitimate trade merely because the federal government would not be justified in pursuing the same activity. What *Shelley* v. *Kraemer* must be understood to mean is that the government may not be called in to enforce those private acts which are in principle wrong, and which people ought not be pursuing even when left to themselves. The government may be called in at times to aid parents who cannot control their own children; and yet the government would not have a license on those occasions to inflict the kind of punishment on the children that a couple of sadistic parents would themselves wish to inflict if they were in a position to carry through their own designs.

The same thing may be said also in relation to contracts. It goes without saying that our courts of law would refuse to enforce Shylock's contract with Antonio, and the Supreme Court indicated long ago that it would not permit contracts for peonage to be enforced.[53] It is taken for granted that a private benefactor may not establish, as part of the condition of a gift, that a college follow policies of racial discrimination that would be forbidden in state and federal law. There has been some concern recently, also, that certain Arab donors may endow programs at major universities, but under the stipulation that no Jews be employed in these programs. The matter is taken seriously enough that it has brought calls for legislation on the subject; but the demand for legal restraint forces us back to the primary ground of principle in the question. We could not say here that the "contracts" are unenforceable because they run counter to public law. It would be our purpose, in fact, *to provide the law that renders these contracts unenforceable*, and so we would have to be drawn back to the ground of principle on which a legal judgment of that kind would have to rest. But in the process we would concede the main point: that contracts ought not in fact be considered valid or enforceable if they ordain things that are in principle wrong. The restrictive covenant in *Shelley* v. *Kraemer* had to be rejected, finally, because it embodied this one decisive flaw: quite apart from any speculations of material injury, the covenant was formed exclusively for ends that were in point of principle wrong—whose wrongness, as we have seen, was grounded in the concept of morals itself.[54]

[53] See *Bailey* v. *Alabama*, 219 U.S. 219 (1911).
[54] See Chapters II and IX above.

Of course the principle that establishes the wrong of racial discrimination would define the nature of the wrong wherever it occurs—in housing, employment, or even the selection of a spouse. And yet it is not entirely clear that the law may vindicate these wrongs wherever they arise. It is not likely, for example, that there will be a certification process—or perhaps even an "affirmative action" program—to insure that people who apply for marriage licenses have not turned away from potential spouses on account of their race. In the case of housing and restrictive covenants, the doctrine in *Shelley* v. *Kraemer* would sweep broadly, and yet it still may not settle the problem of "open occupancy." With restrictive covenants we are dealing with the terms of principle on which legitimate associations may be constituted, and with rules of contract that may properly be made binding on people through the decrees of the state. This kind of problem, however, may be a layer or two removed yet from the case of private owners who set down nothing in writing in a formal contract, but who indulge their personal preferences about race when they sell their own property. In other words, the case would still have to be made for a law that reaches discrimination in housing in instances of this kind. As I have tried to show, that case would not precisely be established by any of the arguments I have reviewed so far; it might be said, however, that we have managed to clear away the most important arguments that do not quite work. But in dealing with them, I think we may have prepared the ground for an argument that finally proves more compelling, and it is to that phase of the argument that I turn in the next chapter.

It is sometimes contended that what is at issue here in the end is a matter of "contract" in a broad sense: not the terms that are established for contracts, but the refusal to enter into contracts with black people and treat them as beings who have the *competence* to contract. That construction is altogether more inventive than convincing, but as I shall try to argue in the next chapter, the invention may be needless: the principle which defines the wrong of racial discrimination would turn out to be quite adequate in itself to establish the justification for its own enforcement, in private spheres and public, for all varieties of housing, wherever the law may practicably reach.

XIII

HOUSING AND THE REACH
OF THE LAW

1. The Private Household and the Limits of Law

It is not uncommon for the law to touch, with its regulations, many acts that take place under private auspices. An industrial plant may be owned privately, and yet the law may enter the establishment in order to enforce regulations for safety and oversee the relations between management and labor. A restaurant may be under private ownership, and yet if it is open to business with the general public it may come under the laws that govern "public accommodations." Even a private home may be entered for the sake of policing certain regulations for fire and safety as well as for seizing evidence of a serious crime. The question in all cases is whether something is occurring under private auspices that will have a "public" effect extending beyond the household (as, for example, in the tolerance of a fire hazard that may be a source of danger to adjacent homes, or in the concert of criminal plans directed outside the household). This guideline is not always very satisfying. There may be a rather widespread and profound "public" effect if every citizen, in the privacy of his household, cultivates a taste for sadomasochistic rituals. It may make a considerable difference to the character of the larger society if the people who are looked upon as the leaders of taste and opinion continue to display, in their highly noticed private lives, a disposition to discriminate on the basis of race or religion. The law does not reach these kinds of cases today, although it reached some of them in an earlier day under the heading of "sumptuary" legislation; and it is not inconceivable that it may one day back into some of the same controls again.

In general, however, the law has restrained itself to the somewhat grosser tests I have mentioned—the presence of criminal acts or extended "public" effects. It can be said of those tests at least that they mark a sensible place from which to begin. In the case of homes that are owned and occupied by single families, the question is: what is it that would open this category of housing to the regulations of the law if owners discriminated on the basis of race or ethnicity in the sale or rental of the property? Would the law be able to reach these transactions even if they were carried on without public advertising of any kind?

There is a tendency on the part of some people to argue that these transactions are open to public regulation because they are already governed by the law at many points. If the house is sold, for example, the title would have to be registered with the government and the sale would have to be recorded. And yet, because a house may be open to public regulation on certain specific points that touch a public interest, it does not follow that the house is open to public controls in all of its attributes and activities.[1] In other words, the presence of public laws is not enough to convert the home from a private household into an agency of the state. Similarly, it has been required by law that marriages be licensed and recorded by the state, but no one would suggest on that basis alone that the government would have a claim to regulate all of the activities that take place within a marriage.

The precise origins of many of our traditions in licensing have become obscure over the years. Some of these requirements apparently do reflect an older understanding of the state, in which the right to undertake any subsidiary activity must flow from the permission of the sovereign. (This perspective may find its most common application today in the chartering of corporations.) A more plausible construction of this principle is that the community may indeed have a profound interest in the terms of principle on which organizations are founded. Corporations may not receive charters if they carry "obscene" names, and the state clearly would not offer the advantages of incorporation to a school for pickpockets or a syndicate for prostitution. On the other hand, certain requirements for licensing or registration seem to proceed from the necessity of establishing an authoritative record of certain facts (such as marriage, inheritance, or the ownership of property) for the sake of aiding the resolution of private disputes. The regulations

[1] See also *Moose Lodge* v. *Irvis*, 407 U.S. 163 (1972). The fact that a private club was the recipient of a liquor license issued by the state was not enough, in the judgment of the Court, to convert the club from a private association into an instrument of the state. As Mr. Justice Rehnquist observed, "The Court has never held . . . that discrimination by an otherwise private entity would be violative of the Equal Protection Clause if the private entity receives any sort of benefit or service at all from the State, or if it is subject to state regulation in any degree whatever. Since state-furnished services include such necessities of life as electricity, water, and police and fire protection, such a holding would utterly emasculate the distinction between private as distinguished from State conduct. . . ." See ibid., 173.

that surround the conveyance of property would seem to be of the latter variety, and so whatever other significance may be drawn from the very act of negotiating the transfer of property, the fact that the transfer is recorded and regulated by the state cannot establish by itself that the transaction ceases to be anything but "private."

At about the same time that the Fair Housing Act was passed by Congress, the Supreme Court took separate steps to strike at discrimination in housing. The Court seemed intent upon making a dramatic liberal gesture, and so it chose to finesse the question of how the law could reach private dwellings which were owned and occupied by single families. The case in question was *Jones* v. *Alfred Mayer Co.*,[2] which was decided in 1968. The Court declared in that case that, in dealing with racial discrimination in housing, the federal government need not be confined by the traditional formulas of the Fourteenth Amendment. The language of that Amendment in its key provisions, spoke in relation to states (e.g., "nor shall any State deprive any person of life, liberty, or property, without due process of law; nor deny to any person within its jurisdiction the equal protection of the laws"). The concept of "state action" had been eroded over the years and yet it was still understood that under the Fourteenth Amendment the federal government was obliged to focus as closely as possible on those acts of discrimination that were taken or fostered by the states or their agents.

But in *Jones* v. *Mayer* Justice Stewart argued for the Court that the government need not be restrained any longer by these traditional requirements. The way around the problem, he thought, lay in the rediscovery of the Thirteenth Amendment. That earlier Amendment, of course, had abolished slavery or involuntary servitude, and in contrast to the Fourteenth Amendment, it did not speak of states. From that small difference Stewart drew a new mandate for the federal government to act more directly on private individuals for the sake of vindicating the rights of black people. It was arguable that the object of the Thirteenth Amendment (the object of forbidding slavery) did indeed require that the federal government act directly on individuals without working through the states. But that was not the only interpretation which was possible from the wording of the Amendment and its legislative history. It was possible to argue, for example, that the Amendment

[2] 392 U.S. 409.

would have been satisfied simply by preventing the governments of the states from protecting the right of property in slaves. And until *Jones* v. *Mayer* reached the Supreme Court no inferior federal court had accepted the notion that the Thirteenth Amendment freed the federal government to act directly on individuals rather than respond to the actions of the states.

Yet Stewart's argument was not without plausibility. For it was the attribute of the federal government as a real government, rather than a confederation, that it had to possess the authority to act directly upon individuals rather than the states. Instead of creating a new mandate, it was possible that Stewart was merely stating anew an understanding that had to be implicit in the idea of a national government all along, but which had been obscured over the years in the fixation on "state action." Of course it was scarcely coherent to argue that the national government bore the attributes of a real government only when it came to protecting the interests of blacks. If the national government could bypass the states and reach the wrongs that were done to blacks by private individuals, it could do that only because it could claim the full competence and legitimacy of a national government; and in that event it had to be assumed that the federal government could act on its own, without the intervention of the states, on almost any other matter as well.

The particular case at hand in *Jones* v. *Mayer* arose from St. Louis County, Missouri. The Jones family alleged that the Mayer Company had refused to sell them a home in a certain section of the county solely because the Joneses were black. The family sought an injunction against the developers, and as the legal basis for their action they cited the Civil Rights Act of 1866, which gave to all citizens of the United States "the same rights . . . as is enjoyed by white citizens . . . to inherit, purchase, lease, sell, hold and convey real and personal property."[3] (It is important to recall that the Fair Housing Act had not yet been enacted.) The petition, however, was rejected in both the district and the appellate courts on the grounds that the Act of 1866 applied only to acts done under the color of state law, and that it could not be brought into play against the refusal on the part of private parties to sell.[4] The Supreme Court then overturned these decisions of the lower courts on the strength of its new reading of the Thirteenth Amendment.

As Justice Stewart made his case for the larger sweep of that Amendment, he argued that its purpose had not merely been to end

[3] 42 U.S.C.A., Sec. 1982 (1964).
[4] See 255 F. Supp. 15 (1965), and 379 F. 2d 33 (1967).

slavery, but to remove its lingering incidents and "badges."[5] He
thought that discrimination against blacks in the sale of housing
constituted a deprivation of a right, and it was no less a deprivation,
in his judgment, because it was suffered at the hands of private
parties rather than at the hands of the state. Beyond that, it was
not unreasonable to find, in the habits of racial exclusion, a custom
that was bound up with the peculiar past of black people in the
United States as a slave population and a stigmatized group. And so
if the Thirteenth Amendment really was committed to the task of
rooting out the incidents and badges of slavery, Stewart thought
that it could encompass, in the field of housing, "every racially
motivated refusal to sell or rent."[6]

This was, on a number of accounts, a doctrine of extraordinary
reach. And yet, as I have already suggested, Stewart could find a
partial defense for his argument in the very idea of a national
government. For the rest, we would discover that his position would
ultimately be supported by the logic of the principle that forbids
discrimination on the basis of race. In the end I think we would be
obliged to conclude that the Constitution would in fact sanction
the sweeping doctrine that Stewart expressed, and that Stewart did
not, in any measure, overstate his case. But his understanding becomes compelling only if we turn the matter around carefully and
consider, in their proper place, the things that are most problematic
in his argument.

Stewart's argument would draw its initial strength from its historical antecedents. In the tradition of jurisprudence that was associated with the first Justice Harlan, the Thirteenth Amendment
was seen as a grand charter of civil freedom, which could do far
more than simply remove the institution of slavery: it would be
used to reach those lingering incidents of injustice toward black
people which were the direct outgrowth of the experience with
slavery.[7] And in exercising the mandate of the Thirteenth Amendment it was Harlan's understanding that the national government
could indeed act directly on private citizens, rather than merely

---

[5] 392 U.S. at 439-40.   [6] Ibid., 421-22; see also 440-41.

[7] In *Griffin* v. *Breckenridge*, for example, Justice Stewart applied this theory of
the "New" Thirteenth Amendment in a case in which blacks were harassed on the
highways of Mississippi by a band of whites in a car. Since the assailants picked out
their victims mainly on the basis of color, it was indeed arguable that the animating
force in these crimes was a prejudice toward black people that arose distinctly out
of the culture of the South and its connection with the history of slavery. See 403
U.S. 88 (1971); and also, Note, "The 'New' Thirteenth Amendment: A Preliminary
Analysis," 82 *Harvard L. Rev.*, 1294-1321 (1969).

react in a remedial way to the actions of a state. But even though the Thirteenth Amendment was quite broad in its reach, Harlan never suggested that it could apply to private acts of any kind, without the need to establish a "public" significance in these acts. In his famous dissent, for example, in *Plessy* v. *Ferguson*,[8] Harlan implied that the Thirteenth Amendment might have been enough in itself to reach a private railroad that discriminated on the basis of race in its treatment of passengers. Of course the policy of discrimination that was enforced by the railroad had been prescribed by the laws of Louisiana, and so the test of "state action" had been easily met. But Harlan took care also to make the point that "a railroad is a public highway, and that the corporation which owns or operates it is in the exercise of public functions."[9] In other words, a railroad provided, in Harlan's view, the functional equivalent of a public highway regardless of whether it happened to be regulated by the state. This minor exegesis on the part of Harlan was wholly unnecessary unless it was his purpose to suggest that the federal courts could have dealt with this case even without the presence of "state action." The Constitution could reach a thoroughly private railroad that separated its passengers on the basis of race, even if the railroad was enforcing only its own, private policy rather than the policy of the state.

In Harlan's judgment the Constitution could reach this private business just as he had argued years earlier in the *Civil Rights Cases*[10] that the federal government could reach inns or restaurants that were open to business with the public. These private establishments were, in the traditional phrase, "public accommodations." Under the Thirteenth Amendment, then, as Harlan understood it, the national government could exercise its sovereign power and deal with all manner of private businesses that discriminated on the basis of race. Still, as sweeping as this vision was, it was not without limits: the federal government could address private acts of discrimination, but those private acts had to be invested with a larger, "public" significance. They had to take place, as Harlan took care to show, in facilities that were at least open to business with the public. Therefore, even if it were conceded that the reach of the federal government was quite as extensive as Harlan and Stewart claimed it to be, that alone would not have disposed of the question that Stewart came to face in *Jones* v. *Mayer*. A private

[8] 163 U.S. 552ff. (1896).   [9] Ibid., 553.
[10] 109 U.S. 3 (1883).

household is not, after all, a business that is generally open to the public. And so even if the Court had managed finally to adopt Harlan's understanding of the Thirteenth Amendment, the question would still remain: How could the law reach the act of a private individual who discriminates on the basis of race in the sale of his own home?

I would suggest that for the beginning, at least, of an answer, it would be helpful to return to a point that was made earlier when the subject under discussion was busing and racial discrimination in the schools.[11] The argument was made then that many things would fall into place if the law could be freed from a concentration on material injuries and the factitious measures of the Commerce Clause. If we could get clear on the nature of the wrong involved in cases of racial discrimination, we would come to recognize, for example, that the wrong of the case would not depend to any degree on the number of employees in the firm (whether it is more or less than fifteen), or the effect of the firm on interstate commerce. Those features are contained in the current federal law on discrimination in employment, and yet they have no relevance to the moral problem they are presumed to gauge. It is arguable, for example, that a law against discrimination on the ground of race would apply legitimately to the proprietor of a hotdog stand, who is open to transactions with the public but who has no measurable "effect" on interstate commerce. On the other hand, the law may not properly reach a gathering at the home, say, of a David Rockefeller, even though the number of people involved may be far larger, and the guests who are collected there may have a very pronounced influence on interstate commerce.

We would see a case to be made for enforcing public law on a business firm (even one as unpretentious as a hotdog stand), while it is hardly imaginable that anyone would think of using the law in order to gain admission for outsiders to David Rockefeller's home. There is a difference in the cases that would be acknowledged instantly, and I think it would be sensed that the distinction would turn on the difference between a business that is "open" to transactions with the general public, and a private household which is not. The difference, it should be clear, does not depend on the presence of private property. Restaurants may represent private property every bit as much as private homes do, and yet they may be open to laws on public accommodation. But of course even private homes may be subject to public regulations, and for pressing

[11] See Chapter IX, Sections 2 and 3.

matters in the public interest (such as evidence of serious crime) homes may be searched, and zones of privacy may be penetrated.

The critical difference does hinge, I think, on the matter of "openness," on our recognition of what Max Weber once defined as the distinction between "open" and "closed" groups.[12] The differences can be marked in the subtlest ways, whether they occur in public or private settings, and yet they can be marked with an evident clarity. In a public restaurant one may come upon two people sitting together and conversing, and even if one knows one or both of the people at the table, there would be a certain constraint on simply pulling up a chair, without a word, and joining them. One would probably feel obliged to ask whether one *may* join them, or whether they are holding a "private" meeting. And in that definite sense that there would be an obligation to ask, one finds the awareness of a gentle barrier: it would not be *presumed* that the conversation is open to any member of the general public who happens along. In the same way, it would never be presumed that any member of the general public would have a claim to enter a private home and attend a party given by the owners. In certain instances the expectations may be reversed: an "open house" may be declared (perhaps for a "garage sale") and even passersby may see a sign and come in. But it is understood that an explicit decision is required in order to reverse the standing presumption that the house is "closed" in its privacy.

The case turns, then, not on the question of whether the establishment is private or whether it is even a household, but whether it is open or closed to transactions with the public. That point may find support in a recent case that drew precisely on the same section of the Civil Rights Act that was engaged in *Jones* v. *Mayer*. This case involved two private secondary schools, which received no money from the government, and which discriminated on the basis of race in the selection of their students. Once again it was argued that the arrangement violated the right of black people "to make and enforce contracts" on the same terms that apply to whites: that the right to contract was denied by the refusal of the school to enter into contracts with black parents.

In his opinion for the court in *Runyon* v. *McCrary*[13] Justice Stewart was inclined simply to uphold the same argument that was

[12] See *Max Weber: The Theory of Social and Economic Organization*, trans. A. M. Henderson and Talcott Parsons (New York: Oxford University Press, 1947), pp. 139-43, especially 141-42.

[13] 49 L. Ed. 2d 415 (1976).

propounded in *Jones* v. *Mayer* and insist that the Civil Rights Act forbids racial discrimination in all species of private contracts.[14] And yet there was also a tendency in his opinion, and in the opinion of Justice Powell, to fasten on those parts of the record which reflected the difference between "open" and "closed" relations. Stewart observed that the secondary schools in this case were notably different from a "private social organization," which may have more freedom to restrict its membership.[15] Stewart cited, in the way of contrast, the language of the appellate court, which pointed up the nature of a school that "holds itself open to the public" for applicants.[16] Justice Powell went on to enumerate the modes of operation that marked these private schools as "open" to transactions with the public:

—"The schools extended a public offer open, on its face, to any child meeting certain minimum qualifications who chose to accept.

—"They advertised in the 'yellow' pages of the telephone directories and engaged extensively in general mail solicitations to attract students.

—"The schools are operated strictly on a commercial basis, and one fairly could construe their open-end invitations as offers that matured into binding contracts when accepted by those who met the academic, financial, and other racially neutral specified conditions as to qualifications for entrance."[17]

As Powell remarked, a far different case would have been presented if the school had been "a small kindergarten or music class, operated on the basis of personal invitations extended to a limited number of preidentified students."[18] Justice Stevens, in a concurring opinion, was willing to support the emerging doctrine of the Court, but he had no doubt, for his own part, that this new coverage of the Civil Rights Act "would have amazed the legislators who voted for it." Stevens was convinced by the historical record that the Congress in 1866 "intended only to guarantee all citizens the same legal capacity to make and enforce contracts, to obtain, own and

---

[14] Ibid., at 423.

[15] However, Stewart in this instance was trying to distinguish this case from the problem of a private club that was presented in *Moose Lodge* v. *Irvis*, note 1 above; see 49 L. Ed. 2d at 423, especially note 5. But the distinction could not be very satisfying.

[16] Ibid., 422.   [17] Ibid., 435.   [18] Ibid.

convey property, and to litigate and give evidence."[19] Shortly after
Jones v. *Mayer* had been decided, Gerhard Casper explained in the
same vein that when the framers of the Civil Rights Act spoke of
the right of black people "to inherit, purchase, lease, sell, hold, and
convey" property, they were still assuming a situation in which
blacks would be dealing with owners of property who were willing
to sell.[20] In the legal theory of their time—and ours—the right of
property could not be understood as the right to compel an unwilling owner to divest himself of his property.

And yet if the matter were viewed, once again, with a concern
for "open" and "closed" relations, it would not be at all clear that
blacks were dealing with unwilling white sellers, either in the cases
on housing or the private schools. Bobbe's Private School in Arlington, Virginia, solicited business with the public just as much as
any restaurant, inn, or used car dealership. The school was not
unwilling, in other words, to offer its services to the public in
general; it was unwilling only to offer its services to blacks. But in
that case it acted upon a principle of exclusion that is inadmissible
when it is employed by other private businesses open to the public;
and if the federal government can reach instances of this discrimination in other businesses open to the public, it can reach, with
the same authority, to this particular business as well. And what
can be said in this respect for the private school can be said for the
owner of a private, single-family dwelling when he enters the domain of commerce and offers his house, in public, for sale. Once
again, it is not the size of the establishment that matters or the
number of units that are being offered on the market. The principle
that establishes the wrong of racial discrimination must be indifferent to the question of whether the individual who discriminates
sells thirty cars a week or only one; whether he has a chain of
supermarkets or a single hot dog stand; or whether he is offering,
at one time only, the sale of his home. What is critical is an openness
to transactions with a public outside the household.

But would that mean that certain acts, which are in principle
wrong, would be insulated from the law so long as they occurred
in the privacy of the household? Of course the proposition in that
form could never be acquiesced in for a moment. But when we
recognize that we cannot accept that understanding, we would

[19] Ibid., 436.
[20] See Gerhard Casper, "Jones v. Mayer: Clio, Bemused and Confused Muse," in
Philip B. Kurland, ed., *The Supreme Court Review 1968* (Chicago: University of
Chicago Press, 1969), pp. 89ff.

recognize why the difference between the public and the private finally ceases, in principle, to matter, and why Justice Stewart was more literally accurate than even he probably knew when he declared that the law may reach "every racially motivated refusal to sell or rent."

It is the logic of a moral principle, as we have seen, that it applies universally, and when anything stands *categorically* as a "wrong," the wrongness is indifferent to places and circumstances. A policy of genocide carried out by private contractors would be no less wrong than the same policy carried out by governments through public facilities. A private murder is no less a wrong, and no less a matter for the law, than a murder carried out in the public streets. However much we hear about the "privacy of the bedchamber," the bedroom would offer no sanctuary from the reach of the law if it were used as a site for the torture of a child or the battering of a wife. As I argued earlier, it is the logic of morals that entails the logic of law. Once it is established that any act is in principle wrong, the logic of that recognition compels us to forbid that act generally with the force of law. It takes no special pleading then for the law to reach the unjustified killing that takes place in a private home. To do something that is in the strictest sense wrong is to define the precise conditions that justify a law in the first place, and at those moments the claims of privacy must recede. The family and the household may be free from legal restraint as they nourish perspectives that are eccentric, unconventional, or deeply unpopular; but they can claim no more license than any other institution to shelter acts that stand in principle as crimes.

It should go without saying that none of this implies any disrespect for the special claims of the family. It merely reminds us that nothing in the life of the family may compel our respect unless it is compatible with the principles of lawfulness. William Lecky suggested, in his venerable *History of European Morals*, that the progress of civilization may be seen in the tendency "to diminish the disparity between the different members of the family"—in the erosion, for example, of the arbitrary power of the Roman father to put his children to death, to sell them several times over into slavery, and generally to treat his wife and children as a species of personal property.[21] To restrain the family from injustice does not interfere with its rightful freedom and autonomy, any more than

---

[21] William E.H. Lecky, *The History of European Morals from Augustus to Charlemagne* (New York: Appleton and Company, 1869), Vol. I, pp. 315-16.

it diminishes the freedom of an individual to be restrained from what he may not properly do. The intervention of the law may even work in some cases to establish the proper ground on which authority and affection may be founded.[22] When Aristotle wrote in *The Politics* that "the polis is prior in the order of nature to the family and the individual,"[23] he was not conveying the view of a statist, but a necessary moral truth: the authority of the family can be accepted as preeminent only if there is no law outside the family, no set of moral standards that would allow others to judge whether the authority of the parents has been exercised justly or unjustly. But if morals exist, those standards of judgment exist, and the intervention of the public authorities marks the recognition that there is indeed a law outside the family. The members of the family may not be abandoned to the arbitrary power of the father or mother, and the presence of the law signifies that the community bears a moral responsibility to preserve for the members of the family the protections of lawfulness.

It is not necessary that the interventions of the law be frequent, but there is no mechanistic standard that defines the limits of these interventions. If we had the space here we might show that the only proper boundary for the law can be found in the limits of our principles themselves—in the clarity with which we can distinguish between things that are in principle wrong (and which merit the response of the law) and the things which are not. If the matter were viewed strictly, we would find that there is almost no type of wrong that has occurred in the privacy of the family which the law has not been called in to redress. At the most dramatic level the list may include incest, battery, torture, and gross neglect. But the record has its prosaic side as well, and the police logs in the country are filled with accounts of policemen who are called in to mediate in families when disputes erupt over the drinking habits of the husband or the gambling of the wife.

Of course not every wrong elicits the intervention of the law. But the omission may result quite as much from the uncertainty of the

[22] Tocqueville offered his judgment on this point "that in proportion as manners and laws become more democratic, the relation of father and son becomes more intimate and more affectionate; rules and authority are less talked of, confidence and tenderness are often increased, and it would seem that the natural bond is drawn closer in proportion as the social bond is loosened. . . . The master and the constituted ruler have vanished; the father remains." *Democracy in America* (New York: Vintage, 1954), Vol. II, Bk. III, ch. VIII, "Influence of Democracy on the Family," pp. 205-206.

[23] 1253a.

"wrong" as from the absence of a complaint (and from the record so far there seems no want of people who are willing to bring the weight of the law to their side in disputes within the family). A child may be sent to bed one night without his supper—and sent, as it turns out, unjustly. But the wrong that was done might have been the product of an honest error on the part of the parent. And yet if the parent keeps the child in his room for a month without food, or if his spanking one day moves across a threshold to serious injury, a design of malice may become evident, a firmer judgment may finally be shaped, and the law would not be obliged to hold back. The difference, again, does not turn on degrees of privacy, but on the clarity of evidence that tells us that there is an intention to hurt, and that a harm is being inflicted without justification. And in certain instances, as we know, the law may go so far as to remove a child from the family.

But we have absorbed all of this as a matter of course by now, and so why should it be so startling to consider that the law may indeed reach even private acts of racial discrimination? I began here by placing emphasis on those private acts of discrimination that are involved in transactions with a public outside the household. But I have sought to suggest, finally, that the household or the family would not provide a defensible barrier to the reach of a moral principle or to a law which embodies that principle. We may be quite willing to concede that the white seller of a house may refuse an offer made by a black family because he finally prefers to sell the house to someone in his own family. However, it would require no special exemption from the principles of the law in order to establish the legitimacy of that preference. The impulse to preserve a parcel of land within the family may arise from the connections of nature and the ties of sentiment that are combined in the family, and it depends on no illegitimate motive. It would not be different from a host of other legitimate preferences that may induce people, for reasons wholly unrelated to race, to turn away a black buyer in certain instances in favor of someone else. (They may prefer, for example, a family that seems likely to take a caring interest in the elderly couple next door.)

But what if the preference for selling to a member of the family was established only as a device for avoiding a sale to a black family? If the evidence is clear on the point, there should be no question that the act of discrimination would be as wrong in this case as in any other, and it would deserve the same condemnation of the law. Consider a situation, for example, in which there has been racial intermarraige within a family and the interracial couple find themselves competing, in effect, with another couple in the family for a home being sold by a relative. Let us say that the white seller of the house makes it plain that he is choosing not to sell to his niece whose husband is black—that he wishes to mark his disapproval of the interracial marriage—and that he decides in favor of his other relatives solely because of his aversion to blacks. If the seller laid out these admissions quite explicitly, and if the black relative brought suit, on what ground could the law possibly hold back from judging his claim? The matter would not be noticeably more difficult or unseemly than any one of that surfeit of other cases in which members of the same family bring complaints against one another to the law, whether it be in disputes over inheritance or in charges of incest and assault. The grounds on which racial discrimination can be known, categorically, as a wrong, are at least as clear as the grounds on which these other wrongs can be known (and in certain instances they are even clearer). It is inconceivable, then, in any strict reckoning, that the law could vindicate this other inventory of wrongs, but that it could not vindicate, in the same private settings, a principle that arises out of the idea of law itself.

Precisely which government acts in this case in the name of the law—whether it is the federal, state, or municipal government—is really a secondary question. The main issue is whether *any* public authority may invoke the obligation of the law to reach these private wrongs. And if they can be reached, the question would have to be raised as to whether there can possibly be a legitimate end of any government in the United States that somehow lies beyond the competence of the national government. To answer that question in the affirmative would be to say that the national government bears a legitimacy that is secondary to the legitimacy of other governments in this country, and that the framers, in 1787, established a confederation rather than a real government which would be competent to address all of the ends of legitimate government. In other words, once it is established that any single public authority can reach the wrong of private discriminations, the question of federal authority can be resolved essentially on the principles that were immanent in the founding, at the national level, of a real government.[24]

[24] For suggestive essays touching on this question see Martin Diamond, "What the Framers Meant by Federalism," and Walter Berns, "The Meaning of the Tenth Amendment," in Robert Goldwin, ed., *A Nation of States* (Chicago: Rand McNally, 1961), pp. 25-42 and 126-48, respectively.

But to say that the federal government may reach cases of racial discrimination in housing is not to say that the jurisdiction of other governments in this country must be displaced. And to say that these wrongs may be reached is not to say that teams of agents should roam the country, carrying out surveillance, setting up violations of the law, and generating a large load of cases. Just what level of enforcement would be adequate to deal with the problem or to teach an important public lesson is a separate matter from the issue of principle. The question in principle is whether an act of racial discrimination in housing may come within the reach of the law when it is carried out by a private owner who is selling the single house he owns and occupies himself. And the answer, in principle, is inescapable. The law may rightly encompass, as Mr. Justice Stewart said, "every racially motivated refusal to sell or rent."

2. "RACIAL" INTEGRATION IN HOUSING: THE TEACHINGS OF PRINCIPLE AND THE LESSONS OF EXPERIENCE

It is entirely possible that a number of white homeowners may accept the principled ground of opposition to discrimination in housing, and yet they may insist that the problem is complicated by the actual experience of communities in responding to integration. They may agree that the aggregate figures on crime and other problems in black communities provide no grounds for discriminating against the black family that seeks to move in next door. They may even concede that the first black families in the neighborhood will be people very much like themselves in their backgrounds and perspectives. But the problem, they may argue, is that racially integrated settlements are inherently unstable. The most liberal communities have used an array of devices, ranging from counseling centers to schemes that verge on racial "quotas," and still the pattern of success has not exactly been striking. There is some evidence that increasing numbers of blacks are living in neighborhoods with whites, and yet where efforts have been made to engineer integration or to bring it about, so to speak, in wholesale lots, the achievements have been more precarious.[25]

[25] See, for example, the case studies of South Shore, Oak Park, and Park Forest, Illinois, in Brian J.L. Berry et al., "Attitudes Toward Integration: The Role of Status in Community Response to Racial Change," in Barry Schwartz, ed., *The Changing Face of the Suburbs* (Chicago: University of Chicago Press, 1976), pp. 231-32, 235-42.

The experience of American communities so far does not inspire confidence that there is some empirically defined level of integration that can be preserved. Once integration becomes substantial it turns into a full-scale transition, with areas going from almost all white to virtually all black. That experience has been widely known, and it accords with the suspicions that most people have about the likely outcome of these arrangements. And so, even if a homeowner had the best motives himself, he could still be affected by his estimates of what other people are most likely to do. If the community begins turning rapidly from white to black, and if the homeowner is one of the last to sell, he may suffer a serious loss in the value of his property. Despite the assurances that have been heard now and then from academics, based on trend studies and aggregate data, there are a good number of known cases in the short run in which people have seen the appreciation on their houses melt away. The point has been conceded more recently by students of the real estate market.[26]

As property values fall and the community seems to be headed for a racial transition, the initial black settlers will be followed quickly by blacks of lower-class standing. The crime rate may go up a bit, there may be certain abrasions and incidents of violence, and some of the problems of the ghetto may be transferred in a small way to the new community. This turn of events may affect the community profoundly in its character and tone, and it would probably accelerate the flight of whites, who fear most of all the invasion of a lower-class culture. As a realistic matter, then, the issue would extend well beyond the character of the first black families who buy property in the neighborhood. These people are likely to be quite acceptable to their new neighbors, but (as the argument would run) the presence of such newcomers would set off a chain of consequences that would prove as unwelcome in the end to the first black settlers as to the old white residents.

There are a number of points in this argument, many of them quite plausible; but it is not clear as to what propositions strictly emerge from this list of "facts," or what conclusions would be entailed by such propositions. The considerations that are drawn here may have a bearing on the problem only as they are converted into propositions and measured against principles. When that is done, some of these considerations may properly give us pause

[26] Anthony Downs, *Opening Up the Suburbs* (New Haven: Yale University Press, 1973), pp. 69-73; Jonathan R. Lang, "Racial Change in Marquette Park," *The Wall Street Journal*, March 2, 1977, p. 14.

before we try to manage integration in wholesale fashion by seeking to open up large chunks of housing with numerical formulas based on race. But it should become clearer, also, in a more exacting inquiry, that none of the facts that arises from the experience of integration could possibly affect the case in principle for a policy of open housing. That case stands on its own ground, and nothing in the putative chain of consequences could provide a justification for receding from the enforcement of the law in any particular case.

In reckoning with the experience of integration, it may be useful to set out a bit more in the way of empirical evidence. The most systematic findings we have on the aggregate features of this experience can be found in a study done by Karl and Alma Taeuber on the pattern of racial succession in nine American cities between 1940 and 1960.[27] The evidence collected by the Taeubers was drawn from housing tracts in the Census, and so it reflected, in the aggregate, the characteristics of the housing and the social backgrounds of the residents. By its very nature, of course, the study could not have been sensitive to many local flavorings, and it might well have missed the sense of the situation that would have been accessible to a perceptive witness on the scene. But it did suggest a number of rudimentary facts, which would probably appear in any process of racial succession.

The Taeubers found, for example, that as housing tracts changed from white to black residents over the period from 1940 to 1960, the characteristics of the population by occupation and education tended to remain essentially the same. In many instances, the change from white to black occupancy brought an *increase* in the levels of education and income among the residents. What the findings of the Taeubers seemed to indicate was that the type of housing tract was far more important than race in determining the characteristics of the population living in the area. The most stable feature of any neighborhood was, of course, the ownership of homes: areas with large numbers of single-family dwellings were likely to have large numbers of homeowners of rather comparable class backgrounds, no matter what the race of the occupants.[28]

[27] Karl and Alma Taeuber, *Negroes in Cities* (Chicago: Aldine, 1965). See also Karl Taeuber, "Population Trends and Residential Segregation Since 1960," *Science*, Vol. 159, no. 3818 (March 1, 1968), pp. 953-56; "Residential Segregation," *Scientific American*, Vol. 213, no. 2 (August 1965); and Taeuber's testimony before the Mondale Committee in U.S. Senate, Select Committee on Equal Educational Opportunity, Hearings, Part 5, *De Facto Segregation and Housing Discrimination*, 91st Cong., 2nd Sess., 1970, pp. 2727-32, 2747-52.

[28] See K. and A. Taeuber, *Negroes in Cities*, p. 180. The coefficients of correlation were all high for home ownership, ranging from .89 to .98.

As might have been expected, there was more variability in the characteristics of people who were living in apartment buildings. But that state of affairs tended to abate or settle down with the end of the Second World War, as the stock of housing was expanded and the different classes in the black community began to sort themselves out. In this respect, the trends within the black community were rather similar to those that were at work among whites. With the shortage in housing during the war, there was a certain amalgamation of people and "classes" in the housing that was available. As I recall the apartment building of my own childhood in Chicago, the tenants included a foreman in a factory, a delivery man for a candy company, two owners of small businesses, and a state senator. But with the expansion of housing after the war, and particularly during the 1950's, families could pursue a wider range of choices, and people could begin to sort themselves out a bit further, according to their means and their preferences.

On a more restricted scale, the same process was at work among blacks as well. In a comparison of housing tracts that were racially mixed, the Taeubers found that where the white populations were higher in economic and educational standing, the black populations were also higher in status than the blacks in other mixed tracts. In Chicago, for example, there were very high correlations between whites and nonwhites in levels of homeownership and "room-crowding." There were also moderately high coefficients between whites and nonwhites in their levels of education and their involvement in white-collar work.[29] The conclusion of the Taeubers, then, was that blacks were distributed among residential areas in much the same way as whites were, presumably as a result of factors that were largely independent of race. And so the dominant tendency was for neighborhoods to retain their economic and class character despite changes in the race of their occupants.

But on the other hand there is a sober expectation that the first black entrants into any area will set off a migration of whites, to be followed quickly by a larger incoming wave of lower-class blacks. We know that this concern reflects no mere fancy. Reactions of this kind *have* taken place, and they are rendered all the more likely by the tendency of many whites to show alarm at the entry of blacks into the neighborhood. This tendency has been documented by Brian Berry, an urban geographer, who has been reviewing over a number of years the turnover in housing in the Chicago metropolitan area.[30] And yet Berry has also found that

[29] Ibid., p. 182.   [30] See, for example, Berry et al., note 25 above, p. 251.

white reactions have not always been indiscriminate or uninflected. He has argued, to no one's surprise, that the flight of whites is affected by the degree to which they have seen, in the coming of blacks, a threat to their own "status." But Berry and his colleagues have also found some evidence to suggest that the reactions of the whites become more restrained in those places where the class standing of both blacks and whites tends to be higher.[31]

This sense of the matter comes through also in the findings of the Taeubers. The Taeubers took the housing tracts that contained substantial numbers of blacks and then ranked them according to the educational and occupational characteristics of their populations (for example, the median years of education or the proportion of people in professional and white-collar jobs). After that, they divided the list into quintiles and compared the top and the bottom fifths in their proportions of nonwhite population. If the housing tracts in Cleveland, for example, in 1960, were ranked in this way, according to the educational backgrounds of their black residents, it would have been found that the top fifth of the tracts had a median of 43 percent nonwhite. (That is to say, blacks composed 43 percent of the population in the "middle" tract in this top quintile.) In comparison, the bottom quintile had a median of 83 percent nonwhite; and that suggested the pattern which generally prevailed in the North. The higher the class standing of blacks, the more acceptable they seemed to be to their white neighbors. The less likely was it, then, that whites would flee in large numbers, to be replaced by lower-class blacks.

Of course, the higher the class standing of the residents, the less likely it would be that blacks could afford housing in the area. The problem of instability is likely to be more substantial in lower-middle-class sections, where more blacks can afford to buy homes, and where the fear of an approaching ghetto is likely to be more acute. Still, the change has been managed in many places, for the residents may have had little choice. But the process of accommodation may be strained by the efforts of the government to tackle the problem in a gross way through the location of subsidized housing. It soon becomes apparent, on entering this problem, that there is an important distinction to be recognized between the "working poor" and the "dependent poor." On the one hand, there are people who accept the responsibilities of working but who bring in a rather low wage; on the other hand, there are individuals who have grown dependent on public welfare, and who manifest all

[31] Ibid., p. 261 and passim.

those maladies we identify, in the culture of the ghetto, with people who cannot manage responsibilities of their own. It is the latter group of people who are likely to foster the presentiment of blight when they are brought into a community in large numbers through public housing projects or through subsidized single-family homes.[32]

The most ambitious effort on the part of the federal government in subsidized housing came with Sections 235 and 236 of the Housing and Urban Development Act of 1968.[33] Section 235 sought to encourage the ownership of homes among people of modest income who were not poor enough to qualify for public housing. Section 236 involved subsidies for rental units, and in defining eligibility for the program the limits of family income were set higher than they were in public housing. (The range was approximately $4,000 to $9,000 for a family of four.) The effect of these two programs on the construction of subsidized housing may be seen in these figures: Between 1950 and 1965, about 42,000 units of subsidized housing were built every year, and almost all of them were constructed under the program of public housing. By 1970, production had increased by a factor of ten; construction began on 431,000 units that year; and two thirds of this increase was accounted for by the programs under Sections 235 and 236.[34]

The experience with Section 235 presents a case study in the limits of what the government may do in seeking to help the poor through the use of subsidies for single-family homes. The animating hope behind the legislation was that the ownership of homes might offer a further incentive to people to help themselves by giving them a stake in something of their own. The houses under the program could be new or reconditioned. They would have a limit in value of $18,500, but most of them would be between $8,000 and $15,000, and the support of the government would be generous. The mortgage would be insured by the Federal Housing Administration; the owner could secure the property with a down payment of only $200; and the government would subsidize the interest rates quite handsomely. The government would pay the lending institution the difference between the subsidized rate of 1 percent and the interest that the lender would have been able to charge at the

[32] In this vein Roger Starr has argued the importance of honoring the distinction between the working poor and the dependent poor in governing admission to public housing projects. See his "Which of the Poor Shall Live in Public Housing?," *The Public Interest* (Spring 1971), pp. 116-24.

[33] 82 Stat., 477-85, 498-503.

[34] See Michael N. Danielson, *The Politics of Exclusion* (New York: Columbia University Press, 1976), pp. 80-81.

going market rate. Under the terms of the policy, the owner would be required to pay each month a sum equal to 20 percent of his monthly earnings or 1 percent interest on the principal of the mortgage, whichever was greater. In practice, this often worked out to monthly payments as low as $65 to $70 for houses with three to five bedrooms. Most or all of the owners, it appeared, were receiving support in welfare funds under Aid to Families with Dependent Children (AFDC).

Within a short time the houses were plagued with problems: faulty wiring, leaking basements, rotting floors and stairways. For some of the occupants the accumulation of disasters soon proved demoralizing, and since they had little or no equity in the property, they found it easier simply to desert the buildings. As one might have expected, a good deal of the work in reconstruction had been shoddily done. Since the owners had little experience with houses, and since they were often not literate, to say nothing of being clever in business, they were not very attentive in guarding their own interests. But as a subsequent study suggested, the faults were not entirely with the contractors. With building costs what they were, any substantial effort at remodeling could drive the price of the house well beyond the range of the program. On inspection it turned out that the markups charged by the contractors were really not out of the ordinary (they ranged between 10 and 25 percent), and in some cases, the charges of the contractors were actually below the estimates of the FHA.[35]

As for the occupants themselves, they were usually living at the margins, so to speak. In some cases their budgets were stretched so tautly that they did not have a reserve for maintenance and repairs, particularly if they were struck at the same time by sickness or by some large, unforeseen expense. In other cases, where the residents did have a bit more margin, it appears that there was an unwillingness to spend any more on the house than the amount that was set aside for the monthly payments.

The result was that buildings were abandoned in large numbers, and the presence of boarded-up houses, in varying states of collapse, could have a demoralizing effect on communities. Those houses could mark, for many people, the first signs of a ready-made slum, and they were potentially destructive of the property values of the remaining homes in the area. Such was the experience very recently

---

[35] U.S. House of Representatives, Committee on Banking and Currency, *Investigation and Hearing of Abuses in Federal Low- and Moderate-Income Housing Programs*, 91st Cong., 2nd Sess., December 1970, especially, pp. 21, 30, 144.

in Marquette Park, on the West Side of Chicago.[36] Around the same time, in a more affluent setting (in the suburb of Park Forest, to the northwest of Chicago), the opening of a large bloc of Section 235 housing managed to disrupt what had been a stable, "integrated" community. In the original plans, the Beacon Hill-Forest Heights section had been intended for development as an industrial park. When that plan had failed, the Beacon Hill area had been developed in the 1960's by a succession of companies, which put up 270 homes at a price of about $17,000-$18,000. The original purchasers were white, but some of the houses were soon abandoned and put on the foreclosure lists of the Federal Housing Administration (FHA). Several of these homes were purchased by black families, and that event seemed to affect the development of the Forest Heights section, which lay to the east of Beacon Hill.

By 1971 a builder had put up 270 units of low cost and poor construction, and the government seemed to have a field for intervention. The FHA was willing to offer Section 235 mortgages on 255 of the houses, which represented about 95 percent of the total development. Homes could be bought for as little as $200 down and $135 a month, and the advertising for these houses was directed at a black audience through "black media." By 1972, as Brian Berry reported, Forest Heights was 99 percent black, Beacon Hill had become 87 percent black, and these sudden changes were made evident very dramatically in the school system. Between 1970 and 1971 the Beacon Hill grammar school changed from 25 percent to 90 percent black, and in a school that was originally built for 350 the enrollment rose to 700. In the Blackhawk and Westwood Junior High Schools the black enrollment went from zero in 1969 to 15 percent in 1971, and the first incidents of racial conflict began to arise.

The disturbances became more serious in the high schools and the strains in the community were enlarged in 1972 when a program of busing was put into effect in order to meet the guidelines of the state on racial balance. More than a third of the students in Park Forest (1,500 out of 4,600) were bused under this plan. The scheme

---

[36] See note 26 above. One family recounted that, even after investing money to add a sleeping porch and improve the house, they were not able to get anything more, after eleven years, than the $14,000 they had originally paid for the house. With the rising cost of real estate, that money was not enough to furnish a down payment in the white area to which they wished to move. The family ended up taking an apartment instead. The Nixon Administration placed a moratorium on the construction of Section 235 houses in January 1973.

seemed to be carried out in an orderly way, and yet it stirred many aversions in the community. White families began drifting out of the area, and those who remained began to consider formulas— some patently illegal—for restricting the number of blacks in certain areas and preserving an integrated community. In estimating the prospects for this scheme, it had to be considered that the residents, as a lot, were rather urbane, tolerant, and well-off (their *median* income in the early 1970's was $30,000). They had taken pride in the past in having an integrated community, and they might not have been moved very easily to panic. Still, communities with a class composition of this nature have rarely formed a stable balance with an enclave of poorer blacks, many of whom may be on welfare. In 1973 one real estate man reported that the number of blacks drawn to the area was increasing, to the point where they could form, at times, more than half the people in his office.[37] If that trend continued, the town would have to recruit white residents largely from a pool of those who were strongly committed to racial integration. For a while, as Berry observed, it seemed to be an open question as to whether Park Forest represented a "breakthrough" in integration or simply "the beginnings of ghetto extension into suburbia."[38]

Before the advent of the Section 235 houses and the complications they created for the schools, Park Forest contained a black population of a little over 2 percent, and it seemed to be accommodating the growth of this population within a framework of stable integration. In that respect, the town offered a prominent lead in a movement that was taking place elsewhere in the metropolitan area. Once again Brian Berry has provided the best figures on this movement, and by his reckoning there were, in 1966, only 100 black families who were living in integrated situations in the Chicago metropolitan region. (The contrast was drawn with those black communities in the suburbs that were largely extensions of the ghetto in Chicago.) From 1966 to the early part of 1972 that number had risen to 1,600, and it was growing by an increment of about 400 families a year. The largest portion of that growth (over 90 percent, as it turned out) occurred in the suburbs which had laws of their own on fair housing. Park Forest was a notable example in this regard, with a statute that was reputed to be one of the strongest in the state. But the importance of laws on fair housing

[37] Berry, note 25 above, p. 241. For the events in Park Forest I have relied on Berry's rather thorough account on pp. 238-42.

[38] Ibid., p. 225.

might have had less to do with their actual enforcement than with the example they held up and the things they reflected to the outside world about the character of the community. The passage of a law on fair housing was likely to signify the presence of a Human Rights Commission which had been active in seeking its enactment. That in turn would have indicated either that blacks were highly influential in the area or that the community itself was receptive to the notion of racial integration. Here, as in other cases, the community could make its character known through its laws, and it could draw to itself, as residents and citizens, people who would reflect in their own lives the commitments of the city.

The whole scheme of things seemed to work well overall. Through a favorable climate of opinion, and with the moderate guidance of law, the community could establish a stable pattern of racial integration by incorporating black households, one at a time, in a setting of ample means. The physical structures as well as the tone of the community would reflect the presence of the educated and the settled, and so long as integration took place within the large borders of this class, it too could become, in its own way, part of the settled order of things. With the sudden influx of black families the proportion of blacks in Park Forest rose from about 2 to 10 percent of the total population. There was an increase in the number of families headed by clerical and manual workers, but Park Forest retained its dominant cast as a community of middle-class professionals, and by 1978 the black population had held steady at 10 percent for several years.[39] In the turnover of real estate, houses that were once transferred from whites to blacks have shifted once again to white ownership—a rather good sign that the community remains open and attractive to both races. By way of contrast, the adjacent community of Park Forest South became tagged very quickly as a place destined for a black succession. In 1970 the town had only one or two black families; by 1978 it was estimated, in a survey, that over 40 percent of the families were black, and it was expected that the town would soon have a black majority.

But then of course the question might have been raised: Had Park Forest produced quite "enough" integration? Or was it a level of integration that served the interests of a small portion of blacks at the cost of excluding many others, who might also have benefited

[39] The estimate comes from a survey carried out in 1978. For the recent figures (and accounts) of the Park Forest area, I am grateful to Brian Berry and to Dudley Onderdonk, the Village Planner of Park Forest.

from homes in the suburbs? The questions must be regarded as plausible because they point back to the original question of just what degree of integration is desirable—50-50? 60-40? 75-25? And the answer again is that one cannot say in principle just which level is better or worse than another. The wrong of discrimination can be seen only in the treatment of individuals, and it is a wrong because of the principle it embodies. The wrong is not measured by the pattern of its results, and it cannot be inferred simply from any distribution of the races. A distribution of 50-50 would be thoroughly reprehensible if, in order to achieve it, blacks were barred from entry in certain areas and permitted to buy only in designated sections (a plan that was briefly contemplated in Park Forest, in a seizure of liberal inspiration). On the other hand, a distribution of 100 percent black and 0 percent white could be wholly legitimate if people had arranged themselves in a pattern of this kind through their own choice. There is no principle that mandates, in the name of "integration", any particular ratio of the races, and therefore there can be no ground on which to say that any given ratio is "better" or "worse" than another. For the same reason, a policy of open occupancy would not depend for its validity on its effect in producing any stipulated ratio of the races. Even if a policy of fair housing had the effect of setting off a migration of whites and creating all-black neighborhoods, nothing in those consequences could possibly efface the ground of principle that underlies the policy of open occupancy. There are ample grounds of prudence, of course, which would encourage the government to avoid setting off massive flights from neighborhoods. But the concerns that argue for a policy of restraint should never embrace any guidelines, however rough, on the ratios that define "more" or "less" integration.

In any event, our experience suggests that there is likely to be "more integration" if we steer away from quotas and act on a more modest scale, in a manner that is more consistent with the principle that forbids discrimination on the basis of race. The violation of that principle can be established only in relation to individuals, and therefore the principle can be vindicated, in turn, only in individual cases. At the same time, if we wish to bring about a situation in which black people are incorporated in larger numbers in a community with whites, the change apparently takes place far more easily when it proceeds through the acceptance of new neighbors in a stream of separate cases. One scholar has already suggested, on theoretical grounds alone, just why a community balanced precisely in its racial composition would be very hard to preserve.[40] And yet the empirical evidence would indicate that integration is far more manageable in some places than in others. The prospects for integration seem to enlarge where communities are more advanced along a scale of income and education, and where there is a fair congruence in the class positions and perspectives of the white and black residents. As it turns out, neighbors do in fact tend to be very sensitive to anything they can learn about the background and character of new members of the community. And so, contrary to the disposition these days to think that only aggregates count, there may be large advantages in "thinking small." One may discover that there is a vast power of persuasiveness in individual cases, and those cases can add up quickly.

To approach the problem of integration with a fixation on magnitudes—to strike forth with the intention, say, of opening up, for blacks, 25 percent of the units in a housing development—is to fall victim to the trap of numerical goals. At their best, as we have seen, those quotas have no particular standing in principle; at their worst they may partake of the same wrong that underlies the practice of racial discrimination: the inclination to assign benefits and disabilities to people on the basis of their membership in ethnic groups. In the test of practice we also know that these departures from principle bring the most severe costs. They are the most likely to set off a panic in local communities and to trigger a process of transition that will see the neighborhood become almost entirely black. Of course there is nothing wrong with that outcome if one's goal is simply to open up a large bloc of new housing for blacks. But it would be self-defeating if the aim is to extend the experience of a common citizenship for blacks and whites in the same communities.

3. On "Opening Up" and "Trickling Down"

The question may still be raised, though, as to what may be done, on a large scale, to open up housing for poorer blacks (and whites) who may not be able to afford single-family homes. At first glance at least, a policy of open occupancy may have little bearing on the situation of these people, and so the inventiveness of different writers has been focused elsewhere. One argument that has been advanced quite vigorously in the last few years has urged the use of

[40] See Thomas Schelling, "On the Ecology of Micromotives," *The Public Interest* (Fall 1971), pp. 61-98.

the law to overcome the regulations on zoning in the suburbs and encourage the construction of cheaper dwellings (most likely in the form of apartment buildings).[41] These proposals are usually predicated on the shifts that have brought more than a third of the population to the suburbs, along with a dominant share of the new jobs created in the country in recent years. The argument has been that the opportunity to secure housing in the suburbs must exist if blacks are going to have access, along with whites, to the jobs that are created in the suburbs. The argument may be overdone in the sense of understating the creation of jobs in the central cities; the access of poor people to cars;[42] and the possibilities that are open already to people of modest incomes to settle in suburban areas closer to their jobs. Very recently, in fact, blacks have been leaving New York City at a rate of 25,000 a year, which exceeds the rate by which whites were departing the city in the 1960's. A similar phenomenon has shown up in Washington, and what has occurred at the same time is a new movement into the city on the part of young professional people in fields such as law, investment, medicine, and architecture. When they come as couples they often bring two professional incomes, and they have been able to bid up the price of housing in New York and Washington. They are converting old brownstones and townhouses, they are attracting new shops and restaurants, and they are turning frowsy areas into chic neighborhoods. This trend, which has taken place largely in the last three years, has been described by Roger Starr as the "gentrification" of the city.[43]

Still, a move to the suburbs would be a notable gain for many people, and Anthony Downs finds, in the prospect of "opening up" the suburbs, the possibility of dealing also with the problems of the inner city: a scheme for settlement in the suburbs may help to dissolve the lower-class culture of the ghetto by dispersing its occupants among a number of smaller enclaves outside the city. This aspiration courts some serious contradictions, and it may lead to some sticky questions of principle. In order to preserve integrated

[41] See, for example, Anthony Downs, note 26 above; Michael N. Danielson, note 34 above; and cf. Nathan Glazer, "On 'Opening Up' the Suburbs," *The Public Interest* (Fall 1974), pp. 89-111.

[42] As Stanley Lebergott has pointed out, automobiles were owned by 41 percent of those families who could have been counted "officially" as poor in 1970. Half a million of these families owned more than one car. See Stanley Lebergott, "How to Increase Poverty," *Commentary* (October 1975), pp. 59-63, at 60.

[43] See Blake Fleetwood, "The New Elite and the Urban Renaissance," *New York Times Magazine*, January 14, 1979, pp. 16ff, at 19.

communities, Downs would prefer to limit what he calls the "multiproblem households," who would bring with them the more violent and corrosive parts of the culture of the ghetto. But if the members of these households are not brought out of the central cities and into the suburbs, it is hard to see how the situation would be very much different from what it is now. Those people with the aspiration to leave the ghetto and its culture depart for another area (in some cases, for the suburbs). On the other hand, those people who are not able or inclined to move simply stay in the central city.

Downs rightly divines that, if these latter people were placed in the suburbs in large numbers—if they were suddenly transported there, for example, by the hand of government—they would probably set off a flight of the middle class. In that event, the ghetto would still exist as before, but it would merely be displaced to a more pastoral setting. Downs is quite as alert to these dangers as anyone else, and so he proposes in his scheme that the prospective entrants into the community be "initially screened." The purpose of the screening would be to filter out the kinds of families that would strain the liberal tolerance even of the most beamish.[44] But with that move Downs may not only back into the very situation that exists already; he would also run the risk of creating forms of selection that are far less neutral in relation to race than the modes of selection that are operating today.

The main thrust of the argument, however, has been to "open up" the suburbs by overriding the power of local governments to preserve their communities in a cast marked by single-family homes and low levels of density. The devices that have been urged in attacking the problem include: the transfer of the powers of zoning or planning to larger units of government (at the metropolitan, state, or federal levels); the development of land in larger lots by single developers (who can be responsible then for making some provision for diversity); and the stipulation, finally, of certain quotas for the provision of less expensive housing. Builders may be asked to reserve a number of units for housing of low or moderate cost if they are developing a large enough tract.[45] Or local communities may be required by their state governments to set aside a portion of their land for settlements with higher density.

On the surface this attack on "exclusionary zoning" may draw

[44] See Downs, note 26 above, pp. 75-76.
[45] Ibid., p. 161 and passim.

on many of the same arguments that apply to discriminations on the basis of race. If we would ask people to spell out the civic ends of their community—whether it is the sharing of a certain moral outlook, the cultivation of excellence in schools, or even the preservation of a certain pastoral quality—there is no decent purpose of a community that depends on selection by race. Blacks as well as whites are capable of sharing these ends, and if the goal were simply that of living in a place that excludes blacks, it could simply not be counted as a legitimate end.

The same argument might be made in part in regard to exclusions that are based, in effect, on wealth, though it would encounter some serious qualifications. People who cannot afford a house (especially a house in a "better" suburb) may still be inclined to share many of the ends that bring people to the community. They may be disposed, quite as much as the owners of homes, to support a certain code of moral obligation, and they may even be willing to tax themselves at a higher rate in order to support better schools and amenities. Of course, it turns out that people who live in apartment buildings will simply not pay as much in property taxes as those who own homes, but that fact arises from the current arrangements for determining the fiscal responsibilities of citizens. It does not establish that people who live in apartments somehow lack the capacity to share the ends of the community or even to contribute additional money in some other way to support those ends. (For all one knows, some of them may be better off financially than people who are living in homes.) Investing in a home may be seen to represent, of course, a stake in the community. But then houses can be quickly sold, investments may be called back, and it would have to be said again, in strictness, that the capacity to commit oneself to the moral purposes of the community is not necessarily measured by the ownership of a home.

That is not to say, however, that there are no cases in which it *may*, and that possibility already establishes an important difference between the exclusions based on race and the exclusions based on financial means. For there may be a variety of legitimate and rather refined enterprises that can be supported only through the presence of significant wealth, and if one of those purposes happened to define the ends around which a community was organized, the levels of taxation that are necessary to support these arrangements could close off the community, in effect, to people of modest means. It is not inconceivable, for example, that a small community may wish to make itself a notable center of research and learning in Renaissance art. That could mean the support, on a full-time basis, of a number of scholars, along with an investment in a library, museum, staff, and ancillary expenses. The presence of such a center could define the dominant character and tone of the town; and it could shape in countless ways many of the smaller activities that fill out the cultural life of the community. In place of Renaissance art one might put the breeding of horses and the cultivation of horsemanship, or, for that matter, any number of other things. Some of them may seem bizarre, but they are not inconceivable, and I mention them only to bring out the possibility that the ends to which the lives of communities are directed need not be as prosaic as the ends we most typically know. And when they are not prosaic, when they do require the massing of wealth for legitimate purposes, they may require levels of taxation that would be forbidding, without disparagement, to people of ordinary means.

In the first instance, then, the attack on exclusionary zoning is flawed by the fact that it is not grounded, as the case against racial discrimination is, on a principle that must be true *as a matter of necessity*. The regulations that encourage lower densities (and higher prices) in the construction of housing may seek ends that are wholly legitimate and unrelated to race; and that point has already been recognized by the Supreme Court.[46] Beyond that, the problem of exclusionary zoning cannot be reached without remedies that bear some of the same defects in principle as policies that seek to discriminate on the basis of race. Downs makes it clear, for example, that any attempt to integrate the poor into the suburbs in a stable way will depend on the explicit use of quotas. It will be necessary, he says, to "adopt explicit legal mechanisms for establishing a desired 'balance' between households of different income levels."[47] What he suggests along the way is that a certain portion of subsidized housing in the suburbs—"say, 20 to 25 percent"—

[46] See *James* v. *Valtierra*, 402 U.S. 137 (1971), *Arlington Heights* v. *Metropolitan Housing Development*, 50 L. Ed. 2d 450 (1977).

[47] Downs, note 26 above, pp. 123-24. Downs is quite frank in acknowledging also that his strategy would depend on the use of racial quotas as well. See pp. 97-98. In this respect he labors under the assumption that the test of the policy is its "results," and that good results mean integration (regardless of what, precisely, integration happens to mean). What he neglects to consider is that the rightness or wrongness of an act can be known only through the principle that it reflects. Next to that, the "results" are secondary, and in any event, they too can be judged only through principles of judgment.

should be reserved for "households from the central city poverty areas."[48] Taking the advice of Downs, governments would make decisions on the distribution of subsidies in the suburbs according to a fixed ratio which reflects the mix of households that seems optimal or stable.

But of course our judgments would have to be governed here by the same tests of principle that applied to cases of racial integration. It would be apparent then that there is no principled ground on which one could say that a mixture of 75-25 (75 nonpoor and 25 poor) is more desirable than any other. And because the numbers are lacking in moral significance they could not properly form the basis of any restriction on the freedom of movement of any person or household. The same conclusion would hold true even if it could be shown that any given ratio was more successful in achieving "stability." For if there is no ground for saying that any one ratio of integration is better or worse than another, there is nothing in the "stability" of integration at any level that can make it, of necessity, good. There is no basis on which to assume as a matter of necessity that any poor person in these optimal, integrated settings would be improved by the experience of integration. Nor is there any ground for assuming that members of the community who are not poor would be rendered more sympathetic or just by the presence of the poor. Someone may argue, perhaps, that the community will become more undesirable in a number of ways as the proportion of poor people grows larger. But even if that were true in the aggregate, it should be evident now, on the principles established earlier, that nothing which is known about the poor in the aggregate could possibly furnish a ground on which to bar any poor family in particular that sought to move in next door. If the government were to follow Downs and provide quotas for the poor, it would find itself acting once again on a theory of "group determinism." Here, as in the past, the government would put itself in the business of conditioning the rights and disabilities of people, not on their own merits, but on the traits displayed in the aggregate by a group into which they happen to fall. And once again a remedy that is offered in the name of justice or sympathy comes to embrace, through indirection, the very principles of that injustice which the remedy purports to cure.

But then what can be done for the housing needs of the poor? The best answer is to make the poor unpoor. In that event they

[48] Ibid., p. 137.

will be able to bid for housing, and the bidding in the market will in turn elicit a larger supply of housing. The best way to make the poor unpoor is to foster growth in the economy and raise the overall standard of living, and that end is most likely to be achieved through a reduction in the rates of taxation and a removal of some of the brakes on capital investment. In the meantime the question may be raised as to whether the needs of the poor in housing are not being met to a large extent already. Our judgment is affected here by what has clearly been a sliding scale of "adequacy" in housing. At the turn of the century only 3 percent of the families in the United States had electricity; by our recent figures there was electricity in the homes of 99 percent of those families who were considered "poor" in the official definition. (In 1972 that meant $4,275 for a family of four.) In 1900 1 percent of the families had central heating, but as Stanley Lebergott has noted, that utility is present today in 62 percent of the households that are counted as poor.[49] We could go on in this vein, and we would come upon the paradox that many poor people live today with amenities that were not considered essential by an aristocracy 70 years ago. None of this is to deny, however, that there are people living in very poor housing. The question, rather, is whether the problems here are of a kind that would be dealt with in the best way through the power of the community, acting directly on housing.

It is often said, for example, that the government ought to undertake at least the modest venture of aiding in the repair and renovation of older housing. But as George Sternlieb and others have pointed out, the costs of renovation are often higher than the costs of building entirely new units.[50] A more sensible approach may be to offer subsidies to people in private apartments of an older vintage, which are being passed on to another generation of tenants. In fact there has been some evidence recently to suggest that one of the best ways of making good housing available to the poor at a cost they can afford is through the turnover of housing that is set off by new construction. The availability of new housing units sets off a chain of moves, and at each step along the way, older, but often very good, housing is abandoned for newer and more expensive units. There is some reason now to believe that the poor may share proportionately in the benefits that are generated

[49] Lebergott, note 42 above, p. 60.
[50] George Sternlieb, "New York's Housing: A Study in *Immobilisme*," *The Public Interest* (Summer 1969), pp. 123-38, at 134.

by new housing, even if the housing is not built specifically for the poor.

The most comprehensive study on this subject was done by John Lansing and his colleagues at the Survey Research Center of the University of Michigan. The Michigan group was able to interview a sample of over a thousand families and then follow the chains of moves from house to house as far as it could.[51] What the researchers found was that the construction of a new home would initiate a sequence of moves that would advance about 3.5 positions on the average. That is to say, for every 1,000 new homes that came on the market, about 3,500 families were able to move (or, to put it another way, 3,500 units were opened to new families). Since new housing is usually more expensive than older housing, the proportion of poor people who are involved in the first set of moves is rather low. But that portion rises with each step in the sequence of moves, and in the study carried out at Michigan, poor people were involved in 14 percent of the moves in the third stage. The study defined as "poor" those families whose incomes were less than $1,000 plus $500 for each member of the family. Another approach was to define as poor all families with incomes below $3,000 a year. By that measure it was possible to identify as "poor" 13 percent of the families in the metropolitan areas that were included in the survey. All of which is to say that, even before the sequence of moves had run its course, the proportion of the poor who were able to move was about the same as the proportion of poor people in the population.[52] The poor do seem to benefit, then, from the turnover in housing, and with the addition of subsidies for rent, as some experts have suggested, the "trickle down" effect may spread even more widely among the poor.[53]

Just how effective, indeed, this process can be has become evident in recent years in Chicago. From 1960 to 1970, over 480,000 new

[51] John Lansing et al., *New Homes and Poor People: A Study of Chains of Moves* (Michigan: Institute for Social Research, 1970). The Michigan group began with a sample of a thousand new homes that were distributed among seventeen metropolitan areas in the United States. The families who moved into these new homes would set off in turn a series of moves by other families, who would advance at each step to fill in the housing that had been vacated. As the Michigan group sought to trace the sequence of moves, it carried out interviews at each level, and by the end it managed to interview over 3,000 families.

[52] Ibid., pp. 65-66. Taking all the moves together, the poor accounted for 9.4 percent of the movers.

[53] See Irving H. Welfeld, "Toward a National Housing Policy," *The Public Interest* (Spring 1970), pp. 31-43.

housing units were built in the metropolitan area; 129,000 in the central city and 352,000 in the suburbs. At the same time, the number of households in the metropolitan area grew by only 263,000, and so the ratio of new housing units to new families was about 1.8:1.0. The result, of course, was a large surplus in housing that set off a vast chain of successive moves, and from there many other consequences began to unfold. The price of older housing was held steady or even reduced, and the "dual housing market" (the convention of charging more to blacks than to whites) was virtually eliminated. A sizable stock of good housing was opened to blacks along a scale of prices that could be suited more precisely to their means. (The government did not have to pay the construction costs of luxury units in order to build apartments for the poor—and then take on the vexing task of determining just who, among the poor, would be selected for the privilege of receiving this housing.) As Brian Berry described the experience in Chicago,

> Not only did a substantial improvement result in the housing condition of Chicago's central-city minorities—for example, over 128,000 units were transferred from white to black occupancy . . . —but 63,000 of the worst units in the city could be demolished at the same time that thousands of additional undesirable units were being abandoned.[54]

These benign effects came about as a result of a surplus of housing, which was produced in turn by a climate of business that encouraged construction. In New York City, where taxes were higher and rent controls were in effect, the city suffered a net *loss* of housing during this same period.

It would be interesting, though, to take a closer look and consider just which type of construction is better or worse at generating turnover in housing. As the Michigan group discovered, the length of a sequence of moves is, on the average, a full position greater when the sequence begins with homes that are owned by the occupants, rather than units that are rented. (The former generated 3.2 moves on the average, compared with 2.1 moves for the latter.) The difference may be explained by the fact that new apartments are more likely than new houses to be filled by young couples who are starting a household, and who are leaving no former home behind. Within each group, the more expensive homes or apart-

[54] Berry, note 25 above, p. 224. See also Berry, "Ghetto Expansion and Single-Family Housing Prices: Chicago, 1968-72," *Journal of Urban Economics*, Vol. 3 (1976), pp. 397-423, especially pp. 416-18.

ments are generally the ones that can give rise to longer sequences of moves. Apartments that were renting in the late 1960's at $200 per month or more could generate, on the average, 3.2 other moves. Those which were renting at less than $100 a month could stimulate no more than 1.7 moves. Houses that were valued between $25,000 and $35,000 could yield an average of 3.8 moves, while houses selling for under $15,000 were giving rise, in all, to an average of 2.2 moves.[55] This all stands to reason, of course, since the chain of moves can advance farther if it begins at a higher level. But it does bring out again one of the ironies that is encountered persistently in public policy: the poor are likely to benefit in the greatest degree by general improvements in the standard of living, and those improvements are often led, or even stimulated, by people with high incomes, who are seeking to satisfy some rather uncommon tastes. I venture no judgment at this point on the question of whether the inventory of federal policies should include subsidies for the construction of apartments for people of middle- and upper-middle incomes—for the purpose, of course, of encouraging chains of moves that will open up even more housing. From the standpoint of equity, there may be reservations about subsidies that are directed for the most part to people with higher incomes. The tendency of subsidies is to produce more of the things being subsidized, and I must leave it to students of the housing market to consider whether housing that is wanted by people with middle and upper incomes would not in fact be built even if there were no subsidies.

In the meantime, the evidence collected by Lansing and his colleagues at Michigan suggests that the "trickle down" effect does not touch all sections of the poor in an evenhanded way. There is a serious question, in particular, about the extent to which blacks have been able to share in the turnover in housing. In that respect the omissions may have the effect of pointing us again to the measures that public law may undertake in the interests of rendering justice. To be strict about the matter, we ought to remind ourselves that the law on open occupancy would not draw its justification from any showing that blacks account for less than some specified proportion in the ownership of homes. There is no number that establishes, in principle, the level of home ownership that is "right," and no statistics, taken by themselves, could prove the presence of

[55] Lansing et al., note 51 above, pp. 17-18. Oddly enough, there was no increase in the average length of the sequence when the houses exceeded $35,000 in value. In the Michigan sample, in fact, there was a slight decline to an average of 3.3 moves.

discrimination. The law on open occupancy would simply stand on its own ground of principle in forbidding discrimination based on race. But the statistics on race and housing may offer some ancillary evidence, which maps out more precisely the field in which public policy may have its effect.

The first thing that stands out in the figures is that blacks do not move into new homes in the proportions that might be expected on the basis of their incomes alone. According to the group at Michigan, blacks made up only about six-tenths of the moves into new housing that they would have figured to make on the basis of their income. In that event there would have to be a far higher turnover in ownership from white to black further along the chain of moves before blacks could come closer to receiving a proportionate share of the housing that comes open. As matters now stand, blacks account for about 70 percent of the moves we would expect them to account for overall on the strength of their incomes.[56] Lansing and his colleagues were rather doubtful that the difference between 70 percent and 100 percent could be explained by racial discrimination. They tended to suspect that the difference had more to do with disparities in the assets of blacks and whites. In the figures on net worth, the average of blacks was less than a fifth of the average for the population as a whole. And young black couples, they thought, were probably less likely to receive a gift or loan from their parents to cover the down payment on a home.

An alternative explanation is that blacks may simply not be as interested as whites in investing their money in homes as opposed to personal property. But the sense of the matter conveyed by the Michigan group is probably accurate on the whole. As the standard of living rises in the country, for blacks as well as whites, blacks will probably come closer to their proportionate share in the chain of moves and the ownership of homes. As it turns out, the level of ownership among blacks is substantial: by 1974 about 44 percent of the black families in the United States owned their own homes. The corresponding figure for whites in that year was 67 percent.[57] The difference between the two figures may reflect a number of conditions. There may be a difference in the willingness of blacks

[56] Ibid., p. 67.

[57] *Statistical Abstract of the United States 1976* (Washington: Government Printing Office, 1976), p. 743. One suspects, of course, that blacks tended to be clustered to a greater extent in homes with a lower valuation. But the data here have not been available, in large part because the values of land vary so widely between one region and another.

and whites to tie up their money in housing; there may be a lag in the purchasing power of blacks, which should diminish, however, over time; or there may simply be, in these persisting differences, the lingering residue of discrimination based on race.

It remains a fact, after all, that real estate does not turn over very frequently from the hands of whites to blacks. The newer the housing, the farther it lies generally from the center of the city; and even much of the older "new" housing is located in areas that have not been receptive traditionally to blacks. And so while the group at Michigan favored some effort on the part of the government to provide housing directly to blacks who were poor, Lansing and his colleagues still reserved a critical role for "measures which facilitate the transition of existing houses from white to Negro occupancy."[58] For that purpose, laws on "fair housing" may be direct and precise instruments. But the amount of housing these laws opened up would not depend solely on the number of homes they managed to reach through the vigor of enforcement. It would depend, also, on the lessons they taught, and the climate of opinion they created about the nature of equity itself and the terms on which a people ought to live together. Here, as in other instances, the law may exert its most pronounced effect through the example it holds up in public and the principles it commends to citizens to incorporate in their private lives.

[58] Lansing et al., note 51 above, p. 68.

FIVE

THE CITY AND REPUBLICAN VIRTUE

XIV

LAW, MORALS, AND
THE REGULATION OF VICE

It may seem at first glance paradoxical that, in a book on the moral dimensions of urban politics, the question of "vices" should be left to the final pages. But it may be apparent now also that this arrangement serves a number of ends that are central to the structure and argument of the book. In the first place it has been part of my purpose to resist that tendency in our current discourse to reduce "morals" to the domain of the "vices," where they may be thought to apply only to matters such as sex, gambling, and drugs. If the province of morals were in fact restricted in this way, then we should render a complete moral account of Hitler, for example, once we explain the nature of his relations with his mistress and his abstention from alcohol and tobacco. And yet any account of that kind would be recognized at once as absurdly truncated: no description of Hitler could purport to be a "moral" account if it left out the monstrous acts of genocide he commanded and the depraved character of the regime he established. It would be recognized, in other words, that the domain of moral judgment in regard to Hitler would have to take in all of his acts for which there were principled grounds of condemnation; and anyone who ignored, in a moral reckoning, this fuller dimension of Hitler's life would probably be derided instantly for moral obtuseness.

As it turns out, this intuitive reaction would reflect an accurate understanding of the proper range of moral judgment. A puzzle for our time is why so many worldly people, whose reflexes would be quite correct in this instance, nevertheless persist in assuming, in formal discussions, that moral matters refer mainly to sex or to conflicts of interest. The same people are not above asking on occasion just why others are intent on mixing matters of morals with matters of legislation.

Part of my object in this book has been to bring about a closer connection between the understanding of morals that governs our public life and the understanding that would emerge from moral philosophy in its more rigorous lights. And what moral philosophy tells us would be in essential accord with our intuitive grasp of what we mean when we commend and condemn and when we cast moral judgments. In the perspective of moral philosophy, questions of morals are raised every time we move beyond issues of merely private and personal belief and begin to speak about the things that are more generally or universally good. And when one moves to the level of politics, when one moves to the point of making policies that will bind others with the force of law, one moves into the domain of morals in the strictest sense, whether one happens to be conscious of dealing with "morals" or not.

The legislator who insists that the "law should have nothing to do with matters of morals" may nevertheless see himself as spending most of his time seeking to improve the human condition—protecting workers from hazardous working conditions, saving children from battering, relieving blacks of discrimination. The discussion of these questions cannot be detached from a consideration of the "rights" and "wrongs" of the matter, which is to say that it cannot be detached from the sense of rendering "justice" (and "justice" is, irreducibly, a moral term). As often as not, the impulse to render justice will take the form of prescribing acts for people that they would not legislate for themselves if they were left to their own inclinations. Whether the legislation in any particular instance is aptly conceived or not, it would seek to establish for many people what amounts to a new principle of action. As I remarked earlier, we are not doing anything less than "legislating morality" when we forbid people to discriminate on the basis of race in the sale or rental of their homes, for so much is implicit in the very logic of legislation. When we forbid discrimination with the force of law we indicate that it is wrong for people to engage in discrimination, even if they themselves find nothing wrong with it. We imply, in other words, that the "wrongness" of discrimination can be established on grounds that are virtually independent of personal choice and subjective feelings—that there are certain principles that a decent people simply must be obliged to respect. The law cannot make decisions binding on the whole society, then, without conveying a moral import and engaging in moral teaching. To come to that recognition is to return (as I have sought to do here) to the classic understanding of the connection between morals and law. In that understanding, as Aristotle made clear, the end of the law is not merely to protect people from mutual injury or to promote commercial intercourse, but to cultivate a sense of morals or justice among the members of the community.

As I have made my way through the preceding chapters, I have sought to show (in case there was any doubt on the matter) that the problem of moral judgment is pervasive in urban politics, as it is in politics more generally. Every practical question, whether it is about the schools or the use of the streets or the organization of the political parties, points outward to the principles or the moral standards that would underlie judgments of public policy. These questions cannot be addressed as practical concerns without entering a chain of reasoning that leads back ultimately to first things—to those substantive understandings that are simply implicit, as Kant would say, in the very notion of a "rational being as such,"[1] a being that has the capacity to give and understand reasons in matters of right and wrong. At the same time, the problems raised in these chapters have made it necessary to sort out questions of principle and "material injuries" that have been confounded in the past. And that recalls my second purpose in arranging this material as I have: I have sought to establish, as I have moved through a variety of cases, that the law can find no tenable foundation—and therefore no convincing justification—if it seeks to identify the presence of a wrong most decisively through the test for material injuries. Whether we are dealing with the defamation of racial groups, the case against discrimination in housing, or the question of "busing," the offenses were to be found essentially in the principles that were being violated. The law achieved its firmest foundation when it rested on premises that were integral to the notion of law itself, as it did, for example, in the matter of discriminations grounded in race. It makes a profound difference, then, that we arrive at the question of "vices" *after* we have come through the series of problems which compel us to sort out these strands of principles and injuries. For once we come to understand, through a cumulative series of cases, that the questions of principle are far more decisive than the estimate of empirical injuries, that recognition alters the very framework in which the question of "vices" must be addressed. Most notably, it would make it untenable to say that the law must recede from the regulation of vices in the absence of any conclusive empirical evidence that these activities are the cause of any immediate material injuries.

But in coming to the question of vices at the end, there is the

---

[1] See Kant, *Groundwork of the Metaphysics of Morals*, 401 and 413. The numbers here refer to the pages of the standard edition of Kant's works published by the Royal Prussian Academy of Science (Berlin, 1902-1938). These numbers can often be found in the margins of more recent editions of Kant's works.

chance to remind ourselves, finally, that the commitment to principles or morals does not necessarily imply a commitment to saintliness. Those very conditions in nature that establish the capacity of human beings for morals make it clear, at the same time, that humans cannot be angels. There is already a disposition in our time to identify the moral with the religious and the ascetic, as though, to be principled or decent, one must be saintly. That perspective threatens to discredit morals altogether by suggesting that they are essentially impracticable for most mortals. But a decent respect for our own nature would lead us to appreciate the capacity for morals that human beings do possess, without committing us to seek more perfection in this world than its materials may properly bear.

1. Kant and the Distinction between Legal and Moral Obligation

The dictum that we "ought not legislate morality" may be the reigning cliché of our own time, but like many clichés it has filtered down to us from the understandings, or even the miscast understandings, of better minds. The separation between law and morals finds a reflection even in the writings of Kant, even though few men have done more to establish the groundwork on which a facile distinction of that kind could have been averted. Of course, on the face of things, one would wish to resist a simple tendency to equate law with morals, as though anything propounded in the name of law could claim the standing of morals. A policy may be enacted in a thoroughly "legal" way, but if it is ultimately baseless or lacking in justification it does not meet the *substantive* requirements of law. In principle, it must always be possible to raise substantive questions about the justification of formal laws in the same way that it must be possible, enduringly, to challenge the justification of those things that have been established in the name of "morals." To that extent, there may be a tension between "legal obligation," in the sense of an obligation to respect the standing law, and "moral obligation," in the sense of a duty to treat certain moral principles as binding, even though they may be neglected or even proscribed by legal statutes.

But the distinction between legal and moral obligation would be seriously misunderstood, and it would work toward the disparagement of morals, if it were taken simply to mean that moral obligations were "weaker" obligations. A child borrows money from his father, and although it may be understood that he is obliged to repay the loan, there is a disposition to say that the obligation is "moral" rather than "legal." But in this understanding, moral obligations are consigned to the domain of commitments that are unenforceable: whether they are treated as binding or not depends on the sentiment or the will of the person who bears the obligation. And yet, taken with strict logic, this understanding would be incompatible with the concept of "morals," as well as "obligations." As we have seen earlier, if a proposition has moral standing (for example, the proposition that "it is wrong to kill without a justification"), its validity does not depend on whether it is accepted by any given person; and the question of whether it will be respected may not be left to the sphere of personal taste or private choice. An obligation that does not bind is not an obligation, and it cannot proceed from any proposition of moral significance.

That is not to say, for example, that the borrowing of money from a parent may not be the source of a "moral" obligation to repay. It is to say, rather, that for one reason or another, this is a moral obligation that people have preferred to keep outside the province of law. Their reasons for that judgment may themselves have moral significance: they may turn on the danger of corrupting the relations of intimacy in the family by introducing surveillance and regulation by public officers. In other words, the reasons for establishing the boundaries of law must themselves have *justifications*, and in that sense they have a moral import. But we tend to suspect, also, that the same considerations that restrained a parent from creating legal obligations for a young child would hold him back also from enforcing that "obligation" with any stringency. In many cases the child is merely encouraged very strongly to honor his commitment; it would be understood that he might not have the capacity yet to shoulder real obligations, and so he is not treated as though he were, in any strict sense, "bound" by his obligation. And yet that is simply to admit that we do not really have here any "obligation" in the strictest understanding.

It would be a misuse of the language, then, if "moral obligation" were understood simply as a responsibility that does not fully oblige—or a binding commitment that does not really bind. But even more gravely, this misunderstanding would run the risk of suggesting that morals have nothing to do with "legal obligation": that the language of justification and the discipline of moral discourse have nothing to do with the grounds in which legal commitments are made and enforced in a community.

That is in fact the misconception which has preserved the slogan in our own day that "we ought not legislate morals." A good measure of confusion has arisen from this tendency to load far more significance on the distinction between legal and moral obligation than that distinction strictly warrants. The tendency had gained respectability in the past because it found a reflection, as I have said, in the teachings of no less a person than Kant. Still, Kant had no disposition to be facile, and his comments on this matter are embedded in understandings that would either question the casual distinction between morals and law or provide at least the foundation from which an alert student could work his way to the proper ground. Kant identified the law with "external actions" and external sources of authority, while he associated ethics with "internal" grounds of action. If laws were directed to mere external actions they were called "juridical," "but when . . . these laws themselves are to be the determining grounds of actions, then they are ethical."[2] The matter may be seen more clearly in regard to incentives: if a person obeys a law only because it is the law (or because he fears punishment), then he is manifesting a sense of legal obligation. But if he obeys a law because he understands the moral proposition on which it is based, he is obeying out of a sense of moral obligation and the act of obedience takes on moral significance.[3]

But when we are speaking of human laws, we are dealing with the realm of "freedom" rather than determinism. That is to say, there is a choice to be made over a course of action, and the existence of a choice points outward to the principles that ought to govern the choice. Whether they are "juridical" laws or "ethical" laws, all valid laws in the domain of "freedom" must then be moral laws, for they imply a judgment about the courses of action that are right or wrong, good or bad. And to be "laws" in the strictest sense, they must proceed from a ground of principle that holds true as a matter of necessity.[4] Therefore, whether we speak of legal duties or ethical duties, they are both duties, and "all duties," said Kant, "*simply because they are duties, belong to ethics.*"[5]

Kant might have introduced some confusion about his meaning when he observed that "duties of benevolence, although they are external duties (obligations to external actions) are reckoned as

---

[2] Kant, *Metaphysics of Morals*, 214. Once again, the numbers refer to the pages in the standard editions of Kant's works published by the Royal Prussian Academy of Science.

[3] See ibid., 218 and 220.   [4] See ibid., 215.

[5] Ibid., 219. Emphases added.

belonging to ethics because their legislation can only be internal
... [E]thics also has duties peculiar to itself (e.g., duties to oneself)."[6]
And yet when Kant addressed, at a later point, the question of
"duties to oneself," he was compelled to say that one could be
bound to oneself only by the same force that bound one to others[7]—
that is, only if there were a moral principle present that one was
simply obliged to respect. In that event, if we follow Kant closely,
there would be no distinct ground of moral difference that would
separate law and ethics, save perhaps on the matter of "duties of
benevolence." There, however, we face a rather different kind of
problem, the problem of "supererogatory" acts: acts of such a rigor
of virtue, of such benevolence and sacrifice, that they are "beyond
the call of duty" as ordinarily conceived. We would not usually
think of establishing these acts as legal duties, and they may mark
for us the prudential limits of law. But the domain of prudence is
subject to contraction in the same way that the domain of moral
imperatives is open to expansion as our moral understanding en-
larges. (In our law today, for example, we clearly acknowledge a
wider range of obligations in relation to black people than we did
in the early part of the nineteenth century. Measures that were
withheld in an earlier day out of a concern for prudence have been
thrust now into the domain of personal duties.)

What we are faced with here is the continuing task of working
out the fuller entailments of moral principles. It might be said that
the exercise of morals, as an ongoing activity, involves the discipline
of drawing out, in concrete cases, the implications that stem from
the notion of morals itself. As Kant reminded us, the discovery of
law in its proper sense proceeds in the same way, by drawing out
the imperatives that arise from the recognition of moral principles
that cannot be otherwise. At the same time, the province of morals
would embrace a concern for those serious moral problems that
would be created if we sought to overreach ourselves and vindicate
all moral interests through the use of formal laws. Therefore, to
recognize the limits we are willing to place for the moment on the
reach of the law is not to suggest that morals begin where law ends.
"Obligations" of any kind can arise only from propositions that
have moral significance, and those moral propositions may—in
fact, *must*—be contained in the law if the legislative acts of the
state would indeed claim the name of "law."

As far as the question of "vices" is concerned, this understanding

---

[6] Ibid., 220.　　　　　　　　[7] Ibid., 417-18.

of the connection between morals and law is as double-edged as it is in any other area where there is a prospect of restricting personal liberty through the law. On the one hand, it would compel us to resist any facile argument to the effect that the law must recede as soon as it comes upon matters of morals (or what are oddly called questions of "private morality"). But on the other hand, we would be reminded of just how demanding the requirements of law would be in the strictest sense: before the liberty of individuals may be restricted in any degree, whether in assigning students to schools through racial quotas or forbidding employers to discriminate on the basis of race, the question must be raised as to whether the provisions of the law are in fact grounded in a principle that must of necessity be true. That question must be asked in the sternest way if the law would be justified in curtailing the freedom of people who do not share the opinions of the men who made the laws. And it must be asked, then, in an equally demanding way, on the question of "vices" as well.

The concept of "vice" derives from the Latin *vitium*, meaning "fault," not in the sense merely of a mistake, but of something morally blameworthy. The irony, though, is that the things which have been branded traditionally as "vices"—the occupations that have been taken almost exclusively to define the province of "morals"—would not all stand out unambiguously as objects of reproach if they were measured by these stringent tests of a moral argument. That is to say, they could not all be shown *categorically* to be wrong in the same way that discrimination based on race could be shown to be morally wrong *as a matter of necessity*. To take one example, it should be clear that there is no ground of principle on which it could be said that the taking of an alcoholic drink under any circumstances, in whatever quantity, must constitute an injury or a wrong. But that is precisely why it was so massively inappropriate to respond to the dangers of alcoholism with a constitutional amendment that forbade, in their entirety, the manufacture and distribution of liquor. The perspective that gave rise to this piece of legislation may have been "moralistic" in its impulses, but it could not have been moral or principled in any strict understanding.

In contrast, the case, say, against prostitution may stand out as more compelling. But even here, I should warn, the argument may not appear to flow with the same force that attended the case in principle against racial discrimination. The argument is still there, and I think it finally holds, but it is, I grant, a more tangled and complicated argument. If I am wrong, then the laws on prostitution may one day be swept from the books, along with other parts of our laws (like most of our regulations on antitrust, and perhaps even the provisions for a graduated income tax) which may not find any grounding in a proposition that holds true as a matter of necessity. My own estimate, however, is that our perfected moral judgment will finally support even more strongly our traditional reluctance to regard prostitution as a legitimate occupation on the same plane of respectability as nursing, carpentry, or tailoring.

2. GAMBLING AND ITS OCCUPATIONS

When we deal with things that are categorically wrong—as, for example, genocide, or any killing that is done "without justification"—it becomes nonsense to say that these acts are wrong only when done *in excess*. The unjustified killing of one person does not represent a lesser crime in principle than the unjustified killing of many; nor does the wrong of genocide diminish in any way when it is done in "moderation." It is simply in the nature of categorical wrongs that they are wrong in whatever degree they are performed.

But that language is already strikingly different from the language in which gambling is ordinarily discussed. The harm of gambling is usually seen only in the effects that may come about when it is carried to excess. The classic and fearful examples, of course, are the people who have become addicted to gambling to the point of throwing over their responsibilities to their families, their jobs, and any decent employment of their faculties.[8] Still, it is apparent that the act of gambling may not be noxious in every instance (in certain cases it may even raise interest in a game and stir people on to a sharper performance); and that is a critical sign in itself that we do not regard gambling as something that is categorically wrong.

One measure of the equivocal nature of the problem is that the very definition of gambling is elusive. There are people who, in effect, gamble on the stock market, and while they contribute to a system of decisions on investment, their motives may be no more elevated than those of people who are seeking windfalls by betting on the horses or playing the numbers. People gamble when they decide to switch jobs at a certain moment or seek to advance their careers by attaching themselves to one political candidate or another. In this sense, all of life may be touched by risk and gambling

[8] A case that may stand as a paradigm is set forth in detail by Robert M. Lindner in "The Psychodynamics of Gambling," in John Halliday and Peter Fuller, eds., *The Psychology of Gambling* (New York: Harper and Row, 1974), pp. 217-38.

at one time or another.[9] Indeed, there is fresh evidence every day that success in life may depend in good part on luck—in being in the right place at the right time—in addition to merit, effort, or wealth. People who have absorbed that fact of life may find a certain rationale, then, in prodding fortune along by laying down a bet of a dollar or two every week, even as they work for a living and raise their families. We may argue with them over whether there might not be a more productive focus for their efforts to tease out a benign fortune, but we could not reproach them with the argument that success always comes through effort rather than luck, or that gambling breeds, in their particular cases, a disposition to avoid work in favor of idle fancies.

There is a difference of course between the kind of "gambling" that takes place on rare occasions at moments of decision in one's life, and the kind of gambling that may form a continuous stream of activity until it becomes the dominant occupation in life. The kind of corruption that may be bred in the inveterate gambler was caught very deftly once by George Eliot in a sketch she drew in

[9] Jefferson was moved to write once on this point that:

If we consider games of chance immoral, then every pursuit of human industry is immoral; for there is not a single one that is not subject to chance, not one wherein you do not risk a loss for the chance of some gain. The navigator, for example, risks his ship in the hope (if she is not lost in the voyage) of gaining an advantageous freight. The merchant risks his cargo to gain a better price for it. The landholder builds a house on the risk of indemnifying himself by a rent. The hunter hazards his time and trouble in the hope of killing game. . . . But the greatest of all gamblers is the farmer. He risks the seed he puts into the ground, the rent he pays for the ground itself, the year's labor on it, and the wear and tear of his cattle and gear, to win a crop, which the chances of too much or too little rain, and general uncertainties of weather, insects, waste, &c., often make a total or partial loss. These, then, are games of chance. Yet so far from being immoral, they are indispensable to the existence of man, and everyone has a natural right to choose for his pursuit such one of them as he thinks most likely to furnish him subsistence.

Jefferson went on, however, to observe that all of the activities he mentioned "produce something useful to society. But there are some which produce nothing, and endanger the well-being of the individual engaged in them, or of others depending on them. Such are games with cards, dice, billiards, &c." As far as these occupations were concerned, Jefferson contemplated the damage they could cause to a person and his family, and he was willing to dispel any hint of libertarianism that might have attached to his teachings: he would have had the society "step in to protect the family *and the party himself*, as in other cases of insanity, infancy, imbecility, &c., and suppress the pursuit altogether, and the natural right of following it." See Jefferson, "Thoughts on Lotteries," in Saul K. Padover, ed., *The Complete Jefferson* (New York: Duell, Sloan, and Pearce, Inc., 1943), pp. 1289-97, at 1290. Emphases added.

Daniel Deronda. She had the occasion to describe there a young woman gambler (Gwendolen Harleth) who had lost heavily at roulette and was moved to sell a necklace that had been left to her by her father. Since she had not known her father, she was able to persuade herself rather easily that she felt no strong attachment to the legacy. "Who supposes," wrote Eliot, "that it is an impossible contradiction to be superstitious and rationalizing at the same time? Roulette encourages a romantic superstition as to the chances of the game, and the most prosaic rationalism as to human sentiments which stand in the way of raising needful money."

In that sense, the passion of gambling may lead on to the most contracted egoism and a profound disordering of character. The gambler comes to recognize no law beyond his own appetites—he may show no sense of the hierarchy of pleasures that may be better or worse; no recognition of the claims of family; no deference to those occupations that would have a higher claim to his commitment. He may become, in fact, the prisoner of his own passions, and he may surrender his self-control in the deepest sense—the sense of a proper ordering of the parts, the governing of his impulses by the higher qualities of reflection and judgment.

Aristotle taught that virtue inhered in moderation, in a golden mean of the passions. But Kant pointed out later that virtue, in this reckoning, would be found somewhere along a scale in which two vices diminish. And yet virtue was not to be found by measuring degrees in the weakening of vice; it was to be found rather in the maxim that was implicit in any act.[10] If gambling or any other pastime is pushed to the point of harm, the evil may result not from people doing "more" gambling, but from their manifesting, in addition, a certain negligence in relation to other responsibilities. The same unwholesome results could occur, after all, if people wasted their fortunes in foolhardy business ventures, or if they became "hooked" on Beethoven or Art History to the detriment of their other obligations.

That is not to say, however, that we can make no discrimination between the cultivation of a taste for Beethoven and the cultivation

---

[10] "... [I]f I regard good management as the mean between prodigality and avarice and think of this mean as one of degree, then a vice would not pass over into its (*contrarie*) opposite vice without going through a virtue; and hence ... If a vice is to be distinguished from a virtue, then not the amount of exercise of moral maxims but, rather, the objective principle of them must be recognized and expounded as distinct. . . . ." Kant, *The Metaphysics of Morals*, Part II, p. 432 ("Concerning avarice").

of a taste for bingo. Any recognition of the notion of morals implies, at the same time, a recognition of the kinds of qualities and pleasures in human beings that are higher and lower. The pleasures of moral understanding must be estimated as higher than the pleasures of a winning streak in Las Vegas. And yet to say that the pleasures of gambling are lower is not to say that they are wholly illegitimate, and it is not to say that gambling cultivates only the lowest faculties. Anyone who has seen skilled bridge players at their highest pitch of subtlety could not imagine for a moment that he was dealing with trifling intellects. Those intellects might not be applied in these instances with their greatest consequence, and yet all minds need relaxation, and there are some pastimes that may cultivate acuity and forethought to a larger extent than others. (The British minister Ian MacLeod was a renowned bridge player, and one cannot say whether politics prepared him for bridge, or whether bridge prepared him with singular aptness to be the Conservative administrator of the National Health Service.)

Even the meaner trade of betting on horses can cultivate, in its more literate practitioners, a knowledge of many worldly things in the care and breeding of horses. When Dr. Johnson was told of a man riding three horses, he was reported to have said:

> Such a man, Sir, should be encouraged; for his performances show the extent of the human powers in one instance, and thus tend to raise our opinion of the faculties of man. He shows what may be attained by persevering application; so that every man may hope, that by giving as much application, although perhaps he may never ride three horses at a time, or dance upon a wire, yet he may be equally expert in whatever profession he has chosen to pursue.[11]

Even the rider of horses in a circus may intimate something further about the range of human competencies, and the knowledge to be gained in occupations of this kind is not all to be scorned. When civilization itself was at stake during the Second World War and it became vital to sabotage the industrial plants of the enemy, whom did the intelligence services call upon in desperation but the former "insurance adjusters" of the world: who would have known better how to undo machinery and plants than the men who had made their livings by discovering just how machinery became bro-

---

[11] James Boswell, *The Life of Samuel Johnson* (New York: Modern Library edition, 1952), pp. 108-109.

ken down and sabotaged? And if the insurance adjusters could be the men of destiny at the hour of the West's need, some useful employment may be found one day for the backgammon addicts and the poker players of the world. For all one knows, the United States might have been better served in the early 1970's if it had Jimmy the Greek negotiating with the Russians over the wheat deal and arms control.

We are often disposed to think of gambling as a less "productive" form of employment than other occupations. In the narrowest or most neutral sense, however, that would not be true, and that is precisely the problem. If almost all forms of gambling were made legal, gambling would probably be one of the most significant growth industries in the country. Beyond the expansion of gambling itself, there are many ancillary industries that would be stimulated by the enterprise of wagering in its various forms. There would be a need for paper, accountants, furnishings, telephones—in short, for many of the same things that ordinary businesses require. The people who earned their livings at this trade would buy automobiles, computers, typewriters, and applicances of every kind. There would be no want of stimulation, in other words, even for the most advanced parts of the economy, and so if the issue were one of "productivity" in the barest sense of producing goods and sustaining the economy, the gambling industry would make its own hefty contribution. And it is hard to see that the activity which stirred all of this production and consumption would be any more trivial or useless than a host of other things, like Sam Ervin sweatshirts or Duncan yoyos, which apparently provide their users with some innocent pleasure.

But if the question of "productivity" were a question of whether people are engaged in occupations that are worthwhile, or which look toward some higher end, the issue would be rather different. If the country came to spend a larger portion of its resources on gambling than on schools and churches, if it found its collective life dominated by its "amusements," we would probably see in this state of affairs the signs of a community that had become disordered: we would have a country that lived for its amusements, rather than a society that made use of amusements as a form of recreation in a fundamental sense—that is, as a means of pointing up the range of possibilities in human achievement and discovering again its own premises and ends (in the way, for example, that plays and sports may provide a kind of moral teaching).

If the situation became inverted and the country lived, in effect, for its amusements, we might expect to see the results that were feared by Rousseau when he contemplated the establishment of a theater in Geneva. As he wrote in his famous *Letter to D'Alembert*,

[T]he theatre is a form of amusement; and if it is true that amusements are necessary to man, you will at least admit that they are only permissible insofar as they are necessary, and that every useless amusement is an evil for a being whose life is so short and whose time is so precious. The state of man has its pleasures which are derived from his nature and are born of his labors, his relations, and his needs. And these pleasures, sweeter to the one who tastes them in the measure that his soul is healthier, make whoever is capable of participating in them indifferent to all others. A father, a son, a husband, and a citizen have such cherished duties to fulfill that they are left nothing to give to boredom. . . . [T]he habit of work renders inactivity intolerable and . . . a good conscience extinguishes the taste for frivolous pleasures. But it is discontent with one's self, the burden of idleness, the neglect of simple and natural tastes, that makes foreign amusement so necessary. I do not like the need to occupy the heart constantly with the stage as if it were ill at ease inside us. Nature itself dictated the response of that barbarian to whom were vaunted the magnificences of the circus and the games established at Rome. 'Don't the Romans,' asked this fellow, 'have wives or children?'. . .[12]

The upshot of all this was that theater and amusements would be good for bad people and bad for good people. If we were dealing with Mafiosi, it might be better for us all if we diverted them by keeping them engaged in theaters and casinos in the evening, and ballparks and racetracks during the day. If we were dealing, however, with a society of citizens, of people who took seriously their responsibilities to their families and their communities, it could only be harmful to the community if they were diverted from their important works.

We might well be a worse nation, then, in some respect, if gambling and its ancillary activities came to take up, in the aggregate, a larger share of our daily exertions. It is entirely possible, of course, that in a time when politics is corrupt, people may still seek integrity

---

[12] Rousseau, *Politics and the Arts*, trans. Allan Bloom (Ithaca: Cornell University Press, 1960), p. 16. For a French edition see *Lettre à D'Alembert* (Paris: Garnier-Flammarion, 1967), pp. 65-66.

in their private lives or in the character of their achievements in sports and the arts. As plausible as that might be for these domains, however, it is hard to imagine a people using gambling as a medium for cultivating a special excellence and integrity. And even if that were the case, one would still have to say of a people of this kind that it expended its virtue on everything except the matters of gravest consequence for the community.

But if it is hard to establish the ground of principle on which gambling can be considered a wrong, it is inadmissible to argue that what is not unambiguously wrong in the particular case becomes wrong somehow in the aggregate. And still less justified would it be to complete the circuit by arguing that, if gambling is undesirable in its aggregate effects, the law may restrain its particular incidents. For myself, I find the life of gambling as appalling as George Eliot found it, and I think the aversion rests on something more substantial than mere distaste. But I have not yet been able to form an argument against it on the basis of a principle that must hold true with inescapable force. For that reason, I would hold back for the moment from any firm judgment on the matter, and I would be compelled, therefore, to hold back the hand of the law as well.

3. Prostitution: Framing the Problem

A firmer ground of argument may be available in dealing with the problem of prostitution; and yet even there, as I have indicated, the matter is more ambiguous than has usually been assumed. Once again, there is a question, initially, about the definition of the activity that constitutes the wrong. The problem of defining prostitution was acknowledged by William Acton in one of the earliest of the "reform" works on the subject in the middle of the nineteenth century.[13] As Acton noted, the French made a distinction between *femmes debauchées* and *prostitutées*. The former group contained those classes of women known as *femmes galantes* and *filles clandestines*, terms which roughly corresponded with the notion of "kept mistresses" and the more "reserved" class of prostitutes. (It seemed to go without saying that prostitutes were women. There was no suggestion that the definitions could be filled also by men, who would have an equal claim, then, to the restraint of the law.) But over the class of "clandestine prostitutes," the courtesans and

[13] William Acton, *Prostitution* (London, 1857; second edition reprinted, New York: Frederick Praeger, 1969).

mistresses and women of cultivation who might be kept by one man, the police sought to exercise no surveillance and control. Gail Sheehy's recent book, *Hustling*,[14] culminates in fact with the case of a woman who managed to make use of her attractiveness at a higher level of refinement and install herself, through marriage, in the best of circles. When she was widowed, she was left a woman of substantial standing and property, with her capital in all senses very much enlarged.

To the extent that this woman was moved by a rather mercenary end outside love itself—and an impulse notably different from that of improving the object of her love—it may well be said that she represented a corruption of love and, therefore, a form of prostitution. With this form of "prostitution," the law has had little to do, mainly because it would be almost impossible in most cases to detect. As the Medical Officer to the British Privy Council testified in the 1860's, it was hard to arrive at any "practical definition of prostitution which could include women wishing to practice clandestinely." What he suggested instead was that the definition of the offense be confined to that prostitution "carried on by women who make it their calling, and live in gangs in brothels, or who publicly solicit men."[15] The "independent" prostitute who was not attached to a brothel might be difficult to distinguish, at times, from a woman in the neighborhood who was known rather widely as promiscuous. Indeed the problem has proved a vexing one in the past under policies of legalized prostitution: almost inescapably the police (or some other authority) had to be assigned the task of declaring just which women in the neighborhood were obliged to register as prostitutes under the law if the zone of prostitution was to be limited and the women were to be subjected to compulsory medical examinations. There was, in these arrangements, no small threat to reputations, and the most intense disputes arose when the authorities designated women who refused to agree that they were in fact prostitutes.[16] As Acton reported, the standard of prostitution that was applied in Berlin covered "all voluntary sexual abandonment for a consideration."[17] By that measure, one could take in the notorious cases of people who seek or accept sexual relations for the sake of advancing their careers; and that says nothing, of course,

[14] (New York: Delacorte Press, 1973).

[15] Testimony of Mr. John Simon, quoted in Acton, *Prostitution*, pp. 30-31.

[16] See Sheldon Amos, *Prohibition, Regulation, and Licensing of Vice* (London: Stevens and Sons, 1877), pp. 83-84.

[17] Acton, *Prostitution*, p. 30.

of the escapades of some recent "secretaries" on Capitol Hill, whose competencies, estimable as they were, did not include typing. Nor does it appear that the "work" of these women was particularly demanding of their time. If the definition of "prostitution" depended, then, on the pursuit of the activity as a "calling," there are many practitioners who can get along quite well on a part-time basis while they make room in their lives for other interests. James and Elizabeth Vorenberg report, in this vein, that in the licensed brothels of Las Vegas there are a number of college women who work on their semester breaks.[18]

The best that William Acton was able to offer as a definition of prostitution was "the legally established and repeated exercise of fornication as a calling, combined with public notoriety thereof, arrest *in flagrante*, proved by witnesses other than the informer or the police agent."[19] This definition was as problematic as any of the others, but one common theme which runs through these efforts to mark off the subject is the emphasis on business with the public. In the last chapter, when the subject at hand was discrimination in housing, I tried initially to establish the boundary between the public and the private, and I suggested that the separation turned on the difference between "open" and "closed" relations: the shelter of privacy was drawn back when the parties opened themselves and their establishments to transactions with a general public outside the household. As we came to see, that distinction between the public and the private did not ultimately establish a barrier that could resist the reach of the law when a real principle was being violated. The public sphere was perhaps the source of the most visible offenses, and public attention may be drawn more easily here to the violation of the law. The violations that are sheltered in privacy may be quite as offensive in principle, but the law may have no practicable way of reaching them without a complaint that emanates from the household itself.

The same arrangement of the problem may apply to prostitution as well. Whatever defines, in principle, the wrong of prostitution would probably have to apply to the fashionable courtesans, as well as to the common prostitute on the street. The courtesan may not seem to present the same difficulty because she may be hidden from public display, and because the prostitute on the street may branch out more easily into muggings and thefts, which will present

[18] See "The Biggest Pimp of All," *Atlantic*, Vol. 239, no. 1 (January 1977), pp. 27-38, at 30. The Vorenbergs neglect to say what these women were "majoring" in.

[19] Acton, *Prostitution*, p. 29.

other problems that the police will be compelled to deal with. But if a law on prostitution were established on its proper ground of principle, the courtesan would not stand so clearly out of reach as she appears to stand today. For the heart of the matter, I think, has to do with the acceptance of sexual intercourse outside the special context of law and intimacy that is defined by marriage and the family. From the free employment of the epithet "whore," it is evident that common usage takes its guide from these very gross, and very clear, markers: women are labeled freely as "prostitutes" when they are promiscuous, and when they engage often in sexual intercourse outside the relation of marriage. That engagement may be extended; it may be offered impersonally, to a larger section of the public, without discrimination, and for the payment of a fee. But no threshold is crossed here; all of these steps merely confirm the criteria that underlay the original judgment: that the movement to prostitution was a movement away from relations of personal commitment and love concentrated in a marriage, and it involved a shift (at the extreme) toward sexual intercourse on an impersonal basis, with members of the public, without commitment and without love.

There is little doubt that it would be far easier for the law to define prostitution if it could use as the core of its definition the unambiguous test of whether sexual intercourse takes place in the context of a legal marriage. But apart from the clarity it would furnish to the law, this standard probably points rather precisely, also, to the moral grounds on which the condemnation of prostitution would ultimately rest. In that event one would arrive at a recognition that one might almost prefer these days to leave undiscovered—namely, that the law which condemns prostitution stood on a much firmer ground in an earlier period, a period characterized by a more stringent regulation of public morals, when the law was willing to condemn as "fornication" all sexual intercourse outside marriage. It seems hardly imaginable, of course, that we could return in our own time to that state of the laws. And yet if the moral rejection of prostitution depends at its foundation on the special significance of *human* love and the unique commitments of family, it is sobering to consider the possibility that the law which restrains prostitution stood on a much firmer ground of principle in an earlier day than it does now, in our own.

The law today must be far less clear about the moral ground on which it would condemn prostitution, and the result is that when the law seeks to address the problem, the tendency has been to deal mainly with the peripheral aspects or the most outward manifestations of prostitution. The inclination has often been to ban "public solicitation" or restrict the zone of solicitation—to treat the problem, in other words, as a matter of "aesthetic regulation" or the abatement of nuisances. Now it is true, of course, that solicitation may be a "nuisance" or a form of harassment on independent grounds, quite apart from whether it would beckon people to activities that are illegitimate. The courts have upheld the rights of communities to ban sound trucks or neon signs, regardless of whether the activities that were being advertised were legitimate. Yet it is virtually inconceivable that the law could ban all forms of advertisement for products and services that are recognized as legitimate.

In the case of prostitution, however, a ban on all public advertising and solicitation has not been considered beyond question. It should be apparent that a measure as sweeping as that could not be separated from a judgment in principle about the legitimacy of prostitution itself, but still there has been no disposition in the law to come to terms with that fact. A case in point has been offered by New York City in its recent efforts to counter the bogus "massage parlors," which have really been brothels in disguise. As the City initially prepared legislation on the subject, its approach was characteristic of the line of attack that would be pursued by most lawyers: in the spirit of Holmes, they would try to banish every word of moral significance from the law altogether, which is to say that they would try to deal with a moral problem while using descriptions and regulations that were notably free of moral import. The result was, and persistently has been, a minor burlesque in the law. The City would require, for example, that "real" massage parlors establish their authenticity by appearing either in hotels with more than two hundred rooms, or in centers that contain facilities for sports, such as swimming pools (with a minimum of 1500 square feet), squash courts (which must be 25 feet wide, 45 feet long, and 20 feet high), or other kinds of courts whose dimensions may be specified with equal precision.[20] The extraordinary precision, of course, reflects the ritual of empty exactitude that the law is forced to undertake in defining the surface features of a problem when the authorities are either unable or unwilling to define the moral essence of the offense itself.

[20] City Planning Commission, December 10, 1975/Calendar #22, CP-23116, pp. 1 and 10.

In point of principle, it is not at all clear as to why a real massage parlor must be annexed to all of these additional facilities if it has a claim to be what it says it is, and therefore a right to stay in business. In the meantime, the return on the bogus massage parlors might be high enough that the owners could afford to build larger establishments, containing hotel rooms and swimming pools and squash courts. After that, the law would presumably have to begin specifying the number of patrons who must make use of these facilities, or perhaps even the proportion of hotel rooms that must be occupied in order to have a legitimate hotel. In this respect the exercise is as ultimately meaningless as the measures that require these "massage parlors" and pornography shops to be at least 1,000 feet apart and no closer than 500 feet to churches and schools. If the businesses in question were law firms, few people are likely to suggest that it would be salutary for the community to keep these businesses 1,000 feet apart—and 500 feet away from churches and schools. The measure becomes plausible only when it is assumed that there is something in the nature of the enterprises themselves that is unwholesome and illegitimate. But if one could explain the grounds of principle on which they are found to be obnoxious in the first place, then these establishments could be banned or restricted without the need for these charades in legal draftsmanship.[21]

The charade becomes ever more functional, however, when the people who are most earnest in resisting the "legislation of morals" become quite insistent, nevertheless, that the culture of prostitution and pornography be removed from their immediate vicinity. In this manner, *The New York Times* has been quite firm in defending the legality of pornography under the First Amendment, but it has also been willing to countenance the use of legal ploys to harass the purveyors of pornography and prostitution and "clean up" Times

---

[21] The same observation would have to be made, for example, in response to the contention of the authorities in New York that "if a land use is so incompatible with the predominant uses of a district's zoning as to change the character of the area, it is appropriate to remove that use." See ibid., p. 3. If one entertains the possibility that the "new" use of a building may be for a law firm or a good restaurant in a district that formerly contained no law firms or good restaurants, the statement would reveal its own vacuity. Once again, the policy of the city would make sense only if it were underlain by a substantive argument as to why brothels are illegitimate businesses. In the absence of that kind of argument, the legal measures of the city become reduced to so many legal formulas, without substance or justification on their own terms.

Square.[22] Similarly, many liberals on the West Side of New York who were inclined to consider prostitution as a "victimless crime" became rather concerned when prostitutes began soliciting in large numbers in the more fashionable precincts of the West 70's and 80's.[23] Doorbells would be rung; neighbors would be awakened in the middle of the night by men looking for prostitutes. As the prostitutes settled into the neighborhood, along with "topless" and "bottomless" bars, they would attract a clientele that had a taste for these services, and the clientele, in turn, would attract muggers and pickpockets. For their own part, the liberal residents of the West Side would have been content to see the police deal with the problem under the cover of "nuisances" without bothering to spell out the grounds on which the law may properly restrict prostitution itself.

Some have argued, of course, that prostitution becomes open to legal restraint precisely because of these ancillary harms that it generates—the increase of street crime, the propositioning of other women in the neighborhood, and the blight that affects the community with this culture of commercial sex. But once again the weight of the argument is placed on empirical effects or material injuries without any account of what would be wrong in principle with prostitution itself. In the absence of that principled argument, the mustering of evidence on the "effects" of prostitution simply yields, once again, a mere collection of correlations that entail no conclusions. It is certainly true, for example, that the presence of prostitutes seems to bring an increase in thefts and muggings. But similar effects may be generated by many legitimate entertainments that happen to bring out large crowds. The incidence of pickpocketing is likely to rise in and around Yankee Stadium when the Yankees are playing an important series, or in Grand Central Station on Friday afternoons; and yet it would be inadmissible to suggest that these legitimate activities ought to be suppressed because of the opportunities they afford for crime. In all strictness, it would be as invalid in principle to ban these activities as it would have been wrong, in the case mentioned earlier, to ban the ice cream wagon because its presence on the town common induced people to tread on the grass.

To speak of the "blight" or "destruction" of the community as

---

[22] See Walter Berns, "Absurdity at *The New York Times*," *Harper's* (May 1973), pp. 34ff.

[23] See *The New York Times*, April 4, 1976, p. 47.

a result of prostitution is to cast, in the images of physical decay, what is really a moral judgment—but a moral judgment arrived at without the benefit of supporting argument. I have many friends who insist that the pastoral quality of their lives was impaired, that their town suffered "blighting" and "destructive" effects, when a strip of "fast food" stands was allowed to develop along one of the main roads. The critics mean to convey their distaste, but they do not suggest that the establishments whose very presence constitutes the "blight" are illegitimate and open to suppression. At the most, they can plead for a policy of zoning that keeps certain kinds of businesses out of designated sections of the town. But it would be hard to ban them entirely without suggesting that the businesses themselves are illegitimate or that the town claims the paradoxical—and untenable—"right" to ban legitimate activities. In the case of prostitution, as we shall see, the efforts to cope with the problem through zoning (through the creation of "red light" districts) have proven largely unworkable and demoralizing. And they have failed to work precisely because they are devices for skirting the question of whether prostitution, as an occupation, ought to be regarded as legitimate or illegitimate.

The argument over prostitution cannot be settled, then, by charting material injuries and pointing to harmful, ancillary effects. None of these items of evidence can have a decisive weight in the absence of a showing that there is something in principle wrong with prostitution itself; and it is on that point, ultimately, that all other judgments must turn.

4. Prostitution and "Plain Sex": The Search for a Principled Argument

Whether prostitution has been legalized in any place or not, "prostitute" and "whore" have always functioned as terms of contempt. And if we sought to account for the source of this aversion, it would probably be found in the disparity that exists, in prostitution, between the special intimacy of the sexual act and a context that is radically unsuited to that intimacy. There are many tiers of closeness, we know, but there is nothing precisely equal to the intimacy of the sexual act and the moral portents that envelop it. The sense of "penetrating" and enclosing, of coupling embraces and fusing bodies, marks a relation quite apart from anything that is accorded even to close friends and confidants. It suggests the image of two bodies seeking to become one, and it draws to itself all of the symbolic import of a "union" or a "wedding." To admit a fusion in that way with another person would be unthinkable unless one were motivated by the deepest personal love. But to say that two people are bound together in love is to say that they are connected by more than a casual attraction. And that connection finds its proper ground when it proceeds from an understanding of those things which make one's partner truly worthy of being loved.

When that deeper source of attachment is present it becomes a proper ground for commitment. And few things express the sense of that commitment as literally as a tie made solemn and binding with the public imprint of law. Nothing could signify more precisely the nature of that commitment than the willingness of lovers to forego their own freedom to quit this relation when it no longer suits their convenience. It might be said that the union consecrated by law stands as the most appropriate symbol of a moral connection between lovers. For as we have seen, law arises in the most proper sense only from imperatives of moral standing; moral propositions entail the existence of law because the logic of morals is a logic of commitment. The binding of a marriage with law may draw to itself then the same sense of solemnity and moral import that invests the notion of "law."

In addition, of course, two people in a marriage will often produce children, who embody in their physical presence, in their mingling of features from both parents, the spiritual union of the two lovers. If the marriage does produce children, then it is all the more important that these children are brought into the world and nurtured in a setting that is already defined by the legal commitment of a marriage. I venture no commentary here on the question of whether "broken" homes are more destructive for children than families in which both parents are present. A single parent with goodness and sense would clearly be better than two indifferent and irresponsible parents. I simply take account of the fact that the first agency of moral tutelage for the child is inevitably the family, and in point of principle it matters profoundly that the child is introduced to the moral world through a structure that embodies visibly, concretely, the meaning of a moral commitment.

Perhaps it has been part of the odd appeal of prostitution over the years that it stands as a reproach to the conventions that reflect these moral understandings; but that is precisely the source also of the wrong that prostitution represents in principle. Prostitution inescapably implies that the intimacy of sexual intercourse need not be connected to any authentic sentiment of love and that it need not take place in a setting marked by the presence of commitment. In that sense it might be said that prostitution patronizes the corruption of physical love: it reduces physical love to the kind of hydraulic action that animals may share, and as it does that it detaches the act of intercourse from the kind of love that is distinctly human. The love that may arise between human beings is not simply a matter, after all, of successful orgasm; it may also involve, at its highest level, a respect for that character or principle of which one's partner is an example.

To the extent that prostitution disparages the notion of a love that is distinctly human, the argument has been made that prostitution strikes at those institutions, like the family, which depend most importantly on the ties of love. But care must be taken here to avoid the form and properties of an "empirical" argument. Principles clearly have consequences, and we ought to be aware that the erosion of certain moral understandings may have serious, adverse results for the family. And yet, the case against prostitution cannot depend on predictions of this kind. It cannot rest on any proposition to the effect that a higher incidence of prostitution will cause an increase in the breakup of families. Even if that notion found some statistical support, it would still represent nothing more than a *contingent* proposition, rather than a proposition that must hold true as a matter of necessity. At the same time, the argument would become vulnerable to any showing that certain people are in fact capable of preserving their families, along with a special love for their spouses, even while they seek other satisfactions in prostitution. The matter of the family becomes pertinent only as it stands as the instance of a larger principle that is engaged in the question of prostitution.

From that perspective, the importance of the family is that it is the most immediate school of moral instruction, and this moral import of the family is in fact central to its definition. A. I. Melden once pointed out that the obligations which children are thought to have to their parents cannot be entailed simply by a biological connection. A man who sires a child and then deserts his family cannot claim later the duties owed to a father. Those obligations are predicated on moral terms, on the understanding that the father has discharged the responsibilities of a parent in the care of his child.[24] Parental rights, then, cannot flow to a father simply by

---

[24] A. I. Melden, *Rights and Right Conduct* (Oxford: Basil Blackwell, 1959), Secs. III-VI, pp. 9-20.

virtue of his biological definition; they can be claimed only by the man who has fulfilled the *moral* definition of a father. We might say here more strictly what any child would understand: that a father who does not satisfy the moral definition of a father is not really a father; or, as the saying goes, he is a father in name only.

In the same way it could be said that a family is a family only in its moral definition. A natural biological group cannot be considered a family if it is not constituted in the first place on terms that recognize the binding force of principle. A man and woman "living together" informally with their child may furnish, for all we know, a sense of affection and care which exceeds that of many legal families. But quite apart from their performance, there is an independent ground of concern for the terms on which this "living arrangement" is constituted. There is something fearful in a family life whose founding doctrine is that no one may be bound ultimately when he chooses not to be bound. This doctrine is at war with the very notion of morals, and it is not hard to consider what its consequences may be if it comes to pervade the life of the family. (And if it is not meant to define the character of the family, we would be left to wonder why the partners would make this understanding the cornerstone of their "relationship.") It may be liberating to know that responsibilities are accepted out of affection rather than compulsion; and yet that sense may be fostered in many legal families as well, while the informal "living arrangements" are incapable of teaching what is manifest in the very constitution of a legal family. The child of an authoritarian father may find his parent disagreeable, but he may come to understand in a number of ways that his father is committed to certain responsibilities for his care by a law outside the family. He may know that the commitments of his parents cannot be discarded at will, and that his claim to their care will not end when he ceases to please them. In that way even some of the least appealing legal families may nevertheless impart to their children the meaning of lawfulness; and children who have absorbed that lesson have cultivated also an awareness of the rudiments of morals.

It does not strictly matter, then, what the evidence may tell us about the "health" of children raised in legal families or informal "living units." As a matter of principle—as an emanation from the very notion of principle itself—a family in its moral definition must be constituted by commitments made manifest in law; it must represent in its very structure an awareness of a moral universe; and if it does not have these features, it is not really a family.

Some critics may intervene at this point and grant all of this to
be true, but they may raise the question of why all sex must be
confined to the family, and why all sex must be "serious" sex. They
may concede, as Alan Goldman does, that sex may be affected with
a much larger significance when it is enveloped by love and commitment, but he would suggest, quite aptly, that many other prosaic
activities may also be transformed when they are animated by deep
personal love. (One thinks of a mother in middle years, anticipating
a visit from her married son, and concentrating all her loving care
in the preparation of his favorite tuna casserole.) And yet sex may
also be, as Goldman says, "plain sex": it may involve simply "a
desire for contact with another person's body and for the pleasure
which such contact produces."[25] What is central here is "the im-
mersion in the physical aspect of one's own existence and attention
to the physical embodiment of the other."

The serious mistake, says Goldman, comes in confusing love and
sex: there can be no such thing as "casual love" as there may be
"casual sex." Love, he suggests, is properly monogamous; it involves "a long-term, deep emotional relationship between two individuals." For that reason it is possible, as he argues, that men
and women may be attracted erotically to a number of people; they
may be drawn by the beauty of others, they may even extend their
love and admiration to people who genuinely merit love; but none
of this may disrupt the unique love and the special relation that
they have with one other person.

Still, what if that "other person" has a different reaction? What
if a wife happens to feel less "unique," and somehow diminished,
if the intimacies she regarded as special and exclusive were now
shared easily with many others? But if the issue really turned on
the injured feelings of spouses, then the problem would essentially
dissolve in those instances when the spouses do not object (and
where they may in fact claim the same franchise for themselves).
When the spouses do feel injured, the pursuit of sexual pleasure
may take on the additional purpose of inflicting injury on another,
and the sexual act, *in that aspect*, would be subject to condemnation. That kind of case would not be different from a class of
other cases in which people pursue their sexual pleasure in ways
that are designed to shock or assault others—for example, the men
who expose themselves in public, or the couples who have inter-

[25] Alan H. Goldman, "Plain Sex," *Philosophy and Public Affairs*, Vol. 6, no. 3
(Spring 1977), pp. 267-87, at 268.

course in the streets—and these people would no doubt be subject to reproach and restraint.

But when sexual intercourse is not used to harm another without justification, then it is Goldman's argument that it must be treated just like any other innocent activity that is pursued for its own pleasure. It has been a necessary part of my own argument in these pages that people have a claim to the exercise of their personal freedom in all of its expressions unless they do something that is in principle wrong, and it is only on the basis of a principle that the law may restrain that freedom. Goldman's argument probably ought to be understood in this light when he seeks to argue that "there are no moral implications whatever [in sex]. Any analysis of sex which imputes a moral character to sex acts in themselves is wrong for that reason. There is no morality intrinsic to sex, although general moral rules apply to the treatment of others in sex acts as they apply to all human relations."[26] That is, there is no morality intrinsic to sex any more than there is a morality intrinsic to driving a car or hitting a golf ball. But the man who drives recklessly, or the sportsman who finds his satisfaction in stroking his golf balls through other people's windows, may suffer the restraint of his freedom. And yet, until they misuse their freedom in this way, they have a right to their freedom to drive or play golf, and Goldman would make essentially the same claim for "plain sex" pursued, with an innocent mind, for the special pleasure that sex may afford.

If we have reservations about an argument of this kind, they would no doubt begin with the conviction, nourished by generations and consecrated by song, that there is, after all, something different about sex. Of course any activity may be innocent until it is directed toward wrongful ends, and on that point there would indeed be no difference between sex and parachute-jumping (though one should be fearful, I suppose, of marrying someone who did not know the difference). But sex may be different in ways that are morally significant, and the recognition that it is different is often borne out indirectly by people who are inclined to take an "advanced" position on matters of sex. A few years ago a group of undergraduate women at Yale demanded that rape should be recognized, in the code of student conduct, as a crime quite apart from others. Presumably assault was already a crime according to the statutes of

[26] Ibid., p. 280.

Yale, and if rape were nothing more than another assault—an unwarranted setting upon the body of another person—then it would have been no more necessary to make any further specifications for rape than it would have been to distinguish assaults directed at the head, say, from assaults directed at the legs. Why then should rape have been different?

There was an awareness, I think, of rape as not merely a striking of the body, but an act of larger arrogance and violation. There *is* something different, after all, about the penetration, the forceful access to an intimacy that is reserved only for people with whom the woman has a special connection. It may be hard to put the matter artfully, but it must be said also that this is an assault in which the assailant presumes to engage the reproductive capacity of the woman. That is, altogether, quite different from the average mugging or the lifting of a wallet: this assault, unlike other assaults, may actually generate new life, and one does not typically engage in anything as grave as that with anyone who just happens along on the street. And in the passions that have ever been aroused over this crime, the child that is conceived as the innocent issue of the crime has often been marked as a fit candidate for abortion, as though he were, in himself, a memorial to the trauma, or as though he somehow shared responsibility for the original crime. In that way there seems to be immanent in the agony of this violation an impulse to efface the original injustice with another one more lethal.

It is hard to account, I think, for the revulsion that marks rape as a crime apart from others without recognizing what is different about the intimacy of sex and the portentousness of reproduction. At the same time it should be apparent that the revulsion would not be diminished in any way by the news that the assailant or the victim was sterile. Our understanding of the crime is formed by our awareness of the special significance and the moral import that invests the act of sex. That is why the moral outrage which the crime elicits is virtually indifferent to any showing that the probability of conception in rape is very slight (which it is) or that the participants were incapable of generating children. The same reason may also inform the traditional objections to casual sexual encounters by people who may not seem impressed with the unique significance of sex, or who are conspicuously less than awed by an inventory of consequences that truly merits their awe.

But the outrage that has arisen traditionally in response to rape has had a tendency also to moderate with the showing that the woman involved was notoriously unselective in admitting people to her intimacies; that her consent, in effect, to enter was usually bestowed with no more hesitation than is shown by the average ticket-taker; and that she was willing to risk the engagement of her reproductive capacities—perhaps even with strangers in the dark— for a price that was not overly demanding. In short, the awareness of a wrong diminishes as the putative victim comes closer to that pattern of conduct which fits, more or less strictly, the sense of prostitution.

Again, the popular understanding here is probably a more ac-curate guide to the nature of the problem than the more ingenious offerings of social scientists. The wrong of prostitution cannot be found in any contingent reckonings about venereal disease, the stimulation of crime, or the breakup of families. It must be found rather in principle—in a principle, we might say, that begins with the awareness of principle itself and of beings that alone have access to the understanding of principles. The aversion to prostitution finds its proper ground in the recognition that there is something of inescapable moral significance about sex in creatures who may have moral reasons for extending or withdrawing their love; whose purposes in conceiving children may be enveloped with a far more complicated understanding than the motives that inspire procrea-tion in animals; and who treat as profoundly serious the terms of principle on which sexual franchises are tendered.

What is finally unacceptable, in principle, about prostitution is that it must deny implicitly this kind of significance in sex. It must reject this understanding because it is compelled to deny the ulti-mate and insistent sovereignty that is entailed in our lives, in all aspects of our lives, by the capacity of human beings for moral judgment. In that sense I think it may be said that the wrong of prostitution would be drawn, in Kantian fashion, from the idea of morals itself and from the nature of that creature which has the capacity for morals. It would arise, that is, as a matter of necessity if one is compelled to acknowledge the special significance of sex in creatures that have access to moral understanding.

5. Child Prostitution, Pornography, and "Legal Paternalism"

A friend recalled for me once, with lingering admiration, the broth-els he came to know in China and Japan after the Second World War. The services in those establishments were rendered with all the delicacy and exquisiteness that comes with the cultivation of a fine art. My friend began to make the case for legalized prostitution along the familiar lines of argument, and he contended, in addition, that the existence of legalized prostitution in China and Japan did not seem to threaten the institution of the family there (although he thought it might have a corrosive effect on that institution in the United States). But could prostitution be regarded, then, as a "business" just like other businesses? Would he have been willing to see his daughter work in a brothel during her vacations from school—as willing as he would be, say, to see her work in a restaurant or an office? The answer, unequivocally, was no.

If the argument I have been offering here is correct, this ultimate aversion to prostitution is grounded in something more substantial than convention, and it is not likely to disappear in future generations. We would expect that, twenty years from now, even parents holding the most advanced views are not likely to offer a standing ovation when their son announces that he is about to withdraw from medical school in order to become a male prostitute.[27] But the opinion of parents cannot be unaffected by the things that society teaches through the law about the kinds of occupations that are respectable; and if the laws become equivocal in regard to matters like prostitution and pornography, we should not be surprised to find even parents taking a more relaxed view of these enterprises, especially if they themselves can turn a small profit. The most bizarre example, which has burst upon us just in the past few years, is the growth of child prostitution and what has been called "kiddie porn" (or child pornography). Parents were found hiring out children as young as three and four years old to perform sexual acts for pornographic magazines and films. In January 1977 a couple in Colorado were arrested for "selling" their twelve-year-old son for sexual purposes for $3,000. In Rockford, Illinois a social worker was convicted for permitting his three adopted sons to perform sexual acts before a camera for $150 each.[28] In some cases the parents performed with their own children, and according to Judianne Densen-Gerber, this new vogue in incest managed to

---

[27] Of course if prostitution should ever become a legitimate profession, we should expect that it will show the same banal urges of other professions to adorn itself with a vocabulary that will support its pretensions to professionalism. Its practitioners will probably carry attaché cases, and state universities will probably offer both preprofessional and M.A. programs in Sexual Therapy, perhaps as part of an overall School of Therapeutic Sciences.

[28] *Congressional Record*, March 31, 1977, p. H2853.

produce, in two grotesque cases, gonorrhea of the throat in infants as young as 9 and 18 months old.[29]

These outrages produced one of the rare moments of unity these days in the political class of the country. Political figures and commentators, on the Left as well as the Right, joined the call for legislation. (The only reservations came from sections of the American Civil Liberties Union, which feared that the government might not merely prohibit the use of children in pornography, but that it might actually go on to prevent adults from viewing these productions!)[30] The result of this rising national sentiment was the act for the "Protection of Children Against Sexual Exploitation," which forbade the employment of children in pornographic enterprises. The act also carried penalties for parents and guardians who knowingly permitted their children to be used for these purposes.[31]

But the consensus that was achieved on this issue temporarily masked the differences among the supporters and the serious difficulties that some of them would have in working out a rationale for the legislation. It was no particular problem to support laws that restricted the use of children in prostitution and pornography if one was generally in favor of restricting both prostitution and pornography. And yet if one happened to believe that prostitution should be legalized or that pornography should generally be available without restriction to mature adults, then it was far harder to produce an argument that came anywhere near the expression of a principle. Dr. Densen-Gerber offered, for example, that children who were engaged in prostitution and pornography were more likely to become prostitutes as adults. But even if the evidence yielded very high correlations, it was obvious that not all of the children would become or remain prostitutes—and besides, Dr. Densen-Gerber thought prostitution ought to be legitimate for consenting adults. Could the "injury" of child pornography possibly inhere in the fact that it might dispose the children toward the adoption of what Dr. Densen-Gerber regarded as a legitimate profession? Could the same argument be made in relation to children who are permitted by their parents to work in Disney films:

[29] Notes on Press Conference, Washington, D.C. (February 14, 1977).

[30] See the statement of Ira Glasser reported in the *Congressional Record*, March 31, 1977, p. H2853.

[31] 18 U.S.C.A. 2252 (1978). The problem of prostitution was covered under the old "White Slave Act," but Congress amended the section on the "Coercion or enticement of minor female" and changed it to the "Transportation of minors." In that way the Act was broadened to take in male children as well. 18 U.S.C.A. 2423.

that they would be condemned to grow into adult actors for Disney?

In the absence of a principled argument, there is a tendency these days to bring forth psychologists who are more than ready to testify about the presence of psychological injuries or traumas. These effects were clearly present and the testimony was duly offered. But this mode of argument suffers persisting embarrassment in the face of evidence that some of these children seem not to have been in the least bit unhinged by the experience, and in fact they might have liked it very much. At this point the resourceful analyst will often come to the revelation that these latter children may be "injured" even more gravely, for they show no discomfort from their involvement in debasing acts. For some reason the point seems usually to be missed that it is the "debasing" quality of the act that elicits our condemnation; the search for psychic injuries comes only after we have formed the judgment that we are in the presence of a wrong, and that normal people, under these circumstances, should probably suffer adverse effects. If we could simply explain in the first place why the use of children in pornography and prostitution is debasing, there would be no need for any psychological testimony: if the act is in principle wrong, its wrongness is independent of the fact that some of the participants and the putative victims find pleasure in it. But then what exactly is that principle? Or how can it be articulated without raising a fundamental question about the legitimacy of prostitution and pornography themselves?

The easiest rationale, for the Left as well as the Right, was that the legislation, after all, was about minors. With a few notable exceptions, it was still common to assume that young people do not have the maturity to manage the most consequential decisions in their lives, and restrictions have been accepted on minors that would not be established for adults. It was thought, in this respect, that the engagement in sexual acts for public display was one such grave matter that minors might not have the maturity to determine for themselves. (This judgment was freely offered, it must be said, even by people who were also quite convinced that minors had the maturity to decide for themselves whether to have abortions, without the knowledge or consent of their parents.) Beyond that, it was argued that the employment of children in pornography could be treated without strain as another incident in the restriction of child labor more generally.

And yet that explanation did not entirely satisfy. The restrictions on child labor carried many exemptions, and some of the most notable were the exemptions granted to children to act in legitimate movies or to model clothes in catalogues. There was reason to believe that children who were thrust, at young ages, into the role of celebrities could suffer alterations in personality and character that were not always wholesome. It was apparent, also, that the parents who sought to propel their children to stardom were often moved by impulses that were no less self-serving than the motivations of those parents who traded off the careers of their children in pornography. But the legislation on child pornography was supported, as I have said, by many people who professed to regard the production of pornography as a legitimate business, as legitimate as making movies for Disney and catalogues for Sears. It goes without saying that there was no move to restrict children from participating in movies for Disney or modeling in catalogues for Sears, and the obvious question must be put: Why this discrimination? Would it not be apparent that the difference between the cases must turn, not on the labor of children, but on the things that separate Disney movies and Sears catalogues from pornography and prostitution? And how could the legislation be defended then unless we were finally able to explain what it is that makes prostitution and pornography *in principle* offensive in a way that Disney movies and Sears catalogues are not?

It is interesting that many people who have often derided "paternalism" in the law have been quite willing in this particular case to displace the judgment made by real parents about the best interests of their children. Of course the opponents of legal paternalism have been concerned about the intervention of the law in relations between consenting adults, when no one is likely to be injured except the participants themselves.[32] Libertarians have insisted in these cases that mature adults be permitted to decide for themselves whether they are injured or gratified by any experience. Still, they have insisted on drawing the line between adults and children, and they have never suggested that the law ought to recede from its responsibility to protect children from injury at the hands of their parents.

But having said all of that, there is still a serious problem here for the opponents of paternalism. Prostitution and pornography are two celebrated examples of the kinds of activities in which governments have been accused of practicing legal paternalism. What must be implicit in this criticism is the conviction that there is no ground of principle that stamps prostitution and pornography

[32] See Joel Feinberg, "Legal Paternalism," *Canadian Journal of Philosophy*, Vol. 1 (1971), pp. 105-24.

unambiguously as wrong, and in that event the law ought to leave
people free to form their own preferences. If that were true, however, on what ground could it be known, unequivocally, that prostitution and pornography must be harmful for children? If the matter must be open to the judgment of adults—if one decision, among
adults, is as plausible as another—why should we not permit the
mature parent to exercise the same judgment on behalf of his child
as the law is willing to let him exercise for himself? How could the
law remove this particular decision from the parents without saying,
as a matter of necessity, that there is a wrong here which does not
depend for its wrongness on the tastes and eccentricities of the
parents? But the law could not say that there is something in principle wrong about prostitution and pornography for children without suggesting at the same time that there may be something about
prostitution and pornography which retains its wrongness in principle for adults as well.

For many years the opposition to so-called "legal paternalism"
has confounded the public discussion of matters like prostitution,
and yet that opposition has been founded essentially on a mistake.
It has depended mainly on the failure to grasp the logic of a moral
principle and the necessary connection between principle and law.
Once that connection is understood, it takes but an additional step
to recognize that if something is in principle wrong, the wrongness
is not affected in any way by the consent of the participating adults.
Nor would it be diminished by a showing that the victim of the
wrong actually found a perverse pleasure in the experience. If a
mugger carries out an unjustified assault on the street, that assault
is still wrong even if the victim turned out to be a masochist who
craved a second helping.

But the most compelling example is one I suggested earlier: it has
been pointed out that, from the standpoint of the prospective slave,
the sacrifice of personal freedom for long-term employment and
security might well be a rational arrangement. And yet even if we
found slaves who wished to be slaves, who willingly offered their
consent to be slaves, we could not honor that insistence, any more
than we have been willing to enforce contracts for peonage. The
problem is that the wrongness of slavery is grounded in principle,
in the propositions which establish why it is wrong to rule human
beings in the way that one may rule creatures that lack the capacity
for reason. The consent of the would-be slave is irrelevent because
he simply lacks the competence to repeal those basic conditions
existing in nature which separate human beings from animals. This

understanding of a right that cannot be effaced or waived conveys the sense of what used to be called an "inalienable" right. A generation schooled to the notion of "inalienable" rights found nothing strange in the notion that individuals may have to be restrained at times from doing injury to themselves. Hence the willingness, for example, to ban dueling, even though it may have the consent of the participating adults. Presumably the same state of mind is reflected in the disposition to require motorcyclists to wear helmets and automobile drivers to wear seat belts, even when they would prefer to take their chances without them. I would not say that these kinds of regulations are as justified as the ban on dueling; I would simply note that this kind of regulation is not apparently regarded as unthinkable, even on the part of people who rail against legal paternalism in the restraint of things like prostitution.

But the heart of the matter here was recognized long ago by Kant, and he put the question in this way: On what ground may an individual properly bind himself or forego his right, as a moral being, to legislate for himself? The answer, very simply, was that he may bind himself on the same grounds by which he may be bound by others and by the law itself: that is, he may be bound on the basis of a moral principle that he, as well as others, would be obliged to respect.[33] And so if it would be wrong for one person to take the life of another because that other person is addicted, irredeemably, to the splitting of infinitives, then it would follow, with inexorable logic, that one could not use the same, insupportable reason as a justification for taking one's own life.

6. Pornography and Its Teaching

In the presence of a principle, then, the law finds its proper ground, and the arguments about "legal paternalism" would essentially be dissolved into irrelevance. If there is a ground of principle for the rejection of prostitution, the concern for the consent of the participating adults would virtually have no moral standing. I have linked prostitution and pornography in this section, for I think it becomes apparent, on reflection, that the same considerations which explain the wrong of prostitution would explain what is wrong in principle about pornography as well. ("Pornography" derives, in fact, from the Greek *pornographos*: writing about the lives of prostitutes.) There is a connection between the willingness to engage in sexual

---

[33] Kant, *Metaphysics of Morals*, 417-18.

acts for money with strangers and the willingness to engage in sexual acts for money with a variety of "colleagues" and near-strangers for the viewing of an audience. But the addition of an audience in pornography raises an issue that was not strictly raised by prostitution. The performers partake of the wrong implicit in prostitution and pornography, but what of the viewers of pornography? They do not themselves engage in the offensive acts, and so the question may be put: What harm do they do, after all, to themselves or to others, through their roles as innocent spectators? On what ground, then, may the law restrict their freedom to command, for their entertainment, the improper acts of others?

It would be hard to find an entertainer or artist who would assent to the proposition that entertainment and the arts are essentially without effect in shaping the culture, the tastes, even the moral understandings of a people. The arts do indeed have consequence. Plays, books, films—all of them teach. They have themes and they hold up models of behavior; they are frequently imitated in ordinary life; and so, in one way or another, they are engaged in moral instruction. If that is the case, the community could hardly be unconcerned about the things that are taught or the culture that is cultivated through entertainments. As Walter Berns put it, "the laws cannot remain indifferent to the manner in which men amuse themselves, or to the kinds of amusements offered them":

> We turn to the arts—to literature, films, and the theatre, as well as to the graphic arts . . . —for the pleasure to be derived from them, and pleasure has the capacity to form our tastes and thereby to affect our lives. It helps determine the kind of men we become, and helps shape the lives of those with whom and among whom we live.[34]

It is widely assumed today that the level of violence portrayed on television can have unwholesome effects, and so steps have been urged to reduce the quotient of violence even though the market among adults would sustain a strong preference for this mode of entertainment. In that respect we are reminded that we have accepted censorship or restraint of quite a number of "public entertainments," even though they threaten no harm to the viewers that is immediately evident. The judgment has been settled for some

[34] Walter Berns, "Pornography vs. Democracy: A Case for Censorship," *The Public Interest* (Winter 1971), pp. 3-24, at 10. Also see H. Montgomery Hyde, *A History of Pornography* (New York: Farrar, Straus and Giroux, 1964).

time that executions generally ought not be treated as public spectacles, and that decision cannot be explained by a simple aversion to taking the life of the prisoner. The prisoner was not meant to be killed for the sake of the crowd, and it is possible, even today, to support capital punishment while holding, at the same time, that executions should not become a new form of public entertainment. The concern, I think, is that even if an execution may be justified in some cases, people should not be encouraged to develop a morbid fascination with these spectacles. There is something highly disturbing about people who can cultivate a certain sadistic pleasure in watching the suffering of others, and one cannot help feeling that people who leave the theater of execution after experiencing this kind of excitement are people who have been made substantially worse. Beyond that, the polity may be a worse place for having them present, among others, as fellow citizens.

For similar reasons, there have been bans on such amusements as bearbaiting and cockfighting. Cockfighting has been going on surreptitiously, but it has been denied the kind of prominence it might well command if the law did not forbid it as a public entertainment. We may properly be concerned for the treatment of the animals in these cases, but that alone does not exhaust our interest. We may be concerned also for the sensibilities of those consenting adults who find their amusement in these rituals of violence.

What is suggestive here is that even people who have described themselves as ardent liberals on questions of censorship and the arts have come to acknowledge recently in public that a legitimate case for censorship might be made. Not too long ago, for example, Gerald Jonas wrote in *The New York Times* about a movie called "The Street Fighter." Jonas had viewed an uncut version of this film, which included scenes in which one man killed an aspiring rapist by tearing off his genitals and then murdered another man by digging his nails into the throat of the victim and pulling out his Adam's apple. In both cases the successful combatant made his flourish of victory by holding up his trophies. The reviewer was finally moved to this admission: "I walked into the theater a firm foe of censorship in any shape or form, especially censorship dealing with the human body and its natural functions. I came out of the theater sick to my stomach at the thought of any child being allowed to see what I had just seen."[35] But what could be said on this point in relation to children surely could be said with equal plausibility

[35] *The New York Times*, May 11, 1975, p. D13.

in relation to older people who may still be rather immature and suggestible. Presumably Mr. Jonas did not think that the film, in its uncut form, should be shown to *any* audience, and it is hard to argue that the film should be available to those adults who *wish* to see it. If we apply the reasoning that underlies our judgments about public executions and cockfights, it is precisely the people who very much wish to have this entertainment who ought not have it.

If it is clear, then, that entertainments may affect the moral sensibilities of the public, and if we have been willing to restrict the entertainment of adults out of a concern for the tastes that are cultivated or the principles that are taught, then the question must be asked: Why not pornography? Why should pornography be exempted from the kinds of questions and regulations we are willing to apply to other forms of public entertainment? Pornography may succeed as well as the others in making its audience suggestible to its themes, and so it is pertinent to consider here, as in other cases, just what is being taught.

When shorn of its larger pretensions, the purpose of pornography is probably nothing more than to arouse the appetite for sex by depicting sexual acts with great variety and explicitness. It may not even be inconsistent with the character of pornography to portray the intensity of sexual experience in situations confined to marriage. And yet it is the condition of this genre that it is incapable of developing with any authenticity the relations of love that add meaning to sexual intercourse. Its own dynamics of justification—its compulsion to develop an ideology for itself—quickly push it, by necessity, beyond the realm of sexual acts confined to the contexts of marriage and love. What is distinct to pornography, finally, is the portrayal of sexual intercourse with uncommon frequency and variety, without the restrictions of marriage or the tethers of commitment. (In the case of sodomy, the intercourse may not even be restricted to members of the same species.) What is taught in pornography is an eroticism detached from any love that is distinctly human—which is to say, a love that is affected by the bonds of loyalty and moral understanding that are uniquely possible in human beings.

In that measure, pornography depends on the same premises that define the wrong of prostitution. The problem posed for the consumer of pornography is that, as he enters vicariously into the experiences portrayed in pornography, he may absorb very readily the principles implicit in the enterprise. And yet even more directly, he may help to confirm, through his presence in the theater, the very premises on which pornography and prostitution rest. He becomes part of an audience of voyeurs, and in that way he participates in the removal of sexual intercourse from a context of intimacy. But if sexual intercourse ought to be affected by a sense of love and commitment, it has been thought to require a shelter of intimacy for the sake of its own integrity. If "intimacies" were to be shared with a larger public, they would cease to hold that special quality they possess when they are reserved exclusively for the relation of two lovers. To admit the public to the sphere of one's intimate relations is to remove the sanctity of those relations, and by exposing to public view the most private acts, one would be manifesting, as Walter Berns argues, a critical sense of shamelessness. To be shameless is to suggest that there is indeed nothing to be embarrassed about, and one can preserve that kind of serenity only if one is unaffected by any sense of the things that truly deserve shame and rebuke.[36]

Shamelessness is possible as a way of life only in the absence of those standards which make it possible to know the difference between the good and the bad, the admirable and the shameful. And the explicit, strident ideology of pornography is that there is in fact no basis for shame or apology because there are no tenable standards of moral judgment. As the advertisement for one X-rated film proclaimed, "Nothing can be bad if it feels good." Blurbs may be no more than blurbs, but this particular aphorism does convey, in its root simplicity, the premises of those who have sought to defend pornography. The defense of pornography has had to take the line that all forms of expression in the arts and politics stand essentially on the same plane of legitimacy, that there are no grounds on which to say with any truth that one publication is more decent or noxious than another. In this view, the only principle acceptable in a democratic government is *that there are no principles* on which to say that certain interests and ideas are any more legitimate than others. By this logic it cannot even be said that a government of law is preferable to a despotism, or that personal freedom is superior in principle to slavery. There is a rejection here, in other words, of those necessary truths that a free people is obliged to respect because they establish the premises on which its own political freedom rests.

To say that "nothing can be bad if it feels good" is to dissolve

---

[36] Berns, note 34 above, p. 13.

the tension that may exist between the moral and the pleasant. It suggests that there is no ground on which to call into question any occupation that happens to give people pleasure, whether it is genocide or torture or even self-mutilation. And of course the position expressed here would have to uphold the decision of the man who finds personal contentment in slavery, and who willingly alienates his own freedom. The defense of pornography is ultimately at odds, then, with the premises of democratic government, and for that reason, as Walter Berns points out, pornography cannot be "politically uninteresting,"[37] even when it would appear to be wholly apolitical. But if the argument for pornography strikes at the premises of democratic government, it is only because it denies, at a more fundamental level, the notion of morals itself and the special capacity of human beings for moral understanding.

7. LIBERALITY AND CENSORSHIP: A NEW SCHEME OF REGULATION

I do not mean to brush aside the vexing question of how one defines more precisely the standards that ought to guide the law in the control of pornography. But the difficulty of the legislative task has largely been overstated in the past. A statute could be drawn with fair precision that covers the range of explicit sexual acts which are portrayed in pornography, but without identifying pornography simply with nudity or with the candid treatment of sexual matters. That is to say, the drafters of a statute may well choose to set forth, as many have done, the inventory of sexual acts that may not be portrayed explicitly (and it would be a sufficient reason to act here simply to avert the debasement or prostitution of the actors themselves). But the statutes could also be sensitive to the distinctive themes that mark the character of pornography.[38] Ordinary terms of art are capable of conveying the sense of a film, for example, in which the story is a thin cover and the "action" is predominantly of that hydraulic kind to which pornography reduces the act of love. A reasonable observer would be able to tell the difference between a production of that type and a film or play

[37] Ibid., p. 10.

[38] A fair model of the more technical and limited statutes may be found in the appendix of Richard Kuh's book, *Foolish Figleaves? Pornography in—and out of—Court* (New York: Macmillan, 1967), pp. 253-56. See also the thoughtful commentary of Harry Clor in *Obscenity and Public Morality* (Chicago: University of Chicago Press, 1969), ch. 6.

in which obscenity may be used as it was by a Shakespeare: sparingly, strategically, with a pronounced, concentrated effect in pointing up what is base.

Reasonable statutes can be drawn with as much precision as one can bring, for example, to problems of defamation or offensive speech, and they can be applied reasonably with the same arts of judgment. The enforcement of the laws can then be left, with advantage, to local governments, in a design very close to the one laid out by the Supreme Court in *Miller* v. *California*.[39] In this decentralized arrangement, any mistakes that are made by officials or juries at the local level may be confined to the neighborhood where the action took place. The mistakes need not be elevated to the level of principle and incorporated in our national law.

What I have in mind, then, is a local licensing board, and I know of no law of nature which requires that licensing boards be filled exclusively with members of the Legion of Decency and the Women's Christian Temperance Union. It is conceivable that the board may represent a wider range of opinion within the local community. It may contain such unfamiliar characters as professors of English and Dramatic Arts, and even liberals who are known to be hostile to the conventions of censorship. Let us suppose, further, that the board may work under rules that require a substantial degree of agreement among the members before restrictions may be imposed on any movies or books. A design of this nature could serve to reconcile a number of ends: as a practical matter, the administration of the law under these conditions would preserve a wide latitude of free expression. The only movies or books likely to be censored would be those which could command a consensus on the board. Borderline cases would probably be dropped, and the law would tend to be reserved only for the most unambiguous cases, which raise the clearest issues in principle.

But if this arrangement would preserve, overall, a large measure of freedom, it would still have the value of establishing the legitimacy of censorship in principle. It would help to dissolve the crude notion that censorship must imply a desire to censor widely; and if it helps to dispel that misunderstanding, a regimen of this kind may have the advantage of fixing attention where it properly belongs: on the questions of principle that are raised by pornography and that call forth the policy of censorship. For the larger purposes

---

[39] 413 U.S. 15 (1973); *Paris Adult Theatre I* v. *Slaton*, 413 U.S. 49 (1973). See also Berns, note 34 above, pp. 23-24.

of the law, it does not matter that only a small number of films may be censored. The purpose of the law is to teach, and it may teach with the most pronounced effect in a smaller number of cases which admit clearer lessons. In the meantime, the fact that censorship is accepted in principle helps to establish many fundamental points of understanding in the public mind, even if the censorship is exercised rarely. It would establish, for example, that the public arts and entertainments are not beyond moral judgment; that standards of moral judgment exist; and that they are knowable. And if the standards of moral judgment can be known, they can be discovered and applied in contexts other than the arts. They can be applied by individuals in their private lives, even on subjects that the law does not strain to reach; and they can be applied by the community in other matters of consequence—in other questions of justice and propriety—that arise among people who are bound together in a polity.

XV

ON PRINCIPLES AND EXPERIENCE: REPUBLICAN VIRTUE AND THE ENFORCEMENT OF MORALITY

1. THE "LEGALIZATION" OF VICE AND THE TRADITIONAL UNDERSTANDING

Those who have resisted the use of the law in regulating "vices" have usually misconceived the ends of the law, just as they have confounded the moral with the moralistic. It is one thing to recognize that human beings have a capacity for morals and principled argument; it is quite another to assume that all human beings may be brought to the perfect virtue of saints. As I will take care to recall more fully in a moment, the concept of law has relevance only for beings who are neither gods nor animals. The logic of the law cannot be detached from the logic of morals, and the law cannot be understood apart from its moral ends and justifications. But if the end of the polity traditionally has been to cultivate a sense of morals or justice in citizens, it has been understood, also, that the law cannot eradicate all vice. What the law has usually sought to do here, with a proper modesty, is to contain vices within acceptable limits. In this understanding, it was thought to be better that vices appear to the public as examples of those shortcomings incidental to human nature, which a decent society puts off to the side, in its seedier precincts. That state of affairs was far preferable to one in which the vices held a place in the center of the society, where they could absorb the wealth and patronage of the best citizens and affect the tone of the community. This older view was conveyed in its essential lines by the statutes established in Florence in 1415. The laws declared that

> Desiring to eliminate a worse evil by means of a lesser one, the lord priors . . . [and their colleges] have decreed that . . . the priors . . . [and their colleges] may authorize the establishment of two public brothels in the city of Florence, in addition to the one which already exists: one in the quarter of S. Spirito and the other in the quarter of S. Croce. [They

are to be located] in suitable places or in places where the exercise of such scandalous activity can best be concealed, for the honor of the city and of those who live in the neighborhood in which these prostitutes must stay to hire their bodies for lucre . . .[1]

The traditional understandings that lay behind these statutes may be set forth rather simply. It was thought, with considerable reason, that if certain vices were made lawful, if the legal inhibitions were removed or lessened, those vices would expand far beyond their present dimensions. They would acquire a position of larger prominence and they would begin to draw off people and resources from other, more legitimate callings. At the same time, it was anticipated that activities of a correlative nature would develop, as one form of vice feeds upon another. When certain vices become legal, a network of illegal vice will often grow up alongside the legal operations, offering services and conditions that are beyond the current limits of the law. This growth of the illegal network has been the most ironic feature in the experience of "legalization." It is the feature that rarely fails to surprise, for it cuts against the common assumption that legalization will bring about atrophy in the underground network or in the operations of organized crime.

Yet there is a very straightforward explanation as to why, persistently, things seem to turn out in this way. The problem may be seen quite clearly in the case of legalized gambling. In the early 1970's New York moved to legalize a system of offtrack betting (OTB for short), with the hope of gathering some revenue for itself and undercutting the illegal network in gambling. After the system was underway it was estimated, however, that six dollars continued to flow within the illegal network for every dollar that moved through the legal betting parlors. When offtrack betting had been in operation for over a year, two economists from the City University of New York discovered that the system had a "devastating" effect on attendance at race tracks and on the revenues that the state collected from parimutuel betting; but the arrangement seemed to have little effect overall on illegal bookmaking.[2]

---

[1] *The Society of Renaissance Florence*, Gene Brucker, ed. (New York: Harper, 1971), p. 190.

[2] *The New York Times*, November 18, 1972, p. 45. In the estimate of the two economists, Gary Ross and Douglas Coates, the state lost $11.4 million in revenue as a result of a decline in business at the racetracks that could be attributed to Offtrack Betting. At the same time, OTB brought in only about $5 million in revenue during its first fiscal year. *The New York Times*, November 3, 1972, p. 46.

Nor should the reasons have been very hard to fathom. When the state itself declared gambling to be legitimate—and when, beyond that, it actually urged the public, in its advertising, to go out and place bets—the state subtly swept aside the moral reservations that still made many people reluctant to gamble. If there was nothing in principle wrong with gambling itself, it was only a matter then of betting at the places that would yield the highest returns. By that measure, of course, the highest return would be available in the illegal network, where the operators did not have to skim off a large share of their earnings in the form of taxes, and where they did not have to work under the parimutuel requirements for dividing the stakes of losers. And since the state had already created the convenience of betting in one's own neighborhood, without the need to visit the race track, one might as well place one's bets with the neighborhood "firm" where there could also be arrangements for credit. But by this point, with most of the moral inhibitions washed away, the main calculation turned on the avoidance of taxes, and everyone, after all, cheated a bit on his taxes.

In New Jersey it was reported that organized crime had been using the legal daily "numbers" game, but with one major difference: the payoffs in the illegal game were ten times higher. For three consecutive digits of the five-digit winning number, a fifty-cent bet could bring a return of $250 in the underground game. The same bet could yield only $25 in the game run by the state. As it was observed by the Superintendent of the State Police, who testified before a legislative commission on gambling, the state lottery had not driven the illegal numbers racket out of business. In fact, the lottery was providing a new convenience for the illegal operators by allowing them to determine and publicize their daily winner on the same day. "Ingenious," said one member of the commission, "simply ingenious."[3]

The same kind of symbiotic relation seems to have developed in New York between the offtrack betting operations and the illegal bookmakers. The bookmakers were apparently willing to spin off many of their small bets of $10 or less to the legal betting outlets (there were reported cases in which bettors were actually referred by their bookies to the offtrack betting).[4] Some surveys showed that with the establishment of legal offtrack betting in New York the share of a bookmaker's business devoted to horse racing declined

---

[3] *The New York Times*, December 7, 1972, pp. 1, 56.

[4] National Advisory Committee on Criminal Justice Standards and Goals, *Report of the Task Force on Organized Crime* (Washington, 1976), p. 221.

from about 50 percent to 10 percent.[5] And yet it is evident that some of this reduction in business reflected the preferences of the bookies themselves, who were specializing in higher bets or moving into newer lines of betting. According to one estimate, the amount of money bet on horses in New York in a year is about $150 million, compared to $1 billion as the total amount bet on sports of all kinds.[6] In any event, it is clear that legalized betting in New York has not had a corrosive effect on illegal betting. On the contrary, by making gambling respectable and exhorting people to bet, the state has cultivated a new interest in gambling. The result is that the volume of gambling seems to have risen, and the illegal network has taken a large share of this new business (as, indeed, anyone of sense would have expected). And so, while the offtrack betting might have reduced the total share of the market held by illegal operations, the policy of legalized gambling enlarged the size of the whole pie, so to speak. In January 1974 it was estimated that illegal gambling had increased by 62 percent in dollar volume since offtrack betting went into effect.[7]

The fact of the matter is that there are rather hard alternatives that block the state at every turn and make it highly doubtful that the state can ever dislodge the illegal network unless it puts itself, increasingly, in the role played by organized crime. The state cannot offer the kinds of payoffs offered by organized crime unless it is willing to take the same kinds of chances that the private entrepreneurs take. But in that case it would be the taxpayers who would have to bail out the state in order to cover its losses in gambling—a situation that would be, on all counts, indefensible. If the state tries to insure itself against losses by using parimutuel regulations and taking care that all of its bets are covered, it will not be able to provide the payoffs that the underground network can dangle before its customers. And if the state taxes the winnings of gamblers, it will clearly lose business to the illegal operations. The recent decline in illegal gambling in Las Vegas has been attributed to the fact that the federal tax on wagers was reduced from 10 percent to 2 percent;[8] and a recent report of the government has urged the

---

[5] Ibid.

[6] David Weinstein and Lillian Deitch, *The Impact of Legalized Gambling: The Socio-Economic Consequences of Lotteries and Off-Track Betting* (New York: Praeger, 1974), p. 141.

[7] *Report of the Task Force on Organized Crime*, p. 234, and letter from Gerald Eskenazi (of *The New York Times*) to the writer, September 20, 1977.

[8] *The New York Times*, January 20, 1975, p. 1.

removal of taxes on gambling altogether.[9] What is awkward in the proposal, however, is that the public would benefit immensely from the removal of taxes from all other businesses (which are mainly passed on to the consumer anyway). The elimination of taxes on gambling may be acceptable as part of a larger design for the removal of taxes on business, but in the absence of a definite move in that direction (which politicians in both parties have been promising, but not providing), it would be indecorous, to say the least, if the government picked out the gambling industry for this special privilege and encouragement. It would be equivalent to a positive decision on the part of the government to make gambling and its ancillary activities a more prominent part of our national life.

The same general dilemmas that attend the problem of gambling would apply to many other cases in which the government seeks an easy cure to certain vices through the simple expedient of rendering them legal. One of the most notable examples here would be the issue of abortion: despite all the glib assumptions that have been broadcast on this question, it is highly unlikely that a strategy of "legalization" will eliminate illegal abortions, and it may not even reduce their number. It is sobering to consider that in Denmark and Sweden, which adopted fairly liberal abortion laws in 1939, there was a large increase in both the number and rate of legal *and* illegal abortions. In Denmark, for example, in the twenty years after 1939, the population had increased by some 20 percent, the number of live births had grown by about 25 percent, but the number of legal abortions had multiplied by a factor of ten, and the number of illegal abortions was thought to be anywhere from two to fifteen times as high as it was in 1939. In 1964, Denmark registered 3,936 legal abortions, against an estimated 12,000 to 15,000 illegal abortions.[10]

To the embarrassment of many people, the same trend began to manifest itself in the initial days of the "liberalized" abortion laws in New York State. The legislature in 1970 permitted abortions up to the twenty-fourth week of pregnancy, and yet, from the number of people who were admitted to hospitals with the effects of botched abortions, it appeared that illegal abortions were persisting even

[9] *Report of the Commission on the Review of National Policy Toward Gambling* (Washington: Government Printing Office, 1976).

[10] See John M. Finnis, "Three Schemes of Regulation," in John T. Noonan, Jr., ed., *The Morality of Abortion* (Cambridge: Harvard University Press, 1970), pp. 172-211, at 183 and n. 31.

under the new legal regimen. The explanation put forth in official circles was that many women were still unaware of the law, and that many of them (especially those with little education) were uncomfortable in dealing with impersonal institutions such as city hospitals and clinics. It was expected that, as the public became more familiar with the law, more women would be drawn away from illegal operations. And, in fact, as time went on, more women were encouraged to come in at earlier stages in their pregnancies, when the operation promised to be safer, and there were some signs that the number of illegal abortions had declined.

An alternative view, however, was that the legislation had simply broken down the inhibitions that many people still had about abortion. Once the public had become schooled to the notion that abortions were morally acceptable—and indeed that one may have a "right" to an abortion—it became hard to understand just what it was in principle that distinguished the twenty-fifth from the twenty-fourth week. It was possible, then, that many women in a more advanced stage of pregnancy simply sought to make other arrangements for themselves, outside of clinics that observed the restrictions of the law. (By that point, of course, complications were more likely to develop, and as the casualties began showing up in hospitals, a rough estimate could be formed of the number of illegal abortions that were taking place.) It bears mention, too, that the cost of an abortion was $500 in the early months of the law. In about a year the cost would be cut to $125-$150 at some clinics, with even lower figures for the poor.[11]

In January 1973 the Supreme Court intervened with its decision in *Roe* v. *Wade*,[12] and with that decision the very structure of things would change. Most of the restrictions on abortion would disappear; the cost of these operations would be driven further downward; and the federal government, through Medicaid, would pick up the cost of abortions for the poor. By 1977 it was reported that the federal government was paying for 300,000 abortions annually (one third of the number every year) at a cost of $50 million.[13] This state of affairs seemed to be brought to a halt in the spring of 1977, when the Supreme Court upheld the refusal of state governments to support abortions with public funds.[14] The result of the decision

[11] See *The New York Times*, October 8, 1972, pp. 1, 20.

[12] 410 U.S. 113 (1973).

[13] *Washington Post*, June 7, 1977, p. A13.

[14] *Maher* v. *Roe* 432 U.S. 464; *Beal* v. *Doe* 432 U.S. 439; and *Poelker* v. *Doe* 432 U.S. 519.

was to sustain, also, the refusal of the Congress to provide federal money for abortions. Still, the right of a woman to have an abortion on her own, with practically no restraint from the law, has been essentially unaffected. The Supreme Court has virtually granted to the pregnant woman (and her physician) what amounts to a right to order an abortion for considerations of convenience that may have little to do with a threat to the life of the mother. By this point, therefore, the concept of an illegal abortion may be nearly outmoded.

And, yet, in view of all these changes, it is astonishing that even one or two cases of illegal abortion crop up every year, as they do, for example, in the District of Columbia.[15] What the incidence of illegal abortion may be even now one cannot tell, for a decision has been made apparently, in the highest official circles of the medical profession, to "eliminate" the problem of illegal abortions simply by refusing to collect evidence on the point.[16] But in Britain, where a policy of legalized abortions has been in effect for a number of years, the experience has been closer to that of Sweden and Denmark. According to some recent testimony from Dr. Margaret White, the figures in Britain for discharges from hospitals for the effects of nonlegal abortions have held steady between 1964 and 1972 at a level of 50,000.[17] Of course there have been slightly more restrictions on abortion in Britain, Sweden, and Denmark than in the United States. There is the need to go through some lingering charade over the "psychological health" of the mother, with the whole business given a more serious and professional cast by the inclusion of medical review committees. The procedures do not apparently contribute much to expose the speciousness of the concepts they apply; but they do serve to delay matters a bit, and in the delay that ensues, women who are inclined to seek an abortion will find an interest in procuring one earlier, even by an operation that is illegal.

It can be expected, generally, that the number of illegal abortions will rise in the United States with every serious restriction that is placed on abortions. For example, the Supreme Court suggested

[15] Information from Warren Morse, Department of Research and Statistics, Bureau of Clinical Services, District of Columbia, April 25, 1977.

[16] The omission was quite noticeable in the study of legalized abortion that was published under the auspices of the National Academy of Sciences. See *Institute of Medicine, Legalized Abortion and the Public Health* (Washington: National Academy of Sciences, 1975).

[17] *Obstetrical and Gynecological News*, March 15, 1977, p. 38.

in *Roe* v. *Wade* that restrictions might be placed on abortions during the first trimester for the sake of providing for the health of the mother. Governed by that understanding, the Supreme Court upheld a statute in Connecticut that required abortions to be performed only by licensed physicians.[18] The decision further undercut the notion that the laws on abortion may be premised on the right of the mother to do whatever she wishes with the issue of her own body. If the state can restrain the mother and enforce its sense of what her own good requires, it is hard to see why it cannot restrain her to protect the life of the human being in the womb.[19] On the other hand, if the "right" to an abortion hinges on the right of a woman to control her own body, it is not at all clear as to how the Court would deny to the woman the right to take the kinds of risks with her own body that she regards as acceptable. And, yet, if the Court does uphold restrictions, if it allows the states to insist that abortions be performed only by physicians in licensed clinics, it may effectively create a dual market for abortions: the abortions can always be performed less expensively through the use of paramedicals and aspiring midwives who are not confined to clinics, and who can operate with lower fees. (And this says nothing, of course, about the appeals that may be exerted by the do-it-yourself abortion kits that are reportedly beginning to appear on the market.)

Of course, for many proponents of abortion the existence of some illegal abortions was always taken as an argument in itself for making the operation legal, and the persistence of illegal abortions, even after abortions are legal, is likely to be taken as an argument for the state to provide the funding for abortion. The tendering of this argument has required no small measure of emancipation from the canons of moral reasoning. We are not generally

[18] *Connecticut* v. *Menillo*, 46 L. Ed. 2d 152 (1975).

[19] See *Raleigh Fitkin-Paul Morgan Memorial Hospital* v. *Anderson*, 201 A. 2d 537 (1964). In this case a pregnant woman in a hospital in New Jersey was found to be in danger of a severe hemorrhage, and unless she could be given a blood transfusion it was likely that she and her unborn child would die. (Her pregnancy was then beyond the thirty-second week.) But as a Jehovah's Witness, the woman refused on religious grounds to have the transfusion. The hospital went to court, seeking authority to administer the blood transfusion if it became necessary. The trial court was reluctant to intervene, but on appeal the Supreme Court of New Jersey authorized the hospital to act. The court conceded a problem in the case of an adult who refused her consent to a transfusion; but the judges argued that the unborn child deserved the protection of the law, and the interests of the mother and the child were so intertwined in this case that it was impossible to act for the sake of the child without compelling the mother, also, to receive a transfusion.

disposed to take the breach of the law in other areas (for example, in civil rights) as a sufficient sign in itself that the law must be repealed. Law does not acquire its sanctity from the test of whether it is universally supported. It acquires its authority from the principle on which it is grounded, and if the principle is sound, if the law is justified, the law cannot offer an exemption to people simply because they are driven, by desperation, to evade its maxims.[20]

In the case of abortion, the argument is made, however, that women endanger their lives when they have back-room abortions, and that if abortions are made legal there may be the advantage, at least, of saving the lives of many of these women. For a while the estimates of these deaths were placed rather high, at a range of 5,000 to 10,000 per year. Christopher Tietze, who has become a leading expert on this matter (and who has been, incidentally, a supporter of abortion), has described these estimates as "unmitigated nonsense." In his own reckoning the number would be around 500-1,000, and some other studies have put the figures, more soberly, between 400 and 600 (and probably closer to 400).[21]

But beyond the matter of the empirical evidence, this argument can be advanced only by preserving the most serene indifference to the fact that it is human lives that are taken, after all, in abortions. The "human" standing of the fetus cannot be regarded in any way as an inscrutable religious question, or as a matter of "opinion." As André Hellegers reminds us, a species can be defined only by its genetic composition, and the offspring of homo sapiens cannot be anything other than homo sapiens.[22] Outside of mythology there is no recorded case of a human being giving birth to a dog, a horse, or a cow. If the fetus cannot be regarded as anything other than human, it has a claim to all of those rights in the law that attach to human beings, and the burden of proof would have to fall upon

[20] A fuller discussion of this issue can be found in my essay, "On the Public Funding of Abortions," in James T. Burtchaell, ed., *Abortion Parley* (Andrews and McMeel, 1980); also reprinted in *The Human Life Review* (Winter 1980).

[21] See Finnis, note 10 above, pp. 172-207, at 186. Dr. Bernard Nathanson, who was one of the founders of the National Association for Repeal of Abortion Laws (later the National Abortion Rights Action League, or NARAL), recalled in his recent book the figures of 5,000 to 10,000 deaths each year which were widely cited in the public debates. Nathanson admitted his own knowledge that the figures were "totally false." "But in the 'morality' of our revolution," he noted, "it was a *useful* figure, widely accepted, so why go out of the way to correct it with honest statistics?" Bernard Nathanson, *Aborting America* (Garden City, N.Y.: Doubleday, 1979), p. 193.

[22] See André Hellegers, "Abortion: Another Form of Birth Control," *The Human Life Review*, Vol. 1, no 1 (winter 1975), pp. 19-25, at 23.

those who would claim that it is somehow less than a human or a "person" in the eyes of the law. The difficulty here is that any feature one would cite in trying to show that the fetus is less than human would turn out to apply to humans who are well outside the womb as well.[23] That is not to say that abortion can never be justified under any circumstances. It is to remind us, rather, that if the fetus cannot be anything other than human, the kinds of justifications that are required for the taking of fetal life must be quite as compelling as the justifications that are usually demanded for the taking of human life more generally.

These requirements would not be met by most of the "reasons" that are put forth today as justifications for abortion. I have dealt with those justifications at length elsewhere, and my purpose here is not to reargue the main substantive issues in abortion. When it comes to the matter, though, of regarding the lives that might be lost each year in illegal abortions, my point is simply that it is human lives that are taken when fetuses are "terminated." Under a policy of legalized abortions, we have now reached a level of approximately 1,200,000 abortions each year.[24] If a policy of legalized abortions is justified by many people as a means of avoiding the deaths suffered by women in illegal abortions, then we are being asked to sacrifice over one million lives each year in order to save 400-600. By a mere calculus alone the decision could not have any warrant.

For some reason these calculations never take into account the casualties that have been produced by *legal* abortions. A recent survey of hospital records found that in 1969, before abortions had been legalized, there were about 9,000 women admitted to hospitals in this country with complications resulting from abortions. In

---

[23] I took up this matter in more detail in "Amend the Constitution" [on the question of abortion], *The Wall Street Journal*, October 26, 1976, editorial page; but I will have to leave the fuller argument on abortion for another occasion.

[24] This figure, for 1977, was reported recently by Christopher Tietze, *Boston Globe*, July 4, 1979, p. 3. Four years ago Tietze had reported for the Alan Gutmacher Institute that the number of abortions, at 900,000 per year, had risen 53 percent above their level of 1972, the year before *Roe* v. *Wade* was decided. It was Tietze's guess that two-thirds of these abortions would have occurred illegally if the law had not been altered. But his judgment nevertheless stands in sharp contrast to the contention offered today that a policy of legal abortions has merely rendered abortions legal and safer without altering their numbers in any way. What Tietze conceded, rather, in his testimony, and what has been borne out again in the most recent figures, is that the policy of legal abortions has indeed raised considerably the total number of abortions in the country. See *The New York Times*, February 3, 1975, pp. 1, 42.

1977—four years after abortions had been legalized—that figure had jumped to 17,000.[25] As the total volume of abortions has risen massively, there have been suspicions that the deaths from botched legal abortions have simply been concealed in hospitals through the device of reporting the immediate, rather than the ultimate, cause of death. And so a woman with a perforated uterus may be described later as suffering the effects of peritonitis or of a pelvic abscess. There are known cases in which deaths resulting from abortions have been attributed to anaesthesia or to "abnormal uterine bleeding"; and one physician in Los Angeles, who had a higher quotient of inventiveness than shame, was willing to report that his patient died of "spontaneous gangrene of the ovary."

There have been ample grounds then to suspect that the casualties from abortion have been vastly understated (or even ignored) in the official records; and these suspicions were confirmed in the fall of 1978, when the *Chicago Sun-Times* brought to light the damages being inflicted by reckless abortion clinics in Chicago, which had turned themselves into the legal equivalent of abortion mills. In the rush to get a quick turnover in customers and perform more abortions in a day, the operations were carried out in as little as five minutes. They were performed before the anaesthetic had taken effect; at times they were done even without an anaesthetic; and on a few occasions they were performed on women who were not even pregnant! (The clinics had neglected to administer pregnancy tests in these cases for the purpose of establishing that the operation was relevant.) The investigators brought in reports of twelve deaths that were attributable to four abortion clinics in their sample.[26] Those deaths, which were uncovered in only four clinics, amounted to nearly half of the deaths that were reported officially for abortion in the nation as a whole.[27] And if, as we suspect, the experience in Chicago can find a modest replication in New York, Detroit, Los Angeles, and other cities, the total deaths due to legal abortion may now exceed the number of deaths that were thought to occur each year as a result of illegal abortions.

[25] *Hospital Record Study, 1969-77*, Joint Publication of the Commission on Professional Hospital Activities (Ann Arbor, Michigan) and IMS, Limited (Ambler, Pennsylvania).

[26] See the *Chicago Sun-Times*, November 12, 1978, p. 1; December 6, 1978, p. 1; and the special edition in summary, "Abortion Profiteers," December 1978.

[27] The most recent figures are reported in *Vital Statistics of the United States 1975* (Washington: Government Printing Office, 1977), Vol. II—Mortality, Part A, p. 1-73.

All of this would become pertinent if the issue were really to be resolved by calculating the casualties on either side. But, of course, it would not be on the basis of a calculus that we would finally decide. If we would hold back from a policy of abortion, it is because we could not establish in most instances a principled ground of justification; and in the absence of that justification, abortions would be wrong even if there were only one or two cases each year. It is sobering to consider, then, that if the main object in a policy on abortions is to eliminate illegal abortions, the measure cannot be maintained in principle as a response to the breach of law; it cannot be justified on a calculus of lives saved and lost; and it cannot even be guaranteed to eliminate the illegal abortions. If public law establishes any restrictions at all on abortions—if only to insure the safety of the operations—illegal abortions promise to continue. But they will continue now in a climate of opinion that upholds the respectability of abortions. In that event, it is entirely conceivable that the number of illegal abortions, even in the United States, will come to exceed the level that was attained under the old legal regimen, in which abortions were severely restricted. Once again, an argument that claims to rise above principle in the name of what is mistakenly called the "practical" will be neither principled nor "practical."

It should be clear by now that the same logic that has been played out in the legalization of gambling and abortion has been present perennially in the efforts to legalize prostitution as well. For some reason, we seem condemned on this matter to reinvent the wheel, in a way, with each generation. In the gatherings of urbane people today it is quite common to hear it said that brothels ought to be licensed by the state; that prostitution should be confined and permitted within its own zone within any city; that there should be a regular system of medical examinations for the sake of protecting people from venereal disease; or that prostitution should be "decriminalized" altogether. One would hardly know from the current conversation that virtually all of these proposals were tried at one time, by rather sophisticated people of an earlier generation, and that they were all eventually abandoned with good reason. Exactly one hundred years ago, Sheldon Amos wrote his classic survey on the *Prohibition, Regulation, and Licensing of Vice in England and Europe*,[28] and what he recorded was a general recession throughout

[28] Sheldon Amos, *Prohibition, Regulation, and Licensing of Vice in England and Europe* (London: Stevens and Sons, 1877).

Europe of the laws that licensed and legitimized prostitution. Characteristic of the movement was the action of the municipal government of Zurich, which, in 1874, abolished its system of regulation as an arrangement that was finally "irreconcilable with the idea of the State as a moral power."[29]

The municipal government that chose to speak here officially spoke out of an understanding, informed by tradition, of what was truly meant by a "city." Whether that understanding would be grasped by the people who are trained to govern our cities today is less certain, but the government of Zurich spoke on the basis, also, of an experience that our own generation may be destined to reproduce. The experience in Zurich apparently paralleled the findings of research done in France and elsewhere, which showed most cases of syphillis deriving from women who were registered and examined prostitutes.[30] (Some recent findings in the United States would suggest that this relation no longer seems to hold true. Only a small portion of cases of venereal disease, perhaps no more than 10 percent, seems attributable to prostitution.)[31] A system of weekly examinations was apparently not adequate to check the disease in Switzerland, and in Belgium, Italy, and France the examinations were being given as often as twice a week. All of this leaves out, of course, the argument made in our own time that if any system of examination is to make sense, the male customers ought to be examined and licensed along with the prostitutes. The argument is perfectly apt, and it may show in itself why any serious system of licensing could never be accepted.[32]

[29] Quoted in ibid., p. 122.   [30] See ibid., pp. 44-45.

[31] See M. Anne Jennings, "The Victim as Criminal: A Consideration of California's Prostitution Law," 64 *California L. Rev.* 1235, at 1242-43 (1976).

[32] For their own part, many prostitutes argue for complete "decriminalization" of prostitution, which would do away with all the problems that attend a system of compulsory medical examinations. In this respect they are more than willing to claim a privilege for their own "business" that they would not abide for a moment in most other businesses in the country that happen to be legitimate. They would probably insist that, in making automobiles or packaging meat, companies must be subject to the supervision of the government in order to regulate the hazardous effects of their operations or their products. And, yet, these companies, too, may value their freedom from regulation, and they could reduce costs considerably if they were relieved of the burdens of administration that become necessary in complying with legal regulations. Here, once again, one finds—as in the proposal to exempt gambling from taxation—that the case in favor of legalizing certain vices goes beyond the plea to put the former vices on the same plane as legitimate occupations. The case often ends up as an argument in favor of lifting the former vice to the position of a "favored" business, which can claim special benefits in taxes and provide, in turn, a more attractive field for investment.

Those people who favor a system of examination and licensing often count themselves as heirs to the libertarian tradition of John Stuart Mill. They have argued that the law may not intervene "merely" to express moral opposition to prostitution or to protect the prostitute from herself. In their view, the law may intervene only to protect second and third parties from harm (for example, to protect customers from venereal disease or neighbors from disturbances). And yet Mill himself did not take this line when the question arose. In testifying before a Royal Commission, he was asked whether a system for the medical examination of prostitutes would tend to do "moral injury." He replied:

> I do think so, because I hardly think it possible for thoughtless people not to infer, when special precautions are taken to make a course which is generally considered worthy of disapprobation safer than it would naturally be, that it cannot be considered very bad by the law, and possibly may be considered as either not bad at all, or at any rate a necessary evil.[33]

As the government of Zurich observed in its official statement, "Whatever advantage may be drawn from tolerated houses in respect of prophylactic measures against contagion can never counterbalance their injurious effect, both immediate and indirect, for it is a recognized fact that the existence of these establishments tends to foster and develop sensuality and to multiply the means of gratifying it. . . ."[34] The effect is rather comparable to that of social programs which aim to reduce illegitimacy by making contraceptives more easily available, especially to teenagers and young people: the program is implicitly (or even explicitly) accompanied by the premise that intercourse among unmarried young people is a fact of life that has to be accepted. The acceptance works inescapably to legitimize the practice, and the incidence of sexual commerce tends to enlarge among young people of this description. The result, in our own day, is that there has been, in many places, an increase in illegitimate births, even in the face of social programs that are launched on the claim to bring those rates down.[35] The

---

[33] Quoted in Amos, note 28 above, p. 54.

[34] Ibid., pp. 121-22.

[35] In September 1977, the National Center for Health Statistics released a study that documented what the Center described as a "puzzling" trend: over the past decade the rate of childbearing among American girls in their mid-teens had risen markedly, even while the incidence of childbearing had fallen off among older women. More than that, the rate of illegitimate births for girls 15 to 17 years old had doubled. What was puzzling, according to *The New York Times*, was that these

practical effect of the policy is inseparable, therefore, from the moral lessons that are taught, and that recognition was brought home again with force to the city of Zurich, as well as to other municipalities in Europe. As the government in Zurich put it:

> Toleration [of prostitution] gives rise to a fatal confusion of ideas; men become accustomed to regard all that passes in houses thus protected as a permitted thing. . . . A moral confusion no less fatal is produced among the employees and agents employed in the *'morals-police'*; the fact of being in constant relations with the tenants of bad houses necessarily leads to a species of intimacy. Moreover, *it is not possible that they should display much energy against unlicensed prostitution while they are occupied in favouring licensed prostitution. Thus the police are placed in a false position* [my emphasis]; they can only truly maintain a repressive attitude towards prostitution by showing themselves frankly hostile to it in all its forms. To admit any sort of compromise with a trade fundamentally evil, to tolerate one description of houses of debauchery and make war upon others, is to enter upon the path of half-measures, compromises, and the equivocal partiality, fruitless of every good result. . . .[36]

In this passage the government hit upon the paradox that undermines the effort to enforce a system of legalized prostitution. As we have seen, a regimen of legal restriction will always generate certain incentives for people to operate in an illegal network: legal brothels may bring taxes and raise prices; the prostitutes may wish to avoid the process of being registered, publicly, as prostitutes, and they may wish, also, to avoid compulsory medical examina-

---

rates of illegitimacy should rise "when cheap, effective contraceptive devices, as well as legal abortion, [have become] widely available, even to teen-agers." But these trends were not so inscrutable to two professors of the Johns Hopkins School of Hygiene and Public Health, who happened to be familiar with the field. As *The New York Times* reported, the two physicians judged the recent trends to be "a result of the increased sexual activity among teenagers that has more than overcome the easier access to contraception." *The New York Times*, September 21, 1977, pp. A1, A15. More recently the same researchers have offered further evidence of this increase in sexual activity among teenagers. In 1971, when the first survey in the series was carried out, about 55 percent of American women were estimated to have had sexual intercourse by age 19. The survey for 1976 showed an enlargement of that figure to 63.3 percent. The sharpest gain was for white teenagers, who showed an increase of nearly 10 percent to reach an overall figure of 60 percent. Reported in *Boston Globe*, July 4, 1979, p. 3.

[36] Quoted in Amos, note 28 above, pp. 120-21.

tions. Even in a system of licensing without legal brothels it has apparently escaped the notice of the people who advocate this arrangement that the prostitutes would be responsible for more than their licensing taxes, since they would be in business for themselves. They would be responsible also for income taxes; and many of the prostitutes would be in the 50 percent bracket or higher. Just why these women should be willing to give half or more of their income to the government when they have become used to operating in a world beyond the law and taxes is something that is never made clear.[37] We can probably expect, then, that the incentives for prostitutes to continue in the illegal market will persist, even under arrangements in which prostitution has become legal.

If the police are charged with the responsibility of enforcing the regimen of legal prostitution, they will have to exert themselves in dealing with the business that spills over the boundaries of the vice zone or the registered brothels. But in that event the charge to the officers of the law becomes morally quizzical to the point of its own erosion. The police are first schooled to the temper of regarding prostitution as acceptable and legitimate, and then they are asked to concentrate their energy and their outrage on those people who merely take their business across the street, out of the designated zone. At that moment the law would be concerned mainly with people who are trying to avoid taxes, and we would seem to ask the police to regard them with the kind of passion that they were once asked to summon over the question of prostitution itself. It is no wonder that the police may lose their zeal for enforcement, and that they may become far more open to corruption.

In one way or another, too, as Sheldon Amos recognized, the police must become enmeshed with the prostitutes and the operators of brothels in the running of their business. As in the case of other establishments open to the public, the police may be called in to deal with unruly customers, and in the anticipation of those emergencies the owners of brothels will cultivate good personal relations with the police. In the process, of course, the police may become, with varying degrees of subtlety, "friends" of the establishment. Some brothels in the past preserved a relation with their employees that was comparable to that of the "company store" as it became known in the South: the prostitutes would become dependent on the owners of the brothels for clothes (and perhaps other things, such as drugs), and they could pile up debts that might keep them

[37] See, for example, the tract written by Jennifer James et al., *The Politics of Prostitution* (Social Research Associates, 1975), pp. 62-63.

in service.[38] That may be rare today, but if any residue lingers from that experience of an earlier time, the police may be called in to enforce the terms of contract and compel service to the establishment in the name of the law.[39]

On the other hand, it may be equally degrading to have the law step in to support customers in challenging the policies of the various houses. According to James and Elizabeth Vorenberg, none of the legal brothels in Lyons County, Nevada, accepts black customers, a practice that has generated a certain tension between local officials and the black men of a military base nearby.[40] It is hard to imagine many prospects more debasing than that of having the federal courts intervene in order to vindicate a constitutional right to gain entrance to a whorehouse.

In Nevada, the police seek to enforce a system of regulations that bars prostitution to girls under eighteen, along with women who have records of felony arrests. As the Vorenbergs concede, regulations of this kind would be very difficult to enforce in cities like Los Angeles, Chicago, or New York, compared to the smaller, more confined settlements outside Las Vegas.[41] But what should be apparent, also, is that rules of some kind would be imposed even under a liberal system of legalized prostitution, and the restrictions would make it necessary for the police to continue in their surveillance over prostitutes. As we have seen, a strong market has apparently developed already for children as prostitutes, and it is clear that the laws in this country will be set firmly against the appeasement of this market. But in that case the surveillance over prostitution may have to become even more intensive, and the police may find themselves involved in almost every stage of prostitution as an operating business. There is considerable truth, then, in the view that was taken by the government in Zurich in the

---

[38] Amos, note 28 above, p. 120. On the aversion of prostitutes today to the costs extracted from them in brothels, see James et al., *The Politics of Prostitution*, p. 62.

[39] In France prostitution is accepted as a legitimate calling, but in a rather paradoxical policy, brothels have been banned. The head of a police unit dealing with prostitution expressed his belief recently to interviewers that prostitution would not be suppressed by legislation. And yet he declared himself to be "absolutely" against a system of legal brothels or "houses of tolerance" of the kind they have in Germany. "If you have an institution of this kind you encourage all sorts of perversion. The girl is shut in and exploited by the owner. If houses are legalized again in Paris, I would quit. It's an immoral system. All the police can do is see that it's working and I would not like to see agents participate in houses of toleration." James and Elizabeth Vorenberg, "The Biggest Pimp of All," *Atlantic*, Vol. 239, no. 1 (January 1977), pp. 27-38, at 36-37.

[40] Ibid., p. 29.   [41] Ibid., p. 38.

1870's: that the chance of containing prostitution would be greater if the police acted on the basis of a simple, categoric rejection of prostitution in principle. Any attempt to introduce finer shades of distinction in the interests of prudential compromise would have the result of legitimizing prostitution, introducing confusion about the moral ground of the law, and rendering the task of enforcement far more difficult.

Despite all of the talk about prostitution as a vice that will always be with us, the fact of the matter is that the incidence of prostitution has been notably lessened in different times and places as a result, apparently, of a vigorous enforcement of the statutes on prostitution. This experience was generally known, also, to the governments that were drawing back from the system of legalized prostitution in the 1870's. In Liverpool, for example, it was estimated that the number of brothels declined from 777 in 1864 to 516 in 1873. The reduction took place even though there was a large increase in population at the same time, and even though Liverpool was a major port of landing for many sailors returning from voyages. In London, the number of brothels was reduced from 2,825 in 1857 to 2,119 in 1868, and a particularly bad class of them was almost entirely closed down (going from 400 in 1857 to only 2 in 1868).[42] A number of factors might help to account for the decline in prostitution, but in the judgment of serious observers at the time, the sharp declines that occurred in England could be attributed most directly to a firm policy of law enforcement. That earlier generation was led to discover again for itself that law enforcement did indeed make a difference. But it came to that discovery, also, with the recognition that principles do, in fact, have consequences; that the climate of enforcement is affected by the state of opinion; and that opinion is molded by the lessons which public men teach. As Sheldon Amos summed it up:

> [T]he public registration of prostitutes is, in respect of the moral influences upon society at large and upon prostitutes themselves, a distinct aggregation of all the moral evils, of an educational kind, which the existence of prostitution itself involves. It must suggest to the young woman as yet unfallen, but not untempted, that a livelihood is at hand, in an occupation not less regular, organised, and publicly recognised than other occupations. It suggests to the young man at critical moments of his life, not only that promiscuous intercourse is

[42] Amos, note 28 above, p. 133.

possible for him (a lesson he could not escape, perhaps, any-how), but that a marked and picked corps of his fellow-coun-trywomen are publicly stamped as available for his use. It suggests to all persons in every part of society that prostitution is not an intolerable and wholly anomalous fact, but that, on the contrary, an order, a caste, a college, of women consecrated to prostitution, are as deeply and lastingly bound up with the fortunes of the State as are the most immoveable bulwarks of the political fabric itself.[43]

The state becomes corrupted then, as Amos says, when it makes itself the sponsor of vice, for "instead of simply commanding, as it best may, what is morally good, it is surprised in the act of a treacherous connivance with what is morally bad. It stands before its subjects in the commanding position of the supreme monopolist and prime minister of sin."[44] Or, as the saying has been recently in New York, the state would become "the biggest pimp of them all."[45]

2. THE EXTENDED EFFECTS OF THE VICES

It is often argued that the problem of prostitution will not abate in any serious way until society becomes far more successful in providing legitimate jobs for the women who turn to prostitution. Some women may, in fact, have been driven to the business in moments of desperation, but one suspects even there that a sense of respectability is more decisive in the matter than the possession of a respectable job. For it should be plain now that if the decision turned wholly on a comparison of the financial returns, very few respectable jobs could compete with the kind of money that pros-titutes can earn—free of taxes. It should not require the testimony of economists to convince us that even people who enter illegal callings are very attentive to the relative costs and benefits when they choose illegitimate over legitimate occupations.[46]

The point holds perfectly well for people who weigh the prospects of prostitution; and even slight changes in the "discount rate," so to speak, may bring very quick results. In New York in the late 1960's, prostitution was reduced from a felony to a misdemeanor, and the penalties were so slight that, as one observer remarked, it

[43] Ibid., p. 39. [44] Ibid., p. 256.

[45] See J. and E. Vorenberg, note 39 above, p. 27.

[46] See Isaac Ehrlich, "The Deterrent Effect of Criminal Law Enforcement," *The Journal of Legal Studies*, Vol. 1, no. 2 (June 1972), pp. 259-76.

was virtually equivalent to the removal of legal restrictions. After paying a small fine (which could be incorporated easily as a business expense), a girl could be back on the streets in a matter of hours. The result was that prostitutes began appearing in vastly larger numbers, and they began flocking to New York from other states. Soon they spilled over into Fifth Avenue and some of the more fashionable areas, and under the press of competition they became noticeably bolder. There was no street, apparently, that they were reluctant to walk, even in the middle of the day, and in many instances they were not even too reserved to solicit men who were walking with their wives.[47]

Before long, the prostitutes began to branch out into other forms of crime. The extension was not altogether surprising, because the circles these women travel in have not been exactly noted for an aversion to illegality in all of its forms. Beyond that, prostitutes may be connected at many points with organized crime, which provides them with a network for disposing of stolen goods. The most likely kind of crime for them was to rob the customers they had lured. (Since they were operating outside the law anyway, it made a certain sense to grab a wallet where they could without rendering service. The customer could not very easily complain to the police.) At times, however, they did not even wait to solicit before they loosed their assaults, and in one celebrated incident, a prostitute attacked Franz-Josef Strauss, the former defense minister of West Germany. All of which seemed to prove that, under the benign laws of New York City, prostitutes could not only become very versatile, but that they were not deterred even by a nuclear capability.[48]

---

[47] A similar pattern developed in San Francisco more recently when the newly elected district attorney pledged not to waste the money of the taxpayers in prosecuting prostitutes. Prostitutes shifted to San Francisco in large numbers and the same aggressive behavior on the streets began to emerge. The Vorenbergs claim that the problem was "eased" by the law of supply and demand as the market became saturated and many prostitutes were encouraged to try other cities. The Vorenbergs do not say, however, that there was a return to the situation as it was, and that the volume of prostitution had not been substantially enlarged. They assume, for some unexplained reason, that the "demand" for this commodity is fixed; they neglect the possibility, known to economists as Say's Law, that an increase in supply may stimulate an increase in demand. See J. and E. Vorenberg, note 39 above, p. 32.

[48] In anticipation of the Democratic National Convention in 1976, New York City established some very tough regulations on soliciting for prostitution. The regulations were apparently applied with effect during the week of the Convention, and they were upheld in the courts. See *The New York Times*, February 18, 1977, pp. A1, A24. But "antiloitering" laws are under constant attack by civil libertarians,

It is simply not realistic, then, to suppose that vices will breed their own form of ennui and grow feebler if the restrictions in the laws are removed. Despite all the predictions, for example, that the legal market for pornographic films will be played out, a survey of most urban centers will show that the audience for these movies shows no signs of diminishing. It may be true that the larger film studios have reduced their interest in the so-called "X-rated" productions, mainly because of the hostility they have encountered outside the major urban areas.[49] But as long as small producers can make a film like *Deep Throat* for $25,000 and bring a return of $5 million in their first year alone, the incentive to make these films will continue to be strong, and the market after the experience of *Deep Throat* seems to be even larger than before.

One index of the strength of the market is that it appears to have expanded rather firmly, even after the decision of the Supreme Court in 1973 that gave local communities a wide latitude in restricting pornographic films.[50] Seven years after that decision, it is surprising how little restriction has in fact taken place. The culture of "porn" seems now to have taken hold: pornographic movie houses can be found in conservative small towns as well as in urban centers. No small part of their influence may come from the considerable financial interest that this minor industry can represent in any town; but the fact that such businesses can be formidable sources of revenue is itself a mark of the new tastes that have been cultivated by these entertainments.

When the restraints of law are removed, a new constituency is likely to be created for amusements and services that were formerly regarded as vices; and once suppliers become used to operating in an illegal market, it would be a rare form of legitimate enterprise that could match the money or the excitement that can be derived from the underground business. What we are more likely to see, then, is an *expansion* of the illegal activities until they consume a larger portion of the resources of the community and draw off people and investment from other callings. In his biography of Pitt, the younger, Lord Stanhope recalled that in England, in 1784, the duties on tea were such that more than two-thirds of the tea that was imported into England came in through illicit trade. It was estimated that forty thousand persons, by sea or land, were engaged

---

and even if the laws survive, the courts have been reluctant to impose substantial sentences on prostitutes.

[49] See *The New York Times*, April 20, 1971, pp. 1, 48.

[50] See *Miller* v. *California*, 418 U.S. 15 (1973).

in this system of smuggling, and the trade became so lucrative that some farmers along the coast found it more profitable to deploy their horses in carting smuggled goods than in cultivating their own farms.[51]

Similarly, in New York City in recent years, the trade in pornography has become so profitable that porn shops have been able to bid up the leases on certain properties, and in a number of cases they have been able to displace establishments such as dress shops and bookstores.[52] The effect of this displacement, of course, on the character and the tone of the city may be pronounced. The denizens of the West Side suffer no strain in deciding just which character they prefer in their own neighborhoods, and they have been quite firm in their resolve to keep the culture of pornography out of these areas. Where they profess uncertainty, however, is over the ground of principle on which it is proper for the law to run these establishments out of respectable neighborhoods. Liberal opinion has denied at its root that the law has any ground of principle on which it can regard pornography as a business that is less legitimate than any other, or less worthy of the protections of the law. The decision to keep pornography out of the better neighborhoods—and direct it in turn toward the poorer sections of the city—is a decision that is often based, then, on nothing more than a contest of political strength.

The question that is raised, however, for the poorer sections of the city is quite a serious one. It is evident, for example, that the expansion of the "vices" will not cause the standard of living to decline in the community in which they are centered. In fact, the situation is likely to bring the kind of outsized returns that are often possible in illegitimate undertakings. We are obliged to call back, I think, the question I had occasion to raise earlier: Would it be a benefit to a community of poor blacks and Puerto Ricans if, thirty years from now, it had a disproportionately large share of the pimps

[51] Earl Stanhope, *Life of William Pitt* (New York: AMS Press, 1970; originally published in 1867), Vol. I, pp. 215-16.

[52] The word going around the police in the Midtown North Precinct in Times Square was that the pressure on the porn shops was purposely eased during the recession of 1973-74: many buildings were losing tenants and having a hard time attracting new ones; and while times were bad the owners of real estate were not anxious to drive even more tenants away. As the economy recovered from the recession, there was a revival of interest among some businessmen in "cleaning up" the area. Other businessmen, however, were more reserved about squeezing out the porn shops, since they seemed to bring a good deal of traffic into the Midtown region.

and prostitutes and numbers runners, and a disproportionately small share of the skilled workers, doctors, and lawyers? The standard of living may go up markedly, and for all we know, the problem of poverty might be dissolved. But would one be willing to say, also, that the community had been "improved"?

If that seems, to many contemporary analysts, one of those hopeless metaphysical questions that no one, ultimately, can judge, it is nevertheless a question that must be faced daily, in a more personal way, by parents in poorer neighborhoods. In this respect there was a suggestive account several years ago in *The New York Times* of how the police managed to uncover a massive narcotics operation that centered on Pleasant Avenue in Harlem. The story has been retold now in fuller detail by David Durk and Ira Silverman in *The Pleasant Avenue Connection.*[53] At the height of its activities, the narcotics ring in this incident was described as a "multi-kilo a week operation," and in tracing out the network, the police had the benefit of some extraordinary intelligence. They were given important names and addresses; they were told how heroin was being distributed to western Harlem, the Bronx, and New Jersey; and they were even told where the heroin was hidden in particular shops that were used as "covers." The information was furnished at some risk by the father of a young man whose friends were deeply involved in the operations. His friends were offering him $3,500 a week (tax free) to come in with them as a courier, and the offer must have seemed irresistible when set against the alternative of going on with school or starting work at an unimposing, but respectable job. The father had seen in his own time the swagger and emptiness of aspiring young criminals, who grew heady for a while on the fast money, but who often paid bitterly. He was resolved, in any event, to have none of it for his son, and he came to the judgment, apparently, that the amount of money his son made was less important than the character of his life. At some point, it became evident to him that the only way to stop his son from joining his friends was to take the steps that were necessary to destroy the narcotics ring itself. And, with that in mind, he finally went to the police.

It may be only academics these days who can afford the detachment of moral relativism; most ordinary people know better. They sense that the distinctions between the legitimate and the illegitimate are not merely conventional, and they recognize in an unlet-

---

[53] (New York: Harper and Row, 1977), chs. 1, 5, and passim.

tered way what the classics sought to teach: that moral questions are by nature practical questions, and that moral judgments cannot be evaded. If the law has nothing to say about matters of morals, it offers no guidance in the most important decisions that are taken every day in the city—namely, the decisions made by people who would govern the character of their own lives, and who bear responsibility, also, for the lives of others. And for those who would make the right decisions, even when it means running against the current of local opinion, the law would be the source of no support.

3. REPUBLICAN GOVERNMENT AND THE CULTIVATION OF MORALITY

A polity that sought to banish morals from the domain of its concerns could not be anything other than an abomination; indeed, it could not even be a polity in the strictest understanding. As we have seen, the very notions of polity and law arise from the capacity of human beings for moral judgment. It is the existence of morals that makes the idea of law necessary, and any statute without a moral or principled foundation cannot claim the name of law in the most proper sense.

Even those in our own time who rail against the "intrusion" of the law into matters of morals are quite adamant in other cases that the law must also render "justice." As I have pointed out earlier, they are no more willing than anyone else to repeal those parts of our law which embody what even they would concede to be moral perspectives. They are not willing to remove the statutes on the battering of wives and the selling of children, or, for that matter, on the purloining of tires or the theft of copyrighted novels. They are quite willing, also, to "legislate morals" when it is a matter of overriding the disposition of people to discriminate on the basis of race in the sale or rental of homes or in the admission of students to private schools. Of course, they may seek to argue that most of these cases involve material harms, but without quite admitting it to themselves they are often willing to impose restraints through the law even when material harms are not present: they may insist on stopping men from "exposing themselves" to children in public; they may act in the name of the "environment" to prevent people of questionable taste from putting up billboards or garish displays in neon; and they may even demand that people who are willing to buy health insurance for themselves be compelled to participate in a compulsory national health plan. (For all we know, these people may also be unsettled, as Woody Allen would say, at the prospect of those refractory persons who persist in dialing Information for numbers they could look up themselves.) In point of fact, it is hard to find any statutes on the books, including the regulations that govern traffic, which do not imply a moral judgment, even on the smallest and most obvious things (as, for example, whether we are justified in restraining freedom on the road in order to avert injuries).

What, then, is the source of the conviction, so prevalent and clichéd in our own day, that one may not "legislate morality"? There is, of course a rich tradition of moral relativism that may be drawn upon in a variety of forms, along with the admonition, lasting through time, that a law which runs counter to the habits of a people may be very difficult to enforce. But when people insist today that it is both wrong and futile to legislate morality, the example they cite most often is that of Prohibition. In that sense, one might say that Prohibition gave morals a bad name. It encouraged the tendency, even among the educated, to confuse "morals"—and the discipline of principled discourse—with a strident "moralism." In point of fact, Prohibition represented a counterfeit morality: it condemned the drinking of liquor in any quantity, under any circumstances—it condemned drinking, in short, with the force of a categorical judgment, even though it was plain that alcohol could not be harmful under all circumstances. It was plain, that is, that drinking could not meet the strict requirements of a categorical wrong, and it was simply incoherent to invoke the language of morals in order to condemn, in a blanket fashion, all instances of the manufacture and consumption of liquor.

In the meantime Prohibition preserved the misconception that morals have nothing to do with the task of employing evidence and reasoning and establishing the truth or falsity of propositions. It fostered the sense of "morality" as a matter of beliefs of an almost mystical or religious nature, which cannot be the subject of reasoned discourse. With this understanding, the authenticity of a moral perspective would be measured by the personal intensity and passion with which it is affirmed. It is one thing to insist that people act morally by establishing the principled foundation of their acts; it is quite another thing to slip into a kind of millennarianism that seeks to eradicate all vestiges of evil from the world. The aim, in this latter case, is not simply to bring about improvement or reduce the incidence of injustice, but to achieve a nearly perfect state—a New Jerusalem, as it were, on earth.

Lincoln, who clearly sought moral ends in politics, preserved his own detachment from the so-called "temperance" movement of his time.[54] The problem for Lincoln, as Harry Jaffa has pointed out, was that the Temperance movement did not seek temperance at all, in the classic sense, but abstinence. Instead of seeking a critical sense of moderation, a golden mean of the passions, it sought, as Jaffa has remarked, "the entire elimination of the influence of passion over human conduct."[55] As Lincoln characterized the movement, it looked forward to the day when all appetites would be controlled, all passions subdued, all matters subjected, and "*mind, all conquering mind*, shall live and move the monarch of the world."[56] The danger, however, with visions of that kind was that the mandates of perfection required a concentration of power that might be incompatible with the conditions of free government. The law had a responsibility to teach, but statesmen had an obligation to be prudent and reasonable. As Aquinas argued in the *Summa Theologica*, the aim of the law is to lead people to virtue, not suddenly, but gradually. One must take care not to "lay upon the multitude of imperfect men the burdens of those who are already virtuous"—namely, that they should abstain, with stringency, from all manner of vice. "Otherwise," he wrote, "these imperfect ones, being unable to bear such precepts, would break out into yet greater evils: thus, it is written (Prov. 33): *He that violently bloweth his nose, bringeth out blood*; and (Matth. ix. 17) that if new wine is put into old bottles, the bottles break, and the wine runneth out."[57] That is to say, if one puts new precepts into men who are imperfect containers, the precepts themselves may come to be despised, and those men may erupt into evils that are worse yet.

To take just one example, there is little question any longer that the smoking of cigarettes is likely to be harmful in the long run to smokers (and, as we are reminded these days, to nonsmokers as well). But as in the case of liquor, it would be hard to argue that it is injurious to smoke in any degree, no matter how moderate the usage, and so there can be no justification for a policy that seeks to ban, in their entirety, the manufacture and sale of cigarettes. There probably would be a justification, however, for policies on

[54] See Harry Jaffa's analysis of Lincoln's Temperance Address in "The Teaching Concerning Political Moderation," in Jaffa, *Crisis of the House Divided* (New York: Doubleday, 1959), pp. 236-72.

[55] See ibid., p. 244.

[56] Ibid., p. 250; emphases in original.

[57] *Summa Theologica* (London: Burns Oates and Washbourne, 1915), Part II (First Part), vol. 8, pp. 66-67.

a more modest scale, which would seek to discourage the use of cigarettes in the quantities—and places—at which they may indeed be harmful. Still, if we tried a number of methods to restrict the use of cigarettes, (for example, limiting their use in public places, restricting their sale to minors) it would be necessary to keep in mind the dependence on smoking that many people have built up over the years, a dependence that cannot be ended overnight without causing many other personal disorders. Like it or not, smoking has become for many individuals a means of calming the nerves, and it is conceivable in some cases that the strains on personal health would be more acute if the smoking were abruptly stopped. In any event, the situation is sufficiently complicated that we would be well advised to be prudent: to recognize that other, and perhaps even worse, kinds of evils may result when the government itself loses a sense of moderation and seeks a thoroughness of compliance that it cannot reasonably expect. The aim of the law, as ever, must be to restrain things that are harmful and wrong—to compress them within limits that are both tolerable and practicable—but without the hope that it can reach every injury or redress every wrong.

But if we lean, in our teaching, toward prudence, if we leaven our laws with a sense of what can reasonably be expected, we do not imply in any way that morals are impracticable. Still less would we deny that the dominant concern of the law can be anything other than moral instruction. The question was raised by Aristotle: What kind of being does not stand in need of a polity? He would be a being who is already so perfect that he does not require the restraint of law, or he would be a being who is cut off decisively from those possibilities of moral instruction that are implicit in the law. He must be, as Aristotle said, "either a beast or a god."[58]

Polity is both possible and necessary because, while we are not gods, neither are we animals. The same things that separate human beings from gods—and put them beneath the obligations of saints—also raise them above the level of animals and establish their capacity for moral learning. "What is government itself," asked Madison, "but the greatest of all reflections of human nature? If men were angels, no government would be necessary."[59] As the Founders understood, the case for government began with the recognition of those differences which separated human things from the things that were either subhuman or superhuman. The natural equality

[58] Aristotle, *The Politics*, 1253a.
[59] *The Federalist*, #51 (New York: Modern Library, n.d.), p. 337.

of human beings inhered in those attributes they shared with other humans, and which separated them from God on the one hand, and animals on the other. In that respect the case for lawful government was in point of principle the same as the case for republican government or government by consent: it began with the recognition that beings which are capable of reasoning over moral things do not deserve to be ruled in the way that one rules beings that are not capable of giving and understanding reasons.

The argument, once again, in all of its aspects, was predicated on the capacity of human beings for morals. The reasoning that established the case for republican government invested the rulers at the same time with an obligation to do far more than preserve the security of the citizens. There can be no incompatibility, therefore, between the notion of constitutional government and the understanding of a government that takes, as its prime concern, the moral character of its citizens.

It has often been observed that, for Jefferson, the greatest threat to republican government came from the usurpations that the government itself might commit if the people lost their vigilance or their capacity for revolution. That understanding had, as far as it went, a certain truth, but it took Lincoln and the experience of another generation to make it more complete. As Harry Jaffa has commented, Lincoln never denied the dangers that were immanent when the government extended its power without justification; but "he placed far more emphasis on the danger of usurpations of a lawless people, which might become the usurpations of the government in response to popular pressure." What Lincoln understood was that "once the government was established upon a popular basis, the great danger was the corruption of the people" themselves.[60] A corrupted people, who were willing to injure some of their members to serve the interests or the passions of the majority, would soon bring forward talented and ambitious men, who were more than content to ride to power by catering to those passions.

Lincoln recognized, perhaps more clearly than his contemporaries, that a lawless people, a people without any sense of restraint, would be governed only by a despotism. But a republican government, which draws its rulers from the people themselves, could not afford to be indifferent to the moral condition of its citizens. It was

[60] Jaffa, note 54 above, p. 323.

the most serious corruption of understanding to say that this government—a republican government—should have less concern than
any other with the moral improvement of its citizens, or that, among
all other kinds of governments, this government alone should deny
its competence to that end. That is a persuasion, as I have sought
to show, which would be inconsistent at its root with the premises
on which a free government rests, and it would render us incapable
of addressing those questions of justice which must form, enduringly, our most urgent business.

INDEX

Library of Congress Cataloging in Publication Data

Arkes, Hadley.
  The philosopher in the city.

  Includes index.
  1. Municipal government—United States.
2. Political ethics.   I. Title.
JS331.A74   320.8'0973   80-8536
ISBN 0-691-09356-3
ISBN 0-691-02822-2 (pbk.)

Hadley Arkes is Professor of Political Science at Amherst College and the author of Bureaucracy, the Marshall Plan, and the National Interest (Princeton).